JOURNAL FOR THE STUDY OF THE OLD TESTAMENT SUPPLEMENT SERIES

45

Editors
David J A Clines
Philip R Davies

JSOT Press
Sheffield

The Confessions
of Jeremiah
in Context

Scenes of Prophetic Drama

A.R. Diamond

Journal for the Study of the Old Testament
Supplement Series 45

To Carole, Ray and Georgia,
Danna, Alice and Lyndall, M'L., G.

Copyright © 1987 Sheffield Academic Press

Published by JSOT Press
JSOT Press is an imprint of
Sheffield Academic Press
The University of Sheffield
343 Fulwood Road
Sheffield S10 3BP
England

Typeset by Sheffield Academic Press
and
printed in Great Britain
by Billing & Sons Ltd
Worcester

British Library Cataloguing in Publication Data

Diamond, A.R.
    The confessions of Jeremiah in context :
    scenes of prophetic drama.—(Journal for
    the study of the Old Testament supplement series,
    ISSN 0309-0787; 46).
    1. Bible, O.T. Jeremiah—Commentaries
    I. Title   II. Series
    224'.206   BS1525.3

    ISBN 1-85075-032-7
    ISBN 1-85075-033-5 Pbk

CONTENTS

PREFACE

The present book represents in substantial form my dissertation accepted by the University of Cambridge in 1984 for the Ph.D. Unfortunately, the recent commentaries on Jeremiah by R.P. Carroll, William L. Holladay, and William McKane could not be incorporated into the present monograph. None of these works significantly alters my own position.

In the host of acknowledgments happily incumbent upon me in the course of research, may I begin by expressing thanks and appreciation to the Committee of Vice-Chancellors and Principals of the Universities of the United Kingdom for the granting of an ORS Award, the Tyndale Fellowship, and my father, Ray Diamond, whose financial assistance made this course of study possible.

Appreciation should be expressed to my supervisor, Professor R.E. Clements, whose steady encouragement to use my time wisely and to work efficiently and whose ability to steer a novice away from false trails have been a great help. Thanks also go to Dr G.I. Davies, who acted as my interim supervisor for one term while Professor Clements was away but whose interest and encouragement have continued throughout the remainder of my work. The thoughtful questions of both scholars have been a great stimulation.

I would like to thank the two scholars just mentioned as well as Professor E.W. Nicholson and Dr R.P. Gordon for encouragement to publish my work. To the editorial committee of the JSOT Press, I express appreciation for accepting my dissertation for publication in the supplement series.

A great contribution to the efficiency and pleasantness of day-to-day work was derived from access to the Tyndale House library and the helpfulness of the staff, particularly the Warden and Librarian.

Finally, I dedicate this book to my wife, Carole, whose steady support is of inestimable value. Lastly, appreciation must be given to our friend, M'Lady, for moral support and personal counsel.

ABBREVIATIONS

For bibliographic abbreviations, see Siegfried Schwertner, *International Glossary for Theology and Related Subjects*, except for:

BDB	Brown, Driver, Briggs, *Hebrew Lexicon*
BibNOT	*biblische Notizen*
CFThL	Clark's Foreign Theological Library
FzB	*Forschung zur Bibel*
GKC	Gesenius, Kautzsch, Cowley, *Hebrew Grammar*
HALAT	Baumgartner, *et al.*, *Hebräisches und Aramäisches Lexicon*
LingBib	*Linguistica Biblica*
SBLDS	Society of Biblical Literature Dissertation Series
TDOT	*Theological Dictionary of the Old Testament*

Standard commentaries/commentators:

Ahuis	Holladay, *Spokesman*
Baumgartner	Hubmann
Berridge	Hyatt, IB
Blank, 'Confessions'	Ittmann
Bright, AB	Nicholson, *Jer. 1-25*
Carroll	Rad, von, *Konfessionen*
Condamin	Reventlow
Cornill	Rudolph
Duhm	Thompson, Nicot.
Eichler	Volz
Fohrer, *Die Propheten*	Weiser, ATD
Gunneweg	

For textual abbreviations and sigla, see BHS and Ziegler, *Septuaginta*, except for:

G	Old Greek, cf. Ziegler.
MT	Masoretic Text, cf. BHS.
Syr	Syriac, cf. BHS.
Targ	Targum, cf. Sperber.
V	Vulgate, cf. Weber.
4QJer.a	Qumran MS, cf. Janzen, *Studies*.

Miscellaneous abbreviations:

Dt.-Isa.	Deutero Isaiah
Dtr.	Deuteronomistic/Deuteronomists
Dtr.-Hist.	Deuteronomistic History
f.n.o.	Foreign Nation Oracles
No.	Number
OT	Old Testament
PN	Personal name

INTRODUCTION

In the study of the book of Jeremiah, the so-called confessions[1] of the prophet (11.18-12.6; 15.10-21; 17.14-18; 18.18-23; 20.7-18)[2] have attracted strenuous attention and have been accorded a central role in the understanding of the prophet's message and significance. The attempt to elucidate their central role has been plagued by two concomitant tasks or problems: the problem of explaining their relationship to the psalms and at the same time, properly discerning their relationship to the prophetic mission—especially in light of the relative uniqueness of the confessions within the prophetic corpus. It is with the problem of achieving a valid reading of the confessions that our present investigation is concerned. In the execution of our study, evaluation of the types of approaches employed—especially those represented in the post-Reventlow period—will be of particular interest for the clarification and focusing of our own reflections with regard to reading Jeremiah's confessions.

Historical Development of the Problem

A brief chronological sketch of confession-research will provide a helpful backdrop to the classification of interpretive approaches and the principal questions and problems used by them.[3] In the modern study of the confessions, the first major period spans the time from H. Ewald (1840) to H. Graf Reventlow (1963). With few exceptions[4] the confessions are taken as primary sources of psychological and biographical data for the construction of a 'life' of the prophet.[5] They are the private prayers and musing of Jeremiah in which are recorded his inner spiritual struggles occasioned by the hardships of his prophetic office. However, two major developments in this period set the stage for the study of Reventlow and those subsequent to him. The first and most important was the application of Gunkel's *gattungsgeschichtlich* method to the analysis of the confessions by W. Baumgartner (1917).[6] He was the first to establish rigorously the organic relationship of the confessions to the psalm genre—lament. As a result, the door is effectively closed on the issue of whether Jeremiah had availed himself of specific psalms in the composition of his own prayers; or *vice versa*, he is to be credited with providing the major creative impetus for the production of the exilic psalter.[7] Instead, the prophet is understood to have availed himself of a longstanding genre and adapted it to express his own uniquely prophetic experiences. Close similarities of form, diction, and theme between the confessions and the laments of the psalter are indications of tropes common to the genre and not signs of direct dependence one way or the other. Still, no difficulty was felt in the continuation of a psychological-biographical reading since amidst the stereotyped idioms and images differences from the normal tropes of the lament genre could be discerned which were to be understood only as distinctively prophetic features and thus deposits expressing Jeremiah's own prophetic experience.

The second major development of this period is the partial modification of the psychological-personalistic interpretation with a greater emphasis upon a theological assessment of the prophet's sufferings in relation to the prophetic office. It is to be suspected that part of the reason for this shift was the greater recognition of the limitations imposed or implied on such psychological approaches once the traditional and stereotyped aspects of the confession were appreciated.[8] The principal studies are those of G. von Rad (1936), H.J. Stoebe (1955, 1964), J.J. Stamm (1955), and J.L. Mihelic (1960).[9] Common to these various approaches is the greater recognition given to the incorporation of the prophet's humanity and whole way of life into his prophetic mission, rendering it as much a witness of God as his prophetic proclamation. As such it represents a reassessment of the confessions as purely private utterances of the man Jeremiah, unrelated to his office as prophet, and as testimonies to the collapse of classical prophecy.[10]

In the second major period of confession-research, spanning from Reventlow (1963) to the present, serious problems remaining below the surface of the consensus burst forth vehemently. But the groundwork for this eruption had already been prepared by the pivotal study of Baumgartner and the theological assessments of the confessions dependent upon it. Reventlow[11] initiated this new phase in the discussion by exploring and stressing more emphatically the relationship between the confessions and cultic lament established by Baumgartner. Of particular interest for Reventlow was the attempt to relate even those elements taken as distinctively prophetic to the stereotyped images and expressions of cultic laments. Thus the language of the confessions was characterized by a radical ambiguity which prohibited their treatment as psychological transcripts, providing insight into the inner spiritual struggles of the prophet. Further, he stressed the institutional rootednesss of lament in the cult[12] and thus attempted to postulate an official function of the prophet as cultic mediator between nation and God. Through the cultic mediator the national complaints are uttered and, correspondingly, divine responses are received. Jeremiah's confessions primarily reflect this process. The individual speaking in them is liturgical and representative in character. The nation's complaints and petitions are presented in individual dress.[13] Reventlow's thesis constituted a major challenge for the traditional reading of the confessions and set the agenda for subsequent research. It was the great service of Reventlow to force to the surface a critical difficulty in the assumptions underlying the psychological-biographical reading of these passages. For, if to a high degree the confessions share the genre characteristics of cultic lament, then how is it legitimate to read these highly stylized and stereotyped expressions as direct psychological transcripts and as 'confessions' in the true sense of that literary genre—i.e. as spiritual biography?

Current Approaches

Having proceeded chronologically in our sketch so far, we would like to discuss the subsequent post-Reventlow study of the confessions from the standpoint of types of approaches employed in order to address the preceding issue pinpointed so well by Reventlow. By and large, his thesis received sharp and effective criticism and generally has not been followed.[14] An overview of the post-Reventlow discussion will reveal, as well, that while some scholars have been content to continue the traditional psychological-biographical reading based upon the refutation of his arguments,[15] others have perceived the key issue pinpointed by him and have attempted various more rigorous analyses of the literary form and setting of these passages in order effectively to relate them to the prophetic mission of Jeremiah and thus to continue the traditional reading in a modified fashion while giving due recognition to their genre characteristics.[16]

In contrast to these, others have accepted Reventlow's observation about the radical ambiguity of the language and coupled this with redaction-critical models which take a positive view of the editorial processes that have shaped the prophetic book. As a result, a direct connection of the confessions to the prophet is denied.[17] Instead they are total editorial compositions placed in Jeremiah's mouth, interpreting him in light of the religious needs of the traditionists' community. In contrast to Reventlow who saw in the confessions the historical prophet presenting the petitions of the community, this approach sees the interpretation of the prophetic person by the community in terms of its traditional piety and liturgical forms.

On both views a direct contact with the inner experiences and personality of the prophet is relinquished. On the latter redactional approach, a direct grasp of the historical Jeremiah is forfeited as well and the problem of how much the editorial portrayal faithfully represents the historical prophet arises.[18] Thus a further problematic assumption of the traditional psychological-biographical approach was pinpointed. That is to say, the more it is recognized that the materials in the prophetic collection have been mediated through a tradition process, that the needs and interests of the tradents have affected the shaping of the tradition,[19] and that quite sophisticated theological and religious motives could be involved on their part, then the more the assumption inherent in the traditional approach that immediate biographical information was accessible in Jeremiah's confessions appears to be too hasty. This remains true unless one could establish in their case that merely biographical and historical interests had controlled their transmission and shaped their presentation. A more nuanced treatment of the pre-redactional and redactional settings of the passages was required. Just such nuanced analyses have been attempted which seek to maintain a connection of the confessions with the historical mission of the prophet on the one hand, but on the other discern a sophisticated editorial process in their present incorporation into the book which allows for development and shift in the meaning of the texts.[20]

Finally, alongside this debate and in reaction to it may be placed the attempt to read the confessions in a rigidly synchronic fashion eschewing the historicist interests that have particularly dominated confession-research. The problem of the relationship between editorial portrayal and historical mission of the prophet is bypassed entirely through an exclusive focus upon the final form of the text and the attempt to elucidate the picture of the prophet presented by it in and of itself as of value and legitimacy.[21]

The major shift in the interpretation of Jeremiah's confessions in the post-Reventlow period from a general consensus to its fragmentation and the generation of diverse approaches could be characterized as a crisis in the search for the proper context in which to read these complex texts. For the traditional approach to the confessions which viewed the texts as psychological and spiritual transcripts, the primary interpretive context was clear—i.e. Jeremiah's inner life. While initially this focus was described in relation to Jeremiah's person apart from, or over against, his prophetic office,[22] subsequently and increasingly these witnesses to Jeremiah's inner life were viewed as constituent parts and reflections of the prophetic office and experience.[23] In both cases, the confessions are treated as a distinct block isolated from the rest of the prophetic book. The rest of the book was employed only in an indirect manner for the illumination of the confessions in so far as the complementary context to that of the prophet's inner life, the historical background of Jeremiah's period, the stages of his mission, and the development of his message, was to be reconstructed from it.[24] Increasing recognition of the literary form of these texts as laments only required slight modification in relation to the question of proper interpretive context by emphasizing a theological assessment as opposed to a psychological one in relation to the preceding context of the prophet's inner struggle within his historically reconstructed mission. However, the greater recognition of the literary genre of these texts, along with the tradition and editorial processes that have presented them to us, theoretically raised a significant barrier to ease of access to the interpretive context of the traditional approach. In the post-Reventlow discussion, instead, a variety of contexts is potentially represented by the texts with a diversity of opinions as to the importance of, and even the viability of access to, any one of the given interpretive contexts. As a result, those basically optimistic about recovering the pre-redactional kernel of each confession and re-establishing its setting within the prophetic mission continue to stress the centrality of this context for a proper interpretation of them.[25] They stand opposed to those fundamentally pessimistic about the same endeavour, who deny the authenticity of confessions, but stress their value as witness to the religious needs and interests of the exilic/post-exilic community who composed and preserved them as their proper interpretive context.[26] On the other hand, mediating approaches to these two poles stress the importance of both contexts in the interpretation of the confessions, are optimistic about the viability of access to both, and employ the pre-redactional and redactional settings of the confessions to illuminate one another.[27] Finally, the synchronic approach has rejected all three of the preceding emphases as inappropriate examples of 'etymologizing' a text[28] and stressed the present literary context of the confessions, covering their relationship within the final form of the book as the primary framework for discovering their intention or point.[29]

Aim of the Present Study

The previous review of confession-research, especially in its post-Reventlow developments, indicates the agenda for the present study. The crisis over the proper context in which the confessions are to be interpreted poses the primary question which we shall seek to address—that is, how is a valid reading of these problematic passages to be achieved? As a theoretical ideal, those approaches which attempt to trace the meaning and significance of the confessions from their original setting within the historical mission of the prophet and then into their subsequent transmission and utilization by the tradents are desirable and commendable. However, the problems, raised by an exclusive focus upon the texts as witnesses to the editorial community and by the further reduction to a focus upon the final form of the text as a witness first and foremost to itself, provide a strong reminder that in the last analysis the text represents a barrier to our immediate access to any other of these potentially significant contexts. Consequently, to address our problem, the text will have to be our starting point with careful attention focussed upon the discernment of the poetic and compositional conventions inherent in it. The point here is not at the outset to reject wholesale the questions, methods, and aims involved in the current exegesis of Jeremiah's confessions, but rather to stress the character of the text as both immediate primary source and potential barrier for current research interests. Thus there is the need to confront repeatedly current research interests, aims, and methods with a close analysis of the nature of the texts themselves, open to the possibility that the inherent characteristics of the text will offer guidelines and place constraints upon our own attempt at interpretation—metaphorically speaking, that the inherent conventions of the confessions will say 'read me this way' and establish by this a hierarchy of priorities in the attempt to achieve a valid reading of them.

In the execution of our investigation, the first phase will be given over to an intensive exegesis of the individual confessional units. By organizing the analysis around the categories of form, redaction, setting, and aim, the complex of issues involved in the current interpretation of the passage will be evaluated more easily. A number of features will be of particular interest. First will be the fore-grounding[30] of each confession against lament poetic tradition from the standpoint of structure, diction, imagery, and thought as a means of illuminating each passage in its particularity and typicality[31] *vis-à-vis* the lament genre. From this standpoint the debate over the detection of distinctively prophetic features and interests *versus* a radical ambiguity can be re-evaluated. Second will be the question of discerning explicit editorial activity within each unit. As yet no consensus has been reached in the current debate.[32] The results of this redactional analysis, coupled with the preceding, can then lead to a third feature of special interest: does the genre of each confession, plus its transmission history, permit one to push back into the historical mission of the prophet to locate the function and significance of it in that context? The evaluation of various attempts to do so mentioned above will be appropriate at this juncture as well as a consideration of the problems attendant on attempts to consider the authenticity question. Our primary aim in this phase of the study will be the consideration of the effect upon the attempt to read the confessions as soon as this is executed by isolating the passages as a distinct block from their present relationship to the prophetic book.

The remaining two phases of the investigation will reverse the direction of our procedure by considering the passages in their contextual relationship to the book as a response to the problems arising from the preceding effort to read them apart from this relationship. Initially an intermediate step will be undertaken by considering the relationship of the confessions to one another as a block. In other words, the possibility of the confessions providing their own interpretive context will be evaluated. Of particular interest here will be the review and critique of previous attempts to discern a significant structural and logical relationship among them, especially with regard to their present literary sequence. If in the latter instance a viable case can be initially established, then further considerations related to the origin and growth of this 'context' will need to be introduced from which to judge the validity and sufficiency of such an approach to reading the confessions. Finally, the relationship of the confessions to their immediate literary context must be considered. The issue at this level is whether the editorial employment of the confessions has effected a significant interpretive framework through its incorporation of the confessions into their respective contexts. By correlating the results of these last two steps along with the careful elucidation of the compositional techniques and intentions reflected in the text, we will then be in a position to compare and contrast the focus of the editorial interest in the employment of the confessions with that of current exegesis which finds in them a primarily paradigmatic significance. Our primary aim in these stages of the investigation is to ascertain the status and role of a contextually oriented reading of the confessions in the effort to establish their meaning.[33]

PART I

DRAMATIC DIALOGUE BETWEEN PROPHET AND GOD

Chapter 1

EXEGESIS OF THE INDIVIDUAL CONFESSIONS

1. *Jeremiah* 11.18-23[1]

18	ויהוה הודיעני ואדעה	And Yahweh[2] made known to me and I knew.
	אז הראיתני מעלליהם	Then you showed me their deeds
19	ואני ככבש אלוף	I was like a docile lamb
	יובל לטבוח	led to the slaughter
	ולא ידעתי	and I did not know
	כי עלי חשבו מחשבות	that against me they had schemed:
	נשחיתה עץ בלחמו	'Let us destroy the tree in its vigour[3]
	ונכרתנו מארץ חיים	and cut him off from the land of the living
	ושמו לא יזכר עוד	that his name be remembered no more'.
20	ויהוה שפט צדק	But O Yahweh,[4] righteous judge
	בחן כליות ולב	Tester of affections and heart
	אראה נקמתך מהם	let me see your vengeance on them
	כי אליך גליתי את ריבי	for to you I reveal my case.
21	לכן כה אמר יהוה על אנשי	Therefore, thus says Yahweh
	ענתות המבקשים את נפשך	against the men of Anathoth who
	לאמר לא תנבא בשם יהוה	seek your life[5] saying: 'do not
	ולא תמות בידנו:	prophesy in the name of Yahweh lest you die by our hand'.[6]

22	הנני פקד עליהם	'Behold I will punish them,
	הבחורים ימתו בחרב	their warriors will die by the
	בניהם ובנותיהם ימתו ברעב:	sword, their sons and their
		daughters will die by famine, and
		no remnant will they have;
23	ושארית לא תהיה להם כי	for I will bring calamity
	אביא רעה אל אנשי ענתות	against the men of Anathoth,
	שנת פקדתם	their year of reckoning.'

Form

The development of our discussion will be carried out in awareness of two major factors. The first relates to considerations of method. Recent discussion of form critical method has criticized the analysis of form which notes only the typical or stereotyped features of a text.[7] So in the present analysis attention will be directed to both the typical and the particular features of each unit. The second major factor relates to the formal classification of the confessions 'in block'. Alongside and over against the consensus following Baumgartner, which understood their primary relationship to be with cultic genre, two additional analyses have been proposed. One, noting the presence of legal terms in the passages, has reclassified the confessions as lawsuits (S.H. Blank; D.H. Wimmer).[8] The other, noting similarities and dissimilarities with cultic lament, has attempted a reclassification which treats the passages as a special genre in their own right (N. Ittmann).[9] In our analysis these three major approaches will constitute the chief points for debate. For the lawsuit view, the central question will be whether the legal imagery provides the controlling pattern of the confession. For the third approach, it will be whether the dissimilarities from cultic genre are significant enough to warrant the rupture of their relationship to it, establishing thereby the confession as a special category.

With regard to the present unit, it has been a frequent practice to rearrange the order of verses—notably the insertion of 12.6 between 11.18 and 19—in an effort to produce a more coherent logical development. This approach remains attractive so long as the abrupt introduction of subject, opaque references to individuals and events, and apparent jumps in logic prevent an intelligible understanding of the present arrangement of the text from being achieved. But the lack of external textual support for rearrangement theories raises a note of caution. It may be that such methods for achieving coherence have relied upon false expectations and misapprehensions of the compositional intention of the passage. We hope to show that attention to characteristics of genre and poetic technique can go far in reducing the problems perceived in the previous approach, thus eliminating the necessity for it.[10]

Typical Form: The passage divides evenly into poetry (vv. 18-20) and prose (vv. 21-23), which invites questions about the genre of each part as well as of the whole. Analysis of the prose divine response seems the least problematic. It exhibits the typical elements of a prophetic judgment oracle: introductory messenger formula (v. 21aα); accusation (v. 21aβ-b); messenger formula (v. 22aα); pronouncement of judgment (vv. 22aβ-23). The situation for the preceding poetic prayer is similar but in relationship to a lament psalm.[11]

v. 19   lament
v. 20a   expression of trust
v. 20b   petition

An exception is provided by v. 18. Instead of the expected introductory address and petition we find a report about the divine activity. Baumgartner, recognizing the anomaly and the lack of parallels in the psalter, continued his classification of vv. 18-20 as lament but explained v. 18 as a distinctive prophetic element reporting the reception of a special revelation from Yahweh.[12] But this is unlikely, since no other parallels exist in Jeremianic poetry which indicate that we have to do here with a revelational reception formula or even an experience that is peculiarly prophetic.[13] Reventlow's alternative seems more promising. He argued that vv. 18-20 constitute a segment from a thanksgiving psalm.[14] If the main section of a thanksgiving psalm is considered, with its elements of portrayal of distress (cf. v. 19), cry to God (cf. v. 20), and answer (cf. v. 18), then his view appears to account for the problem of v. 18.[15] However, v. 18 still remains partly unexplained. In thanksgiving, the normal orientation has the worshipper fully aware of his distress, initiating the plea for help: 'I cried to God in my distress and he answered me' (Jon. 2.3). Verse 18 is just the reverse. Yahweh is the initiator of aid to an individual oblivious of his danger: 'Yahweh told me and I saw'. For this reason, it is difficult to classify the verses as only lament or thanksgiving. Given the close relationship between lament and thanksgiving,[16] it seems best to regard the passage as a borderline case. In two thanksgiving psalms such a stress is placed upon the portrayal of distress that it becomes difficult to distinguish them absolutely from laments (Ps. 41; and esp. Ps. 120—cf. v. 1: קראתי ויענני).[17] The existence of such potential for overlap and other borderline parallels suggests the legitimacy of a similar classification for 11.18-20. As such, the typicalities of both genres affect the tone of the piece, since it reverberates between confident expectation and alarmed plea. However, the association with thanksgiving seems slightly to the fore.[18]

Though the preceding borderline classification seems to account best for the confession, reclassification as a lawsuit has been attempted, based on the presence of legal terminology (שפט, בחן, ריב, פקד) and its trial procedure structure.[19] The immediate legal background of the passage is found in Deut. 19.16-19.[20] However, this view does not seem legitimate. Jer. 11.18-23 and Deut. 19.16-19 sustain no material connections. Their only point of connection is the common sharing of the general principle of *lex talionis*. Their immediate connection is remote. Further the confession lacks the characteristic motifs of Hebrew law and any explicit allusions to the scene of a trial.[21] The presence of a few legal terms does nothing to invalidate the associations with cultic poetry already observed, since the Psalms also make extensive use of legal imagery.[22] It seems best to regard the legal terms as directly mediated from cultic psalm practice with the original legal sphere as remote.[23]

Finally, there still remains for discussion the relationship of the prayer and following oracle in relation to formal patterns. The best parallel to which comparison can be made is the well-attested prophetic liturgy which has incorporated elements from national lament and the divine oracle into a single structure.[24] Precedent for this pattern exists elsewhere in Jeremiah as a method of clothing judgment oracles with cultic forms (Jer. 3.21-4.2; 14.1-10; 14.17-15.4).[25] Three of the other confessions are constructed in a similar way (12.1-6; 15.10-14; 15.15-21). The presence of divine oracles or allusions to the same in individual laments (Pss. 12; 35.3b; cf. national laments Pss. 60//108; 85) blunts the initial difficulty for comparing these patterns in the confessions to the prophetic liturgy since the latter consists of national lament.[26] Perhaps it would be best to say that 11.18-23 have been structured under formal influence of a cultic pattern, attested primarily by the prophetic liturgy, that has been mediated through the example of the other Jeremianic confessions cited above.

Particular Form: The divergence from typical features of lament and thanksgiving in vv. 18-20 invites consideration of the particular structure of the passage. Traditional typicalities seem to have been subordinated in order to achieve a particular effect. We begin with a schematic illustration of the prayer:[27]

Present	v. 18	יהוה	ידע, ידע ידע		
				ראה	מעלליהם
Retrospect	v. 19	ואני			
			לא ידע		מחשבות
					Citation
Prospect	v. 20	יהוה		ראה	
			גלה		ריב

The major controlling structural factors are the disjunctive markers (ואני, יהוה) plus the shift of temporal perspective in the development of ideas (present—retrospect—prospect). This framework is integrated further by the repetition of key verbs and ideas. The citation lends specificity to the general terms ריבי, מחשבות, מעלליהם. Verses 18 and 20 form an inclusio around the whole by use of the key verbs. In v. 18 Yahweh is revealing/showing, but in v. 20 the poet requests to see divine vengeance based upon his own revelation to Yahweh. As a result, v. 19 is set at the centre of the prayer.

The following divine response exhibits a similar integrated structure:[28]

v. 21	— לכן —	messenger			אנשי ענתות
		formula	מות		
					— inclusio
v. 22	(— לכן —	messenger)		פקד	
	(	formula)	מות		
			מות		
v. 23				פקדה	אנשי ענתות

If the second messenger formula is retained (see text), then the logical division of the oracle is explicitly marked. The whole oracle is framed by an inclusio with אנשי ענתות. The accusation and pronouncement sections are tied together by the key verb מות, suggesting a crime-punishment correspondence. And the pronouncement is itself integrated by the repeated key term פקרה/פקד.

The formal connection (noted above) between the prayer and its answer is complemented by a number of additional features. First, the initial conjunction (v. 21—לכן) invites perception of a logical connection between the sections. Second, both sections employ oblique 3rd pers. references to the poet's enemies. The suspense created by the abrupt oblique reference in vv. 18-20 is resolved in vv. 21-23 by their identification as the men of Anathoth. The progressive development of the prayer ends in petition. The contacts with thanksgiving genre lend to the prayer overtones of confident expectation. This high degree of expectant tension receives its fitting climax and resolution in the following oracle. Parallelism between the use of the citations of the enemy (vv. 19, 21) can be observed.[29] In both cases they lend greater concretion to the general intentions of the enemy (v. 19—חשב; v. 21—בקש). Similarly, a crime-punishment correspondence is effected across the sections. As in v. 19, the intentions of the opponents are articulated with three members—two positive, one negative—as also the pronouncement of judgment, vv. 22b-23a. Those who plotted the prophet's destruction will themselves be destroyed.[30]

Still certain dissonant features, which can be discerned between the sections, lead to a consideration of redactional issues since these very dissonances could be an indication that their connection is secondary and not original. Explanations for these features must be sought if an original connection is to be maintained.

Redaction

In the evaluation of redactional issues, the related but distinct issues of original/secondary and authentic/inauthentic must be kept separate. Theoretically, originally separate authentic material could have been redacted together at a subsequent stage. Naturally if one unit is known to be inauthentic, its secondary connection to another would be demonstrated; but inauthenticity is not a necessary factor in the discernment of editorial activity.

In our view, the most probable candidate for evidence of editorial activity is in the connection between vv. 18-20 and 21-23. Evaluation of proposals related to this problem will be our main concern. However, suggestions have also been made with regard to vv. 18-20 and so we begin with a brief consideration of these, though they do not seem as probable.

U. Eichler and F. Ahuis have argued that vv. 18-20, in block, represent a Dtr. composition. For the latter, the chief indication of this lies in the prose character (nowhere demonstrated) of vv. 18-19 into which has been incorporated the poetic doublet (v. 20) drawn from 20.12. Supporting evidence is seen in alleged late literary contacts (v. 19; cf. Isa. 53.7) or signs of integration with the wider Jeremianic context (11.16; 12.1—agricultural images/v. 19; 12.3— צאן לטבחה/11.19—כבש לטבוח; 11.18—*waw* connection to 11.1-17; v. 19 חשב מחשבות/18.18).[31] However, the ease of scanning vv. 18-19 into three bi-cola and one tri-colon with 3 + 3 or 3 + 2 metre makes analysis as prose unlikely. Emphasis upon late literary contacts takes the direction of influence for granted and ignores numerous points of contact with Psalms and especially other Jeremianic poetry (see diction analysis below). The integration into the wider context will be the focus of our attention in the second and third stages of this study, but in and of itself it does not require that a given unit is the total compositional product at this stage of the redactional process. The doublet with 20.12 is difficult to evaluate but seems best understood as formulaic repetition. Our preceding formal analysis shows that it is fully integral to the passage.[32]

The most elaborate redactional model for 11.18-12.6 has been proposed by J. Vermeylen.[33] Restricting our attention to vv. 18-20, he discerns a two-stage post-exilic redaction. First, vv. 18-19 were added as commentary to the following oracle (vv. 21-22) followed by a second stage in which v. 20 was added to the prayer plus the marginal gloss או הראיתני in v. 18. However, Vermeylen's proposal, based upon alleged logical inconsistencies and late literary contacts, is unconvincing. Our formal analysis suggests a higher degree of structural integrity than he recognizes.[34] As with the position above, he has assumed a uni-directional influence for the late literary contacts and ignored other Jeremianic parallels in the poetry.[35] It seems best to regard the prayer as an integral unit with no discernible signs of internal editorial activity.

The situation for the divine oracle seems different. The parallelism between the citations is disturbed by v. 19 depicting a secret plot while v. 21 portrays open confrontation and threat.[36] Further, the crime-punishment correspondence would have been stronger had consistent imagery been used for both. Verse 19 is executed in agricultural terms, while vv. 22b-23 employ military-war categories. The logical connector in v. 21 (לכן) is just the sort of binder a later editor would use. And finally, the other confessions which are patterned similarly are completely poetic; but this one has its divine oracle in prose. In this regard, important phraseological and stylistic parallels between vv. 21-23 and the Jeremiah prose traditions exist.[37] However, Hubmann has argued against viewing the whole of vv. 21-23 as secondary. For him only vv. 21 and 23bβ (אנשי ענתות) constitute editorial additions. The remaining vv. 22-23bα constitute the original poetic oracle.[38] Besides the internal tensions with v. 19, v. 21 exhibits exclusive contact with Jeremianic prose in style and vocabulary.[39] Verse 23bβ was added to integrate v. 21 with vv. 22-23bα and 12.6.[40] For his poetic kernel he observes rhythmic parallelism and parallels with other poetic texts in Jeremiah.[41] But the structural integration of the oracle observed above raises difficulties for Hubmann's reconstruction. The repetition of מות and the resultant crime-punishment correspondence indicate an integral connection between vv. 21 and 22. The validity of excising אל אנשי ענתות (v. 23bβ) is not so clear in the light of prose and poetic parallels (48.44; 23.12b) which suggest that the construction אביא רעה אל/על is normal and expected. This in turn makes excision of v. 21 unlikely because of the inclusio with אנשי ענתות (v. 23).[42] Finally, Hubmann's vocabulary analysis and poetic reconstruction are not entirely satisfactory. True, individual words have parallels in Jeremianic poetry, but stylistically the contacts with the prose traditions are much stronger.[43] A tolerable poetic parallelism can be reconstructed, and the existence of poetic parallels suggests that Hubmann's proposal cannot be entirely excluded.[44] However, the smaller frequency of poetic parallels compared to the greater stylistic affinity with prose may suggest a complex process of the editor's rhetoric showing influence of Jeremianic poetic vocabulary. Thus the existence of such poetic precursors would still not require the reconstruction of the whole back into poetry. Given the difficulty in certain cases of distinguishing poetry from rhythmic prose, the poetic-like effect of some of these verses in the oracle may be more the result of the editor affecting speech characteristic of oracular prophetic utterance.[45] But even if the validity of the poetic reconstruction is granted, the dissonant features between the oracle and the prayer do not seem to be entirely eliminated; for the crime-punishment correspondence still does not mesh in terms of imagery. On the whole, it seems best to view the connection between vv. 18-20 and 21-23 as secondary.

used in public defence.[50] Wimmer also stresses his formal analysis of
the passages as lawsuits which indicate their role as 'public
declamations', and the social role of the prophet as imparting a
necessarily public character to whatever transpires between prophet
and Yahweh.[51] This proposal is very plausible, particularly in the
light of a prophetic employment of lament motifs to enhance their
oracles of judgment and the apologetic role of prophetic call
narratives. But the primary test of its validity must be the suitability
of its application to each of the eight confessional units. It is possible
to anticipate difficulties with aspects of the proposal. That the last
four units (17.14-18; 18.18-23; 20.7-13; 20.14-18) all lack divine
responses raises questions about Berridge's stress upon this feature.
And already, Wimmer's reliance upon the lawsuit pattern seems
invalid for 11.18-23 as a result of our preceding formal analysis.
Finally, the effects of various redactional models upon this approach
must be considered. Final assessment of their approach must await
our discussion of each unit.

The other main variation relates to the establishment of a special
sub-genre of lament (*gerichtsprophetische Klage*). Eichler and Ahuis
isolate authentic Jeremianic kernels from the confessions and then
postulate a prophetic setting within the messenger function approach
to prophecy. As a messenger the prophet is potentially susceptible to
crisis at two points: when he delivers the message it may meet
outright opposition and rejection; or, having delivered it, he may
experience opposition arising out of delay in its fulfilment. At both
these points, the setting for lament in prophetic mission is to be
found.[52] The organic connection of the lament to each of these crisis
points is exhibited in two literary patterns.[53] The first pattern is
narrative in character depicting the stages of the messenger event
(*Botenvorgang*) viewed as: commissioning of the messenger, execution
of the task, and report (Gen. 24; 32; Num. 20; 22; Judg. 11; Ruth 3;
1 Sam. 25; 2 Kgs 8).[54] In cases where the messenger meets with
rejection, the 'report' (*Rückmeldung*) can take the form of a lament.
The lament is characterized by accusation of the one who commissioned the messenger (1 Sam. 10.1-5; Exod. 5.6-18; Num. 11.11-
13; Exod. 5.22-23).[55] The second pattern, determined by the
expectation of outstanding judgment, centres on the accusation of
the prophet's enemies and appeals for his vindication by their
destruction. Yahweh's apparent silence has subjected him to ridicule
and persecution (1 Kgs 19.8-18; Isa. 6.11; 8.16-18; Ezek. 33.23-33;
Hos. 9.1-9; Mic. 3.1-12).[56]

In principle, this attractive theory offers a potentially recurrent sociological institution (i.e. prophet as messenger) plus a recurrent occasion (i.e. the two crisis points) for the occurrence of a special prophetic-lament. Thus Jeremiah's complaints would become an intelligible phenomenon. While the applicability of this approach, as with the other, to each of the units must await our respective analyses, at least initially the question can be raised about the successful establishment of a special sub-genre of lament that is organically related to prophetic mission. Major problems appear to be present. For the first pattern (*Botenvorgang*), it must be recognized that the occurrence of lament within the structure is exceedingly rare in the OT. Ahuis can list only four examples, none of which occurs in prophetic literature.[57] Only one of the four really seems to fit the requirements (Exod. 5.22-23). This comes at the end of a section depicting the initial call and failure of Moses' mission to Pharaoh.[58] In the other examples, either no lament is actually present (1 Sam. 10.1-5);[59] or the lament does not occur within the structure of the messenger process (Num. 11.11-13);[60] or the commissioning does not relate to that of messenger and the complaint does not arise out of opposition to the task (Exod. 5.6-18). On this basis, it is questionable whether the one clear example (Exod. 5.22-23) constitutes evidence of a fixed form. The lack of any clear examples in other prophetic books is also surprising since the messenger function should fundamentally apply to them.

Turning to the second pattern, the extra-Jeremianic examples seem equally unsatisfying. In some, no situation of opposition to prophetic mission is involved (Isa. 6.11; Ezek. 33.30-33; Hos. 9.1-9); in others the problem of delayed fulfilment is not a question (1 Kgs 19.8-18; Hos. 9.1-9; Mic. 3.8); and none of the examples is in the literary form of individual lament (see above, and Isa. 8.16-28; Mic. 3.1-12).[61] While the general framework could render Jeremiah's complaints understandable in the context of prophetic mission, it still necessitates explaining the uniqueness of the confessions *vis-à-vis* other prophetic literature. Why did the postulated setting of this approach produce lament in Jeremiah's case? Posed this way, the problem leads back to the traditional approach which explained the uniqueness of the confessions within the personal experience of the prophet himself. The preceding approach of Eichler and Ahuis would allow discussion of the texts within this framwork unencumbered by the difficulties of an overly psychological reading. But this raises again the question of viability for the older approach and its underlying assumptions.

Criticism of the latter is the strength of the second theoretical approach to the confessions—i.e. as total editorial compositions. This approach has stressed variously the problem of the psalm language as private utterances, the radical ambiguity of the idioms *vis-à-vis* any detectable 'prophetic elements', and the lack of any clear rationale for the inclusion of such private musings in the Jeremiah tradition. Thus it seems preferable to this approach to see the confessions as editorial compositions employing pre-existing lament psalms, placed on Jeremiah's lips, and interpreting the prophet in relation to their own needs and problems.[62] Such a process is theoretically possible (cf. 1 Sam. 2.1-10; Jon. 2.3-10) and the suitability of such an explanation for each of the confessions will need to be considered.[63] But in relation to the present unit, 11.18-23, problems already arise. For the prose oracle, numerous contacts with Jeremianic poetic diction and themes have already been observed (see notes 42-44). Ways in which the prayer, vv. 18-20, diverges from normal laments have been noted. This will prove true for the diction as well, and parallels at this level with Jeremianic poetry can be observed.[64] At least for this confession a certain allowance for the employment of authentic material or even reworking of pre-existing Jeremianic units would have to be made on this approach.[65] If such problems continued to arise in analysis of the other units, a serious modification of this second theory would seem to be required.

On the basis of the preceding general survey, we can now turn to consider the setting of 11.18-23 more directly. At the outset, the secondary relationship of vv. 18-20 to vv. 21-23 requires looking for a setting for each section independently. The question of the setting for vv. 21-23 seems the most straightforward, so we shall begin there. Its characteristics correspond perfectly to the typicalities of a judgment speech. The motif of a prophet announcing judgment upon his opponents is well attested in Jeremiah and other prophets (Jer. 20.1-6; 28.12-17; 29.24-32; Amos 7.10-17). The oracle clearly reflects a setting of conflict over the prophetic mission.

The clarity of details in the preceding is in sharp contrast to the opaque character of the prayer. Taken by themselves, vv. 18-20 provide no stimulus to search for a setting within the prophetic mission. This latter connection seems to be a factor primarily based upon its secondary association with the prose oracle and its present literary setting within the prophetic book. None of the positive proposals for a setting in prophetic mission seems applicable. As a dramatic apologetic form in situations of conflict, the whole passage could be serviceable, but not vv. 18-20 alone. Nothing in these verses would seem to alert its listeners to concerns distinctively prophetic except the fact of their utterance by a prophet. But no indication of the speaker's identity is given. A conflict situation is indicated, but nothing suggests that a prophetic figure is at its centre. As noted above, v. 18 need not be taken as an allusion to prophetic revelatory experience; and any encouragement to do so seems to be a result of the present contextual setting for the passage. Such difficulties raise serious questions for the attempt to view the unit as a special type of prophetic lament. On the other hand, the stylistic and vocabulary contacts with Jeremianic poetry could permit the assumption that the passage originally bore some relationship to the historical mission of the prophet. In any case, the present literary setting seems dominant and any hypothetical setting prior to it has been rendered indeterminant. Consideration of the remaining confessions may be more profitable in this regard.

Interpretation

Since the basic meaning of this confession seems clear, our primary concern in this section will be the foregrounding of the lament against lament and cultic poetic tradition in general to highlight the continuity and discontinuity,[66] illuminate the particular force of the imagery employed, and evaluate various possibilities of inner Jeremianic allusions.

The prayer opens (v. 18) with a report about a divine initiative on behalf of the poet to warn him aginst the activities of an unspecified group. Verse 19 moves retrospectively to describe his situation prior to v. 18 and in so doing lends a progressive note to the prayer. The oblique references to an unspecified group are clarified now as the poet's enemies whose deeds consist of a plot to destroy him, articulated by a citation motif.[67] The prayer concludes by turning from the past to look forward in urgent petition to Yahweh for vindication over against these enemies.[68] The divine oracle provides the crucial climax. The expectations and tensions of the prayer are resolved. This occurs not only because the oracle confirms the preceding plea, but also because the opaqueness of the poetry is made concrete. By it the prayer is firmly rooted in Jeremiah's prophetic experience, his opponents are explicitly identified, and the occasion of conflict is rooted in the prophetic mission.[69]

Against the backdrop of the Psalms, at no point is Yahweh ever depicted as warning the psalmist prior to the plots of his enemies coming to fruition.[70] The imagery employed within the citation has exploited overtones associated with the destinies of the righteous and the wicked. Obliteration of the name and removal from the ארץ חיים—the sphere of blessing for the righteous (Pss. 27.13; 116.9; 142.6)—is the fate reserved for the wicked.[71] The prophet's enemies plot for him the fate appropriate to the wicked. Usage of כרת and שחת may imply that they view their actions as enactments of divine judgment.[72] However, these overtones are in tension with the description of the prophet as כבש אלוף and עץ בלחמו.[73] The former labels him as an unsuspecting innocent, and the latter as a fruitful tree, which are common images of the righteous.[74] From the standpoint of the poet, his appeal to Yahweh is motivated by a portrayal of distress as the unthinkable, i.e. a righteous man threatened with the fate of the wicked. On the other hand, as a citation of the enemy, insight into their view of the prophet is granted—i.e. he represents the problem of the prosperous wicked.[75] The petition fits well with the preceding images related to the righteous and wicked in its use of terms with legal overtones (שפט, ריב, בחן) and its assumption of integrity of the one so praying.[76] The prayer reflects a blend of similarity and dissimilarity to psalm technique. And even some of the similarities are not represented in a widespread fashion in the Psalms. None of this invalidates paralleling this passage and lament-thanksgiving genre,[77] but it does suggest that we are not dealing merely with a typical psalm. This in turn suggests the need to modify previous views which have regarded it as the transfer of a typical lament or a fragment of one into the present setting.[78]

Aim

The text presents a dialogue between prophet and Yahweh. Its composite genre affinities of lament, thanksgiving, and judgment speech lend a complex tone to the whole of confident certainty, urgent plea, assurance, and threat. It would be incorrect to view the central issue of the confession as a conflict between prophet and

Yahweh. On the contrary, these two occupy positions of solidarity. The prophet is consistently presented as an innocent litigant who is wrongly threatened. It is only natural that Yahweh, who is just and the proper judge of men, will side with such a one. The prophet is Yahweh's threatened spokesman. It is only to be expected that divine support will be forthcoming. At no point does the prophet engage in accusations against Yahweh for permitting this threat to occur. There is no need. From the outset it is the prophet's God who has taken steps to warn and protect him and who ultimately will destroy his persecutors. The prophet's 'case' is set within a framework which at no point leaves its beneficial outcome in doubt. The conflict and tension which are present lie solely between the prophet, Yahweh, and the men of Anathoth. The latter constitute the oblique or explicit third partner to the dialogue. And it is to the issue of opposition to prophetic mission that the confession speaks.[79] This is particularly underlined by the oracle which lends to the confession the character of testimony or witness. Literarily speaking, a 'private' interchange between prophet and God has taken on public import.[80] The witness given is that opposition to Yahweh's prophet seals one's doom with the general impending judgment of the nation (שנת פקדתם).[81]

2. Jeremiah 12.1-6

1
צדיק אתה יהוה
Innocent are you, Yahweh

כי אריב אליך
If I lodge a complaint before you.

אך משפטים אדבר אותך
Yet sentence must I pass on you!

מדוע דרך רשעים צלחה
Why does the way of the wicked succeed,

שלו כל בגדי בגד
Why at ease are all those practising treachery?

2
נתעתם גם שרשו
You planted them so they took root,

ילכו גם עשו פרי
they grew up, even produced fruit.

קרוב אתה בפיהם
Near are you in their mouths,

ורחוק מכליותיהם
but far from their inmost being.

3
ואתה יהוה ידעתני תראני
But you, O Yahweh, know me, see me[1]

ובחנת לבי אתך
and test that my heart is with you.

התקם כצאן לטבחה
Drag them away like sheep for butchering,[2]

והקדשם ליום הרגה
consecrate them for the day of slaughter.

4
עד מתי תאבל הארץ
How long must mourn, the land,

ועשב כל השדה ייבש
and the grass of every field wither,

מרעת ישבי בה
because of the wickedness of its inhabitants,

ספתה בהמות ועוף
they perish, beast and fowl.

כי אמרו
For they say:

לא יראה את אחריתנו
'He does not see our end'.[3]

5
כי את רגלים רצתה וילאוך
If with footmen you have run and they have wearied you

ואיך תתחרה את הסוסים
how will you compete with horses!

ובארץ שלום אתה בוטח
If in a peaceful land you feel secure,

ואיך תעשה בגאון הירדן
how will you act in the Jordan's thicket!

6   כי גם אחיך ובית אביך   For even your brother's and your
father's house
גם המה בגדו בך   even they betray you
גם המה קראו אחריך מלא   even they call after you:
'assemble, help!'

אל תאמן בם   Do not believe them,
כי ידברו אליך טובות   though they offer to you terms of
friendship.

Form

Analysis of the preceding unit (11.18-23) as an integrated and well-rounded composition necessarily conditions the approach to 12.1-6. Problems arise for the common practice of removing verses from the latter (esp. v. 3b) to insert into the former. The question of whether such verses as vv. 3, 4, 6 are fully appropriate within the present confession must be faced, but such attempts as the preceding to preserve them within the context seem ruled out.

Typical Form: As with 11.18-23, this confession represents a complex blend of different genre motifs. The passage divides again into the poet's prayer (vv. 1-4) and the divine answer (vv. 5-6). The problem of poetry-prose shifts is once again represented by v. 6. But whereas the genre affinities of the preceding prayer (11.18-20) were primarily with lament-thanksgiving motifs and secondarily with legal motifs, the balance shifts in 12.1-4 to a blend of lament and legal speech forms to the total exclusion of thanksgiving.

The bulk of the confession can be related to the typicalities of the prophetic liturgy with its components of lament and answering oracle:

v. 1a	disputational introduction
vv. 1b-2	complaint
v. 3a	profession of innocence
v. 3b	petition
v. 4	complaint
vv. 5-6	divine oracle

From the perspective of lament typicalities, however, vv. 1-2 are unusual compared with the normal introductory address and petition. There is a concentration of expressions and imagery drawn from the sphere of jurisprudence (דבר משפט את, ריב אל, צדיק אתה),

מדוע). The theme of the prosperity of the wicked narrows the lines of
affinity to certain wisdom psalms (37; 49; 73) and the book of Job.[4] In
light of such features, the continued classification of the prayer as
lament must be considered as well as the possibility of discerning
some other genre which has been more constitutive in the structuring
of this text.

Adequate comparative texts are difficult to find. No lament psalm
opens in a way similar to vv. 1-2. Even the wisdom psalms above
handle the problem at issue within a different framework.[5] All of
them draw back from explicit accusation of Yahweh. For this,
examples from Job must be included (Job 19.6; 21.7-26; 24.1-12).
Even so, a more precise analysis of genre, other than simply 'near-
lament', does not result.[6] Because of these difficulties and the
presence of legal imagery, a reclassification of the passage as a
lawsuit has been attempted.[7] The elements of the passage are
illuminated by the courtroom scene in which the litigants bring
accusation, counter-accusation, and defence before the judge.[8] The
presence of the legal terms makes such an approach attractive, as
well as providing an explanation of troublesome features. The caveat
to the צדיק of the judge becomes understandable as an attempt
favourably to dispose him to the poet's plea. Verse 3a, which seems
out of place as a profession of innocence in relation to the theme of
the prosperity of the wicked, becomes understandable in this trial
context of confrontation between litigants.[9]

Nevertheless, it does not seem that a trial process pattern actually
exercises a controlling influence upon the text. The use to which the
legal speech forms have been put is striking. צדיק אתה, the formula of
acquittal, reflects a sentence of the court and implies that Yahweh is
the defendant. But ריב אל represents Yahweh as the judge before
whom the litigation is presented. The picture is reversed again by
דבר משפט את, which indicates the intention of the poet to pass
sentence upon God. Elements drawn from the trial process have
been used in a jumbled and ironic fashion. Elements expected only at
the end of the trial occur mixed up with elements of the pre-trial
encounter. Motifs associated with speeches before the court seem
entirely absent. If the 3rd pers. references to the wicked are taken as
this,[10] then their point is misconstrued, for Yahweh is not being asked
to decide between the poet and his enemies; rather the wicked are the
'crime' which he lays to the blame of Yahweh. The 2nd pers. address
fits the pre-trial encounter. Yahweh is represented as both judge and

accused. The legal metaphors have been strained to the breaking point.[11] Attempts to reclassify the passage as a lawsuit do not seem to have taken adequate account of the way the legal speech forms are normally used, nor of the question whether their employment here is really intended to represent a normal portrayal of trial procedure.[12] Instead of exercising a controlling influence, the lawsuit pattern appears to have been subordinated to the lament with the juridical picture turned on its head. As a result, the petition receives a driving force and much of the potency of the prayer is affected. But this returns one to a classification of near-lament relative to typicalities of form.[13]

Particular Form: A structural schematic of the passage illustrates the integrated character of 12.1-6:[14]

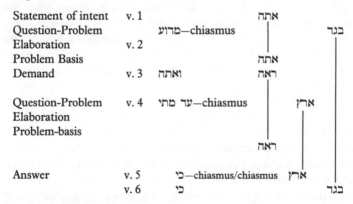

Statement of intent	v. 1		אתה
Question-Problem		מדוע—chiasmus	בגר
Elaboration	v. 2		
Problem Basis			אתה
Demand	v. 3	ואתה	ראה
Question-Problem	v. 4	ער מתי—chiasmus	ארץ
Elaboration			
Problem-basis			
			ראה
Answer	v. 5	כי—chiasmus/chiasmus	ארץ
	v. 6	כי	בגר

Verse 3 occupies the centre of the prayer, set off by the disjunctive ואתה. Verses 1b-2 and 4 constitute parallel formulations. They share a common threefold development of question-problem, elaboration, and problem-basis. The parallelism is strengthened by the chiastic structure of the question-problem elements (שלח־צלח־דרך רשעים ;בגדי בגר) and the execution of the problem-basis elements with their depiction of the true nature of the wicked in relationship to Yahweh. The inclusios of אתה and ראה help round off the prayer into two sub-units (vv. 1-2; 3-4). The divine answer is linked to the preceding by the conjunction in v. 5 (כי). The two 'if . . . how' clauses of v. 5 are structured chiastically, suggesting a parallelism with the two question-problem elements above (vv. 1b, 4a). Verse 6 is linked to v. 5 by the conjunction (כי) and the apparent shift from a figurative statement (v. 5) to its concrete explanation (v. 6). The only link of v. 6 to vv. 1-4 is the inclusio with בגד, suggesting nevertheless that the whole of 12.1-6 is integrated together. This consistent and integrated structure raises serious difficulties for exegetical approaches which proceed by radical rearrangement and/or expunction of various verses like portions of vv. 3, 4, and 6.[15] Even if these elements are shown to be secondary, their present placement would suggest a composite artistry whose intention would be misconstrued if such radical emendations are employed.

The presence of dissonant features still must be evaluated, and this will be the focus of much of the rest of our discussion, especially in the sections on Redaction and Interpretation. In anticipation, the profession of innocence (v. 3a) in relation to the problem of the prosperity of the wicked is troublesome. Its function must be clarified. How are the situations depicted in vv. 1b-2 and v. 4 really parallel and integrally related? Does the divine answer really supply a fitting response to the prayer? Especially problematic is the prose or poetry status of v. 6 and the question of its material connection to the preceding.

Redaction

The primary focus of attention in this section will be the status of v. 6 in the divine answer. Dissonant features noted for vv. 3-4 can be treated best in the Interpretation section, where the possibility of viewing their meaning in a way that complements the signs of formal integrity can be addressed.[16] To my knowledge, no one has questioned the originality of v. 5 in its present context. The formal analogy to the prophetic liturgy pattern plus the particular structural parallels with vv. 1-4 provide a strong presumption in favour of this judgment.

Formerly the only way of preserving v. 6 in some fashion in context, besides radical rearrangement, has been through radical separation of 11.18-23 and 12.1-6.[17] It is questionable, though, whether this reckons seriously enough with the present contextual association of the two confessions and the apparently close links between 11.21-23 and 12.6. However, recent redactional models have been proposed in the effort to provide an alternative explanation of the difficulties occasioned by v. 6. On these approaches, 12.6 is considered an editorial expansion linking 12.1-5 back to 11.18-23. The position has been most persuasively argued by W. Thiel and F.D. Hubmann. For Thiel, the verse has been displaced by the Dtr. from 11.18ff. The close contact with the subject matter of 11.18, 21-23 indicates that 12.6 represents the original divine warning mentioned in 11.18. Its prose character provides further indication of secondary character since this contrasts to the normal poetic form of the confessions.[18] Hubmann has modified Thiel's position in so far as 12.6 is attributed to the same editorial hand as 11.21, 23; and 12.5 is taken as the primary stimulus for the expansions. The lesser-to-the-greater logic of the latter has been incorporated into the plan of the larger composition. So the secret plot of 11.19 intensifies to open threat (11.21), and then the circle of opponents spreads from the prophet's townsmen (11.21) to penetrate his immediate familial circle (12.6).[19] He elaborates Thiel's line of argument in support. Analysis of the vocabulary in 12.6 is inconclusive since it is too general or too rare to permit definite conclusions.[20] This permits him to stress the primary objection to v. 6 in its lack of an organic connection with the preceding.[21] The verse only sustains a relationship with v. 5. It is thematically unrelated to vv. 1-4.[22] The echo with בגד in v. 1 is purely mechanical, catchword association.[23] The only explicit thematic connection is with the mention of Anathoth in 11.21.[24] Thus the point of comparison in v. 6 is different from that of v. 5. For the latter, the 'lesser' problem is reflected in vv. 1-4; but in v. 6 it is in 11.21. Verse 5 is oriented toward the future, but v. 6 assumes a present reality.[25] Finally, the redactional character of 11.21 suggests that 12.6 is redactional as well, since they are both intrinsically related.[26]

The great advantage of this approach is that it avoids textual rearrangement, comes to terms with the present structure of the passage, and, at the same time, provides an explanation of the apparent dissonant quality of v. 6 in its present setting.[27] Nevertheless, certain factors are present which suggest that this solution is not as satisfactory as it seems. First the classification of v. 6 as prose, which is so important in many of the redactional studies, is problematical.[28] The strong contacts of 11.21-23 with Jeremianic prose were an important factor in discerning the redactional character of that oracle. The situation is not so clear for 12.6 since, as Hubmann's vocabulary analysis shows, there is no distinctive Dtr. vocabulary in it.[29] Still, if the vocabulary is evaluated strictly in terms of individual

Setting

The attempt to establish the setting of each of the confessions must be executed in a judicious manner. For once the transfer and borrowing of genres from one setting to another is recognized, a given genre of a text can no longer be taken as providing immediate indication of its setting within the prophetic mission. The primary and secondary uses of a genre must be kept in mind. And even at the end of a search for these pre-literary settings it may turn out that they have been subordinated to the present literary employment of the passage, thus rendering a given primary or secondary use opaque.[46] Some indication of the problem the confessions have presented to current research in this regard has already been indicated in our Introduction. Increased recognition of the stereotyped and abstract nature of these passages in their relationship to cultic genre, plus the difficulty of explaining the rationale and manner of publishing what were taken originally to have been purely private utterances, have led to attempts to reach a new understanding of their setting and aim. Two major competing theories have been articulated.[47] The first continues to see the confessions or a reconstructed pre-editorial kernel as authentic and postulates a distinctive setting within the prophetic mission. The second denies their substantial authenticity, detaches them from the historical prophetic mission, and views them as total editorial compositions placed in the mouth of the prophet. At the outset of our discussion it will be helpful to survey these approaches in more detail, particularly from the standpoint of overall theoretical viability.

The first theory has a number of variations placing emphasis upon a public apologetic function or upon the classification of the confessions as a special sub-genre of lament. J.M. Berridge has drawn attention to the use of lament forms in Jeremianic oracles (4.19-22; 8.18-23; 9.1-8; 10.17-21; 15.5-9; 22.28-30; 23.9-12; 3.21–4.2—prophetic liturgy) and argued that their occurrence as a constituent part of the prophetic message suggests an equally integral connection of the confessions to his public proclamation. As proclamation, they constitute a symbolic portrayal of the impending judgment, with the stress placed upon the divine response.[48] This approach has been developed further by D.J.A. Clines and D.M. Gunn, and Wimmer who see the confessions as the prophet's public defence in a situation of conflict over the prophetic word.[49] Corroboration is found in the analogous use of call narratives—i.e. apparently 'private' experiences words, it is clear that they have a distinctive prose character, though not exclusively so.[30] And if the specific idioms of the verse are analysed, then with one exception (רבר אל טובות—Jer. 52.32//2 Kgs 25.28) they occur only here in Jeremiah.[31] But this is where Hubmann's analysis does not go far enough. For if the verse is evaluated stylistically, particularly in regard to the repetitive usage of the particle גם, then distinctive traits of Jeremianic poetry emerge.[32] If the first level of analysis suggested the prose character of the verse without excluding the possibility of poetry, the second level raised the problem of the distinctive character of v. 6 *vis-à-vis* the prose represented elsewhere in the book (contrast 11.21-23). And now the third level raises the possibility that 12.6 constitutes poetry rather than presupposing an original poetic oracle lying behind it.[33] A tolerable poetic structure and parallelism appears capable of re-construction:

a	גם אחיך ובית אביך	
a'bc	גם המה בגדו בך	4 + 3 + 4
a'b'c'd'	גם המה קראו אחריך מלא	
ab	אל תאמן בם	2 + 3
cde	כי ידברו אליך טובות	

The metre represented by this scansion matches the mixed metre elsewhere in 12.1-5. The semantic parallelism in the bi-colon is comparable to other poetic lines in the passage (see v. 2a-ab//cde; v. 4bα-ab//cde; v. 4bβ-ab//cde) and that of the tri-colon represents the staircase pattern exhibited elsewhere in biblical poetry.[34] An example of anaphora with גם in the tri-colon can also be observed. It may be that classification of this verse as prose has been unduly influenced by its apparent logical connection with the preceding confession whether textual rearrangement has been employed or not. While the warrant for reconstructing poetry in 11.21-23 was not so strong, the situation in 12.6 is different since clear contacts with Jeremianic prose idiom and style are lacking. This distance from the prose tradition on the one hand is matched on the other by stylistic affinity with other Jeremianic poetic texts. Thematic parallels with Jer. 9.3-8 are to be noted as well.[35] Were clear contacts with Jeremianic prose present, the supposition of rhetorical prose affecting authentic poetic motifs would be more probable.[36] In conclusion, if v. 6 is taken as poetry, one of the main supports of the preceding redactional models falls away.

The second issue for re-evaluation is the question of the lack of organic connection between v. 6 and vv. 1-5. While the thematic contacts with 11.21-23 and its commentary-like function in relation to v. 5 could indicate its secondary character, other factors in v. 6 suggest that such arguments are not as conclusive as they seem. The verbal link with בגד in v. 1 is part of a larger chiastic structure spanning the whole passage: בגד—עשה—ראה—ראה—עשה—בגד—דבר—דבר.[37] These verbal links revolve around the central theme of the passage and suggest that neither mechanical catchword linking, nor fortuitous association, is involved. For, as we hope to show in the section on Aim, the complex structure of the poem develops much of its potency around the idea of tension/contradiction. In the poem, nothing is right: matters are not what they seem; and normal values and expectations are turned on their head. The בגד is intrinsically related to this. Not only is attention redirected to the problem of the treacherous at ease (v. 1), but it also relates to the motif of the hypocrisy of the wicked (v. 2b). The appearance of piety is not matched by an inward reality, just as the apparent positive posture of the relatives (v. 6) in reality conceals treacherous intent.[38] The usage of בגד in a social (v. 6) and a theological sphere (vv. 1b-2) does not seem difficult given a similar intertwining of the themes in 9.3-8 and the usage eleswhere to characterize the theme of Israel's apostasy (3.20).[39] The suitability of the divine answer to the prayer also seems less difficult than at first glance. Given the nature of the answer as a rebuke of the preceding complaints and a reassertion of divine aid by virtue of the warning of treachery, the discordant nature of the oracle is not so surprising since it is not attempting to provide an explicit answer to the problems raised.[40] And finally, while the link with 11.21-23 seems valid, it is not clear that this requires the precise model of growth suggested by Thiel and Hubmann. The secondary expansion, 11.21-23, could just as well have been added under the influence of the pre-existing structure, 12.1-6, in the effort to bind the passages into a larger composition. We suggest that the factors normally observed which suggest the secondary character of v. 6 are not conclusive. On closer inspection, structurally and thematically, v. 6 would seem to be a fully integral part of the passage.[41]

Setting

Recollection that the discernment of clear indications of a setting for the previous confession prior to its present literary setting appears extremely problematical suggests that the discussion of 12.1-6 must focus upon the discovery of any internal features that would provide clues about its hypothetical setting within the prophetic mission. Along with this, the applicability of the proposals surveyed above to the present unit must be considered.[42]

A certain distance from the normal cultic setting of lament is already indicated by the way in which the unit diverges from the usual execution of such laments. Reventlow's consistent corporate interpretation seems excluded by v. 6.[43] The affinities in v. 4 to national drought liturgies do not necessarily require his approach since it would not be altogether surprising to find Jeremiah as a prophet agonizing over the ill-effects of the nation's sin in these terms (cf. 23.10). The affinities with Job are instructive since the individual plaintiff there can lament the prosperity of the wicked, not in terms of their effect upon the poet but in terms of widespread ill-effects in society (Job 24.1-12).[44]

The post-Reventlow proposals seem equally unsatisfactory. A view of the confession as a dramatic apologetic form clashes with the passage as it now stands. The problem does not seem to be a conflict over the prophetic mission but rather the miscarriage of divine justice with reference to the wicked. Verse 3a implies a contrast between the prophet and the wicked, but it need not refer to personal suffering at the hands of his enemies. Classification as a lawsuit is unlikely in view of our preceding formal analysis. It would be possible to imagine an apologetic role for vv. 1-4 as a variant form of judgment speech, employing lament in emblematic fashion. The implicit petition for the judgment of the nation would be endorsed by the presuppositions of the prayer since the only thinkable response would be an affirmative one. However, the divine response in vv. 5-6 complicates the situation, for the element of rebuke undercuts the force of the preceding. Why should the wicked be concerned to heed the prophet's plea and threat when Yahweh himself has apparently set the burden of the petition aside? Verse 6 alone could permit such an apologetic role to operate, but not v. 5; and the latter cannot be so easily expunged in light of our formal and redactional analyses. Similarly, classification as a special prophetic lament related to either the *Botenvorgang* or *Warten auf das Gericht* is problematical. Both themes seem intertwined if a prophetic setting is assumed. Verses 4bβ, 6 could imply opposition to mission, but vv. 2-3, 4abα could imply a delay in fulfilment. And, still, no explicit mention of a commissioned messenger is made.[45]

The latter point raises the chief difficulty for this approach and the previous one, for the poem contains nothing which is appropriate only to a prophet, even in v. 6.[46] It is really the present literary setting of the passage which is essential for its interpretation in relation to the prophet. On the other hand, those viewing the passage as a pre-existing liturgy transferred to the prophet by the editors must find a way to explain the many thematic contacts of the passage to Jeremianic poetry.[47] The present literary employment of the confession has apparently obscured whatever setting in the prophetic mission it may have had as a whole or in part. Discernment of additional inner-Jeremianic allusions and contacts may strengthen the assumption that such a setting existed but in the last analysis may provide no additional concrete definition of it.

Interpretation

Three categories of problems present themselves for discussion in this section. First is the discernment of additional signs of integrity for vv. 3, 4, 6 at the level of content in relation to the rest of the unit. Second is the possibility of determining more concretely the identity of the wicked. And third is the possibility of concrete references behind v. 5.

The use of the three legal phrases in v. 1a dramatically affects the tone of the lament. Yahweh is both judge and defendant, acquitted and sentenced. This near-blasphemous address to God is striking.[48] Verse 1b continues the altercation. The problem which has provoked the poet's accusations derives from a contradiction in terms. The בגדים/רשעים prosper (צלח) and are secure (שלה). Normal expectations are overturned. Such 'rewards' are normally reserved for the righteous alone. A fate for the wicked other than destruction is unthinkable. That Yahweh would be faulted for the prosperity of the wicked occurs only in the speeches of Job.[49] This draws the accusation and tone of Jeremiah's complaint much closer to Job than to the psalter. Finding a more explicit identity for this group is difficult. The abstract nature of the vocabulary employed precludes a firm decision because of a lack of explicit contextual indications.[50] Wider usage of the terms in Jeremiah may supply possibilities that can be tested further as we proceed through the passage. Particularly interesting is the usage of the בגד root, which uniformly refers elsewhere in Jeremiah to the nation as a whole (cf. Jer. 3.7, 8, 10, 11, 20; 5.11; 9.1).[51]

Verse 2 continues to elaborate the preceding problem, presenting the incongruous picture of the wicked enjoying the blessings of the righteous, and is articulated with agricultural imagery. The poet holds Yahweh directly responsible for this state of affairs (נטעתם). Verse 2b grounds the injustice of Yahweh's blessing to this group in the hypocrisy of its relationship to him, for their external piety masks an inward orientation to Yahweh that is one of fundamental opposition.[52] Given the wider use of the hypocrisy motif in Jeremiah to refer to Israel's religious posture (cf. 3.1-5; 5.2; 6.20), additional evidence for the identification of the wicked as the nation may be present, particularly in light of the usage of בגד in v. 1. Similarly the wider usage of the divine planting motif in v. 2a in reference to the establishment of the nation in the land continues to strengthen this suggestion (cf. 1.10; 2.21; 11.17; 18.9; 24.6; 31.28; 32.41; 42.10; 45.4).[53] If these allusions can stand, then the complaint has accomplished its effect by blending two sets of images. The first are the themes related to the wicked and righteous and their respective fates. The second, more subtly articulated, are the themes associated with Israel as Yahweh's vine—established, blessed, and fruitful in the land. They have been blended so as to place the latter into the former just at the point occupied by the wicked. The challenge to divine justice has to do not with the prosperity of the wicked in general but rather with the justice of Yahweh permitting 'wicked' Israel to remain under divine blessing. The role of v. 4 as a structural parallel to vv. 1-2 will be important for the corroboration of this view.

With v. 3 the central petition of the prayer is voiced. But the presence of the innocence motif in relation to the problem of the prosperous wicked has occasioned difficulties. Usually understood as a reflection of the persecution experienced by the prophet, it has seemed hard to integrate it with the preceding, even though part of its function as a motivational motif[54] seems clear.[55] However, the use of innocence motifs in psalms wrestling with this problem of the wicked's prosperity can be found (Pss. 37; 73).[56] In both psalms the troubles of the poet are not so much personal suffering as anxiety over the success of the wicked. Similarly, Ps. 139 includes a declaration of innocence (vv. 17-22) motivated not so much by the personal persecution from the wicked as by their opposition to God.

The poet has made Yahweh's enemies his (v. 22). This last example
parallels Jer. 12.6 best.[57] The point of the contrast in the latter is the
difference between the poet and the wicked. לבי אתך stresses the
poet's faithfulness over against their hypocrisy (cf. BDB, p. 861dγ;
Judg. 16.15). No further characterization is given and the prophet's
persecution need not be in view. Finally, if allusions to the prophet's
call (1.5; cf. ידע, קדש)[58] and murder plot of 11.19 (cf.12.3b)[59] are
allowed to stand, then the nature of the opposition involved would be
more a question of the prophet as divinely commissioned opponent
of the wicked. As such he must even seek to prosecute Yahweh if his
task requires it. Such allusions would also strengthen the identification of the wicked as the whole nation.[60]

According to our formal analysis, v. 4 begins the second section of
the complaint element in the prayer formulated in a parallel fashion
to vv. 1-2. with the reference to ישבי בה, we appear to have the most
explicit reference to the identity of the wicked encountered so far.
And with it we appear to have confirmation of our proposal that the
whole nation is in view. All the inhabitants of the nation seem singled
out rather than a particular sub-group.[61] The structural parallel with
vv. 1b-2 argues for an identification of רשעים and ישבי בה without a
need to postulate two distinct groups.[62] Such an expedient is required
only so long as vv. 1-2 are concerned with the prophet's own
sufferings from a select group of enemies. The preceding discussion
suggests that this is not the case.[63] And if this view is correct, one of
the major difficulties relative to the contextual appropriateness of
v. 4 drops away. However, the more serious problem relates to the
appropriateness of the content of v. 4 with that of vv. 1-2. Examination of the imagery and its usage seems to offer a resolution of the
conflict.[64] The picture of the land languishing under its inhabitants'
sins reflects an important prophetic motif. A disturbance in the
divine-human relationship through man's misdeeds is mirrored by a
disturbance in the natural order (Hos. 4.1-3; Isa. 24.4-6; 33.7-9; Jer.
23.10). In addition, the approach of Yahweh for punishment or
chastisement is presaged by upheavals in nature (Amos. 1.1; Joel
1.10; Jer. 4.28).[65] Thus the prophet can appeal to such disturbances
as evidence of disturbance in the nation's relationship to Yahweh and
of the need for repentance before impending judgment (Jer. 3.2-3;
5.23-25). As v. 4bβ indicates, the significance of the upheaval in the
natural order has been rejected. The 'signs of the times', as it were,
have failed to produce repentance.[66] The nation rejects this inter-

pretation and denies the imminence of doom.[67] So the plaintive question challenges the perpetuation of these ineffectual portents. A miscarriage of divine justice is implied by the delay of this heralded judgment, for the inhabitants are permitted to continue in wickedness with apparent impunity. A material shift in the subject matter of the lament does not seem present. Both vv. 1-2 and v. 3 relate to the imperilling of divine justice in the face of the nation's continued impunity with respect to its wickedness. There is no need to see v. 4 as contextually misplaced.[68]

The basic logic of the divine answer seems clear, issuing a challenge based upon a lesser-to-the-greater argument. If present 'lesser' difficulties cannot be surmounted, then how will future 'greater' troubles be handled? It seems best to treat v. 5 as an intentionally abstract and cryptic, almost proverbial, statement[69] and v. 6 as its more concrete explication (כי). The frequent attempts to find various historical referents to which v. 5 alludes—such as the foe from the north/Babylonians[70] or Jeremiah's prophetic opponents, and a situation where Yahweh's presence cannot be perceived[71]— though attractive, are ultimately unsuccessful. In each case the proposal results in a misrepresentation of the logic and focus of the complaint. The identification of the greater threat with an imminent invasion requires, according to the logic, that the lesser problem be related to the prophet's personal troubles in his conflict with the wicked and the related devastation of the land by natural calamity.[72] However, our previous exegesis has argued that these are not the fundamental problems involved but rather the miscarriage of divine justice represented by Yahweh's apparent failure to judge the nation.[73] Thus, it is not clear how a threat of an imminent Babylonian invasion would represent further testing for the prophet, since it is just the delay of this invasion (12.3—יום הרגה) which constitutes the trial for his faith. Similarly, identification of the lesser threat in v. 5a with Jeremiah's prophetic opponents requires the allocation of vv. 1-2 and v. 4 to two different groups of people and problems. But our exegesis makes this unlikely due to the parallelism of the sections and the greater probability for viewing רשעים and ישבי as the whole nation. Thus, there is no encouragement to see an allusion to the prophetic office behind רוץ. Again, identification of the greater threat in v. 5b (גאון הירדן) as a future situation where evidence of divine action and rule is lacking clashes with the logic, for it would not represent a situation materially different from his present one where the hiddenness of divine justice is specifically the problem at issue. Thus, none of the proposals permits the discernment of a consistent pattern of allusion behind the terms that also gives due regard to the logical pattern of the answer and the point of the preceding complaint. Each of the proposals must select a few of the terms as significant and leave the others as undifferentiated abstract images.

It remains to establish how v. 6 provides an intelligible explanation of the impending, more severe, troubles announced in v. 5 and at the same time continues to provide a suitable and consistent response to the prayer. Clarification of two obscure idioms must be provided before such an explanation can be offered.

The first is קרא אחר מלא and the discernment of a coherent meaning for מְלֵא. Normally the latter has been taken in an adverbial sense—i.e. 'cry aloud', 'cry with a loud voice'.[74] The biggest difficulty for this view is its contextual inappropriateness, for there would seem to be no deception, no necessity for warning the prophet if his relatives were so obviously in 'full cry' after him. An alternative solution seems preferable which depends in part on finding an alternative nuance for the root מלא of 'collect', 'gather', 'assemble'.[75] For the other part, מלא would be taken as a sg. imp. or inf. absolute in the *pi.* with the same force (מַלֵּא) and viewed as a one-word citation, meaning 'assemble! help!', with the implicit connotation of assemble for mutual help or defence (cf. Jer. 4.5—קראו מלאו).[76] The only other occurrences of the phrase קרא אחר (1 Sam. 20.37, 38; 24.9) serve to introduce direct speech in address to the person concerned.[77] Not only are citation motifs features in this confession (v. 4) and the preceding (11.19, 21), but they are characteristic of Jeremianic poetry (2.20, 23, 35; 5.12, 13; 6.16, 17; 23.17). If it was right to view the pattern of 12.5-6 as the stimulus for the addition of 11.21-23, the citation in v. 21 could aso be an indication that a citation is to be expected in vv. 5-6.[78] These converging considerations suggest a high probability for this view of מלא. As a result, it becomes possible to perceive a need for the divine warning. While the citation, 'assemble!, help!', could refer to a banding together in order to destroy the poet,[79] it could alternatively be an invitation to the poet to gather with his family for defence/help. The divine warning labels this as בגד and not to be trusted. מלא as a citation with its deceitful positive offer would parallel nicely the closing phrase 'say nice things to you'.[80]

Second, the latter phrase should also be given a more technical

nuance based upon other biblical parallels and international treaty-
covenant terminology, where the idiom has reference to the
establishment of 'friendship' or 'good relations' on the basis of a
treaty-covenant.[81] It may be going too far to see the offer of an actual
pact in 12.6, but a nuance of 'establish good relations' should be
maintained.[82]

On this view of the two idioms it becomes possible to see the
relationship of v. 6 to the preceding. The more severe trial is located
in an impending attempt[83] by the poet's family to ruin him through
the ruse of a false offer of help, i.e. a 'defence pact'. The enhanced
severity *vis à vis* the problem of the prayer (vv. 1-4) is to be located
through the verbal echo with v. 1 (בגד). It suggests a parallel between
the treachery of the wicked nation and the poet's own family. In both
cases an external positive orientation masks hostile intent or
opposition (cf. vv. 2b and 6). Consequently, the prophet's experience
of treachery appears destined to become a reflection of the treachery
which Yahweh experiences at Israel's hands.[84] Thus at the heart of
the complaint is reflected a crisis in the prophetic mission due to its
failure to effect national repentance and the continued impunity of
the nation as a result of delay in the threatened judgment. The oracle
summons the prophet to a more difficult threat and task. If the
prophet cannot successfully carry out his mission in the face of
challenges to the authenticity of the word of judgment, how could he
expect to survive the greater burden of having his experience become
a symbol of Yahweh's betrayal by Israel?[85]

Aim

The dialogue between prophet and Yahweh in this confession is in
stark contrast to that of 11.18-23. The prophet initiates a dispute in
which he approaches Yahweh as another Job. The previous picture of
solidarity and certainty has given way to turmoil and antagonism.
The poem as a complex structure develops its potency around the
idea of 'tension'/'contradiction'. Confrontation and opposition are
effected at every level of the passage. The prayer places a demand at
its centre which is ignored by the divine response. Near blasphemous
accusations go unanswered. If the previous confession resolved its
tensions in the climax of the divine answer, 12.1-6 leave nothing
resolved. There is only challenge and counter-challenge. Legal forms
of speech are used in a surprising, unusual fashion. Motifs are joined

in ways that produce contradictions in terms. The wicked nation enjoys the rewards of righteousness under the beneficence of God. A constituent of salvation history, the land-gift, is hinted to be the height of divine injustice. The wicked reject warnings of doom, and Yahweh's delay of judgment aids the nation in its apostasy. Instead of God and prophet against the nation, Yahweh is depicted in collusion with the enemy and the primary threat to the prophet. A crisis in the prophetic mission is implicitly present. The text is not so much concerned with the problem of innocent suffering, nor the persecution of the prophet, but rather the miscarriage of divine justice in perpetuating the life and well-being of Israel in the land in view of her apostasy. The prophet is scandalized by a threat to the veracity of his mission. However, the divine response moves in opposition to the complaint. The prophet's attention is directed to the requirements of the prophetic mission in the future as a challenge to continue successfully in the way of that mission in the present. The prophetic mission is to be a mirror of the conflict between Yahweh and Israel.

10	אויli אמי כי ילדתני	Woe is me! my mother, that you bore me,
	איש ריב ומדון לכל הארץ	A man of strife and contention[1] to the whole land.
	לא נשיתי ולא נשו בי	I have neither lent, nor have they lent to me
	כלה מקללני	(but) each one curses me![2]
11	אמר יהוה	Yahweh said:[3]
	אם לא שרותך לטוב	Surely, I have set you at odds for good,[4]
	אם לוא הפגעתי בך	Surely, I have inflicted you
	בעת רעה ובעת צרה את האיב	in time of trouble and in time of distress with the enemy.
12	הירע ברזל	Can iron be broken,
	ברזל מצפון ונחשת	Iron from the north, and bronze?
13	חילך ואוצרותיך לבז	Your wealth and treasure for booty,[5]
	אתן לא במחיר	I will give without price.[6]
	ובכל חטאותיך ובכל גבוליך	even for all your sins throughout all your borders.
14	והעברתי את איביך	I will cause your enemies to pass over,
	בארץ לא ידעת	into a land you do not know.
	כי אש קדחה באפי	For a fire burns in my wrath,
	עליכם תוקד	against you it is kindled.

Form

Solutions to the difficult textual problems of this passage materially affect the nature of the form present for analysis. The cumulative result of the preceding textual discussion was the general retention of the present text according to MT. Our discussion of form must test these proposals by discovering an intelligible, integrated structure in the unit.

Typical Form: Though the basic prophetic liturgy pattern of complaint (v. 10) plus divine response (vv. 11-14) seems clear, it has been effected through a complex blend of genre typicalities. Verse 10a corresponds to the normal pattern of a cry of lamentation: ל + אוֹי with suffix + כִּי—clause of reason/ground.[7] Verse 10b consists of the usual complaint-psalm motifs of a profession of innocence (v. 10bα) and complaint (v. 10bβ). Affinities with Psalm laments are overshadowed by the divergences—i.e the lack of address to God, petition, or motifs of confidence, plus the use of the woe cry, which is very uncharacteristic (only once, cf. Ps. 120.5).[8]

The divine response is composed of three major features. First, in addition to the introductory formula, v. 11 contains two parallel, abbreviated affirmative oaths (אִם לֹא).[9] Second, v. 12 is a rhetorical question expecting a negative answer, which apparently employs elements of wisdom rhetoric since it functions through appeal to phenomena of the natural order for disputational purposes.[10]Third, features common to prophetic judgment oracles are exhibited in vv. 13-14. The announcement of judgment is expressed in vv. 13a, 14b with the former articulated concretely and the latter abstractly. The element of accusation plays a minor role occuring only in v. 13b. The pattern is broken, however, in v. 14a according to its present formulation. In contrast to its context, it appears to function as a prediction of salvation, executed similarly to elements in an oracle of salvation,[11] especially the verbal clause directed toward substantiation and the outcome which indicates the consequences for the supplicant and/or his enemies.[12] This raises the problem of whether judgment and salvation are addressed to the same individual. Verses 11-12, 14 and the shift from 2nd pers. sg. suffixes (vv. 13-14a) to 2nd pers. pl. (v. 14b) suggest a subtle blend of addressees in vv. 13-14 resulting from the adaptation of the judgment oracle into a promise of salvation as an appropriate response to the complaint of v. 10. Such a rhetorical device can be observed elsewhere in Jeremianic poetry where complex changes of voices/speakers occur in the development of oracles.[13] This must be tested further in subsequent analysis.[14]

This use of various genre typicalities in the composition of the unit matches that encountered in the previous confessions (11.18–12.6). Still, in contrast to the preceding, hardly any legal imagery is employed (except possibily אִישׁ רִיב) from which a lawsuit classification could be sustained or that would permit discernment of a trial process as the controlling pattern.[15]

Particular Form: As further accumulative corroboration for treating 15.10-14 as an integrated unit, we offer the following schematic outline:

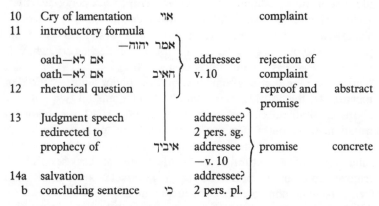

Verse					
10	Cry of lamentation	אוי		complaint	
11	introductory formula				
	—אמר יהוה				
	oath—אם לא		addressee	rejection of	
	oath—אם לא	האיב	v. 10	complaint	
12	rhetorical question			reproof and	abstract
				promise	
13	Judgment speech		addressee?		
	redirected to		2 pers. sg.		
	prophecy of	איביך	addressee	promise	concrete
			—v. 10		
14a	salvation		addressee?		
b	concluding sentence	כי	2 pers. pl.		

Stylistically, the passage is characterized by a doubling of synonymous expressions: ריב/מדון and לא נשה (v. 10); doubled oath and אוצרותיך/חילך (v. 12); ברזל/ברזל (v. 12); עת רעה/עת צרה (v. 13).[16] The brief and compact[17] v. 10 functions to present the complaint and establish the problem for discussion. The bulk of the text constitutes the divine response. The lack of verbal links between it and v. 10 draws attention to their relationship primarily on the basis of subject matter, besides the formal prophetic liturgy pattern.[18] Each of the three genre components provides an appropriate response to the complaint:

v. 10   —negative destiny/cf. v. 11—positive destiny;
v. 10   —opposition and alienation/cf. v. 12—undefeatable
           supplicant;
v. 10   —unjustly cursed/cf. vv. 13-14—enemies will be removed.

The possibility of a loosely structured editorial composite in the response is countered by the logical development to be observed within it. There appears to be a movement from rejection/rebuke (v. 11) to promise/assurance (vv. 13-14) with v. 12 the logical pivot and transition. Understood as a reference to the supplicant's impregnability, it both rebukes the fear of the opponents in v. 10 and promises his vindication over them.[19] The relationship to the following is one of abstract to concrete application in the failure and

destruction of his enemies (vv. 13-14). Finally an inclusio of האיב/
איביך knits the oracle together since the same group appears to be in
view. It still remains to decide if these indications of integration are
sufficient to offset the apparent tensions of the abrupt changes in
addressees and the doublet phenomenon which raise possibilities for
detecting redactional seams in the confession.

Redaction

While the preceding formal analysis suggests that the older
approaches which practised radical removal of certain verses (vv. 12,
13-14) are invalid, the possibility of intentional editorial expansions
remains a serious question. By far the most probable candidate for
detecting editorial seams is the doublet, vv. 13-14. On the other
hand, the remaining verses (vv. 10-12) most probably sustain an
original connection. This seems most likely for vv. 10-11, based upon
their logical and formal pattern.[20] However, the secondary character
of the connection between the stereotyped complaint (v. 10) and the
divine oracle (v. 11), which exhibit no strong verbal links, is a
conceivable possibility. Recent arguments for such a view have been
put forward by Eichler and Ahuis.[21] Taking vv. 11-14 as a Dtr.
expansion, Eichler stresses that v. 11 is totally inappropriate to the
context and Ahuis relies upon the classification of the verses as prose.
Eichler's position depends upon reading v. 11 as continued prophetic
speech and thus as an unnecessary repetition of the innocence motif
in v. 10. But we hope to show that MT אמר יהוה makes the best sense
and that a fully intelligible meaning as the beginning of the oracle
can be detected.[22] And the attempt to view any of the verses as prose
does not seem to be required, given the nature of the parallelism and
mixed metre through the verse.[23] None of the diction appears to be
distinctively Dtr.[24] Similarly, v. 12 sustains a crucial transitional and
pivotal function, related both to the preceding and following verses.
Its obscurity probably is not a sufficient consideration for classifying
it as an addition.[25] The perceived disturbance of the verse in its
present setting appears to lie on the same level as that encountered in
the rhetorical question of 12.5. As such it could even be viewed as a
fitting conclusion to the answer without vv. 13-14. There is no need
to see the verse as a corruption of 17.1 for the correspondences
between them are too slight.[26] By its very nature, the prophetic
liturgy pattern (complaint + divine response) involves the blending

of various genres. It may be that certain 'tensions' are endemic to this complex genre pattern so that caution is advisable before any and every 'tension' is taken too quickly as a sign of editorial activity.

This returns us to the problem of the doubletted tradition (15.13-14/17.3-4). At the same time that the doublet phenomenon raises the redactional question, it also complicates the attempt at a solution.[27] Logically, either one of the doublets may be original and the other secondary, or both could be secondary; or again both could effectively be original if the material involved were of such a formulaic nature that it facilitated repeated use in various contexts. In the present text it is difficult to discern a clear path through the alternatives.[28] Comparison of the two units will show that 17.3-4 is consistently articulated corporately. Those features are absent in 15.13-14 which clearly identify the nation as addressee.[29] Viewed in terms of its setting within the larger judgment speech, 17.3-4 seem fully appropriate to the context.[30] 17.1-4 as a piece is just what we should expect of a prophetic oracle. There seem to be no grounds for doubting the originality of vv. 3-4 in this setting (textual problems notwithstanding).[31]

The relationship of 15.13-14 to 15.10-12 must be evaluated in a similar fashion. The re-addressing and remodelling of vv. 13-14 into a promise of salvation already create the impression of an integral contextual relationship. Given the focus of v. 10 upon conflict with the community and the concern of vv. 11-12 to respond to this very issue, the presence in the divine answer of a prophecy of judgment against the supplicant's opponents seems entirely understandable. On the other hand, the verbal links between vv. 13-14 and the preceding are not as strong as those observed for 17.1-4. The inclusio with איביך/האיב may not be sufficient to compensate for this. And though a logical function is discernible for vv. 13-14 in relation to v. 12 (abstract to concrete), it is still possible to view vv. 11-12 as a complete thought with vv. 13-14 a supplementary development.[32] Arguments either way seem inconclusive.

The common elements between the passages consist of fairly general announcements of judgment. It may be that viewing the doublets as an expression of formulaic judgment motifs could provide a way through the preceding impasse.[33] Some of the doublet phenomena in Jeremiah seem explicable on these terms (see esp. 5.9/5.29/9.8).[34] A helpful parallel is provided by 23.19-21/30.23-24, which show the multiple use of fairly abstract judgment imagery.[35]

Such an understanding of the doublet would push an evaluation of them beyond the secondary-original debate. However, this attractive possibility will need to be tested further by an analysis of divine wrath/judgment imagery in Jeremiah (see below, Interpretation). In the meantime, the length of the doublet and its attestation only twice raise problems for the label 'formulaic'. And the feature of re-addressing rules out an explanation that appeals to simple multiple anchoring in the tradition. At present, there appears to be a slight tipping of the probabilities in favour of seeing vv. 13-14 as a secondary expansion.

The difficulties encountered in this discussion in an effort to bring forward considerations that would firmly exclude one alternative or the other provide an interesting illustration of certain problems adhering to the fundamental assumptions of redaction-critical method. Since the discernment of redactional activity relies heavily on the discovery of compositional 'seams', as evidenced by 'tensions' in the articulation of a text, it means that cases will arise where it is difficult, if not impossible, to distinguish composite redactional artistry from rhetorical-compositional complexity. The present passage could be seen as a prime example of such a case. What, after all, theoretically excludes the possibility that the prophet is responsible for the readdressed doublet?[36]

In this regard, the role of the authenticity question in redactional analysis is instructive. Of all the parts of the unit, it is the doublet which has the strongest attestation for authenticity. Not only the nature of the doublet with 17.3-4, but also the content and imagery fully accord with Jeremianic oracles heralding the despoiling and exile of Judah. The situation for vv. 10-12 is only slightly different. The stylistic compatibility of v. 12 with its employment of wisdom rhetoric and other Jeremianic poetry has been noted above. There is potential in vv. 10-11 for inner-Jeremianic allusions to the call narrative and other thematically parallel motifs (cf. 20.14-18; 15.9 to v. 10; and cf. 18.20 to v.11 if אמן יהוה is read with G). Apart from unique expressions, contacts with the diction of Jeremianic poetry can be observed.[37] Such signs of compatibility raise the possibility, though short of demonstration, that the verses are authentic or have incorporated authentic material. At least the possibility cannot be excluded absolutely on this level. But even so, a resolution of the redactional problems is not achieved, for it is entirely possible that an editor has worked exclusively with authentic materials—in this case

vv. 13-14. In this instance, the authenticity-inauthenticity question seems of little use. While it is not very satisfying to end the discussion in a stalemate, it appears to be due as much to problems inherent in redaction-critical method as to the nature of this very difficult text.

Setting

The problems encountered already in attempting to determine the setting of the preceding confessions afflict 15.10-14 as well.[38] The apparent lack of explicit prophetic concerns within the unit represents the Achilles heel for proposals associating the confessions with the prophetic mission as a special type of prophetic lament or an apologetic form.[39] There is no suggestion that we have to do with a commissioned messenger. Legal forms are virtually absent, as well as any hint of a trial process. The hypothesis of an apologetic form at least has in its favour that a situation of conflict is in view, and the focus of the divine answer upon vindication of the supplicant makes it conceivable that we should visualize a prophet uttering the 'conversation' as a threatening witness against his opponents (even if vv. 13-14 are secondary). However, nothing in v. 10 or the divine response explicitly identifies the supplicant as a prophet. The divergence of the passage from normal lament, the potential inner-Jeremianic allusions (esp. to the call narrative), the prophetic character of the speech in vv. 13-14 (if they are not secondary) could combine to encourage the search for a setting in prophetic mission and even be taken as corroboration of the apologetic theory. But such a proposal is not likely to succeed unless more explicit prophetic concerns can be discovered (esp. in v. 11). Otherwise, the 'success' of the allusions depends more upon the present literary setting than upon their inherent characteristics. The search for more explicit references will be a special concern of the Interpretation section.[40]

Interpretation

In addition to the evaluation of possible allusions to prophetic concerns, the chief tasks of this section must be the resolution of the interpretive crux represented by v. 11, the justification of our proposal concerning a complex alternation of addressees, and the examination of the judgment imagery in vv. 13-14 for evidence of its formulaic character.

The import of v. 10 seems clear. Working back from his present lot of conflict and rejection by the community, the supplicant challenges the value of such a life. Signs of allusions to prophetic concerns seem completely lacking for v. 10b. The lending-borrowing imagery appears to represent a figurative transfer. The innocence motif has selected in a representative fashion a part of the social activities liable to misdeeds or criminality and implicitly claims that none of the supplicant's social dealings has been amiss or a cause of approbation (synecdoche).[41] While such figurative transfer need not require the assumption of a later hand, it does not help in the discernment of prophetic motifs.[42] The potential for v. 10a is more promising. It is attractive to see an allusion to the call narrative in the birth imagery (cf. 1.5) and to view the cry as a lamentation over his selection as a prophet.[43] איש ריב in association with מדון[44] would also complement the political and military imagery that permeates the call narrative designating the prophet for 'war' with the nation and as an object of siege on their part.[45] Still, for all this, the success of such allusions depends upon the present literary setting of the unit.[46] Given that context, appeal to such contacts seems legitimate though they are not explicit enough for aid on the question of setting above.[47]

The chief difficulty of v. 11 is whether an interpretation of שרותך can be achieved which still permits taking the verse as the beginning of the divine response.[48] Older approaches either followed the *Qere* reading שרה ('loose, free') or saw a defective writing of the verb שאר, or noun שארית (cf. α′ σ′ Targ V). Alongside these was the proposal to derive it from שרר (intensive—'strengthen'). As a consequnce, such solutions worked best on the understanding of the verse as divine speech.[49] The next two solutions tended in the opposite direction, accommodating a view of the verse as prophetic speech. On the one hand a derivation from אשר ('lead', 'guide'; cf. G) was advocated[50] or on the other, from שרת (*pi.*—'serve'). The latter has been the most popular among recent studies.[51] Finally, there has been the attempt to put forward, anew, a derivation from שרר attested only in the participle שורר ('enemy') and so to see a causative verb or a noun for 'enmity' in 15.11.[52] The last comes full circle in the proposals and favours taking v. 11 as divine speech.

The validity of any one of these proposals seems to rest heavily upon the force given to the parallel oath, הפגעתי בך,—i.e. negative or positive. Normally, it is taken in a positive sense of 'make intercession for' and so favours very much taking v. 11 parallel to 18.20 as a prophetic statement with שרותך related to שרת.[53] The chief difficulty for this is that the normal expression with this meaning is not represented here,[54] and instead הפגע .... ב .... את is found which has its only parallel in Isa. 53.6 (הפגיע בו את עון).[55] The latter implies a translation for Jer. 15.11 of 'I caused the enemy to fall upon you'. As a result, viewing the statement as divine speech seems best and would produce a contextually appropriate response. The complaint of an unjust fate is countered by a claim that the supplicant's experience accords with the divine will and purpose. Given the precise grammatical parallel (Isa. 53.6) and the context, a negative nuance or, more properly, a more concrete meaning of פגע as 'meet', 'encounter', 'touch' seems preferable.[56]

Returning to v. 11a, the nature of the parallel oaths suggests that a similar negative nuance be sought for שרותך. Though the parallelism need not be synonymous, the stylistic feature of doubled synonymous expressions in vv. 10-14 would seem to provide the necessary warrant for viewing them as such. Of the various solutions which would preserve v. 11a as divine speech semantically complementary to הפגעתי, a derivation from שרר ('Make an enemy'/'set at odds') meets these requirements beautifully and is preferable.[57] Though their force can be blunted, certain philological problems remain; for a geminate root, שרר, is not generally attested[58] and the causative meaning required for שרותך (presumably *pi.*—שֵׁרוֹתִיךָ) from a geminate verb normally would have expected a *po.* form (שׁוֹרַרְתִּיךָ).[59] In spite of these difficulties, this proposal makes the best sense within the context, particularly in comparison to the difficulties afflicting the other proposals.[60] As a result of this view, the structural connection between vv. 10 and 11 is considerably strengthened. A life of open hostility and alienation from countrymen, viewed as a lamentable lot (v. 10), receives its rebuttal with Yahweh's reinterpretation of that lot as an agency of his purposes for good. Still, potential allusions to the prophetic vocation seem to remain on the same level as those of v. 10.[61]

The rhetorical question of v. 12 expects a negative answer and so asserts the superior, indestructible character of northern iron-bronze. The issue remains of whether a more concrete allusion lies behind the imagery. The diverse usage of the imagery in Jeremiah suggests that the present context must be decisive in reaching a solution.[62] As a reference to the nation's unbreakability, it would clash with the following vv. 13-14 which appear to announce just the opposite.[63] As a reference to the invading national foe, Babylon, it would be more appropriate since it could be viewed as the abstract expression of the more concrete vv. 13-14. However, ברזל ונחשת are never associated elsewhere in Jeremiah with the northern foe; and מצפון could be explained differently as a reference to the source of quality iron.[64] The most appropriate possibility lies in an allusion to the prophet. Yahweh's statement that he has 'hit'/'inflicted' (v. 11b) the supplicant with the enemy leads to the logical expectation that a reference to the superior strength of the iron-bronze, as a further development of the oracle, would most naturally be a reference to the supplicant and provide an appropriate rebuttal of his fears, implying the defeat of his enemies, which is at least the focus of the following verses.[65] Such an allusion to the prophetic vocation finds explicit encouragement in the next confession (15.20) and in the call narrative (1.18) where the prophet is designated an iron pillar and bronze wall. This would fit nicely with the potential allusions to the prophetic vocation discerned in vv. 10-11. Nevertheless, such an allusion may be due more to the present literary setting; and, given the proverbial character of v. 12, it may be preferable to see a simple metaphor for indestructibility without an intentional concrete reference. In this case, the supplicant of v. 10 remains the focus of the saying and is compared to shatter-proof northern iron-bronze over against his opponents. As a simple metaphor, a reference to Babylon would be definitely excluded.[66]

The remaining verses of the oracle complete the development from rebuff/challenge to promise/reassurance as well as provide a concrete explanation of the abstract rhetorical question of v. 12. On the strength of the surprising shift from singular to plural between vv. 14a and 14b, the possibility of an alternation of addressees was proposed in our formal analysis. Verse 14a seems totally incomprehensible with the land/nation as addressee according to the present text.[67] Viewing v. 14 in connection to v. 10 would favour taking v. 14a as direct address to the supplicant and v. 14b as address to the former's opponents. However, the extent of such alternation in the oracle is difficult to ascertain. Our exegesis of vv. 11-12 makes any such alternation in them unlikely—both are best understood as addressed to the supplicant of v. 10. It remains to decide if a change of addressee occurs in v. 13. As announcement of judgment parallel to v. 14b, it is attractive to see the former addressed to the same plurality as the latter. The problem of the singular suffixes in v. 13

could be explained as a personification of the whole land/nation as an individual.[68] The most serious difficulty for this suggestion is that the singular suffixes (vv. 11-12) which have the individual of v. 10 in view provide no preparation in their logical development for a shift in addressee as one reads through to this verse.[69] Because of this, Hubmann has argued that the prophet continues to be addressed in v. 13 with עליכם (v. 14b) including both prophet and land/enemy.[70] His proposal appears to represent the only viable alternative to the explanation above. He develops his own view by interpreting the two prepositional phrases of v. 13 (ובכל . . . . ובכל) as fully co-ordinate goals of the divine action.[71] Taking the double-conjunction construction as 'not only . . . but also',[72] he understands the loss of property for both prophet and nation as a penalty and atonement for their sins.[73] However, it is not clear that his grammatical point is really required or yields the result that he wants. Assigning a suitable nuance to the prepositions in support of his view does not seem possible.

Though Hubmann does not say, he has apparently derived the idea of atonement from בכל חטאתיך. Presumably, he has understood the prepositions (ב) as Beth of price (BDB, p. 90.III.3) or cause (BDB, p. 90.III.5). In either case his interpretation of two co-ordinate goals runs into trouble. The first understanding of the preposition conflicts with the explicit לא במחיר and the second is unintelligible for גבוליך, since it is not obvious how the prophet's possessions could be a basis for punishment. It would be totally uncharacteristic elsewhere in Jeremiah.[74] Still, Hubmann's explanation implies a subordination of גבול to חטאות rather than coordination since he wants atonement through judgment for both prophet and land. Beth of price would make גבול part of the terms of atonement. His appeal to doubled synonymous expressions appears actually to work against his view. So it seems that on his interpretation of the double waw construction, the options for the prepositional functions either fail to support his overall view or appear unintelligible in context.

Contextually it is preferable to see separate nuances in the prepositions (causal for the first; locative for the second) with the second phrase subordinate to the first, thus: 'because of all your sins throughout all your territories/borders'. The two conjunctions need not provide any difficulty since the first could be taken explicatively and the second pleonastically, thus left untranslated.[75] The latter point permits the retention of the traditional understanding of the verse and removes the stimulus for Hubmann's interpretation of it.

This brings us to reassess the appropriateness of our suggestion to the context.[76] The key issue is the analysis of the function of עליכם within the oracle. Verse 14a can only be addressed to the supplicant of v. 10 as an announcement of judgment upon his enemies. The announcement is grounded (כי) in the divine wrath directed to עליכם. It does not seem likely that a promise of deliverance from enemies (v. 14a) would be followed immediately by a statement of wrath directed to these very enemies and the one who is to be delivered (v. 14b). Consequently, the concomitant of exile (v. 14a), despoliation (v. 13), would seem best understood as directed to the same group as in v. 14b.[77] The weakness remains in our argument that v. 14b could be related in a general way to the preceding oracle (concluding characterization) and thus עליכם could still include both the prophet and his enemies.[78] Given the considerations of logic and the relationship of the oracle to v. 10, we favour viewing v. 13 as an apostrophized address to the prophet's enemies.

The possibility that these verses could represent a formulaic expression of judgment in order to account for the doublet phenomenon does not seem likely on closer inspection. The best possibilities lie in v. 14b as a near citation of Deut. 32.22[79] and the use of אש and אף as standard idioms of divine wrath.[80] However, the bulk of v. 13, apart from לבו אתן לא במחיר, does not come close to being formulaic. And v. 14a is similar with בארץ לא ידעת the only possibility.[81] The most that can be argued is that some traditional stereotyped expressions lie behind vv. 13-14, but not completely so since many of the images and expressions cannot be paralleled. Consequently, the scales continue to be tipped slightly in favour of taking the readdressed doublet as a secondary expansion.[82]

Aim

The dialogue between the prophet and Yahweh is articulated somewhat differently from the preceding units. The complaint is articulated more obliquely as an anguished cry of mourning. There is no direct address or petition to God. Nevertheless, the points of contact with the supplicant's call to prophetic mission contain an implicit challenge. The prophet's appointed destiny as combatant of the nation is reinterpreted in terms of a mistaken life—one which should never have been. The problem is not so much a question of enemies and persecution but rather a crisis in prophetic mission occasioned by the former. At the heart of the crisis is Yahweh's deed of appointment.

The divine rebuff and promise are directed immediately to the substance of the complaint. Stylistically it combines elements encountered in the previous oracles of both rebuke (12.5) and promise (11.20ff.), direct address to the prophet (12.5; 11.20) and to his opponents (11.20ff.). The complaint is countered by the assertion that the prophet's destiny as combatant is not a mishap but divine purpose for good. The combatant is invincible. His assailants will perish. The divine response refutes any suggestion that this specific prophetic mission of fundamental opposition to the nation is ill-conceived or mistaken. The strife engendered by it represents the divine intention to shatter the nation before its prophetic opponent and to carry it away into exile. The apostrophized address to the nation underlines the promised deliverance for the prophet, and at the same time testifies to the threat to national existence contained in the latter's opposition to the prophetic mission.

4. Jeremiah 15.15-21[1]

15	אתה ידעת יהוה	You know, Yahweh![2]
	זכרני ופקדני	Remember me, and take notice of me,
	והנקם לי מרדפי	Avenge me on my persecutors!
	אל לארך אפך תקחני	Do not—on account of your forbearance[3]—take me away,
	דע שאתי עליך חרפה	know that I bear reproach for your sake.
16	נמצאו דבריך ואכלם	Your words[4] were found and I ate them;
	ויהי דברך לי	your word was to me,
	לששון ולשמחת לבבי	for the joy and delight of my heart.
	כי נקרא שמך עלי	For I am called by your name,
	יהוה צבאות	Yahweh of Hosts.
17	לא ישבתי בסוד משחקים ואעלז	I have not sat nor rejoiced in the circle of merry-makers,
	מפני ידך בדד ישבתי	because of your hand, I sat alone;
	כי זעם מלאתני	for you have filled me with wrath.
18	למה היה כאבי נצח	Why is my pain perpetual,
	ומכתי אנושה מאנה הרפא	and my wound grievous, refusing to be healed.
	היו תהיה לי כמו אכזב	Surely, you have been as a falsehood to me,
	מים לא נאמנו	unreliable water!
19	לכן כה אמר יהוה	Therefore thus says Yahweh:
	אם תשוב ואשיבך	If you return, I will restore you,
	לפני תעמד	before me you will stand.
	ואם תוציא יקר מזולל	If you bring forth the precious without the base,
	כפי תהיה	as my spokesman you will be.
	ישבו המה אליך	Let them turn against you!
	ואתה לא תשוב אליהם	But you must not turn to them;

20	ונתתיך לעם הזה	So I will make you to be for this people
	לחומת נחשת בצורה	a fortified, bronze wall.
	ונלחמו אליך	They will war against you,
	ולא יוכלו לך	but not overcome you,
	כי אתך אני	Since I am with you,
	להושיעך ולהציל לך נאם יהוה	to save you, to deliver you— says Yahweh[5]—
21	והצלתיך מיד רעים	I will deliver you from the power of the wicked
	ופדתיך מכף עריצים	and ransom you from the grasp of the terrible.

Form

As a result of the preceding analysis of 15.10-14, attempts to view a portion of the preceding along with 15.15-21 as a single unit have been seriously weakened. It remains to consider 15.15-21 for signs that it too constitutes an integral unit comprising a lament (vv. 15-18) with answering oracle (vv. 19-21).[6] Such a view of the structure of the passage and its relationship to cultic lament has been widely recognized, following the analysis by Baumgartner.

Typical Form: A schematic of the passage illustrates the controlling role of features typical of cultic lament.[7]

v. 15　　　—introductory address and petition
v. 16　　　—profession of innocence
vv. 17-18　—lament
vv. 19-21　—answering oracle

Recent attempts to divorce completely this confession from cultic lament (Ittmann) or to reclassify it as a lawsuit (Blank and Wimmer) seem inappropriate in light of the ease with which the typical pattern of a lament psalm can be paralleled in the text and in view of the virtual absence of legal metaphors, as our analysis of the diction will show (see below).[8] Among those who have basically followed Baumgartner's analysis, some have experienced difficulty in the precise classification of v. 16 and esp. v. 17. The problem presented by v. 16 seems to lie primarily in the nuance to be given to דבר.[9] However, its overall logical and structural function as a profession of innocence seems independent of this latter difficulty. Whatever its nuance, its motivational function of setting forth the supplicant as among the pious, responsive to the divine word, fits nicely with analogous sentiments in Psalms (40.8 ff.; contrast the wicked—Pss. 50.17; 54.5; 55.20; 119.139, 150, 158). The classification of v. 17 has encountered difficulty because of its superficial similarity to Pss. 1.1 and 26.4, which relate the poet's separation from fellowship with the wicked as a profession of innocence.[10] But the harmless nature of the referents in Jer. 15.17 (משחקים) introduces a surprising element if a classification of profession of innocence is attempted.[11] For this reason, it seems preferable to include the verse in the lament section as further expression of the troublesome circumstances of the supplicant. The analogy to the professions of innocence noted above is to be explained as part of this lament's characteristic of ironic misinterpretations.[12]

Another aspect of interest in regard to the typical features of this confession *vis à vis* lament is its total lack of confidence motifs: confession of trust, assurance of being heard, or vow of praise. The presence of such motifs is the rule in psalm laments, though in Ps. 88 they are so attenuated as to be virtually absent.[13] If one then contrasts to Jer. 15.15-18 those psalms which emphasize personal innocence and thus express exuberant confidence in their vindication (Ps. 69), and those penitential psalms which exhibit a general reduction of innocence and confidence motifs (Pss. 51; 38; 39, in order of reduction), the tone of unrelieved despair and complaint is highlighted emphatically, even though prominence has been given to innocence motifs to the total exclusion of motifs of penitence. Based upon the tendencies in the Psalms noted above, the presence of confidence motifs would have been expected.

Finally, the typical features of the answering oracle can be analysed further. By containing an oracle, the overall prophetic liturgy pattern noted for the preceding three confessional units can continue to be applied in the analysis of 15.15-21. The appropriateness of this appeal to the prophetic liturgy as an explanation for the form of these four confessions is particularly evident in this fourth instance since the bulk of the divine oracle contains motifs drawn from the salvation oracle genre.[14]

v. 19	—summons to repentance
v. 20aα	—substantiation (verbal clause in the perfect)[15]
v. 20aβ	—outcome (normally in the imperfect)
v. 21	—substantiation (verbal clause in the perfect)

A marked divergence from the normal elements of a salvation oracle is provided by v. 19, for instead of the expected assurance of salvation formula, 'fear not', we find a summons to repentance:[16] v. 19aα— messenger formula; v. 19aβ—admonition and promise; v. 19aγ— admonition and promise; v. 19b—admonition. Extra-Jeremianic biblical parallels to the pattern of the oracle are lacking.[17] None of the salvation oracles in Dt.-Isa. contains a summons to repentance, and the assurance formula is always present.[18] The only similar articulation of conditional promise of salvation is to be found in Jer. 3.21–4.2 (3-4), which also appears to be a prophetic liturgy.[19] Appeal can also be made to the partial doublets in the call narrative (1.8, 17-19) where at one point the assurance formula (1.17) has taken on an admonitory force. On this basis, it still seems legitimate to maintain the affinity of the divine response to the salvation oracle pattern in spite of its divergences.[20] However, these divergences raise difficulties for analysing the syntactical and logical relationship of v. 19 to vv. 20-21. The latter, coupled with the doublet phenomenon observed previously, will require consideration of the implications for redaction and interpretation below. Analogous to the divine oracle in 15.10-14, the present one comprises a blend of genre affinities.

Particular Form:[21] While the primary features integrating the confession together appear to be those of lament and prophetic liturgy typicalities, certain special features can also be observed which complement the former:

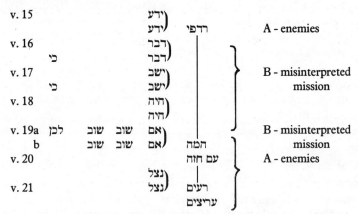

As the schema illustrates, the major divisions of lament and divine

response are marked by the conjunction (לכן) in v. 19. Major
overarching verbal echoes are lacking, though a general stylistic
feature of repetitions limited to individual verses or between
adjoining verses is observable.[22] The abstract, stereotyped references
to the supplicant's enemies are altered at one point by a more
concrete reference to the nation. However, the primary integrating
feature complementary to the typical pattern is the chiastic development of the central themes. For the complaint begins in relation to
the prophet's enemies (v. 15) but gradually shifts (vv. 16-18) the
emphasis to Yahweh and the ironic misinterpretation of his mission;
and then the answering oracle responds by addressing this misinterpretation first (v. 19a) and finally the problem of the prophet's
opponents (vv. 19b-21).[23] The latter feature illustrates well the
integral relationship of the oracle to the lament and combines with
the typical features to create the general impression of the passage as
an integrated unit.

Redaction

The apparent unity of the confession has been vigorously contested
in recent redactional analysis of the passage, without, however,
achieving a consensus. Though the most significant problems and
possibilities relate to the divine oracle (vv. 19-21), not a single verse
has gone uncontested. The overall effect of any given redactional
model on the passage has ranged from viewing only one or two verses
or a part of a verse as secondary to ascribing the entire confession to
an editorial composition.

In our view the various proposals for the lament section (vv. 15-
18) have been the least convincing apart from the initial phrase
אתה ידעת (v. 15).[24] Both Eichler and Ahuis have argued that vv. 15-
16 are Dtr. expansions, in their attempts to reconstruct vv. 10, 17, 18
as the original kernel from 15.10-18.[25] However, the results of our
analysis of 15.10-14 already render their approach problematical.
Their primary criteria for the secondary nature of vv. 15-16 are the
lack of logical connection between them and vv. 17-18 and their
prose character.[26] For Eichler and Ahuis, Dtr. has expanded the
original complaint by giving great prominence to the theme of the
prophet's enemies and thereby has reduced the force of his
accusations against Yahweh.[27] However, the interweaving of complaint
toward enemies and toward God is not unusual for the lament

genre;[28] and, coupled with our preceding formal observations about the chiastic development of these, this observation causes the description of the verses as a loose collection of self-standing elements to lose its force.[29] In addition, Ahuis provides no basis for his reclassification of the verses as prose.[30] The ease of discerning the parallelistic lines with fairly balanced metre makes such a proposal unlikely. The diction of the lament contains nothing distinctively characteristic of prose or Dtr.[31]

The situation for the divine oracle (vv. 19-21) is much more difficult to evaluate. Some overlap in the various analyses can be observed.[32] Eichler views the original kernel as vv. 19b, 20; Ahuis, as vv. 19b, 20aα; Vermeylen and Hubmann, as v. 19; Ittmann, as vv. 19-20. As a rationale for excluding v. 19a, its prose and/or Dtr. affinities are noted (Eichler, Ahuis). For all or parts of vv. 20-21 the primary evidence of editorial activity is perceived in its doubletted character with the call narrative (1.8, 18-19) and mechanical catchword associations (v. 21 to v. 20—נצל).

The merits of these various proposals are not uniform. For v. 19a, Ahuis's atttempt to classify it as prose suffers from the same weaknesses as those noted on vv. 15-16. Viewing the repentance theology[33] and its articulation in the conditional format[34] as signs of Dtr. character loses its force when the widespread use of the summons to repentance among the prophets is recognized (Isa. 1.19-20; 55.6-7; Amos 5.4-7, 14-15; Joel 2.12-13; Zech. 1.2-6) as well as its occurrence elsewhere in Jeremianic poetry (3.12-13; 3.22a; 4.3-4; 4.14)—especially in 4.1-2, where there is an analogous conditional construction and verbal play on the root שוב.[35] Positively, the verbal play on and echoes of the root שוב appear to bind the whole of the verse together. The removal of v. 19a disrupts the chiastic development of themes and produces a divine response which formally does not address the ironic and bitter accusations against Yahweh in the lament. Thus the integral connection of the answer to the complaint is much weakened.

The case for v. 21 is slightly stronger since it exhibits a generalized and formulaic character (עם הזה .vs עריצים/רעים), a partial verbal echo with 20.13 (הצל ... מיד מרעים); and the verbal repetition of נצל (vv. 20-21) could be explained as due to a mechanical catchword process of association.[36] In addition, the zero variant in G at vv. 20bβ-21 could be taken as a further indication of explicit editorial activity, though in this case the alternative reading seems to have occurred through mechanical error (see above note 5). However, the formal relationship of both this verse and v. 20 to the elements of a salvation oracle coupled with the verbal repetition of נצל—now viewed as a further sign of original integration—could argue strongly for their unity. The correspondence between 15.21 and 20.13 is not extensive enough to consider the verses within the doublet phenomenon encountered in discussion of 15.13-14. And the generalized character of the terms could permit an explanation of the echoes as due to the formulaic usage characteristic of a particular genre or authorial style.[37] Finally, the generalized terms for the opponent fit the pattern in the rest of this confessional unit (סוד משחקים, רדפי, חמה). It is actually עם הזה which provides the exception.

As a result of our discussion so far, attempts to isolate a portion of v. 19, or v. 21 as a whole, from the oracle as an editorial expansion seem highly unlikely. The remaining issue for discussion is whether the connection between v. 19 and vv. 20-21 is original or secondary. In the excellent discussion of this problem by Hubmann, a cogent case for viewing all of vv. 20-21 as a secondary expansion has been made.[38] In primary support for this view, appeal is made to the doublet[39] of 15.20 with 1.8, 17-19, coupled with certain internal tensions within its present confessional context. The latter consist primarily of the apparently abrupt shift from a conditional to an unconditional reinstatement of the prophet in his office[40] and a shift in the identity of his opponents from false prophets (v. 17—סוד משחקים) to the whole nation (v. 20—עם הזה).[41] Additional corroborative support is sought by appeal to the parallel structure between the divine oracles in 15.11-14 and 15.19-21; since the prior pattern resulted from the editorial expansion of vv. 13-14, the similar patterns in vv. 19-21 may also indicate the same editorial hand affecting the parallelism through the addition of vv. 20-21.[42]

Evaluation of any given doublet phenomenon is a difficult task, as was illustrated in our previous analysis of 15.13-14/17.3-4. A nuanced approach to each case is required instead of assuming that the mere occurrence of a doublet indicates the secondary character of the text in question. In the present case, it seems inappropriate to attempt an explanation of the doublets as due to a mechanical multiple anchoring in the tradition since the verbal divergences between them clearly indicate adaptation of each to its present context.[43] Similarly an explanation based upon simple repetition of set formulas encounters some difficulty in the extent of text involved and more particularly in the unique expression חומת נחשת בצורה, which is not used outside Jer. 15.20 except for its close analogue in Jer. 1.18. This raises the possibility that one or both doublets are secondary in their present context. Considering each doublet from the standpoint of appropriateness to context, its occurrence as part of the answering oracle in 15.15-21 seems completely commensurate, formally and logically, based upon its affinities with the salvation oracle genre. The close contacts of the salvation oracle with cultic lament[44] and the overall prophetic liturgy pattern of 15.15-21 suggest that the occurrence of vv. 20-21 within that structure is just what one would expect. The chiastic development of these strengthens this impression further. On the other hand, the connection within a call narrative is not so obvious or expected.[45] The overall impression made by Jeremiah 1 as a compositional unity made up of independent units, designed to provide an overview and introduction to the prophetic message and book, further reduces the value of the doublet phenomenon as an aid to detecting editorial layers in 15.19-21.[46] But even if 1.18-19 is secondary, it does not automatically require the originality of 15.20-21. The importance of supposed internal tensions between 15.15-19 and 15.20-21 takes on more significance in the analysis since on the level of the doublet phenomenon *per se* an original connection within a prophetic liturgy seems more probable than one within a call narrative. In this regard, a tension in the shift from conditional to unconditional reinstatement—that is to say, v. 20 appears to promise what v. 19 made explicitly contingent and thus assumes the fulfilment of those conditions —exists only so long as simple co-ordination of v. 20 to v. 19 (ונתתיך) is assumed. However, the clause could be taken as the result of the admonition in v. 19c[47] ('so/thus I will make you . . .'). This would be expected, in view of the patterns in v. 19ab which stipulate the behaviour required and announce the result of compliance. On this basis vv. 20-21 would be fully integrated into the conditional promise of salvation.[48] The remaining internal tensions can be treated more properly in the Interpretation section. Our discussion so far permits a tentative conclusion that sees vv. 20-21 as integral and original to the divine oracle. Subsequent discussion must seek further corroboration of this judgment. Apart from אתה ידעת (v. 15a) no other signs of redactional activity seem detectable.[49]

Setting

The discernment of the pre-literary setting of the confessions has been plagued, so far, both by the lack of external information corroborating a given proposal[50] and especially the problem of internal ambiguity of the units *vis à vis* the prophetic mission. Explicit contact with prophetic concerns has been more a factor of editorial activity (11.21-23; 15.13-14) and the location of the passages within the prophetic book (11.18-20; 12.1-6; 15.10-12).

For the present unit, the situation is only slightly different. Most of the proposals seem unsatisfactory. The consistent corporate interpretation of Reventlow is excluded by the answering oracle which sets an individual over against the nation (עם הזה), thus precluding his cultic mediator theory. The lawsuit/ריב classification of Wimmer suffers from the lack of legal imagery. Ahuis's theory suffers primarily from the lack of external evidence for a lament as *Rückmeldung* within a *Botenvorgang*. Internally the lament includes both report about opposition (דע שאתי עליך חרפה) and the problem of delay on Yahweh's part (אל לארך אפך תקחני) but emphasizes the prophet's own conflict over the conditions of his prophetic mission (vv. 17-18). Thus the patterns which Ahuis would like to keep distinct (*Botenvorgang* and *Warten auf das Gericht*) have been woven together in one unit. If his attempt to understand this confession as *gerichtsprophetische Klage* is to be followed, the more generalized model of Eichler would need to be employed.

However, the real difficulty to be faced is whether the content of the unit encourages the search for a setting within the prophetic mission. For the lament section (vv. 15-18), the diction is plagued by the same ambiguity encountered in the previous units. Even דבר in v. 16, which could be a reference to the prophetic word, is capable of an alternative explanation, thus removing the best possibility of a distinctive prophetic element from it.[51] On the other hand, the divine oracle, especially in v. 19, seems to provide the best unambiguous indication that a prophetic individual and his mission are in view, regardless of how the redactional status of vv. 20-21 is assessed.[52] While the expression עמד לפני indicates some type of official functionary, the phrase כפי seems best interpreted as reference to a prophet.[53] On this basis the ambiguous idioms within the complaint would become fixed to a greater degree in the direction of the prophetic (esp. v. 17b). The many points of contact with the vocabulary of Jeremianic poetry[54] and the play of מים לא נאמנו (v. 18) upon the Jeremianic formulation מקור מים חיים (2.13) combine with the preceding to enhance the explictly prophetic character of the confession, thereby inviting a search for a setting within the prophetic mission.

Given the more explicit character of the prophetic element, the proposal of J.M. Berridge, Clines and Gunn becomes more attractive, especially perhaps in combination with Eichler's general observations about the potential crisis points within prophetic mission.[55] In contrast to the confessional units studied so far, this one presents the least difficulty for the supposition of a dramatic form of proclamation with apologetic intent in a situation of conflict over prophetic mission. Even the emphasis upon the prophet's conflict with his mission, countered by the divine summons of repentance, could be accommodated within an apologetic perspective as the prophet's statement to his opponents that no other manner of executing the prophetic task has been permitted him. Finally the problem of the limitation of such a dramatic form to the Jeremiah tradition could be blunted somewhat by appeal to the prophetic liturgy pattern and its use elsewhere as a method of articulating prophetic proclamation.[56] The occurrence of such a form elsewhere in Jeremianic poetry (3.21–4.2) could render more intelligible such a further development in the defence of the prophetic message as that envisaged for this confession of Jeremiah.

Interpretation

While the general import of the confession seems clear, further details for discussion remain which present problems for a more precise understanding of the text and of its implications for the problems afflicting the redactional analysis and the determination of a pre-literary setting within the prophetic mission discussed above. The principal questions relate to establishing the identity of the prophet's opponents more precisely and to the analysis of the supposed prophetic elements with their ambiguous character. Along with these central issues must be included the further clarification of v. 19bc and the way in which the confession oscillates between continuity and discontinuity with the normal lament tradition.

Some indication of this continuity and discontinuity with lament tradition has already been illustrated by our formal analysis and

vocabulary statistics.[57] Broadly speaking, the complaint section
exhibits more continuity than the divine oracle apart from the
contacts of the latter with salvation oracle motifs. The lack of formal
elements expressing confidence already sets the complaint on the
borders of normal Psalm laments and intensifies the negative tone of
this lament. The negative slant is enhanced further by biting ironic
plays upon divine epithets. In v. 15,[58] the phrase ארך אפך should
probably be seen as an allusion to the divine predication of Yahweh's
forbearance (Exod. 34.6), normally celebrated in hymns expressing
confidence in divine aid (Pss. 103.8; 145.8) and employed as a
motivational theme in lament (Ps. 86.15) and prophetic liturgy (Joel
2.13). In this case, its normal connotations have been set on their
head, since it is precisely Yahweh's forbearance with the poet's
enemies that constitutes the threat and works against him.[59] Again in
v. 18,[60] מים לא נאמנו should probably be understood as a parody of
מים חיים[61] (Jer. 2.13; 17.13) and thus a direct denial of Yahweh's
emphatically asserted reliability over against man's falseness (Num.
23.19; Deut. 7.9—האל נאמן; Deut. 32.4—אל אמונה; Pss. 89.36; 93.5;
111.7; contrast Pss. 5.7; 58.4). Though accusations in the Psalms
come close, they never go so far as to depict Yahweh explicitly as a
liar (cf. Pss. 44.10ff.; 88.7ff.; 89.39ff.). In effect, the accusation
reduces Yahweh to the status of Israel's idols (cf. Jer. 2.13—
בארת נשברים).[62]

Discernment of further ironic motifs is bound up with potential
allusions to the prophetic mission and the bitter 'misinterpretation'
of the same developed across vv. 16-17. An elucidation of these ideas
first requires the resolution of major difficulties related to the
ambiguity of terms alluding to prophetic concerns. Normally, v. 16 is
understood in relation to the prophet's call, especially with the
positive response to דבר as the prophet's response to the prophetic
word.[63] In support, appeal can be made to analogous expressions
such as מצא דבר יהוה (Amos 8.12), מצא חזון (Lam. 2.9), and call
narratives which depict the prophet eating the prophetic word (Ezek.
2.8–3.1) or having the word placed in his mouth (Jer. 1.9).[64] Though
such evidence seems compelling, this understanding has two major
difficulties. First, the picture of the prophet as positively responsive
to the prophetic mission contradicts the picture elsewhere of
reluctance (1.5; 17.16) and outright opposition to the mission with
the divine word experienced as an oppressive power (20.7-9).[65]
Second, it leaves unexplained the peculiar impersonal and passive

form of the expression נמצאו דבריך.[66] The only parallel usage is in
2 Kgs 22.13 and 23.2 in reference to the rediscovered law book during
the Josianic reform (דברי הספר הנמצא). In light of the paucity of
parallels, it might be legitimate to view Jer. 15.16 as an allusion to
this very event.[67] Rather than a statement about the receptivity to
the prophetic word, the profession of innocence would depict the
poet as a loyal supporter of the law book and accompanying reform.[68]
The problems encountered in the normal understanding would be
removed. The transition from v. 16 to v. 17 also would become
smoother.[69] Though the probability of this view is difficult to
assess,[70] we prefer it in light of the problems afflicting the usual
approach. Thus, explicit reference to prophetic concerns becomes, at
the least, very ambiguous.

A similar problem arises for v. 17b. Viewed in terms of lament
tradition, the expressions ידך and זעם could be understood as
references to an experience of Yahweh's judgment.[71] On the other
hand, in light of v. 19 and their present context within a prophetic
book, they could be understood as references to prophetic inspiration
and the messsage of divine wrath.[72] Verse 19 provides the strongest
indication that the ambiguity should be resolved in the direction of
the prophetic. However, instead of entirely excluding the other
potential nuance, it is suggested that the same use of poetic irony
observed in v. 15 is also at work here. In other words, the poet is
referring in v. 17b to the isolation and alienation from the community
which have been imposed by the prophetic mission, but in such a
way as to freight the reference with overtones of judgment and curse
motifs. In short, he is characterizing his office as a divine curse and
affliction.[73]

This developing picture of the bitter, ironic misinterpretation of
the divine character and the prophetic mission (vv. 15, 17b, 18) leads
us to the consideration of v. 17a and the problem of the prophet's
opponents. As noted above, the general practice of stereotyped
references to the opponents is altered only in v. 20 with the reference
to the nation (לעם הזה). On the surface, this would suggest the same
referent for the other labels (עריצים, רעים, המה, רדפי).[74] Against this,
Hubmann has sought to identify the סוד משחקים in v. 17a with the
false prophets.[75] His most important reason for this is the absolute
necessity, in his view, of understanding v. 17 as part of the profession
of innocence.[76] The problem lies in the apparently innocent activities
of משחקים and עלז which do not seem to provide adequate bases for

self-vindication before Yahweh.[77] Since זעם and יד יהוה understood in
relation to the prophetic mission provide the key points of antithesis
(מפני) for the prophet and the סוד משחקים, Hubmann proposes the
false prophets of peace and salvation (contrast Jeremiah as a prophet
of doom—זעם) as the concrete referents behind the phrase.[78] A major
weakness of this proposal is that the remaining usages of the
participle in Jeremianic poetry (30.19; 31.3) have nothing to do with
the false prophets but preserve the more natural nuance of general
merrymaking.[79] The appeal to Jer. 23.18, 22 for the סוד יהוה as sign of
a true prophet is promising,[80] but סוד need not be connected with
prophecy or prophetic knowledge in Jeremiah (cf. 6.11—סוד בחורים).
This conflict between the supposed function of v. 17[81] as a profession
of innocence (cf. Pss. 1.1; 26. 4, 5) and discerning an appropriate
meaning for שחק/עלז may be resolved better by recourse to the
technique of poetic irony already so well attested in the lament. Verse
17a creates an expectation that it is indeed a profession of innocence
but then frustrates the expectation with the disavowal of participation
in innocent activities. A play upon a normal hallmark of the pious
seems in force; for instead of separation from the wicked and
enjoyment of community of the righteous, his covenant loyalty
(v. 16) has been rewarded with exclusion from the community and its
blessings.[82] Understood in this ironic fashion, the verse should be
joined with v. 18 as part of the complaint section.[83] The basic
requirement for Hubmann's proposal drops away.[84] And a consistent
interpretation of the prophet's opponents as the nation can be
maintained.[85]

Aim

The dialogue between prophet and Yahweh reaches the sharpest tone
of agitation and conflict encountered in the confessional units so far.
The prophet stands against both Yahweh and the nation. The biting,
negative tone of the complaint is emphatically underlined by the
exclusion of normal confidence motifs and the employment of poetic
irony. The latter draws attention to the heart of the complaint, a
crisis in the prophetic mission. Arising out of the threat to the
prophet from his national opponent and the threat of Yahweh's
forbearance delaying divine aid to the prophet, the prophet engages
in a bitter 'misinterpretation' of the prophetic mission. Yahweh's
commission has set him at odds with his community and prohibited

any solidarity with it. As such it constitutes a violent frustration of the legitimate expectations of any loyal member of the covenant community. Coupled with the factor of Yahweh's delayed succour, the prophetic mission is shown to be a divine pestilence or curse and challenges Yahweh's reliability. The virulent attack of the prophet is countered by an equally sharp divine response. Though it is similar to previous answers with the mixture of rebuke and promise, the summons to repent upon which the promise is contingent implies a stinging charge of blasphemy and infidelity to the mission on the prophet's part. No other way is held out to the prophet for executing the mission other than the present one of total conflict with the nation. No exercise of mission in support of the nation is open to him. Paradoxically, hope of deliverance for the prophet lies not in the restoration of community solidarity but in the shattering of the nation in its war against the divine messenger. The overall effect of this prophetic liturgy is to provide a massive vindication of the manner of the prophetic mission in terms of the realities depicted in the complaint with, however, a refutation of the prophet's misinterpretation.

12	כסא כבוד	A glorious throne,
	מרום מראשון	an eternal height
	מקום מקדשנו	is the place of our sanctuary.
13	מקוה ישראל יהוה	O hope of Israel, Yahweh,
	כל עזביך יבשו	all who forsake you will be ashamed.
	יסורי בארץ יכתבו	Those who turn from me,[1] in the Netherworld
	כי עזבו מקור מים חיים את יהוה	shall be recorded; for they have forsaken the Fountain of living water, Yahweh.
14	רפאני יהוה וארפא	Heal me, Yahweh, and so, healed shall I be!
	הושיעני ואושעה	Save me, and so, saved shall I be!
	כי תהלתי אתה	for you are my praise.
15	הנה המה אמרים אלי	See they taunt me:
	איה דבר יהוה יבוא נא	'Where is Yahweh's word? Let it be fulfilled!'
16	ואני לא אצתי מרעה אחריך	But I did not hurry away from being a shepherd after you;[2]
	ויום אנוש לא התאויתי	yet I did not crave the calamitous day.
	אתה ידעת מוצא שפתי	You know the utterance of my lips,
	נכח פניך היה	before you it has been
17	אל תהיה לי למחתה	Do not be a cause of a terror to me!
	מחסי אתה ביום רעה	you are my refuge in the evil day.
18	יבשו רדפי ואל אבשה אני	Let my pursuers be ashamed but do not let me suffer shame
	יחתו המה ואל אחתה אני	Let them be shattered but do not let me be shattered.
	הביא עליהם יום רעה	Bring on them the evil day;
	ומשנה שברון שברם	and with a double breaking, break them!

Form

Of particular note in the examination of typical and particular features of this passage is the problem of the precise extent of the unit and the contrast of the overall pattern to that encountered in previous confessions.

Typical Form: Baumgartner's analysis of vv. 14-18 in relation to individual lament has won acceptance by most scholars and, in our view, rightly so as follows:[3]

v. 14	introductory address and petition (with expression of confidence)
v. 15	lament
v. 16	profession of innocence
vv. 17-18	petition

More problematical for Baumgartner's approach was his view of vv. 12-13 as a hymnic introduction to the lament. On the face of it, such a view is totally acceptable, particularly since significant parallels exist for such a practice.[4] However, most scholars have not followed Baumgartner and have excluded the verses as part of the confessional unit based upon their supposed inauthenticity.[5] But this is not appropriate methodologically since even as an inauthentic editorial expansion they could still have a formal function as part of the confessional unit, even if it is a composite.[6]

Returning then to more formal considerations, there does appear to be one feature of the verses which proves fatal for Baumgartner's view. While vv. 12-13a represent direct address to Yahweh and a corporate worshipper (מקרשנו), MT וסורי/יסורי in v. 13b breaks the continuity with a change of speaker. Contextually the shift to 1st pers. sg. makes best sense as divine speech. Reventlow has suggested that this change of speakers indicates the dialogical-liturgical character of the passage. Verses 12-13a are seen as an expression of national lament and v. 13b as the divine response of judgment.[7] Reventlow's view of vv. 12-13a as veiled lament and petition seems a bit strained. It would probably be better to regard the motifs of praise as citations of the national false piety used as grounds for accusation and thus to view the whole as a variant form of judgment speech (cf. the similar use of the *vox populi* in the oracles of Jer. 2.20-37). Reventlow's attempt to carry a consistent corporate interpretation throughout vv. 12-18 founders on the exegesis of vv. 15-16 as previous criticisms have made clear.[8] This being the case, it would seem best to regard vv. 12-13 and vv. 14-18 as two distinct formal units. Verses 12-13 would be viewed as a judgment oracle, articulated in dialogical fashion with the aid of the motifs from cultic genre (cf. the analogous oracles in Jer. 8.19; 9.16-21; 10.19-22). As a judgment speech to the nation it contradicts false national hopes centred on Zion as the throne and guarantee of Yahweh's presence, with the implied corollary that the nation would not be numbered among the wicked who forsake God nor be subjected to their shame.[9] Formally distinct from this are vv. 14-18, articulated according to patterns of individual lament but, as we hope to show, in such a way as to bring issues related to the heart of prophetic mission to the fore. This approach would not rule out that these units may be purposefully related in the present context, rather only that vv. 12-13 are to be treated as a constituent part of the confession.[10]

Particular Form: While the overall framework of the passage appears to be controlled by the typical elements of lament, these typical elements seem to be integrated by two major features. One is the contrasting interplay of the three subjects of lament—thou (Yahweh), I, they (enemy)—especially as this is illustrated by the use of the personal pronouns. The second is the verbal/subject links set up by the repetition of the related phrases יום אנוש (v. 16)—יום רעה (vv. 17, 18) and, as well, between דבר יהוה (v. 15) and מוצא שפתי (v. 16) if the exegesis of the former as 'prophetic' word can stand.[11] We offer the following schematic:

The interplay of the pronouns characterizes the relationship of the 'three subjects', consistently presenting Thou–I in a positive relationship and the I–they in a negative, oppositional one. The repeated phrases provide the central issue around which the 'three subjects' are oriented to one another. A further stylistic feature bears mention, that of the 'negative petition' which in reality constitutes a veiled complaint.[12] It introduces a note of threat and uncertainty into the

Thou-I relationship. Finally, in contrast to the confessions previously examined, the prophetic liturgy pattern of lament plus answering oracle is absent.

Redaction

On the basis of our discussion of form, the case for vv. 14-18 as an integrated original unity appears very strong. This also requires that questions of authenticity be discussed in terms of the whole unit.

Some objections to its unity have been raised. B. Duhm (p. 149) and C.H. Cornill (p. 218) argued that v. 18 represented an editorial expansion because it flatly contradicted v. 16. Whatever theological or psychological explanations one might use to attempt an integration of the two statements, at least on formal grounds such a 'tension' is a characteristic of lament and does not constitute grounds for questioning the original unity of the verses (see Pss. 35; 109).[13] A more thoroughgoing questioning of unity has been raised more recently by Vermeylen, who proposes a two-stage post-exilic redaction with the original kernel consisting of a petition in general distress (vv. 14, 16-17) and the second layer focusing attention on the fate of those who forsake God because of persecution (adding vv. 12-13, 15, 18).[14] Though space did not permit him to document his case, his basic rationale appears to lie in supposed post-exilic literary contacts and internal integration. However, this does not give due weight to the inner-Jeremianic literary contacts of the passage (see below) nor to the integrating features noted above in our schematic on Particular Form. On the face of it, there appears to be nothing in the character of vv. 14-18 which would require such a complex theory of development—even if it were post-exilic in origin. Finally, we may note that the attempt of Ahuis to view vv. 12-13 as a Dtr. expansion which redirects the focus of the confession to serve as the development of judgment proclamation is misplaced if our argument about the independence of the two units stands.[15] On our view, Ahuis's comments would pertain more to the compositional intention in the present context and not so much to a supposed redactional development of the confession proper. We will readdress ourselves to Ahuis's proposal later in considering compositional intention in the larger context.[16]

Setting

Indication of the difficulties pertaining to the question of determining a setting for Jeremiah's confessions has been illustrated by the problems already encountered in the previous units. However, viewing the present confession internally on its own terms, it seems hard to avoid the conclusion that it is intentionally concerned to reflect problems related to a prophetic situation—i.e. conflict arising out of the delay in fulfilment of prophetic proclamation (v. 15). Then if one proceeds to consider the confession from the standpoint of its inclusion in the book of Jeremiah, it seems that it is meant to be read in terms of Jeremiah's prophetic situation. We think here particularly of the allusion to the call narrative in v. 18 with the double use of תחת (cf. 1.17). The passage would seem to provide strong warrant to search for a setting within the prophetic mission of Jeremiah.

It remains problematical, though, whether the passage actually provides enough information to determine the specific setting. Here I must express a certain amount of dissatisfaction with the attempts mentioned previously.[17] The approach that would see this confession as a constituent part of the prophet's public proclamation—in this case as a public declaration for apologetic purposes in a situation of opposition—does not seem very workable. The lack of an affirmatory answering oracle (cf. 11.21-23) or even one with a mix of challenge and promise (cf. 15.11-14; 15.19-21) constitutes a serious problem for this approach. For it does not seem likely that the bare lament-petition for vindication would provide any type of effective defence before his opponents, unless one assumes that the lament is functionally equivalent to a curse uttered for the benefit of one's opponents. However, the negative petition in v. 17 with the element of uncertainty it introduces relative to divine-prophetic solidarity seems an odd approach to defending one's legitimacy as a prophet before those who question this very legitimacy. Furthermore, one would also like to see examples, external to the book of Jeremiah, where a lament formally addressed to Yahweh is used in a way functionally equivalent to curse and uttered for the benefit of one's opponents in a dispute or conflict. To my knowledge, there is no such example.

The latter lacuna in external parallels also constitutes the primary problem for the alternative of viewing this confession as a special prophetic lament. So while the present passage gives some general

indication of the type of occasion in the prophetic mission lying
behind it—i.e. delayed fulfilment—still the determination of its
precise setting (oral function) in the life of the prophet no longer
appears to be possible as the passage is preserved. The present
literary setting has become dominant in shaping the significance and
role of the lament.

Once a certain amount of indeterminacy relative to the setting of
this confession in the life of the prophet is accepted, this still does not
require acceptance of the second major theory of origin as editorial
composition. To see this passage as a transfer to the prophet of a
normal individual lament—which originally had nothing to do with a
prophetic figure, but whose stereotyped idioms provided the necessary
ambiguity to make such a transfer possible—in my view does not
deal adequately with vv. 15-16. While some of the idioms of this
confession are ambiguous (for example: יום רעה; allusion to call
narrative, חתת) and their character as 'prophetic' could be a factor
solely of the context, the attempt to argue the same for דבר יהוה
seems very unlikely.[18] And if one is going to argue that the presence
of such features is the result of editorial adaptation to make the
lament more applicable to prophetic concerns,[19] then on what basis
can the very same process be denied to the prophet himself? The
examination of this passage so far indicates that none of its features
necessarily excludes its connection with a prophetic and Jeremianic
setting—indeterminate though its precise nature may be.[20]

Interpretation

The primary problems for discussion are the validity of the supposed
'prophetic' elements of vv. 15-16, and a clear analysis of the precise
issue, or concern, about which the lament revolves. Bound up with
these primary questions is the nature of the diction of the lament,
especially as this oscillates between continuity and discontinuity
with the usual diction of Psalm laments.

Since vv. 15-16 seem critical for an overall synthetic understanding
of the passage, we shall begin our discussion there. Already we have
had occasion to mention our dissatisfaction with the attempt of
Reventlow to interpret these verses in a way completely free of
reference to a prophetic situation.[21] Though he points out correctly
that דבר as a divine word in the Psalms can refer to helping/saving
power (Ps. 107.20) or perhaps more accurately to saving utterance/

promise (Pss. 130.5; 56.5, 11) and thus the enemies' taunt in Jer.
17.15 could be equivalent to 'where is your God?' (Ps. 42.4, 11),
nevertheless J. Bright and Berridge are right to criticize him for
failing to consider the phrase דבר יהוה in conjunction with בוא. Usage
provides strong evidence for the exclusive referent of the association
being fulfilment or non-fulfilment of prophetic utterance.[22] Once
Reventlow's argument breaks down here, his approach to the passage
as a whole becomes improbable. So the profession of innocence,
v. 16, is similarly best understood in relation to prophetic mission
rather than in the more generalized sense of his view.[23] Though
admittedly awkward, the basic sense of v. 16aα is to claim loyalty in
pursuance of the prophetic office.[24] The unusual usage of רֹעֶה in
reference to a prophet is perhaps more comprehensible when one
recalls the employment elsewhere in the confessions and the call
narrative of political-military imagery with reference to Jeremiah's
vocation.[25] Also if Berridge is right to see the usage in Jer. 23.1 as a
reference not only to the king (i.e. the usual recipient of the label) but
to officials generally and in 2.8 to view הרעים as strictly parallel to
הנביאים in light of תפשי התורה//הכהנים, the the apparently singular
usage in our present verse would be totally understandable.[26]

Verse 16aβ is disjunctive and sets up a contrast to the preceding. In
light of the predominant usage of אנוש in Jeremiah to refer either to
the sufferings/wounds of the nation under judgment or to the
prophet's suffering, יום אנוש should probably be understood in
relation to Yahweh's day of judgment on the nation.[27] While the
preceding clause affirmed the prophet's loyalty to his prophetic
vocation, this clause provides a disclaimer that the judgment
announced corresponded to his personal desires or cravings.[28]

The expressions examined so far in vv. 15-16a appear to be
unambigously concerned with the affairs of prophetic mission. Many
of the remaining expressions and images throughout the lament,
which admittedly have an ambiguous character *vis à vis* 'prophetic
concerns' or 'typical concerns' of individual lament, should be
interpreted in light of the clearly prophetic features in order to gain a
proper appreciation of the integrated structure of the whole lament.
Thus the second half of v. 16, which could be a simple declaration of
innocence of speech מוצא שפתי, (Pss. 17.1; 34.13) or more particularly
loyalty to one's vows (Pss. 66.14; 89.35; Lev. 30.13; Deut. 23.24),
should be viewed more immediately in terms of דבר יהוה (cf. Deut.
8.3) and so a statement that Yahweh knows and approves the

prophet's proclamation (נכח פניך היה).[29] Again, the introductory
petition, which could be understood totally in traditional lament
categories, receives a more pointed force since the 'healing' requested
should be understood in terms of the crisis arising from delayed
fulfilment (v. 15) and so consists essentially of the realization of the
announced judgment (v. 16aβ). That this is the concern of the
petition is indicated further in the petitions of vv. 17-18 which
appear to contain allusions to the call narrative (1.17) through
repeated use of the root חתת. The 'healing' of the prophet is
essentially his vindication over against the opponents through
bringing on the day of judgment (v. 18b).[30] The allusion to 1.17
suggests that the present situation of delayed fulfilment threatens to
realize the discomfiture of the prophet as the punishment for failure
to carry out faithfully the prophetic commission. Yet v. 16 rejects any
such suggestion. The veiled complaint of the negative petition (v. 17)
is enhanced further by the possible conscious contradiction or
reversal of such 'mini-confessions' as Ps. 94.22—ויהי יהוה לי למשגב or
Ps. 118.14, 21—ויהי/ותהי לי לישועה.[31] Further special nuances which
probably are to be detected relate to the vocabulary cluster ישע, רפא
(v. 14); אנוש (v. 16); חתת, שברון, שבר, יום רעה, בוש (vv. 17-18). This
block of vocabulary is especially associated in the book of Jeremiah
with the destruction/judgment and restoration of the nation.[32] This
provides a strong indication that the opponents (המה; רדפי) referred
to so obliquely are in actuality to be identified as the whole nation.[33]
This lends even more (ironic) force to the prophet's petition, for his
'healing' (i.e vindication, v. 14) will mean the 'breaking' (v. 18b) of
the nation.

In sum, the analysis of the passage argues that the problem about
which the lament revolves is the delay in fulfilment of the prophetic
proclamation which has subjected the prophet to the taunts of the
nation and thrown his legitimacy into question (v. 15). Correspondingly the petition calls for vindication of the prophet and his
proclamation by Yahweh's execution of the promised judgment
(vv. 14, 18). The profession of innocence motivates the petition and
underlines the veiled complaint (v. 17) that the real threat lies in
Yahweh's failure to act, especially so since the proclamation was
divinely approved utterance (v. 16b) and not merely the prophet's
own desires (v. 16aβ). On the contrary, he is preaching in faithful
pursuance of his prophetic vocation (v. 16aα). The causes for lack of
fulfilment do not lie with him.[34]

Aim

While we have been able to discuss the aim of previous confessions in terms of a dramatic dialogue between prophet and God, this confession is the first to break that pattern through the absence of an answering oracle. The search for an appropriate explanation of this feature will have to be taken up later after our detailed exegesis of all the confessions is complete. At least, the absence of the prophetic liturgy pattern raises questions for any assumption that the divine answer is essential for Jeremiah's confessions. As lament of the individual, formally speaking, it need not have an answering oracle however much it may create a climate of expectation for one.

As we have sought to argue, the central aim of this confession is vindication of Jeremiah's prophetic proclamation of judgment. The delay in fulfilment has created a crisis of legitimacy before the nation who now can taunt an apparently misguided or even self-styled prophet. The structure of the lament portrays the relationship of prophet and nation, and nation and Yahweh in exclusively antithetic terms. However, the relationship between prophet and Yahweh is presented, at least in its main thrust, as one of solidarity and confidence. Yet an undercurrent to this main thrust is introduced by the negative petition and the profession of innocence in relation to it. A certain amount of tension and uncertainty is suggested. There is a veiled accusation that the cause of the present crisis in prophetic mission lies with Yahweh. Remedy of the present crisis will mean the inbreaking of divine judgment on the nation as announced in prophetic proclamation.

18   ויאמרו לכו ונחשבה על ירמיהו
מחשבות כי לא תאבד תורה מכהן
ועצה מחכם ודבר מנביא לכו
ונכהו בלשון ואל נקשיבה אל
כל דבריו

And they said: 'Come! Let us devise against Jeremiah schemes, for neither instruction from priest nor counsel from the wise, nor utterance from the prophet will perish. Come! Let us smite him with the tongue and give no[1] heed to any of his words.'

19   הקשיבה יהוה אלי
ושמע לקול יריבי

Give heed, O Yahweh, to me!
Listen to the voice of my adversaries:[2]

20   הישלם תחת טובה רעה

'Will he reward with calamity instead of good?'

כי כרו שוחה לנפשי

for they have dug a pit for my life.[3]

זכר עמדי לפניך

Remember my standing before you

לדבר עליהם טובה

that I might proclaim on their behalf good,

להשיב את חמתך מהם

thus turning your wrath from them.

21   לכן תן את בניהם לרעב

Therefore, appoint their children to famine;

והגרם על ידי חרב

bring them down by the edge of the sword;

ותהינה נשיהם שכלות ואלמנות

and so may their wives be barren widows!

ואנשיהם יהיו הרגי מות

As for their men, let them be slaughtered by death

בחוריהם מכי חרב במלחמה

their warriors smitten by the sword in battle.

22   תשמע זעקה מבתיהם

May a cry be heard from their homes;

כי תביא עליהם גדוד פתאם

when you bring upon them suddenly raiders.

כי כרו שיחה ללכדני

For they have dug a pit to capture me,

	ופחים טמנו לרגלי	and snares have they hid for my feet.
23	ואתה יהוה ידעת	But You, Yahweh, know
	את כל עצתם עלי למות	all their schemes against me for death.
	אל תכפר על עונם	Do not forgive their iniquity
	וחטאתם מלפניך אל תמח	nor blot out from before you their sins,
	ויהיו מכשלים לפניך	and thus may they be hurled down before you;
	בעת אפך עשה בהם	in the time of your wrath, deal with them!

Form

The overall structure of this confession is similar to the preceding one in its lack of an answering oracle. However, the affinity of the lament itself to psalms of individual lament has long been recognized. What is problematical for the formal analysis is the precise role of v. 18 which appears to be prose (cf. *BHS*) and which appears to provide the setting or background for the prayer which follows. Closely bound up with the previous issues are the problems related to discernment of the redactional history of the confessional piece. *Typical Form*: We begin by first offering a schematic of vv. 19-23 in relation to lament patterns:

v. 19   —introductory address and petition
v. 20a   —lament
v. 20b   —profession of innocence
vv. 21-23 —petition including lament (v. 22b) and expression of confidence (v. 23aα).

Of particular note is the central and emphatic role that petition elements have, so that even the lament sections are subordinated to them. In addition, the bulk of the petition is articulated in a fashion analogous to the curse sections of imprecatory psalms (vv. 21-22a) plus the use once again of a negative petition (v. 23aβ). This view of the typical features would find general agreement among scholars regardless of their particular analyses and hypotheses about the redactional growth of the text.[4] As noted above, it is the place of v. 18 within this typical pattern that is problematical. In recent exegesis, the verse is generally viewed as a prose introduction but not formally as a part of the lament itself. On the other hand, some attempts to see it as part of the lament proper have been made. Baumgartner recast the verse into poetry and considered it an introductory *Klage* section. Similarly, Eichler discerned a poetic kernel (v. 18a) which was to be re-connected to v. 19 as a *Situationsschilderung im Zitat*, while Ittmann attempted a total reclassification of the typical characteristics of the confession, accepting the prose-poetry shift as a legitimate confessional characteristic with the prose introduction (v. 18) providing a *prophetische Situationsbeschreibung*.[5] Aside from the question of the prose-poetry status,[6] the chief difficulty for the approaches of Baumgartner and Eichler is the completely untypical way of introducing lament that v. 18 would then represent. While it is true that a lament can open with lament proper (Ps. 3) or even with a self-reflective semi-biographical statement (Ps. 39),[7] to my knowledge an introduction consisting of a bare citation of one's enemies without any address to God is totally unparalleled.[8] Besides the serious difficulties noted earlier for Ittmann's formal approach, in our view he has also failed to deal adequately with Thiel's observations about the redactional character of the verse (see below). So while logical and verbal links (קשב v. 18b-19a) are sufficient indications that v. 18 is part of the whole confessional unit, it still seems best to view it as formally distinct from the following lament. This raises, however, the question of its redactional status.

Particular Form: Leaving v. 18 aside for the moment, we turn our attention to a more detailed analysis of the patterning of the lament vv. 19-23. The smooth development of the passage from a typical standpoint is matched by its particular details:

There are two major features by which the structure of the lament is articulated: major units in the thought development are marked by

the conjunction לכן (v. 21) and the adversative *waw* (v. 23), and
integration of the subject matter of the lament by verbal-subject
repetitions. Of particular interest is the way in which vv. 21-22 are
set off as a distinct block. The conjunctions לכן and כי frame the
verses. The subject matter of the petition is formulated as a curse (cf.
imprecations in Pss. 109.6-20; 35.4-8; 69.23-29).[9] The formal
emphasis upon petition, noted above, is particularly underlined by a
cluster of imperative and voluntive verbal forms in this section.
Reference to the enemy is focused in the section by the concentration
of 3rd pers. pl. pronouns. Finally, the general 3+3 metre increases in
the curse to a predominantly 4+4 metre, again serving to set off the
whole unit.[10] On the other hand, though a distinct unit, it is still an
integral part of the structure of the lament, being connected to the
preceding by the repetition of the clause כי כרו שוחה (vv. 20, 22), and
to the following by the verbal echo with מות (vv. 21, 23) which
parallels the fate plotted by the supplicant's opponents for him
(v. 23) and that which he petitions for them (v. 21).

It would appear that vv. 19-23 form a nicely integrated unit. Yet
the question of redactional development is not absolutely excluded
thereby. The clearly demarcated sub-units of the lament, integrated
though they are, permit possibilities for discerning editorial activity.
Various proposals have been presented which take their starting-
points from one or more of the above particular features.

Redaction

Attempts to discern redactional activity within the confessional unit
have been proposed relative to v. 18, v. 23, and vv. 21-22a.

First, as noted above, the prose character of v. 18 plus its formal
distinctness from the following lament raise significant questions
about the editorial status of the verse. In the studies of Thiel, and
more recently Hubmann, it has been argued persuasively that the
verse not only introduces the following confession but also provides
an important structural link back to the preceding prose material of
vv. 1-12. There is the developing pattern of prophetic sermon (vv. 1-
11) plus response of the people (v. 12 ויאמרו), followed by a second
prophetic speech (vv. 13-17) and again a response of the people (v. 18
ויאמרו), creating an overall picture of rejected message and messenger.
This pattern is held together further by the repeated interplay upon
the root מחשבה/חשב (vv. 8, 11, 12, 18). This integral relationship to

the wider context, expecially the prose material, would appear to
provide strong evidence for the secondary character of v. 18 in
relation to the following lament.[11]

Second, Ittmann has argued recently for the redactional status of
v. 23.[12] The decisive factor in his argumentation relies on the validity
of viewing v. 18 as part of the original confession.[13] Once this is
granted, he argues for a contradiction, or tension, in the nature of the
enemy plots as present in the respective verses. In v. 23 it is a
question of a murder plot (למות), but in v. 18 it is a question of
subverting and ignoring prophetic activity and preaching.[14] It should
be noted, however, that the murder plot of v. 23 is internally
consistent with the other depictions of the enemy's activity since the
'snares' and 'pits' are intended for the capture and presumably
destruction of the supplicant (v. 20 לנפשי; v. 22 ללכרני, לרגלי). The
imagery is that of the hunt.[15] Ittmann's observation then could work
to the opposite effect and provide further evidence for the redactional
status of v. 18.[16] In light of our previous considerations for v. 18, this
seems a much stronger line of argumentation to follow. And yet it is
not so clear that an unacceptable tension exists between v. 18 and
v. 23, whatever one makes of the redactional status of the former
verse. If one recalls the imagery in the Psalms of the tongue of the
wicked as a weapon by which the innocent are destroyed (Pss. 57.5;
64.4), then the relationship between the plot in v. 18 to נכהו בלשון and
that of v. 23 (עצה עלי למות) may not be all that disharmonious.[17] One
could view the former in terms of immediate goal and the latter in
terms of ultimate effect. It seems best, then, to view v. 23 as part of
the original confession.

Third, Ahuis and Eichler have attempted to argue for the
redactional status of vv. 21-22a, though for different reasons. The
chief weight of Ahuis's argument lies upon the contention, nowhere
demonstrated, that these verses are Dtr. Prose.[18] Further subsidiary
evidence is seen in the repetition of v. 22b in v. 20 aβ. In the latter
case the parallelism of v. 20 is interrupted and represents the attempt
by the editor to smooth out the prose insertion (vv. 21-22a) between
the original v. 22a and v. 22b (p. 34). He also suggests that the
location of the curse before confession of trust and concluding
petition is ill-fitting (p. 34). In addition, the parallel content of the
prose insertion with Jeremianic judgment speech, esp. 11.22ff.,
suggests that original judgment speech (N.B. לכן) has been reformed
into lament-petition (p. 35).

While Ahuis is correct to point to the somewhat different character
of these lines from the surrounding ones, it is not clear that the
evidence will support his contention about their prose character—
especially as Dtr. prose. The vocabulary of the verse is distinctly free
of clichés or expressions that would label it as Dtr. Certainly the
vocabulary is of a very common nature with a general tendency
toward a widespread distribution in Jeremianic prose. Yet the
vocabulary is also consistently represented in Jeremianic poetry. At
least one could not make a decisive judgment about the prose-poetry
character of the lines on this basis. But it should be noted that some
of the vocabulary and expressions either occur only here in Jeremiah
or only in Jeremianic poetry.[19] It would seem better to couple these
features with the ones observed in regard to form and recognize that
the difference of these verses from the surrounding is not one of a
shift from poetry to prose but rather one of a shift in metre. Note as
well the relative ease of scanning the parallelism into a tri-colon and
a bi-colon compared to the problems encountered in v. 18. Verse
20aβ appears just as necessary to the content of the verse as v. 20b
for explaining the nature of the plaintiff question (v. 20aα).[20] Its
repetition is not necessarily problematic when one recalls the
presence of identical, or slightly altered, refrains in Psalms. The
location of the imprecation is also consistent with other imprecatory
Psalms which place a curse unit prior to expressions of confidence
and further petitions or complaint (see Pss. 35; 69; 109). The
question of parallels to Jeremianic judgment speech leads us to
consider the proposal of Eichler, but we can sum up our discussion
on Ahuis by concluding that his arguments are unconvincing on the
whole and insufficient to demonstrate vv. 21-22a as a secondary
expansion.

The weight of Eichler's argument, who similarly views vv. 21-22a
as editorial, lies in their similarity to 11.22-23.[21] Also for her, one
member of the repeated refrain must be rejected as an unnecessary
doubling. In her case, it is v. 22b which is the doublet drawn from
v. 20 (contrast Ahuis, above).[22] In our view, her approach to
Jeremianic doublets is not nuanced enough, since for her the
presence of a doublet constitutes demonstration of the secondary
character of a text (p. 71).[23] This is only one of the possibilities.
Further, it is necessary to distinguish between passages whose
formulations are identical or correspondent to a high degree and
passages which exhibit similarity but still are formulated in distinct

ways. Otherwise it becomes difficult to discern a special literary phenomenon, 'doublet', from the correspondences one would naturally expect to be exhibited in an author's style, images and ideas.[24] It is this latter category into which our passages fall. Though they share much of the same vocabulary, and the basic ideas are certainly similar enough to evoke comparison, the difference of formulation and the presence of features in one not shared by the other argue for a relationship founded upon the general vocabulary of judgment in Jeremiah (cf. 3.24; 5.12, 17; 14.18; 15.7-9).[25] As with Ahuis, the argument of Eichler does not appear well-founded.

If one were to argue for the editorial character of the verses, it would seem preferable to begin with the rhetorical peculiarities noted on form—i.e. distinct structural block, metrical shift, לכן introducing petition.[26] These at least raise the possibility of seeing an editorial expansion, though this is short of decisive demonstration. Then based on the textual irregularities noted for G relative to the phrase כי כרו שוחה (v. 20), we could appeal to the phenomenon of *Wiederaufnahme* or resumptive repetition—the device for introducing an insertion into the flow of a text by repeating a word, phrase, or extended clause before and after the insertion drawn from the point of interruption[27]—as an explanation for the text variants. In other words, they reflect the disturbance in the location of the v. 20aβ-v. 22b parallel due to the insertion of vv. 21-22a. As Ahuis's diagram illustrates (p. 34), removal of the verses would still leave one with a normal, complete lament. This argument is more attractive but in the last analysis still seems inadequate. A more accurate example of *Wiederaufnahme* would require the location of v. 20aβ at the end of v. 20, not in the middle. There seem to be no reasons for suspecting v. 20b as an insertion. The 'doublet' could be read as a slightly varied refrain. The text variants are capable of simpler explanations (see above, n. 3). Irregularity of metre is not uncommon in Psalms (cf. overall metre in Pss. 35, 69, 109) and the functioning of imprecation as a sub-unit within a lament has already been noted (see previous psalms). In sum, it seems best to view the attempts to discern redactional activity within the confession, besides v. 18, as unsuccessful.

Setting

The editorial introduction to the lament (v. 18) clearly intends us to read the confession against the backdrop of opposition to prophetic mission and Jeremiah's prophetic mission in particular. The problem, however, is whether this prophetic setting can be discerned for the pre-literary lament (vv. 19-23). The recent attempts to provide a positive answer to this problem seem, on the face of it, particularly attractive.[28]

Wimmer's development of an apologetic role in the public proclamation of the prophet represents the more attractive application of this approach to the problem. For him, the emphasis upon imprecation/curse functions, as it were, as a type of 'propaganda technique' which threatens the enemies of the prophet. Presumably, the concern of the 'propaganda' is to warn these enemies from the course of opposition lest they experience the dire consequences of the curse.[29] For Eichler and Ahuis, as with 17.14-18 the setting is viewed as one of the delayed fulfilment of prophetic proclamation.[30] The aim of the confession would then become the vindication of the prophet through fulfilment of the announced judgment. Both approaches have their strengths, and it may be that they could be formulated in a way that is not mutually exclusive. In favour of the former is the use of curse as an oral or written threat in a variety of public and personal settings[31] plus the close correspondences between the content of the imprecations and the content of Jeremianic judgment speech.[32] This latter feature might also explain the lack of an answering oracle similar to 11.21-23, since the imprecation itself carries the judgment expected.[33] Still, we do not have simply a curse but rather an imprecatory psalm; and to my knowledge there are no attested usages of imprecatory lament in the manner proposed. The second approach appears to have discerned correctly the problem of delayed fulfilment, since v. 23b assumes that the judgment (עֵת אַפְּךָ) is still outstanding; and the negative petition (v. 23aβ), which contains a veiled complaint against the meting out of forgiveness instead of judgment, argues aginst the legitimacy of delay and annulment of the judgment proclamation.[34] The most serious obstacle for this latter approach is the question whether the contents of the lament at any point require a prophetic situation in order to be intelligible. In other words, the success of Ahuis's approach may be more a result of the present literary setting of the passage. Analysis of the diction of the lament would appear to favour the latter possibility. Even the mention of intercessory activity in v. 20 cannot be reserved exclusively to a prophetic individual.[35] Apart from its present contextual setting, it is difficult to see how one would receive any warrant to search for a prophetic situation.[36] This evaluation, however, is based upon the normal exegesis of v. 20. Hubmann has recently challenged the older approach and offered a new proposal which, if valid, greatly affects the evaluation of the setting of the passage *vis à vis* a prophet.

Interpretation

The usual understanding of this confession takes as its starting-point the occasion indicated by v. 18. The plot against the prophet is apparently engineered with greater subtlety than the one in 11.18ff. for the concern is to catch the prophet in some inadvertent statement which can provide grounds for the slander, discrediting, and ultimate destruction of the prophet before the nation. In light of the reference to official sources of guidance, there is a general preference for seeing Jeremiah's opponents consisting of these various three groups. The prophet's prayer of complaint labels such activity as heinous ingratitude which violates normal expectations of reward (v. 20aα), since the prophet has laboured in intercession before Yahweh to preserve his enemies from wrath (v. 20b) while they have repaid his praiseworthy actions with an insidious plot. In intense outrage over such treatment, the prophet alters his posture toward his enemies and now imprecates them before Yahweh with an extensive curse that includes not only his immediate antagonists but either the whole nation or at least the dependants of the enemies as well (vv. 21-23).[37]

This view of the passage seems fairly straightforward, which no doubt accounts for the wide consensus it has enjoyed. The only real difficulty the confession has caused—in common, we might add, with imprecatory laments in the psalter—has been the theological offence of such strong imprecation of the prophet's enemies.[38] But recently Hubmann has argued, very convincingly, that on closer inspection the traditional understanding suffers from a number of questionable features.[39] The central difficulty lies in proper identification of the יריבי and the referents of the 3rd pers. pl. pronouns, especially in vv. 21-22a. The use of v. 18 to infer their identity is problematic on two counts.[40] First, as part of the redactional aspect of the chapter its use for interpreting the details of the pre-literary confession is highly questionable. Second, even if one were to allow consideration of it, the wider contextual function of the verse within 18.11-12 clearly suggests that the citation has been put into the mouth of the whole people not just some official sub-group. Within the lament proper, the oblique 3rd pers. pl. references in v. 20aβ and vv. 22b-23 seem clearly to refer to יריבי (v. 19). As the immediate context for vv. 21-22a, this may seem determinative for the further 3rd pers. pl. references requiring a similar identification with יריבי. However, the parallels with Jeremianic judgment speech elsewhere strongly suggest that the judgment depicted by the curse is none other than the general judgment upon the whole nation. Once again problems arise for the traditional approach. On the one hand, viewing the יריבי as a group of the prophet's personal enemies conflicts with the contextual indications in vv. 21-22a that a whole nation is involved; and on the other, explaining the social categories (vv. 21-22a) as the dependants of the יריבי[41] requires the softening of indications that the general judgment is in view. Finally, Hubmann observes that within the book of Jeremiah prophetic intercession is exclusively directed toward the national distress and toward averting Yahweh's wrath from total obliteration of Israel.[42] This requires a different under-standing of the identity of יריבי or a new understanding of the logical development of the verses since the intercessory activity is normally taken in reference to these very antagonists.[43]

Hubmann attempts to resolve these problems inherent in the traditional understanding in the following manner. A distinction is still maintained between the יריבי and the 3rd pers. pl. references in vv. 21-22a. The national allusions and the distinct, structured character of the curse as a logical sub-unit argue for this. Further, the intercessory activity of v. 22b cannot be referred to the יריבי, since it too involves national associations (as noted) and so must be connected with the following. As a result, vv. 20b-22a no longer are to be as closely connected with their surrounding statements as the prophet's reaction to the persecution by his enemies. A new function is discerned for them by first reinterpreting v. 20aα as actually a citation of Jeremiah's opponents (קול יריבי) and no longer as a statement by the prophet. The significance of the question is to be found by interpreting רעה and טובה,[44] in light of usage elsewhere in the book, as the corresponding terms for judgment and salvation.[45] Thus the rhetorical question, which expects a negative answer, opposes any suggestion that any expectation for Yahweh's action toward Israel other than salvation is appropriate. The pitfall laid for the prophet is theological in nature and aims not only at refuting the Jeremianic proclamation of judgment but carries further threat of legal prosecution for false prophecy.[46]

Once Hubmann establishes this approach to v. 20aα, he can proceed to review the overall development of the lament as follows: vv. 20b-22a are fundamentally Jeremiah's response to the question of the antagonists and situation of threat it raises for his prophetic mission. The profession of innocence, analogous to 17.16a, establishes his fidelity to his prophetic mission (esp. intercessory activity) and that his expectation of judgment has its ground in Yahweh and not personal desires. Further, it points out the contradictory situation resulting from his intercesory activity since by doing so he has played into the hands of his opponents. For if he is a true prophet, will not his intercession on behalf of the nation be effective, thus confirming the expectation indicated in the citation (v.20aα)?[47] The petition of vv. 21-22a now becomes a request for vindication of the prophet's judgment proclamation before his enemies through realization of the judgment upon the nation. The petition is not directed, in the first place, toward the punishment of his opponents.[48] Only in v. 23 do they receive specific attention, since the prophet now requests that in the time of the general judgment they too should not be excluded. But just as they attempted to make the question of divine recompense the downfall of Jeremiah, so they are to receive their appropriate recompense—their own destruction by the very רעה which they denied as a legitimate action of Yahweh.[49]

Hubmann's new proposal is very attractive in many respects. The קול יריבי creates a strong expectation for a citation.[50] His approach offers a rationale for the sectioning of the lament and explains why the petition exists in doubled form (vv. 21-22; v. 23). The approach also makes significant strides in reducing the theological offence of the imprecation and relates it more closely to the requirements of opposition to prophetic mission. However, there are two features of his explanation which seem unsatisfactory.

The first problem relates to the idea of two separate referents for the 3rd pers. pl. pronouns. The structural integrity of the lament observed previously on form plus Hubmann's evidence for the association of vv. 20b-22a with national concerns seem to argue more strongly for a consistent identification of יריבי as the whole nation.[51] While admittedly the imprecation of vv. 21-22a forms its own sub-section, the profession of innocence falls outside it and it cannot be separated too easily from the preceding. It is also arguable that the 3rd pers. pl. prounouns in הגרם (v. 21) and עליהם (v. 22a) link back precisely to the ירִיבִי (v. 19). In short, it seems most natural to see a consistent reference all the way through and to see their identity as the whole nation.[52] Once this is said though, a great deal of Hubmann's impetus toward viewing v. 20aα as a citation drops away. The remaining factor in its favour is קול ירִיבִי, and one may well prefer the normal understanding as speech of the prophet.

A second, slightly less troublesome feature relates to the precise role of the profession of innocence on Hubmann's view of v. 20aα. The traditional understanding provides a smooth development of the thought since the profession provides content to the preceding statments. His beneficial intercessory activity for them is returned by evil, seditious schemes toward him. If v. 20aα is a citation, then some slightly different understanding for v. 20b must be found. But להשיב את חמתך seems to tie one to the intercessory idea.[53] In light of the previous criticism, Hubmann's procedure of connecting the profession more with the following than the preceding will not work. Perhaps it is of some help to observe the relationship and overlap between prophetic intercession and consultation of a prophet for an oracle.[54] The citation might be best understood as arising from a request for an oracle or at least as a response to the previous intercessory activity of the prophet. Thus it could be viewed as the antagonized response to frustrated expectations about the efficacy of true prophetic intercession (cf. Jer. 27.18) and prospects of receiving a hopeful oracle.[55] This would provide a more integrated way of viewing the role of the innocence profession and continue to clarify the nature of the defence and motivation it provides relative to the complaint and petition along the lines of Hubmann's approach noted above.

In sum, while we prefer a consistent interpretation of the identity of ירִיבִי throughout, Hubmann's proposal about v. 20aα is attractive and seems to provide a better understanding of the passage than the traditional view. This approach touches once again on issues related to setting. By and large the situation remains the same. Internally the lament provides little unambiguous warrant for discerning a specifically prophetic situation. However, on this alternative approach to v. 20 there is at least a slightly better indication of issues relevant to prophetic mission. This in turn certainly lends more weight to the inner-Jeremianic contacts with judgment imagery. One might even be more inclined to see the confession as a form of oral defence and warning within the public mission of the prophet. Nevertheless, distinctively prophetic characteristics are not as prevalent as those encountered in previous confessions. There are no potential allusions to the call narrative in 18.19-23 as were detected in other confessions. Yet our notes analysing the diction of the lament illustrate once again that curious characteristic of the confessions: their vacillation between continuity and discontinuity both with Psalm lament and Jeremianic poetry.[56]

Aim

This confession stands in a close relationship to 17.14-18. It too breaks the prophetic liturgy pattern. Once again the nation is portrayed as antagonistic to Jeremiah's prophetic mission. Similarly the general situation for the conflict appears to be delay in fulfilment of the prophetic word—at least the opposition occurs within the gap between proclamation and fulfilment. Yet the immediate crisis does not seem so directly occasioned by delay *per se* but rather is predicated more on the rejection of the message of judgment itself and the concomitant concern to do away with the messenger. The central concern of the petition dominated by imprecation is once again the deliverance of the messenger through vindication of the message. The negative petition of v. 23aβ introduces the only hint of threat *vis à vis* prophet and Yahweh, since forgiveness in this case would have a distinct purpose in the suspension of the judgment proclaimed, thus ostensibly invalidating the prophet's expectation of judgment over against the nation's false hope of salvation. Yet it is difficult to detect a veiled accusation against Yahweh (cf. 17.14-18) that somehow the fault lies with him for the present crisis in the prophetic mission. The picture of solidarity or confidence approaches much more that found in the first confession, 11.18-23. Finally, it is worth noting that the redactional incipit, v. 18, is fully compatible with the internal concern of the lament.

7. Jeremiah 20.7-13[1]

7	פתיתני יהוה ואפת	You forced me, Yahweh, and I was compelled!
	חזקתני ותוכל	You o'er-powered me and prevailed!
	הייתי לשחוק כל היום	I have become a continual laughing stock,
	כלה לעג לי	everyone mocks me.
8	כי מדי אדבר אזעק	As often as I must speak, I cry out:
	חמס ושד אקרא	'violence, destruction', I call.[2]
	כי היה דבר יהוה לי	For Yahweh's word has become to me,
	לחרפה ולקלס כל היום	cause for reproach and scorn, continually.
9	ואמרתי לא אזכרנו	I had said: 'I will not mention it'.
	ולא אדבר עוד בשמו	I will no longer speak in his name.
	והיה בלבי כאש בערת	But it became within me[3] as a fire, burning,
	עצר בעצמתי	imprisoned within my bones.
	ונלאיתי כלכל	I have become weary with restraining it,
	ולא אוכל	and cannot prevail.
10	כי שמעתי דבת רבים	For I have heard the whisperings of many:
	מגור מסביב	'terror on every side'
	הגידו ונגידנו	'Let us inform against him';
	כל אנוש שלומי	All my compatriots
	שמרי צלעי	watch for my stumbling:
	אולי יפתה ונוכלה לו	'Perhaps he will be induced that we may prevail over him;
	ונקחה נקמתנו ממנו	and take our vengeance upon him.
11	ויהוה אותי כגבור עריץ	But Yahweh is with me as a dread warrior,
	על כן רדפי יכשלו ולא יכלו	therefore my pursuers will stumble and not prevail!
	בשו מאד כי לא השכילו	They will be utterly shamed, —Yea, they will not succeed,

	כלמת עולם לא תשכח	—with a perpetual, unforgettable shame.
12	ויהוה בחן צדיק	O Yahweh,[4] who tests the righteous,[5]
	ראה כליות ולב	who sees inmost being and heart,
	אראה נקמתך מהם	Let me see your vengeance upon them,
	כי אליך גליתי את ריבי	for to you I have revealed my case.
13	שירו ליהוה	Sing to Yahweh!
	הללו את יהוה	Praise to Yahweh!
	כי הציל את נפש אביון	For he has rescued the life of a poor-man,
	מיד מרעים	from the power of evil-doers.

Form

The classification of this confession as a lament or at least as related to lament has been generally accepted by most scholars since the work of Baumgartner. Differences among scholars have existed more at the level of labelling the various elements of the lament and discerning its actual extent. This problem of delimiting the confessional unit(s) has especially related to vv. 7-13 and vv. 14-18 with the dramatic shift of tone represented by the former to the latter, and within vv. 7-13 toward a similar shift in tone between vv. 7-9 and vv. 10-13.[6] The various approaches to form have also been affected by views regarding redactional interference with the original confessional material which naturally complicates the accurate analysis of the structure and genre relationships of the text. To facilitate the discussion of these interlocking problems, we begin by attempting a formal analysis of the confessional unit as a whole and then proceeding to questions of redaction.

Typical Form:[7] The recent study of Clines and Gunn provides, in our view, a significant improvement over previous approaches which sought to subdivide vv. 7-13 into a series of separate units, or which sought to treat all of vv. 7-18 as one unit.[8] They distinguish two originally independent units (vv. 7-13; 14-18) and are able to analyse vv. 7-13 beautifully in line with the typicalities of individual lament.[9]

v. 7aα	—address
vv. 7-10	—lament
v. 11aα	—confession of trust
vv. 11aβ—11bβ	—certainty of being heard
v. 12a	—confession of trust
v. 12bα	—petition
v. 12bβ	—confession of trust
v. 13	—praise

This analysis also draws attention to a shift in tone from complaint (vv. 7-10) to confidence and praise (vv. 11-13). Such shifts of tone within lament are characteristic motifs[10] and thus provide no basis, on formal grounds, for questioning the unity and originality of these verses.

Particular Form: This initial isolation of vv. 7-13 as a unit on the basis of formal lament typicalities finds further corroboration from observation of the integrating and unifying patterns at verbal, thematic and logical levels of the lament:

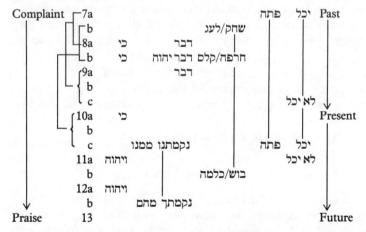

As the schema is concerned to illustrate, the lament is intricately structured. The central focus of the lament upon 'power' and 'overcoming'[11] is developed through a series of verbal repetitions with פתה and יכל.[12] The prophet protests at this domination by Yahweh (v. 7) against whom he cannot prevail (v. 9). The prophet's enemies too expect the 'delusion/persuasion' of the prophet so they may prevail over him (v. 10). That these verbal links effect a certain parallelism between Yahweh and the enemies as oppressive forces over against the prophet is not to be missed.[13] This parallelism is also sustained by the manner in which the complaint section (vv. 7-10) is developed, for the problems of the prophet—suffering under Yahweh's word and under persecution of his enemies—are presented in an alternating, juxtaposed fashion (vv. 7a, 8a, 9; and vv. 7b, 8b, 10 respectively).[14] Note too that the positive-negative alternation with יכל partly underlines the parallelism.[15] What Yahweh is said to accomplish positively *vis à vis* the prophet is also the positive intention of the enemy (פתה, יכל). On the other hand, the alternation concludes by breaking the parallelism, for while Yahweh succeeds with the prophet, they will not (לא יכלו v. 11). The thematic repetition of words for shame/insult (vv. 7, 8, 11) further underlines this contrast since the enemies of the prophet must suffer what they have made him suffer, including the vengeance (נקמה vv. 10, 12) which they sought. This shift in parallelism between Yahweh and the persecutors *vis à vis* the prophet corresponds to two additional developments which bring the whole lament to its climax—i.e. the progression from complaint to praise, and the temporal progression[16] of past, present, and future. In light of all these features, there appears to be an extremely strong case for taking vv. 7-13 as one integrated and original unit. These features must be kept particularly in mind when we examine the various redactional models that have been proposed. A major question that these various proposals will have to face is whether any aspect of the passage can be viewed as secondary without seriously damaging the structure of the lament as the preceding analysis has attempted to present.

Redaction

In the discussion of the integrity of vv. 7-13 as a unit, most attention has been focused on the last two verses[17] with sporadic questioning of vv. 10 and 11[18] also raised as possibilities. This may be somewhat surprising in light of the previous formal analysis and one may well wonder what possible grounds one could have. However, a quick glance back at the typical form of the passage will show that the location of petition (v. 12) following certainty of hearing (v. 11) is somewhat unusual.[19] And, in terms of particular form, it is worth noting that v. 13 exhibits no verbal or tonal/assonantal links with the preceding.[20] Formal considerations[21] aside, it has been the doublet of

v. 12 with 11.20 and the hymnic-psalm character of v. 13 which have been decisive criteria for most who evaluated one or both of the verses as secondary.[22] But before evaluating these arguments for vv. 12-13—especially as recently argued by Hubmann—we turn to consider the view of Eichler and Ahuis as the most recent and emphatic challengers of vv. 10-11 as a whole block.

Both of these scholars have argued that vv. 10-13 represent a secondary expansion by the Dtr. redactor, with vv. 7-9 remaining as the original kernel. While the main thrust of each of the arguments differs somewhat from the other, at least with regard to vv. 12-13 the approach of each is parallel to the other and in line with most approaches. Since we will focus more particularly on the problems of vv. 12-13 below, our concern here will be with their arguments with reference to vv. 10-11. Eichler argues that structurally vv. 10-13 are modelled upon the previous confession 11.18-20; 12.6.[23] And, since that confession is a total Dtr. composition, so must this one be. However, it is neither clear that the material of 11.18; 12.6 can be ascribed to Dtr. nor that structurally they represent lament and corresponding divine response.[24] This treatment ignores the present redactional arrangement of 11.21-23 as a response to 11.18-20 and 12.6 as an integral part of 12.1-5. Even granting the previous points, for the sake of argument, it is still not clear that both are formed on the same pattern though certain elements common to lament genre are shared.[25] The present-past-future temporal sequence of the former contrasts with a present-future sequence in 20.10-13. 11.18-20 opens with v. 18 in a manner more akin to thanksgiving genre while 20.10 represents characteristic complaint motifs.[26] Finally, the attempt to label 11.18 as a confession of certainty parallel to 20.11 overlooks the formal associations and function of the former with the thanksgiving motif of report about the divine action on behalf of the supplicant;[27] and it is questionable whether the motif of praise (20.13) can truly be compared to 12.6 as a divine response.[28] The former may presuppose an answer and may obviate the need for explicit reporting of an answer, but it is not the same thing.

Ahuis, on the other hand, builds his judgment on the assertion that vv. 10-13 are a mixture of prose (vv. 10-11) and poetry (vv. 12-13). This constitutes for him clear signs of Dtr. redactional activity to which the rest of his arguments can be added. Unfortunately, he makes no attempt to justify this claim about the prose character of vv. 10-11.[29] The majority of commentators have treated them as

poetry,[30] though irregularity of metre has been noted with some
resorting to textual emendation in order to produce greater balance.[31]
But it is questionable whether the irregularity is of such a nature as
to force one to re-evaluate the lines as prose. Only מגור מסביב
produces a longer line in v. 10 (3 + 4). The others are easily laid out
in 3 + 2, 3 + 3 bi-cola. The only metrical oddity in v. 11 appears to be
its increase to balanced bi-cola of 4 + 4, 4 + 4 metre. In short, Ahuis's
assertion does not seem to be required.[32] Further, his observations on
the details of the verses do not seem to be decisive factors. On v. 10
he notes the numerous verbal links with the preceding and following
context and concludes that the verse exhibits a *Verklammerungs-
funktion*.[33] But just these factors could argue for the opposite
conclusion that v. 10 is firmly anchored in its present setting.[34]
Similarly his observations on v. 11 are meant to show its verbal
echoes (יכל) not only with the preceding but also with vocabulary of
other confessions (cf. עריצים 15.21; רדפי—15.15; בוש—17.18) or other
texts in Jeremiah (cf. גבור—32.18; 20.11bβ—23.40b).[35] Thus, the
verse is to be seen as a newly constructed editorial confession of
certainty. While such considerations helpfully raise the question of
the relationship and connections with preceding confessions, a
possible challenge to the originality of v. 11 results only if such
contacts have to do with material equally demonstrable as secondary.[36]
But only 15.21 represents the strongest case here in light of our
previous analysis. On the other hand, all these connections could
provide an indication of the originality of the verses in light of their
verbal compatibility with the confessional material. The vocabulary
itself cannot be labelled as distinctly Dtr. or Jeremianic prose;[37] and
since the doublet in 23.40 is a prose text, one would have to be open
to the priority of the poetic example functioning as part of the
substrata upon which the prose tradition has drawn.[38] In sum,
neither Ahuis's nor Eichler's evidence appears sufficient to offset the
formal characteristics observed previously for vv. 10-11 which
illustrate their integral connection within the confession.

Evaluating the status of vv. 12-13 is more difficult for the evidence
seems much more finely balanced. Serious formal reasons for
questioning originality are not present. Even the order of petition
following certainty of hearing is not all that significant given the
great diversity of arrangement within laments.[39] Objection to v. 13
because of shift in mood or because of its hymnic character fails to
consider seriously the many connections of this passage with cultic

lament motifs or the similar occurrence of just such features there.[40] Similarly, the mere fact of the doublet, v. 12, with 11.20 is not an automatic demonstration of its secondary character. It could be the other way round, and a decision is hard to reach since both contexts are fully appropriate locations for the verse.[41] An explanation of the doublet as free re-utilization of formulaic expressions is attractive but most probable only for v. 12a, for v. 12b/11.20b have no parallels outside each other.[42] Even for v. 12a, differences from 11.20a are to be noticed, which, while slight, may reflect a more deliberately motivated alteration in light of the context.[43] One is still left with the problem of which use is primary and which secondary and thus which usage represents the conscious adaptation to context.

This apparent stalemate in evaluation of probabilities may have found some resolution from the new considerations offered recently by Hubmann. He has attempted to show that vv. 12-13 are not as firmly anchored in the context by attempting to lend more precision to the formal classification of the passage. For him, the formal affinities of the passage lie more toward the side of thanksgiving than lament.[44] The past narrative mode of vv. 7-9 parallels the narrative of past distress;[45] contrary to expectation, there is no petition or cry of 'how long!' in relation to the prophet's oppression under the word, if in fact vv. 7-9 are intended as complaint against this.[46] Contrary to previous treatment of the persecution theme, there are no expostulations about prophetic innocence and fidelity to the mission, nor pleas for vindication through fulfilment of the proclamation, only confident assertion of personal vindication and discomfiture of opponents.[47] Thus the basic reclassification of the passage as close to thanksgiving permits Hubmann to view vv. 7-11 as a complete unit in which vv. 12-13 play no essential role.[48] In other words, if vv. 7-11 do not require a classification as lament, then one of the key reasons for demanding the preservation of v. 12 (petition) falls away[49] and thus v. 13 which is dependent upon it.[50] As a redactional expansion, vv. 12-13 intensify the character of the preceding which gives a résumé of the prophet's struggle now resolved in acceptance of the prophetic word and mission and confidence in vindication by interpreting the process as trial/test of the Righteous (בחן צדיק).[51]

Hubmann's observations are extremely useful for drawing attention to some of the peculiar features of this passage. However, certain questionable features in his analysis must be noted which render his conclusion unconvincing. The narrative mode of vv. 7-9 is not

sufficient in itself to establish the thanksgiving-like character, for, as
Gunkel–Begrich observed, within laments the form of the complaint
section can occur both as *Schilderung* in the imperfect and as
Erzählung in the perfect. The distinguishing mark of the latter from
the portrayal section of thanksgiving is that the perspective of
distress never restricts itself to the past but reaches into the
present.[52] The past-present temporal progression for our verses
seems to be commensurate with this observation.[53] Further, to my
knowledge, a thanksgiving psalm normally does not open in direct
address to Yahweh. When it does, the tone is one of praise and
describes the divine saving actions (cf. Pss. 30; 138). In our passage
the direct address to Yahweh carries a description of the divine
actions which have been anything but beneficial, for, as the
alternating structure and common imagery make clear, the prophet
suffers under two enemies—Yahweh and the human opponents. In
fact, it is the prior action of the former which provides the ultimate
cause for the latter's activity. It is difficult to see how one can
eliminate the tone of complaint from these verses. A more problematical feature for Hubmann's view is the lack of praise and
celebration for deliverance. As stridently confident as v. 11 is, still it
is in the mode of expectation; the deliverance itself is outstanding.[54]
Expressions of trust and certainty of hearing motifs are to be found
in thanksgiving but they presuppose past deliverance and take on
more of an instructional testimonial function (cf. Pss. 32.6-9; 34.9ff.;
41; 92.12ff.; 138.7). Though the progression from complaint to praise
takes some of the sting out of the complaint proper and shifts the
genre affinities of the whole confession to what one might call a
borderline area between lament and praise,[55] these features are not
sufficient to nullify its overall lament character (cf. again Ps. 22).
Even if Hubmann's reclassification is correct, there is still the
problem of the thematic and verbal links[56] of v. 12 with the
preceding; and though possible it is difficult to see how this is merely
a matter of a superficial catchword link. But this returns us to an
apparent situation of stalemate in the evaluation of v. 12. If
preference is still to be given to the doublet feature, the tentative
character of such a decision requires recognition. The originality of
v. 12 could not be ruled out.[57]

Setting

As we have had occasion to observe in discussion of previous confessions, the question of discerning the original setting for these texts is particulaly vexed both by the lack of internal specification and by the lack of sufficient external information. In the absence of these we must accept the speculative character of the solutions that one is forced to engage in with regard to the problem. This state of affairs seems no less promising for consideration of the present passage. The strong internal warrant that we have to do with a prophetic situation seems incontestable,[58] but attempts to specify this typical occasion are not completely satisfying.

The attempt of Clines and Gunn to elucidate an apologetic function in the face of opposition to prophetic mission seems a very plausible suggestion.[59] It is not difficult to imagine the defence function of the confession, moving as it does from complaint to praise, underlining the unavoidable compulsion to prophetic mission, the irresistible superiority of the divine word against human opposition, and the confident anticipation of the vindication of the prophet against his antagonists. This pattern certainly obviates the potential weakness of the lack of a divine response noted for this approach relative to 17.14-18 and 18.19-23. Nevertheless, there is the major weakness of the complete absence of any such parallel usage of lament outside the Jeremianic material.

Similarly, as a special prophetic lament, it is questionable whether Jer. 20.7-9 really reflect the imagery and process of commissioning messenger, rejection of messenger, report as explicitly as Ahuis argues.[60] No doubt vv. 7-9[61] reflect upon the prophetic call and the prophet's struggle against it in face of opposition and rejection, but the language of compulsion and overpowering seems to portray the prophetic mission in different imagery from that of the messenger. More serious for Ahuis's view is that it is argued only for vv. 7-9, but we have already found his view of vv. 10-11 unconvincing. The problem of vv. 12-13 aside, the integral unit of vv. 7-11 with its progression even there from complaint to confidence[62] poses severe difficulty for formal comparison with a *Botenvorgang* (cf. Exod. 5.22-23).[63] In light of these difficulties, Ahuis's approach must be judged unsatisfactory in the last analysis. In sum, attempts to postulate a specific setting within the prophetic mission seem fully warranted on internal considerations; and though the approach of Clines and

Gunn seems the most attractive of proposals to date, finally one is left with a situation of indeterminacy in regard to the problem owing to drawbacks afflicting even the most plausible of suggestions.[64]

Interpretation

Interpretive analysis of the details of the passage has focused primarily upon the semantic import of the thought and imagery of the text. Has the borrowing of Psalm idiom produced such a stereotyped and ambiguous picture that the distinctively 'prophetic' characteristics are a matter of the present literary setting? Are the images of compulsion and overpowering to be read in terms of sexual, seduction imagery? In light of this, how is the prophetic mission represented? What precisely is the nature of the opponents' conspiracy against the prophet?

The formal relationship of the confession with cultic lament plus the many contacts of idiom and imagery raise, legitimately, the question of ambiguity *vis à vis* the prophetic character of the passage.[65] It is just such features which lend plausibility to the approach of scholars who view the confessions as total editorial compositions.[66] The success of their approach depends, though, upon the existence of consistent ambiguity in the diction of the passage. But as many have pointed out, such expressions as דבר יהוה[67] and אדבר בשמו[68] seem incontrovertible indications that the plaintiff of the lament is a prophet.[69] It seems best to view the genius of the confession in its ability to employ the typicalities of lament genre as a backdrop against which to portray the particular concerns of prophet mission.

The startling portrayal of the prophet as the victim of a divine enemy is usually understood in terms of sexual seduction (פתה) and assault (חזק) with the prophet's anguished cry (חמס ושד) as effectively equivalent to a girl's cry of 'rape!'[70] In light of usage, the presence of such overtones is possible.[71] But in light of explicit usage of פתה elsewhere in relation to prophets, it is not likely that such sexual connotations exert a dominant influence in the present passage.[72] As Clines and Gunn have recently argued,[73] the idea of 'persuasion' is central for the root with the connotation of 'deceit' more a factor of the context.[74] The emphasis in the present passage upon the prophet's inescapable domination by Yahweh to be a speaker of the word suggests that a connotation of deception is also not appropriate for פתה here. A neutral translation such as 'persuade'[75] catches the basic idea but leaves unrepresented the tone of reproach and criticism with which the context presents this act. Perhaps a loose translation such as 'you pressured me and I was compelled' would bring out more forcibly the idea of persuasion/manipulation of the prophet's will to take up the prophetic function. This subjugation to the prophetic task is clearly associated with the social victimization of the innocent[76] in the cry of חמס ושד.[77] It seems best to view this cry for assistance and of protest as ironically addressed to Yahweh, because of the alternating parallelism of the passage[78] (see previously in Form). These verses (7-9) present us with a conflict in prophetic mission; but the portrayal of this conflict with the imagery of overwhelming compulsion, forcible persuasion, and victimization of the innocent, raises questions about the degree of influence the model of prophet as 'messenger' has had upon the present confession. If such a picture is present at all, it appears preferable to view it as a remote influence at best. Ahuis's attempt does not seem to account adequately for the nature of the imagery actually employed.[79]

The victimization of the prophet also includes personal suffering from human opponents who have responded with bitter opposition to his proclamation. As the structural and verbal parallels indicate, this latter victimization is bound up with his victimization by the divine word. It is a constituent part of it. In vv. 7b, 8b this rejection and this opposition take the form of personal vilification. However, the connection of this with the following development in v. 19 is somewhat problematical. Normally, it is understood as a plot to encourage Jeremiah's friends (אנוש שלומי) to play the informant (נגד) so that by some personal mis-step (צלע) the delusion (פתה) of the prophet would become clear; and thus an opportunity for his enemies to have their vengeance would be provided (v. 10bβ).[80] Recently, Hubmann has questioned this interpretation based upon its inappropriateness to the context. In his view, it does not seem logical that the enemies required some pretext before they could denounce Jeremiah since they had apparently already found sufficient grounds for personal vilification in the prophetic word itself (vv. 7-9).[81] In addition, no special nuance for נגד other than 'announce, report' is to be observed and the co-ordinated imperative-cohortative sequence is to be taken, similar to באו ונבאו (Jer. 35.11) with the initial voluntive understood adverbially thus: 'Auf, wir wollen es verkünden'.[82] As a result, the plot consists now of a deceptive ruse of announcing judgment in agreement with Jeremiah's proclamation so that an opportunity for mastery over him as false allies might present itself.[83]

Though Hubmann's new proposal helpfully brings to attention an apparently rough edge in an aspect of the development of the passage (i.e. on the normal view of v. 10), it is not clear that his own approach significantly resolves the problem. A contextual shift from open hostility to a treacherous alliance seems equally lacking in internal motivation and plausibility. If the prophet and his word are merely objects for derision and scorn, why the need for so elaborate and subtle a plot? Also an attempt to remedy the problem of connection between vv. 7b, 8b, 10 by postulating two separate groups of opponents appears to run foul of the parallelism between כל לעג// כל אנוש שלומי//רבת רבים.[84] Perhaps the difficulty can be reduced by recourse to the temporal progression (past into present and future) of the passage as depicting various stages,[85] realized or expected, between the prophet and his opponents rather than searching for a suitable interpretation of the plot (v. 10) which exhibits some inherently logical development in the portrayal of hostility. If this is right, then one may well view either the traditional understanding of v. 10 or Hubmann's as permissible. In this regard, many of Hubmann's observations about the details do not successfully exclude the traditional understanding; and one is left with a bit of a stalemate in evaluating probabilities. However one understands the syntax of הגידו ונגידו,[86] the verb can mean either 'announce, proclaim'[87] or 'inform'.[88] Hubmann's understanding of פתה in v. 10b as a result of the direct action of the enemy rather than some careless mis-step of the prophet is attractive. The parallelism between Yahweh and the human opponents[89] favours this as well as the parallelism of v. 10aβ (מגור מסביב הגידו ונגידו) with v. 10b.[90] The supposition of the latter seems based in some way on the former. Even in light of our previous semantic discussion on פתה, his exegesis is a workable explanation of this relationship even though one translated the verb as 'be persuaded' rather than 'be deceived'. On the other hand, a more technical nuance to נגד and אנוש שלומי may be present which would still render viable the normal understanding of the plot. It is possible that both expressions should be given a distinctly political nuance drawn from the sphere of treaty-covenant bonds. Illustrating the former from Deut. 13.10 (LXX הגר תגירנו)[91] which provides for the formal denunciation of anyone who incites treason/sedition to the treaty/covenant[92] and the latter from Obad. 7 (אנשי בריתך//אנשי שלמך) which speaks of political allies,[93] the plot of v. 10 could be understood as the attempt by Jeremiah's compatriots to induce him (פתה) to speak or act seditiously, thus providing legal grounds for the execution of vengeance (נקמה). Though both approaches have their weaknesses, we prefer the normal understanding of the plot in light of the previous considerations.

Aim

In keeping with the previous two confessions, the dialogue pattern of petition plus divine response is absent from 20.7-13. While an explanation of this lack of a divine response in these preceding confessions appears unclear on internal grounds, the situation for the present text appears more hopeful. The temporal progression plus the shift from complaint to praise bring the whole confession to a climax. Any explanation of the focus of the passage which places the emphasis upon a preceding sub-section misconstrues the emphasis of this complaint.[94] The confident petition for deliverance from persecutors is buttressed by the climactic, anticipatory invocation to praise. This contrasts with the preceding confessions where increasingly intense opposition is met by passionate cries for vindication which persistently increase in severity and professions of innocence which protest prophetic fidelity and carry veiled complaints that the true problem lies in the failure of God's righteousness.[95] The irony of this confident appeal in 20.7-13 is that it is grounded in the very problem from which the persecution has taken its occasion.[96] For it has been the whole way of Yahweh with Jeremiah, as a way of violent (חמס ושד) domination (יכל) and compulsion (פתה), forcing him to be the bearer of the word (דבר יהוה), which has spawned the attempt of the opponents to carry out a similar attempt at violent oppression and mastery toward the prophet. And yet, it is precisely the prophet's inability (לא אוכל) to withstand Yahweh, the dread warrior (גבור עריץ)[97] whose word has proved to be an irrepressible power, which guarantees that the bid for victory against the bearer of this word will fail (לא יכלו).[98] This rehearsal[99] of Yahweh's treatment of the prophet and the prophet's unsuccessful struggle against and suffering under the prophetic task is now resolved by the interpretation of this 'way' as the test and trial (בחן) of the righteous (צדיק) which will surely result in his deliverance.[100] The lack of an answering oracle becomes comprehensible in view of the internal characteristics of this passage.

14	ארור היום	Curse the day,
	אשר ילדתי בו	on which I was born.
	יום אשר ילדתני אמי	The day, my mother bore me,
	אל יהי ברוך	let it not be blessed.
15	ארור האיש	Curse the man,
	אשר בשר את אבי לאמר	who announced to my father, saying:
	ילד לך בן זכר	'Born to you—a male child!'
	שמח שמחהו	He made him very glad.
16	והיה האיש ההוא כערים	May that man be as the cities
	אשר הפך יהוה ולא נחם	which Yahweh overthrew without mercy.
	ושמע זעקה בבקר	May he hear a cry at morning,
	ותרועה בעת צהרים	an alarm at midday!
17	אשר לא מותתני מרחם	Because he did not slay me in the womb[1],
	ותהי לי אמי קברי	that my mother would be my grave,
	ורחמה הרת עולם	her womb, perpetually pregnant.
18	למה זה מרחם יצאתי	Why now, did I come forth from the womb,
	לראות עמל ויגון	to see trouble and sorrow,
	ויכלו בבשת ימי	and waste my days in shame?

Form

We observed previously that the present passage comprised a unit formally distinct from that of the preceding (vv. 7-13). Already in the study of Baumgartner the formal distinction of the unit from cultic lament genre was recognized. He proposed a classification of 'self-curse'.[2] This basic classification has been borne out in subsequent research with the closest parallel to be found in Job 3.[3]

Typical Form: The passage can readily be analysed in terms of the elements typical for the curse.[4]

vv. 14-15   —doubled curse formula
v. 16   —curse-developments
vv. 17-18   —curse-substantiations

Crucial markers of the genre curse are the basic single curse formularies ארור האיש/ארור היום, each developed by relative clauses (אשר) which characterize in more detail the nature of the day and man in view. In the context, these descriptions probably carry some overtones as further justifications or grounds for the curse just uttered.[5] The two bi-cola of v. 16 develop the preceding curses[6] by specifying the intention of the curse more concretely.[7] The remaining verses provide reasons/motivations for the curse. Verse 17 articulates this with a causal relative clause (*GKC* §158b) and provides the presupposition for the second development of the motif in v. 18 with its 'why-question'.[8] While Baumgartner found in this verse the only points of contact with lament psalms, some modification appears necessary for the affinities of this particular למה-question.[9] The למה-question is certainly attested in Psalm laments but is usually directed expressly to Yahweh in accusation for his failure to act, or absence, or allowing the psalmist to suffer, but never uttered as a lament over self and existence.[10] C. Westermann and W. Schottroff find closer parallels outside the psalter (Gen. 25.22; 27.46; Tob. 3.15; 1 Macc. 2.7, 13; *4 Ezr.* 5.35).[11] At least the unusual character of the content of the verse *vis à vis* normal cultic lament should be observed.[12]

Particular Form: While it is the typical pattern which seems to dominate the present curse, further integration and complementation of it can be observed by the repetition of key words and the development of ideas:

The whole unit is framed nicely by repetition of the key idea of the calamitous day of birth, sustained throughout by the repetition of ילד and רחם. Of further interest is the parallel way in which the two curse formularies develop their ideas. Each consists of two bi-cola with the thought articulated in chiastic fashion. In v. 14 the basic synonymity of the 1st and 4th cola and the 2nd and 3rd producing an ABBA pattern seems fairly straightforward.[13] In v. 15 the chiasm functions more synthetically with the 1st and 4th cola providing the fact and consequence of the birth annunciation, and the 2nd and 3rd related to the content of the annunciation (ABBA').[14] Finally, this self-curse or curse on the day of one's birth, which is clearly the main thrust of the passage, has the odd feature of a detailed focus upon the messenger of birth. As the MT now stands, the central core of the curse (vv. 15-17) is taken up with this subject (האיש אשר בשר). The question must be raised of the relationship of this imagery and thought to the framework of the curse and lament upon the day (היום/ ימי) about which one might have expected to receive further explicit comment. Ever since the objections of Duhm,[15] it has been customary for scholars to emend conjecturally v. 16aα to read either היום for האיש, or simply והיה omitting האיש alone, or both האיש ההוא as an incorrect explanatory gloss.[16] The curse-developments of v. 16 now refer directly back to v. 14; and the causal clause (v. 17), which seems to require a personal subject—i.e. האיש, can be taken as an impersonal predicate obviating a further need for retaining the איש reading.[17] The question of whether such emendation truly represents a superior reading can best be discussed along with questions about the redactional development of the passage since this feature of the curse raises in a significant manner the question of the integrity of a text which at first glance seemed so incontestable.

Redaction

To my knowledge, it has been only with the recent study of Ahuis that anyone has attempted to discern major redactional activity within the unit. For him, the whole of v. 16a[18] is to be seen as a Dtr. expansion.[19] Consonant with his method previously discussed with the other confessional material, he argues for its redactional character based upon its prose form and supposed contacts with Dtr. diction.[20] Particularly in his favour are the near parallel with Deut. 29.22 (אשר הפך יהוה באפו ובחמתו),[21] the corroborating considerations of the supposed logical disturbance of האיש ההוא noted above, and the increased length of the line.[22] Further, removal of the bi-cola is conceivable without serious damage to the unit. However, Ahuis's

arguments do not appear to be of equal weight. The classification of
v. 16a as prose is highly questionable for again the analysis appears
mistakenly to equate irregularity of metre with indication of prose
character.[23] This does not follow of necessity.[24] The vocabulary in
general does not exhibit characteristics distinctive of Jeremianic or
Dtr. prose as Ahuis attempts to show.[25] However, the partial parallel
with Deut. 29.22 constitutes the best candidate he has adduced in his
study as a whole for classification as Dtr. Of texts which treat the
Sodom-Gomorrah theme in the OT, this one is closest in wording. It
may be that here his approach cannot be ruled out. On the other
hand, when one considers how widespread the Sodom-Gomorrah
image is—especially in the prophets[26]—with some of the key
vocabulary shared, plus the character of Deuteronomy 29 as part of
the blessing and curse section of the book and the broad similarities
of the latter with Ancient Near Eastern curse motifs,[27] then one may
well speak of Deut. as composed of numerous traditional (i.e. pre-
existent) formulations and motifs. It is probably more accurate to
view Jer. 20.16a as reflecting a 'traditional malediction'[28] rather than
a distinctively Dtr. sentiment.

But this leads us to re-evaluate the usual emendation of האיש ההוא.
The view of v. 16a as an editorial expansion could have offered an
explanation for the supposed illogic of the statement in context and
obviated the need for the emendation. The chief difficulty of MT
appears to lie in discerning an adequate rationale for such an
emphasis upon the messenger of the birth when the expectation
raised initially by the curse is the focus upon the day of birth itself.[29]
Perhaps some help can be had by considering more carefully those
features which lend the curse its poetic force. It seems proper to view
the emotional genius of the curse in its utilization and reversal of
normal expectations associated with the birth of a child, especially a
male—i.e. an occasion normally of great joy, a sign of blessing.[30] The
curse radically challenges the normal evaluation working back from
the quality of life subsequently experienced (v. 18 בשת, יגון, עמל).[31]
Our text executes this effect by depicting the key participants of the
event in relation to one another (mother, father, bearer of joyous
news) as perpetrators, as it were, of a great misdeed. The isolation
and extended development of the joyous messenger component allow
the poet to underscore the very theme of cause for joy/blessing-
reversed/overturned which lies at the heart of the poetic dynamic of
the curse. In other words, it seems probable that the apparently 'odd'

emphasis upon the 'messenger' rather than explicitly the 'day' should be understood as part of the complex development of the imagery—perhaps as an involved metonymy where the bearer of joyous news associated with the day is substituted for the joyous day itself. If this is correct, then the need for emendation drops away as a mistaken attempt to impose improper canons of strict rationality upon this curse.[32]

Setting

Throughout the previous discussion of setting for each of the confessions serious difficulties were encounterd in the attempt to discern their pre-literary significance and function. Even the most attractive proposals were not entirely satisfactory. The present passage is particularly instructive in this regard since its character seems to require an approach distinctly different from the previous passages. It presents serious problems for the previous models offered as explanations of setting. Legal associations and patterns seem totally absent so that the defence function of a lawsuit appears to be ruled out. Curses may serve a legal role[33] as an oath of innocence, etc., but this one as a virtually unconditional self-curse seems an unlikely candidate for such a function.[34] Even as a generally formulated proclamation intended for prophetic self-vindication, this passage seems totally unsuited. The recipients of such a message as in vv. 14-18 more probably would have heard their prophetic antagonist's announcement of defeat. There seems to be little indication in the curse that it has been called forth within a context of conflict over prophetic mission.[35] In this regard, there seems to be no indication at all of the messenger function and its accompanying tensions which Eichler and Auis sought to employ as the background for the confessions.[36] In fact, just at the point where reasons/motivations are given for the curse (v. 18), the language is highly traditional and stereotypical, with efforts to pin down a more concrete background for them apparently doomed to frustration.[37]

Further recognition that vv. 14-18 require a different approach to the question of pre-literary setting is provided by Clines and Gunn.[38] They draw attention to the literary conventions associated with the report/hearing of bad news[39] (cf. Jer. 6.22-26; 49.23; Isa. 13.7f.) and similarly with the prefacing of judgment oracles with laments (Jer. 4.19-22; 8.18; 10.19-20; 23.9) and argue that such conventions are designed to emphasize the disturbing, distressful nature of the message rather than to provide a personal emotional transcript of the prophet.[40] Closer examination of the imagery within Jer. 20.18 suggests a similar function for this passage, for the vocabulary is associated elsewhere in the book with national calamity and religious apostasy (יגון—cf. 8.18; 31.13; בשת—cf. 2.26; 3.24, 25; 7.19; 11.13).[41] Thus for Clines and Gunn the curse is not so much bound up with the prophet's personal despair but rather represents 'a conventional utterance of distress accompanying a judgment-speech or woe-oracle'.[42] Their proposal is very attractive and has much in its favour. The dominance of the birth theme, especially as it is formulated in v. 18 (מרחם יצאתי) suggests inner-Jeremianic allusions to the call narrative 1.5 (בטרם תצא מרחם)[43] and other confessional material (15.10—אוי לי אמי כי ילדתני). This is further suggestive evidence of a specific prophetic connection. Similarly or analogously formulated external parallels such as 1 Macc. 2.7; *4 Ezr.* 5.35; and Jer. 45.3 seem to provide very strong corroboration that such a setting could be workable for our present text.[44] Still these factors appear to find their warrant from the present setting of the passage within the prophetic book rather than from internal characteristics which demand a setting within prophetic mission. The parallel with Job 3 at least provides a strong indication that such a formulation as 20.14-18 does not necessarily require a prophetic situation in order to be understood properly. It seems that a certain indeterminacy for the pre-literary setting must be postulated.[45]

Interpretation

The basic meaning of the self-curse is not in doubt. The formal distinction of the passage from cultic lament, already noted, receives further corroboration from the lack of lament psalm connections at the level of diction, except as already noted for v. 18.[46] Working back from the experience of a life bereft of normal blessings, the poet utters a curse upon his birth, heralded as a joyous occasion but in reality shown to be a criminal event. The culpable party/parties is/are to be brought under the power of curse as redress for the crime perpetrated.[47] However, in light of our discussion on Setting where we noted the absence of clear internal characteristics which can be viewed as distinctively prophetic, it is difficult to discern just how the details are to be pressed further in terms of the prophet Jeremiah.

For example, if the pre-literary setting proposed by Clines and Gunn is followed, the question arises of the extent to which this original thrust has been preserved.[48] The original setting would preclude the attempt to read the curse more personally of the prophet's own feelings. However, the present close literary association with the preceding confession, vv. 7-13, and the narrative of 20.1-6 strongly suggest that editorial constraints have been placed upon our passage so that now it is meant to be read so personally.[49] The contacts with the call narrative provided by the birth theme only strengthen this impression further. But does this mean, as Clines and Gunn argue,[50] that the content of יגון, עמל and בשׁת is to be drawn from 20.1-6 and no longer speaks of national calamity but rather of personal persecution at the hands of Pashur and thus creates a confessional unit of vv. 7-18 whose dominant mood is one of despair? Or should we find, with L. Prijs, continuing national overtones and associations and view האישׁ as a representative of the whole nation?[51] So Jeremiah commiserates and confirms the curse[52] upon the 'man/ Israel' because in effect his birth announcement heralds the arrival of the one destined to utter Yahweh's word of judgment—i.e thus signalling the downfall of the nation.[53] Or again, while Clines and Gunn stress as primary the relation to 20.1-6 and Prijs stresses more general inner-Jeremianic connections, Hubmann stresses the immediate connection with vv. 7-13 and modifies these approaches by viewing vv. 14-18 as response to the asseveration concerning the invincibility of the divine word which he has proclaimed (vv. 7-13). If it is impossible for anyone to withstand successfully the prophetic word—both prophet and his opponents—then the judgment is inescapable; and vv. 14-18 provide an asseverative function in response.[54]

Each of the approaches makes attractive points and raises the need to consider the total contextual relationships rather than just one over against the other. But this need calls for further consideration of the editorial placement of the passage before an adequate basis for evaluation can be attempted. The internal ambiguities of our text illustrate well the impossibility of ranking these levels of meaning as to probability and predominance in the passage based solely upon internal considerations.[55]

Aim

In a similar fashion, the determination of aim under these circumstances would be hazardous and only tentative at best. The idea of asseveration of national doom seems very attractive, and we will want to evaluate this further after subsequent questions about the editorial intention relative to all of the confessions have been addressed. At present, however, it is worth observing that a third explanation or category for understanding the aim of Jeremiah's confessions seems required by our passage. For, if the initial passages presented the prophet in dialogue with Yahweh with both parties verbally 'present' in the 'conversation', the previous three texts witnessed an absence of the divine speech and now this last passage witnesses the cessation of the dialogue entirely since it no longer provides us with even a bare address to Yahweh—the prophet speaks a self-curse or lament. It is not apparent why such a diversity is to be found in the literary form of the confessions—especially on internal considerations.

9. Summary of Exegetical Section:
Overall Results and Intermediate Observations

With the completion of the initial exegetical phase of the study, it will be helpful to provide a review of our overall results and to attempt some intermediate observations about the reading of these passages as a transitional development to the remaining sections of this study.

The formal analysis of the confessions continues to confirm their strange quality of continuity and discontinuity with lament psalms when foregrounded against that poetic tradition. In most cases an organic relationship to that tradition is indicated with the differences arguably a matter of degree only. From this standpoint, many of the divergences could not be viewed as reflections of a distinctive prophetic character. Nevertheless, the confessions do not comprise a uniform formal group. Half of them were articulated under the influence of the prophetic liturgy pattern (11.18-23; 12.1-6; 15.10-14; 15.15-21). The other half divides into two groups. Most are executed as single complaint psalms (17.14-18; 18.18-23; 20.7-13); but the last one (20.14-18) breaks the connection with cultic lament entirely as a self-curse. Discerning clear reasons for this alteration of formal patterns at least on the basis of the individual unit involved was not immediately possible. Description of the units in these broad terms should not obscure the fact that in most cases they represent a complex blend and intricate interweaving of diverse genre characteristics to produce well-integrated structures.

The last point marks out a major difficulty encountered in the attempt to discern signs of editorial activity in the units and probably lies at the heart of the lack of consensus reflected in the various editorial models proposed for each confession. The well-integrated structure of the confessions has raised a theoretical problem for the elucidation of editorial seams since it was not possible in every case to distinguish clearly complex rhetorical artistry from editorial, compositional skill. Even the presence of doublet phenomena (11.20/ 20.12; 15.13-14/17.3-4; 15.20/1.8, 18-19), while raising the possibility of additions, carried further complications for a proper assessment of them, so that a judgment of 'redactional expansion' was not required in every case. The numerous recent attempts to detect extensive editorial activity in each confession was found unconvincing. In half of the units, discernment of any editorial activity does not seem feasible; and it is more likely that, in these cases, original units are present (12.1-6; 17.14-18; 20.7-13; 20.14-18). For the remaining block, only two units exhibit major expansions (11.21-23; 15.13-14), while the remaining are limited to a verse or part of a verse, respectively (18.18; 15.15 אתה ידעת). The effect of each addition varies from the creation of the prophetic liturgy pattern (11.21-23) to the concretizing of the confession in relation to the historical mission of Jeremiah (11.21-23; 18.18), to the explanation and development of abstract elements in the divine oracle (15.13-14) and finally to the apparent linking of confessional units to one another (15.15).

Determination of the origin of these expansions is equally problematic on the basis of their internal characteristics. Clearly distinctive Dtr. characteristics do not seem evident to support the contentions of Eichler and Ahuis, though in two cases (11.21-23, 18.18) extensive contact with the Jeremianic prose seems evident which could permit assignment to a Dtr. editor. Nevertheless, the editorial method is characterized by extensive utilization of Jeremianic material (15.13-14) or, at least, shows influence of Jeremianic themes (11.21-23) and the style of other confessions (15.15).

A no less vexing problem has been the determination of the pre-literary setting for the confessions—i.e. their hypothetical setting within the historical mission of the prophet. The impetus to search for such a setting is provided by three levels of characteristics. The first two testify, at least, to the explicit editorial connection of the confessions with Jeremiah, first by editorial expansion (11.21-23; 18.18), and second, through successful exploitation of potential allusions to the prophetic mission (12.1-6; 15.10-14; 20.14-18) as a result of their contextual location. The third level consists of unambiguous references to prophetic concerns, corroborating the previous editorial connections (15.15-21; 17.14-18; 20.7-13). The latter passages point to the invalidity of applying the label 'radical ambiguity' consistently and uniformly to each unit. The feature of discontinuity with lament idiom is not merely a question of degree in every instance.

For all these indications, a more precise description of their setting remains opaque. The recent proposals, on this score, were found to be unsatisfactory. The isolation of a special prophetic lament genre suffered from the most theoretical drawbacks, and neither it nor the apologetic model was capable of uniform application to all of the confessions. The problem of delayed fulfilment and/or opposition to prophetic mission is exhibited in the units; but in the absence of legitimate parallels, the problem of uniqueness to Jeremiah remains as well as the problem of adequately determining the concrete oral setting for the lament. Those passages exhibiting the prophetic liturgy pattern worked best for the apologetic theory (11.18-23; 15.10-14; 15.15-21) but not consistently so (12.1-6). The absence of the liturgy pattern in some units or its presence only on the basis of editorial expansion further undermined the applicability of this theory in a comprehensive fashion. And finally, that five of the eight units failed to encourage a search for a prophetic setting apart from editorial indications exposed the major weakness in these speculative attempts.

On the other hand, the consistent stylistic compatibility of the confessions with Jeremianic poetry, plus the ease with which they can be interpreted in terms of the prophetic mission (contrast 1 Sam. 2; Jon. 2), given their present context, repeatedly suggested the need for modification of the total editorial composition approach. It is not clear that such a close 'fit' would be expected had the units originally been totally unrelated to their present use. At the least such approaches need to make more allowance for the editorial incorporation and/or overworking of prior Jeremianic passages to produce the present confessions. And it is not clear that evaluated on these levels such theories could absolutely exclude the authenticity of the present units apart from the few discernible editorial additions. Even here redactional approaches have assumed too quickly that the label 'redactional' automatically indicates inauthenticity. More attention must be given to a rigorous establishment of the criteria used on questions of authenticity. Many of the studies exhibit method relying on too superficial features, suggesting at times an exaggerated tendency to find inauthentic elements.

For all this, the significance of the authenticity question is ambiguous in relation to the determination of setting and aim. For even if their substantial authenticity were granted, the confessional units would remain opaque in terms of their setting within the historical mission of the prophet. Unfortunately, the more one isolates the confessions from the book the more opaque and unsuccessful such a reading becomes. Though numerous warrants for making such an attempt are provided, the information necessary for its successful execution is not. This information appears to have been suppressed for other interests. While it remains possible to see the primary aim of the confessions in the depiction of a crisis or crises in prophetic mission, nevertheless it is their contextual utilization which appears crucial for the stimulus to take such an interpretive approach. So it must be the task of the remainder of our study to explore more fully the interpretation and significance of the confessions in light of their present contextual employment.

Chapter 2

THE INTER-RELATIONSHIP OF THE CONFESSIONS: THE SIGNIFICANCE OF THEIR PRESENT LITERARY SEQUENCE

Introduction

Until recently, scholarly approaches to these passages have been seriously hampered by the failure to consider the contextually conditioned nature of the confessions through their determination to read the passages in isolation from the book against the hypothetically reconstructed context of the historical mission of the prophet.

As a first step in considering more carefully the contextual utilization of the confessions and for discovering the nature of the editorial conventions employed, we would like to explore the possibility of their inter-relationship with one another. More specifically, do the confessions provide their own interpretive context, among themselves, through their present arrangements? This question has been variously approached in the past, and it will be useful to begin our discussion with a critical review of the types of answers attempted. Broadly speaking, answers have been found either through discovery of a significant relationship, or order, by means of rearrangement of the present texts or through explanation of their existing arrangement. It is interesting to note, at the outset, that the types of problem attendant on the assumptions already criticized in the preceding exegesis of the confessions resurface again in relation to the present question.

Significant Sequentiality by Rearrangement

Common to the advocates of this view is that their reconstructed order is viewed, to a greater or lesser extent, as directly corresponding to a historical, chronological, and psychological sequence in the mission of Jeremiah himself. This approach thus exhibits the greatest affinity with the assumptions of those exegetical approaches which attempt to interpret successfully the confessions within the setting of the prophet's historical mission. And so the difficulties attendant upon those approaches will apply in this specific question as well.

Our first representative is the classic English exposition of the confessions as biographical memoir, by J. Skinner. For him, the confessions not only sustain a 'psychological continuity' among themselves, but also, 'they form a connected series, recording the stages of a definite, though more or less protracted crisis in Jeremiah's life'.[1] This crisis was produced by the conflict within Jeremiah between loyalty to his prophetic calling and his human desires and feelings.[2] The climax of the crisis is to be found in Jer. 15.15-21. It represents the 'turning-point in his life' which 'solves the problem of his personal relation to God'.[3] Skinner located the prophet's spiritual crisis in the last twelve years of Josiah's reign, at the end of which Jeremiah emerges in victorious self-mastery ready to continue the prophetic mission with calm courage and self-possession.[4]

For all its personal attractiveness and widespread popularity,[5] his reconstruction seems inappropriate methodologically in its disregard of the nature of the confessional material itself—particularly in light of the recent debates over these passages. The most problematic aspect for his approach is the reconstruction of the various stages of the spiritual crisis by drawing various motifs here and there from all the texts without regard to their internal integrity. The rearrangement into a progression of crisis to resolution of crisis, then, is not based ultimately upon the present structure of the passages but is derived from his assumption about the nature of these texts as spiritual biography and the supposed sequence which would be thought most likely. However, if such means are employed, it is conceivable that almost any model which seeks to reconstruct a significant and logically plausible progression could be produced.[6] In addition, the fact that he does rearrange the passages is a tacit recognition that the confessions, as we now possess them, do not provide direct access to the prophet's inner life and historical mission. But this would suggest the need to provide some type of external warrants—such as clearly datable historical markers[7]—that would substantiate any particular reconstruction of a supposed original psychological and historical sequence. Our discussion of the problems encountered in the search for the pre-literary setting within

Jeremiah's mission illustrates the great difficulty that scholars have in the discovery of just this kind of crucial data. Skinner did not provide any, and it is unlikely that reliance upon logical plausibility is a sufficient criterion on its own.

In the two very recent studies of Ittmann and Ahuis, greater cognizance is taken of the need for external warrants if a particular reconstructed order is going to begin to approach success. Both scholars proceed on the basis of form-critical considerations as justification for the rearrangement. Recalling our earlier discussions of the formal analysis of the confessions, for Ittmann the passages were to be divided into three groups based upon their similarities (No. 1: 18, 11, 12; No. 2: 17; No. 3: 15, 20).[8] He then argued that a thematic development can be observed for the above order which represents the personal intellectual development of Jeremiah's own self-understanding.

Alongside Skinner's criterion of a progression of thought that is logically plausible, Ittmann offers his formal analysis as the underpinning of the former. But we have already sought to show that his approach to the form criticism of the confessions is deficient.[9] And once this aspect of his approach falls away, the validity of the reconstructed series suffers from the same difficulties as Skinner's in its inability to provide compelling justification for the procedure.

Similarly, Ahuis seeks to underpin his reconstruction with formal criteria. Unlike Ittmann, he preserves the present order of the confessions and resorts to rearrangements only in relation to the contextually adjacent narratives of symbolic prophetic actions. On the basis of the formal pattern of *Botenvorgang* and catchword associations, the pre-redactional confessional units, 12.1-4bβ, 5; 15.10, 17, 18, 19b, 20a; 20.7-9, are arranged into three complexes, each with the narrative of symbolic prophetic action preceding (13.1, 2, 4-7; 16.5, 7; 18.2-4/19.1-2a respectively) to yield the normal sequence of commission, execution, and report.[10] The kernels of 17.14-18 and 18.19-20, 22b-23, relating to the formal pattern of *Warten auf das Gericht*, can be connected to the preceding complexes to produce one original literary complex: 13/12; 16/15; 17/18; 18/19/ 20.7-9; 20.14-18.[11] The sequence of 17/18 and its insertion between the second and third *Botenvorgang* complex are justified from consideration of thematic development.[12] Literary echoes between the first and second *Botenvorgang* complexes justified their association,[13] but no connections could be found to the third (18/19/20).

This gap is filled by 17/18.[14]

Again the inadequacies, discussed earlier in relation to his formal analysis, seriously weaken the viability of his reconstructed *Botenvorgang* complexes (13/12; 16/15; 18/19/20). In any case, their arrangement together plus the inclusion of 17/18 technically do not arise from formal consideration but once again primarily from logical development of ideas and partially from verbal echoes. However, the fact that he did not need to resort to rearrangement of the confessional units themselves in order to discover significance in their serial arrangement is interesting. For while the criterion of logical plausibility may be insufficient to substantiate a hypothetically reconstructed order on the one hand, it may, on the other, provide important means to discover whether the present arrangement of the confessions is significant. Thus, specific observations of Ahuis may be useful, however unconvincing his overall reconstructed literary complex may be. If a significant sequentiality can be discovered in the present arrangement of the texts, then the subsidiary question he raises of the existence of such a complex prior to its inclusion in its present literary setting would need to be addressed.

Significant Sequentiality Without Rearrangement

The possibility raised by the preceding study of Ahuis that the present arrangement of the confessions might be significant has been pursued prior to him, and independently of him. While each of the three studies under review answers the possibility in the affirmative, the details of the progression, or pattern, perceived differ. The two studies of von Rad and Wimmer can be discussed profitably together, while the different orientation of W.L. Holladay's study can best be exhibited as a following contrast to the others.

Both von Rad and Wimmer discern a significant progression in the present order of the confessions which depicts sequential stages in the prophet's experience.[15] What is striking is that they come to different conclusions about the nature of the progression. For von Rad the progression is emphatically one of ever-increasing despair.[16] In the final passages where a divine response is no longer present and despair reaches its peak, the prophet takes on 'typical significance', mirroring Israel's relationship to Yahweh—i.e. 'God's whole way with Israel hereby threatens to end in some kind of metaphysical abyss'.[17] In contrast, Wimmer finds a progression where despair is resolved into acceptance and hope.[18] Following the initial confession (11.18-23), each subsequent passage has as its occasion the failure of the solution offered by the divine response. The problem of suffering is the central issue with the progression constituting a 'quest for *neqamā*' which is finally resolved in the last confession (20.7-18) with the rejection of any solution in terms of 'vengeance; vindication' (נקמה).[19] The apparently despairing cry of 20.18 is interpreted as the prophet beginning 'a new life by rejecting his old way of life'. 'Here Jeremiah starts anew by accepting his prophetic life *for what he has experienced it to be.*'[20]

That both scholars have reached opposite conclusions raises suspicion about the validity of both attempts since it may be that each has improperly emphasized one element over another in the confessional sequence. Features in favour of each approach seem to be present. The first four confessional units (11.18-23; 12.1-6; 15.10-14; 15.15-21) are structured in terms of complaint plus divine response with each subsequent confession responding to the preceding divine oracle. Furthermore the tone does increase in the bitterness of its vituperations against Yahweh. Numerous verbal echoes between the passages plus the contextual pairing of two sets further encourage the perception of a progressive literary relationship.[21] However, it seems fatal to Wimmer's view that the last four units (17.14-18; 18.18-23; 20.7-13; 20.14-18) lack a divine response so that the posited dialogical pattern is not sustained throughout; furthermore his approach to 20.14-18 does not reckon seriously enough with its face-value import as self-curse. This latter unit would support von Rad's view much more easily. But the penultimate unit (20.7-13) is equally problematical for von Rad with its internal progression from complaint to hopeful praise. Had this unit been the very last, Wimmer's contention of despair resolved into hope would have been on surer ground. Additionally troublesome for von Rad is the marked shift in tone at the mid-point of the confessional series (17.14-18; 18.18-23). The prophet's bitter complaints directed at Yahweh have receded into the background (17) or are virtually absent (18). Finally, before greater confidence can be placed in von Rad's theological interpretation of the lack of divine responses in the last half of the units, closer attention needs to be given to other possibilities that might negate his assumption. Formally speaking, there would be no technical reason why any one of these complaints has to have an explicit answer reported. Already we suggested that the internal character of 20.7-13 obviated the need for an answer.[22] And it may be that factors in the immediate context of the other units would account for the change in formal pattern rather than indicate the presence of an ominous theological silence. In order to argue more successfully for a significant sequential arrangement in the present order, there is a need to take better account of such problematic features as the arrested movement in the flow of the sequence at 17.14-18 and 18.18-23, the inconsistency of the lament-divine oracle pattern, and the significance of the abrupt shift in tone between the last units, 20.7-13 and 14-18, for the proposal of a progressive sequence.

Holladay's analysis of the present arrangement of the confessions proceeds along entirely different lines from those of the preceding approaches.[23] Instead of attempting to trace out a progressive pattern in the development of the ideas, he focuses more strictly on the elucidation of pattern or structure alone. Because of this, it is difficult to discern the significance he would see in this static structure for interpreting the actual meaning of the confessions.[24] Employing a rhetorical critical methodology,[25] he attempts to isolate an initial stratum[26] consisting of confessional and quasi-confessional material, which serves to organize structurally the whole of Jeremiah 11–20. The initial stratum consists of six blocks of material: 11.18–12.1-3, 5-6 (Father complex); 15.10-12, 15-21 (Mother complex); 16.1-9 (Integrating passage); 17.5-10 (Man complex); 17.14-18; 18.18-23; 20.7-13 (Day complex); 20.14-18 (Integrating passage). The remaining intervening materials between 11–16 and 17–20 are taken respectively as secondary additions to the initial stratum.[27] His labels indicate either key rhetorical markers or functions. In 11–16, the Integrating passage, 16.1-9, maps out, or indexes, the structure of the preceding material[28] with the reference to fathers/mothers of the nation (16.3, 7)—the key terms respectively in the Father complex (12.6) and Mother complex (15.10).[29] Just as the Father complex precedes the Mother complex, so the integrating passage reproduces this pattern with the Father complex echoed by the funeral section (16.1-7) and the Mother complex echoed by the subsequent wedding section (16.8-9).[30] As support, Holladay points to the infrequency of references to Jeremiah's parents; further verbal echoes between the Father complex, the Mother complex, and the funeral section and wedding section of Jeremiah 16, respectively; and the absence of any further links between 16.1-9 and other intervening material in 11–

16.[31] Similarly in 17–20, key terms in the Man and Day complexes are positionally indexed by the Integrating passage of 20.14-18.[32] Finally, 20.14-18 also supply the larger function of integrating the whole of the complexes in 11–20 by echoing each one in reversed order[33] and by exhibiting a parallel sequence of time-related words in the pattern ABC // ABCD // BCD.[34]

While the pioneering and provisional nature of Holladay's method and proposals is recognized and welcomed in relation to this vexed issue of discerning a pattern of organization in the Jeremianic tradition, serious questions must be raised on both aspects of method and result. The first relates to his selection of key rhetorical markers. The problem is not whether such literary devices as verbal echoes, word plays, and symmetrical patterns exist, for they do, especially in the poetic medium. Rather, the problem is determining what actually constitutes key rhetorical markers in the delineation of structure. When a particular datum is selected as a structural counterpart to another and yet other occurrences of the same feature exist, the risk of an arbitrary subjectivity in method arises. At this point, Holladay's treatment of the texts has not been sufficiently accurate or consistent. For example, why is the echo of the Father complex in 16.1-9 significant and not similar intervening references to fathers (13.14; 14.20)? Also, 16.1-9 do not seem to index the Father and Mother complex as claimed. While the wedding section (16.8, 9) does share common vocabulary with 15.15ff., it does not have Holladay's key term, Mother. Instead it occurs along with Father in the funeral section (16.1-7) which is supposed to echo 11.18ff. Again the supposed lack of connections between it and 16.1-9 and the material interposed between the Father/Mother complexes is contradicted by the presence of substantial links. The burial-nonburial theme, the non-mourning and corpses-for-food themes of 16.1-9 also occur in 14.16 and 15.1-9. These more proximate connections seem more plausible and probable than the ones suggested by Holladay. Similarly, his selection of the time-related words for the sequence binding 11–16 and 17–20 together passes by other occurrences of the same words in context for which he provides no justification (עת— 11.12, 14; 14.8, 19; יום—16.9, 14, 19; 17.11; 18.17; 19.6). Factors like these quickly efface the neat sequential pattern offered.

A second problem related to that of the selection process is the determination of whether an alleged rhetorical marker is intentional or fortuitous as far as the creation of structure is concerned.[35] Some verbal echoes, etc., might pertain more to characteristic authorial diction associated with common themes or to stylistic conventions associated with the particular genre of the material.[36] Holladay is aware of this alternative explanation and employs it on occasion to eliminate certain repetitions or echoes from having structural significance.[37] It is not clear, however, that he has demonstrated why the terms he has selected do not fall into the same category.

Third, the distance separating his alleged markers also introduces difficulties. Many of the suggested rhetorical devices are quite possible, especially within poems or between adjacent ones. But as separating distances increase, the improbability of a given association also increases, since the relative obscurity of an immediate correspondence between the two points becomes more difficult for the collection to overcome successfully. Hence, there is need for a convergence of factors in the collection for such structural markers or allusions to succeed. For example, if a proposed structural device could be intelligently related to the argument or the message of texts involved, this would greatly enhance the validity of the proposal. Holladay's thesis suffers from its restriction almost exclusively to matters of form in the elucidation of structure.

Finally, his attempt to employ rhetorical-critical means in order to elucidate an initial stratum which constitutes the earliest layer of material in 11–20 to which the rest has been added raises the question of the proper interface between rhetorical- and redaction-critical methods. Can rhetorical considerations, on their own, go beyond an explanation of existing structures to provide information about the historical growth of a literary work? Recent redactional studies of the Jeremiah tradition need to be brought into interaction with his theory of growth for they could be viewed as suggesting an alternative view of the development of the text. The approaches of Thiel and E. Nicholson, who see Dtr. editorial activity as constitutive for the present form of the book, suggest that the confessional materials play a subordinate function within the larger Dtr. complexes rather than constituting an initial stratum into which the other material has been inserted.[38] If Holladay's initial stratum did exist at some point, redaction-critical considerations might suggest that this prior structure has been subordinated to other structural and organizing principles. In any case, the successful demonstration of a significant pattern in the present arrangement of the confessions is a separate question from that of the origin of that pattern and the possibility that it indicates the existence of a prior literary confessional collection.[39]

Progression in Two Cycles[40]

While the preceding survey of approaches provides a useful illustration of characteristics of our passages in relationship to one another, still we have had to register our basic dissatisfaction with each of the attempts, based either upon considerations of method or upon the failure to explain certain features, or both. If problems such as these cannot be overcome, then the attempt to find significance in the present arrangement of the text may need to be viewed as a dead end.[41] It will be the concern of the following to attempt an alternative explanation of the literary sequence of the confession which does take into account the problems previously encountered. Yet any new attempt to find significant sequentiality in the present arrangement of the passages must face the question whether there are explicit factors in the texts themselves which encourage such an attempt and thus provide hope of viability.

The necessity of reading the confessions in series would have been indicated more strongly had all eight units been found as one connected collection instead of distributed through chapters 11–20. Nevertheless, six of the units have been immediately juxtaposed to one another (11.18-23 and 12.1-6; 15.10-14 and 15.15-21; 20.7-13 and 20.14-18). The implication of the preceding—that they should be read in relation to one another—is further strengthened by the presence of significant verbal echoes between the members of each pair[42] plus possible redactional additions which indicate a pattern of literary growth oriented toward establishing an explicit relationship between the two. For example, if our perception of the editorial character of 11.21-23, developed upon the model of 12.5-6, is correct,[43] then an explicit effort to link the two units together seems indicated, involving the theme of persecution by clansmen and family. Also, the zero variant in G at 12.3bα, though probably haplographic, could also be taken as an editorial attempt to tie the two units together with the association of 'lamb to the slaughter' (11.18). Similarly, in the second pair the probable additions of 15.13-14 and 15.15aα (אתה ידעת) fill out 15.10-12 in relation to 15.19-21, with the latter as model of rebuke and promise, and orient the second complaint as 'response' to the preceding divine oracle (אתה ידעת). No such explicit editorial expansions are discernible in the third pair. Only their immediate contextual association and verbal links[44] could be taken as an invitation to read them in relation to each other. Even if these features suggest that at least the relationship of the units within each pair is significant for interpretation, the question still remains whether warrant exists for linking the separated confessional blocks together.

On the latter question, two features could be taken as encouragement for making such links. In the first four units a consistent pattern of complaint plus divine oracle (prophetic liturgy) has been followed. This raises the possibility, argued by Wimmer,[45] that an on-going series has been constructed which carries the issue raised in one unit forward into the next through the alternation of prophetic and divine speaker. Second, in the exegesis of 20.7-13 its synoptic quality in the presentation of Yahweh's whole way with the prophet could be an indication that the entire group of the preceding confessions is in view. The doublet of 20.12 with 11.20, whether it is redactional or not, seems to provide an explicit link back to the first unit. If such initially positive encouragements can be combined with an increasing convergence of verbal, thematic, logical and redactional links across all eight units, then the legitimacy of such an approach to the confessions would be greatly enhanced. Nevertheless, it would be crucial for these factors to indicate a sequential pattern which can take into account more successfully the kinds of problem which led us to reject previous attempts along these lines. We have in mind particularly the problem of inconsistency in the prophetic liturgy pattern plus the complex oscillation of tone which seems, in one case, to arrest any discernible movement at the midpoint of the units (17.14-18 and 18.18-23) and, in another, produces an abrupt shift from hope to despair between the last two units which is difficult to understand at first glance. An approach to the sequentiality of the confessions must succeed through the discernment of a more complex pattern of movement.

In light of these initial considerations of valid warrants and problems, we would suggest as a working proposal the attempt to discern a complex progressional pattern articulated in two movements or cycles. The first cycle would consist of the series of prophetic liturgies (11.18-23; 12.1-6; 15.10-14; 15.15-21) rounded off by 17.14-18, which not only functions to give the concluding prophetic response to the preceding but also provides the transition to the second cycle. This second cycle comprises the remaining three confessional units (18.18-23; 20.7-13; 20.14-18). Abandonment of the prophetic liturgy pattern and shifts in the progressive tendency in tone and outlook are to be explained as related to corresponding shifts in the thematic focus of emphasis from one unit to the next and one cycle to the next.

Cycle One and Transition
As noted above, the four units of this proposed block are grouped into two pairs in ways which suggest explicit concern to establish an interpretive relationship. The chief task before us, at this point, must be the discernment of accumulated links between these two blocks and the proposed transitional passage, 17.14-18, organized around a dialogical pattern.

Between the first two units numerous points of similarity exist which render intelligible and possible the apparent editorial attempt to associate the two meaningfully. Both share themes of opposition to prophetic mission depicted as treacherous plots. The depiction of the prophet, his opponents, and Yahweh is carried out with imagery associated with descriptions of the righteous and wicked and their respective lots.[46] Much of the impact of the two poems is brought about by the contravention of normal expectation with regard to the previous theme. That this potential for association has been exploited seems indicated by explicit verbal echoes.[47] Particularly instructive are the verbal echoes between 12.3 (התקם כצאן לטבחה) and 11.19 (כבש אלוף יובל לטבוח) which immediately draw a connection in the categories of punishment suited to the crime.[48] Those who schemed against the innocent prophet (11.19) are to receive their deserved reward in similar terms (12.3). It is the next verse, 12.4, however, which appears to provide the key thematic point for effecting a logical connection and development between the two units. This verse challenges the justice of continued delay in punishment of the wicked opponents. As the citation of the wicked indicates, the situation of delay has thrown into question the validity of their imminent doom (לא יראה את אחריתנו). Thus, a logical development seems indicated: the initial complaint of the prophet (11.18-20) receives the divine promise of the destruction of his enemies (11.21-23). The failure of this promise to materialize, seen in the continued prosperity of his opponents, elicits the second complaint of the prophet (12.1-4) which shifts the crisis in prophetic mission from opposition and persecution, per se, to that of Yahweh's justice in delaying[49] to vindicate the prophet over his enemies as deserved. The rebuke and challenge of the second divine response (12.5-6) appears to shift the basis of the dialogue once again by directing attention to the nature of the prophetic mission. A sense of progression and development is further underlined by shifts which suggest an escalation of the problem at issue: the relationship of the three subjects[50] of the first lament is a consistent one of prophet/God vs. the opponents. This shifts in the second to prophet vs. God/ opponents which the second divine response rejects. Parallel to this is a shift in tone from motifs of confidence and trust drawn from thanksgiving (11.18-23) to one characerized by strident, biting challenge and counter-challenge. Finally, the nature of the crisis shifts from the lesser to the greater (secret plot of clansmen, 11.19; to open opposition, 11.21; 12.4; to the faithlessness of his own household, 12.6).

Establishing connections between 12.1-6 and the third unit, 15.10-14, is complicated by their separation, the lack of editorial additions which would tie them together, and though possible, the verbal echoes which do not seem as obvious.[51] Still, the woe-cry operates through the contravention of normal expectations about the fate proper for the innocent. If it was correct to find present allusions to the call narrative (1.4) of the prophet, then strong thematic reasons emerge for viewing 15.10 as the prophet's response to 12.5, 6. Instead of a direct response to questions about Yahweh's righteousness, the oracle of 12.5, 6 directed attention to the nature of the mission with a challenge about the prophet's ability to hold up under the prospect of solidarity with Yahweh's experience with Israel. 15.10 directly responds to the challenge, countering with his own interpretation of the prophetic mission as a mistaken life, a woeful fate.[52] It thus contains an oblique accusation of Yahweh. The subsequent oracle (15.11-14) rejects any suggestion of legitimacy for this view of the prophetic mission. The prophet as combatant of the whole nation represents the divine intention to shatter Israel in her rebellion. Again a sense of development is supported by the removal of any expressions of confidence and the ironic interpretation of the prophetic mission in the woe-cry. Again there is a shift in the three subjects: 12.5-6 challenged the preceding representation by placing the prophet at the centre of its focus. 15.10 picks up this focus but turns it into an oblique accusation.[53] The overall effect is to continue the picture of prophet vs. God/opponents. The doubled oath, rhetorical question, and remodelled judgment speech (15.11-14) counter by reasserting the initial depiction of prophet/God vs. opponents.

The continuing development from the third unit to the fourth (15.10-14; 15.15-21) once again seems more explicit. Besides the editorial expansions (15.13-14; 15.15 אתה ידעת), there is the more important verbal link חומת נחשת בצורה/נחשת (15.12; 15.20)[54] which continues the picture of the prophet besieged by the nation (cf. 15.11). The doublet of 15.20 with the call narrative (1.18) indicates that the nature of the prophetic mission is still the focal point. As the preceding oracle ended with the promise of his enemies' judgment, so this complaint opens with explicit reference to his enemies (15.15). Reference is made to the threat of delay (cf. 12.1-4) in the realization of this promise due to divine forbearance. The addition of אתה ידעת[55] seems to refer this back to 15.13-14 as a dissatisfied refutation and rejection. The rest of the complaint (15.16-18) then turns to interpret once again the mission as a contravention of normal expectations (cf. 15.10). The mission is depicted as a divine pestilence and curse inflicted upon a loyal member of the covenant community, and so it radically questions Yahweh's reliability. As such, this depiction of the mission represents the counter to the preceding divine interpretation (15.11-12). The divine oracle admonishes the prophet with the summons to repent and implies that in the preceding the prophet has imperilled his official status. 15.20-21 reassert the original terms of the prophet's call and in that context promise deliverance.[56] Further indications of development can be perceived; the virulence of the complaint reaches its highest pitch yet in the ironic play on the divine epithets and the bitter interpretation of his mission, concluding in the explicit blasphemous accusation (15.18). Correspondingly, the degree of censure in the divine oracle is the most pronounced of them all.[57] The picture of prophet vs. God/opponents seems to have reached a climax in its development.

The climax in the struggle between prophet and Yahweh reached by the preceding unit now seems to receive its resolution in 17.14-18. The lack of explicit editorial additions and the separation by intervening materials are compensated by extensive verbal echoes.[58] Particularly interesting are the terms for the opponents which are employed. For the first time, they overlap between units (רדפי, המה). As the divine oracle issued a summons to repent, so the plea of 17.14

for restoration/deliverance could be taken as the immediate response. As the admonition of the oracle refers to the terms of the prophet's call (1.18), so the petition, 17.17, 18, alludes to the threat of discomfiture (1.17—חתת) as punishment for lack of courage and fidelity to the mission. A marked shift back to the situation in 11.18-23 is to be observed. Instead of a despairing mood, the ironic play upon divine epithets, and ironic 'misinterpretation' of the prophetic mission, there are once again repeated expressions of confidence (תהלתי/מחסי אתה). The attempt to struggle with the mission is replaced by the stress upon its fulfilment in the realization of judgment (הביא אליהם יום רעה; cf. 11.23 אביא רעה אל). The initial relationship of the three subjects in 11.18-23 is restored to prophet/ God vs. opponents. The picture of tension and conflict between prophet and God is subordinated to a veiled, implicit level in the negative petition. It would seem legitimate to view 17.14-18 as the prophet's positive compliance with the summons of 15.19-21.[59] That a further divine response is lacking further suggests that the dialogical series has come to an end.

Still the undercurrent of tension between prophet and Yahweh (17.17-18a) imparts a certain unresolved quality to the cycle. Though he no longer attacks the nature of his prophetic mission by 'misinterpretation', the prophet has not entirely given up the complaint against Yahweh. The situation of delayed fulfilment is at the heart of the complaint, and the profession of innocence eschews any suggestion that the cause of that situation lies with the manner of his execution of the prophetic office (17.16). The verbal echoes between 17.16 and 15.19[60] suggest a contrapuntal role with 17.16 rejecting the implicit accusation of 15.19 that the prophet's speech has been amiss, or that he has attempted to abandon his office. If 17.14-18 resolve the crisis escalating through the preceding dialogical series and present the prophet's repentance, it is only a partial one at best. This feature raises the possibility that our working hypothesis of a transitional function[61] for 17.14-18 may have some validity.

Transition and Cycle Two
The burden of our discussion must turn now to the discernment of appropriate additional indications that 17.14-18 do represent a transition to a second series of confessions when, on the face of it, the previous crucial structural pattern of complaint/answer/counter-complaint has been relinquished.

The impression that 17.14-18 mark the close of the preceding cycle by the return to the situation of 11.18-23, at least partially, seems corroborated further by similar links of 18.18-23 and 11.18-23. The return of 17.14-18 to the situation of prophet/God vs. opponents is preserved. The issue of plot against the prophet, which gradually recedes in the attention of the first cycle, re-emerges in 18.18. Broad similarities of the imprecation (18.21-22a) with the judgment speech of 11.21-23 also direct attention back to the beginning of the first cycle. A description of the relationship between 17.14-18 and 18.18-23, the midpoint of the confessional material, as an arresting of the movement of the first cycle and initiation of a new beginning seems appropriate. The question is whether signs can be detected that the sixth confessional unit has picked up and has begun to develop concerns raised in a transitional manner by 17.14-18.

Our suggestion is to view the use of citations of prophetic opponents with their focus upon rejection of the prophetic message as the key datum of the new cycle (17.15; 18.18, 20aα). The use of citations gradually disappeared in the first cycle corresponding to the increased focus upon the prophet/God conflict but re-emerges with 17.14-18. The verbal links between 17.14-18 and 18.18-23 revolve around the prophetic message and its execution (17.15—דבר יהוה; 18.18—דבר מנביא, דבריו; 17.18—הביא עליהם; 18.22—תביא עליהם).[62] The probable redactional status of 18.18 as a citation and as the main contributor of verbal links between the two units underlines, all the more, the possibility of explicit association of the two confessions based on these features. A development appears in the course of the citations: in 17.15, delayed fulfilment allows the opponents to question the veracity of the prophetic message; therefore, in 18.18 Jeremiah's prophetic word can be discounted (אל נקשיבה) and disputed (נכהו בלשון); in 18.20aα the intention of dispute is executed in the rejection of judgment (רעה) as the legitimate content of prophetic proclamation. Further sense of development is indicated by the professions of innocence which focus upon the prophet's orientation from which he has made the proclamation of judgment,[63] the increased place given to petitioning the judgment announced (18.21-23), and the subordination of the threat of delay/non-fulfilment theme to a more implicit level in the negative petition (18.23).

The potential for significant association with the next unit, 20.7-13, is provided by the presence in the latter of the plot theme (20.10), the central focus of the whole unit upon the irrepressible power of the divine word, and important verbal echoes, esp. דבר יהוה (20.8) and יכשלו (20.11).[64] Again the nature of the citation (20.10) focuses upon the opponents of the prophet in their dispute with the prophetic message. The challenge inherent in the enemies' rhetorical question (18.20aα) seems developed further in 20.10 by the attempt to induce prophetic utterance which can be construed as seditious speech. The development from complaint to confident praise in 20.7-13 suggests a climactic function for this unit in Cycle Two. The petition of 18.23, יהיו מכשלים, is resolved in the certainty of hearing 20.11aβ-11b, רדפי יכשלו. The dispute with the prophetic word carried forward in the citations is also resolved by certainty of failure (20.11—לא יכלו) in light of the irrepressible power of the divine word (20.7-9). Emphatic profession of innocence and elaborate petitions for his enemies' destruction give way to confessions of trust (20.11aα; 12bβ) and anticipatory praise for the deliverance from his opponents.

Besides a climactic function for the unit in relation to Cycle Two, earlier observations about the résumé-like quality of 20.7-13 may mark out a synoptic function which further links together the double Cycle progression of the confessions. The unit sustains important verbal links with all of the preceding units.[65] The central issues of the preceding two cycles are all reflected in the focus of 20.7-13 in a way which appears to mirror[66] the course of the progression already discerned in the two cycles. Just as the first cycle presented the prophet's struggle with Yahweh against his mission through an increasingly bitter, ironic 'mis-interpretation' of that mission which culminated in the prophet's compliance to the divine rebuke, so 20.7-9 depict, ironically, once again, his compulsion to take up the mission as a victimization of the innocent against which he is powerless so that he must capitulate before the divine demand. Intertwined and juxtaposed with this theme are the opposition and struggle of his opponents with the bearer of the divine word. As already argued, this reflects the focus of the second cycle. The struggle of prophet vs. God/opponents in the first cycle gives way to the struggle of prophet/ God vs. opponents in the second as in the change from 20.9 to 20.10 and the confident resolution of the latter in 20.11. The defeat of the prophet in his struggle with the mission provides the basis for the sure defeat of the nation in its struggle against the prophetic word.

However, if 20.7-13 really does bring the second cycle to a climax as well as provide a synopsis which ties both Cycle One and Two together bringing the whole complex of issues to a confident resolution, then what is the rationale of 20.14-18 with its marked change of tone? Its immediate contextual juxtaposition argues against its too hasty exclusion from any significant association and function with the other confessional units. The allusions to the call narrative in the self-curse once again suggest the ironic 'mis-interpretation' of the prophetic mission through the device of a contravention of normal expectations. Thus the unit seems to have a more personally directed focus as the prophet's response to his mission, particularly akin to sentiments expressed in 15.10-14 and 15.15-21.[67] If such an understanding is correct, then a certain amount of inconsistency is introduced in relation to the editorial development of the second cycle. As 18.18-23 linked back to the initial situation of 11.18-23 and 20.7-13 resolved that situation in hope, 20.14-18 seem to return the reader to the situation in 15.10ff.

On the other hand, our earlier exegetical discussion of the unit raised the possibility of a more externally, non-personally directed orientation for the passage as a response to an announcement of doom. The observations of Clines and Gunn, and Prijs as modified by Hubmann, would suggest a function for this unit which is more in keeping with the direction of the second cycle. In this view, the unit draws out the implication of the preceding conclusion of the invincibility of the prophetic word against all opposition in an asseverative manner—the nation's destruction is inescapable. Thus 20.14-18 would relate directly to the central concern of the second cycle with the fate of the prophetic word. The possible verbal and thematic links of עמל, יגון, בשת with כלמת עולם, באר מאר בשו in 20.11 might provide more explicit reasons for such an understanding.[68]

Nevertheless, troublesome features still persist on this question of the relationship of the final unit to the two cycles. Even as an asseverative conclusion to Cycle Two, it is executed in a manner which reflects ironically on the nature of the prophet's mission—the birth of the one destined for the prophetic office is a harbinger of national doom. The résumé/synoptic function of 20.7-13 seems to extend into 20.14-18. Yet strong verbal contacts spanning across both cycles are not as strong as was the case for 20.7-13.[69] And along with associative connections with the preceding cycles, this unit also introduces a major break with the preceding since one of the major structural elements was the progressive alteration in the orientation of the three subjects. 20.14-18, as a self-curse, have dropped this pattern entirely. Perhaps the break with the progressive cycles and the ambiguity of aim can be explained through more extensive structural functions for the unit than just as a 'postscript' to the double confessional cycles.

Summary

Our initial encouragements to search for a complex inter-relationship among the confessions have found corroboration in the discovery of two progressive cycles (11.18-15.21 and 18.18-20.18) which have been integrally related together by a transitional passage at their midpoint (17.14-18) and at least by one, if not two, concluding synoptic units (20.7-13; 20.14-18). The focus of the first cycle is upon the nature of the prophetic mission depicted by a struggle between prophet and Yahweh. The second cycle shifts the focus to the fate of the prophetic word depicted as disputed, challenged, and rejected by the nation. If a situation of delayed fulfilment led in Cycle One to a dispute over the nature of prophetic mission, in Cycle Two it led to a dispute over the nature and fate of the prophetic word. Cessation of the prophet-God dialogical pattern in Cycle One may relate, in part, to the shift of attention to the conflict between prophet and nation over the message. If there is any sense in which the label 'dialogue' is proper for Cycle Two, it would have to be in relation to the implicit dialogue between the prophet and his opponents witnessed by the citations, the chief linking/structuring elements of the second confessional block. The final unit of the confessional sequence resolves the central issues of the preceding progressions in a way which mirrors the course of development itself. The nature of the prophetic mission and message supplies in both cycles the basis for the resolution of the crisis points for the prophet. The convergence of verbal, thematic, logical and redactional factors points at least to the tentative substantiation of this working hypothesis. But additional problems need to be considered before more satisfaction with it can be expressed.

Implications and Problems

The preceding review and critique of attempts to find a significant structural relationship among the confessions, in addition to our own similarly oriented new proposal, raise important additional questions which we would like to discuss in concluding the present section.

Genetic Implications

Frequently, those who have discerned significant sequentiality in the confessions or at least have viewed them as a structured complex of textual units also infer that this reconstructed sequence or present arrangement represents an earlier literary or tradition block, ultimately going back to the prophet, which has subsequently been incorporated into the present context (Ittmann, Ahuis, Holladay). Even among those who do not go so far in their analysis, it is common to assume that from their very nature these complex texts constitute an earlier tradition block of some type before receiving their present location.[70] Assuming for the moment, then, that our proposal about the inter-relationship of the passages is correct, the question arises anew whether it is legitimate to take the step, often argued, and to view this structure as an indication of an earlier literary complex.

While such an inference is not logically or theoretically impossible, consideration of the role of redactional factors in the formation of a progression in two cycles makes it highly unlikely. We have taken such passages as 11.21-23; 15.13-14; 15.15aα; 18.18 as the most probable indications of editorial additions. They occur at crucial points in the progressional series (esp. 11.21-23 and 18.18), and their removal would seriously affect the validity of our working hypothesis. Acceptance of other possibilities, even the proposals of other scholars which we have not followed, would only enhance this situation.[71] Thus the confessional complex must be viewed as a product of editorial compositional activity. Still, as an editorial composition, the collection could have taken place prior to their incorporation into the present setting. The question remains undecided. However, attention again to the nature of these additions would suggest as well that the present literary sequence is a product of the major and comprehensive redaction of the book by Dtr. editorial activity.[72] While most of the additions are of a nature which prevents their secure classification as Dtr., in two crucial instances, 11.21-23 and 18.18, a strong case can be made which would tie them to the rest of the prose traditions in the book. The role of the first in providing the initial divine response and the premise for the ensuing dialogue and the role of the second in providing the movement of return and shift to the issue of Cycle Two illustrate the critical nature of the additions if our perception of sequential literary complex is to succeed. So it seems more appropriate to speak of the inter-related complex as the result of the major final redaction in the book.

Problems of Validation

As mentioned above, the legitimacy of our proposal about the present sequential arrangement must be accorded only tentative validity. Additional features still need to be discussed before more confident affirmation can be made. These outstanding issues are pressed all the more by the redactional factors just discussed in relation to the origin and growth of the confessional complex. We have had to work out the hypothesis so far by disregarding the presence of intervening materials between most of the confessions. But if it was really the intention of the major final editorial action to construct such a pattern, why did they not preserve the integrity of the complex rather than distributing units through the surrounding literary material? As a distinct textual block the potential for the collection to succeed would seem to have been greater as far as a reader is concerned.

Similarly, the adequate understanding of the place of 20.14-18 needs further consideration. What is the need for such a 'postscript'? The internal dynamic of the double-cycle progression does not seem sufficient reason to account for the presence of the unit—i.e. from this angle it appears slightly redundant. Its ambiguity plus the formal-logic break with the double cycle might argue for the existence of additional redactional intentions at work. If it is important to relate supposed rhetorical patterns to redactional considerations,[73] so too must one redactional interest and complex be related to others. Exegesis of individual confessional units pressed us to explore their contextual utilization. This present section began that exploration by considering the literary sequence of the confessions as providing their own interpretive context. The concern for additional indications of validity in our reading suggests that the search for a contextual understanding is not adequate on this level alone. Initial indications appear to require that a valid contextual reading of these texts will have to proceed along two axes: present literary sequence and immediate contextual setting.

PART II

DRAMATIC DIALOGUE—PROPHET AND GOD VERSUS ISRAEL

Chapter 3

THE COMPOSITIONAL FUNCTION OF THE CONFESSIONS IN THEIR IMMEDIATE LITERARY CONTEXT

1. *Jeremiah 11.18-23; 12.1-6*

Introduction

As our next step in the exploration of the editorial utilization of the confessions, we turn to consider their immediate literary setting. The necessity of doing this was indicated particularly by the previous chapter. There the problem of explaining the fact of intervening passages rather than an integral collection forcefully presented itself.

The first question that must be addressed is that of elucidating what constitutes the immediate literary context for the confessional complex—in this case, 11.18–12.6. In other words, what extent of the material preceding and following a particular confession is to be considered relevant in the attempt to discern the editorial conventions employed in, and the significance of, the incorporation of a given text into its present location. For 11.18–12.6 it is suggested that chapters 11–13 provide this editorially created context in which the investigation is to be carried out. The main evidence in support of this suggestion is the occurrence of the editorial superscription in 11.1.[1] The next superscription, at 14.1, indicates that a new section has begun. In chapters 7–25, at least, a consistent pattern of marking off new sections by use of the superscription appears to be in force (7.1; 11.1; 14.1; 18.1; 21.1; and 25.1 slightly different). The two stereotyped patterns used in 11.1 and 14.1 also occur elsewhere in the book as editorial incipits to collections of smaller or greater extent (to 11.1 cf. 30.1; 32.1; and to 14.1 cf. 1.2; 46.1; 47.1; 49.34).[2] If further evidence from verbal-thematic echoes to logical and redactional markers can be accumulated as we proceed in the analysis, then the validity of this initial suggestion can be viewed more confidently.

11-13: Overview of Units[3]

Before proceeding to a more concerted analysis of 11.18–12.6 and its place within 11–13, it will be helpful to survey briefly the other material by delineating the individual units, their order of occurrence, and signs particularly of a catchword or thematic nature which would provide additional indications of purposefulness in the collection or complex, even if only on a mechanical basis.

The complex is composed of eight basic units. The first is the prose sermon (11.1-13) about the broken covenant followed by a composite of prose and poetry (11.14-17) focused upon cultic activities. The cultic subject matter of the latter sustains verbal and thematic links with the preceding prose sermon (11.14—אל תתפלל, בעת קראם אלי/ קטר לבעל—11.17; זעק אל—11.14/איני שמע—11.11/לא אשמע—11.17; 12—11.11, מקטרים להם—11.14, רעתם, קטר לבעל; רעה/11.11—11.17, 13—11.12, בביתי—11.15; מזבחות/11.13—בביתי; רעתם—11.15; רעה, 11.12). Passing over 11.18–12.6 for the moment, the fourth unit is a poetic judgment speech (12.7-13) in the form of Yahweh's lament over Israel as his rebellious house/inheritance (בית, נחלה), consequently deserving punishment. This is followed by a prose oracle of hope (12.14-17), directed to Israel's neighbours, which reflects concepts in the preceding (12.14, 15—נחלה, כרם, חלקה, ארץ/12.7, 8, 9, 10, 11, 12—נחלה; 12.14, 15, 17—נתש an agricultural term/12.7-13—Israel depicted under agricultural figures; 12.14—שכני רעים נגעים בנחלה/12.9-12—invading neighbours).[4] If the units so far provide some indications for their association with each other, the next two prose units consisting of the symbolic action of the linen waistcloth (13.1-11) and the parable of the wineskins (13.12-14) appear to offer a break. The association of these two with each other on first sight could be related to their common parabolic-symbolic nature. But connections with the preceding units (12.7-13, 14-17) seem lacking unless one is to be found in the verbal echo of שחת (12.10; 13.7, 9, 14).[5] On the other hand, the association of the eighth and final unit (13.15-27) with the preceding seems to lie in the appeal of the poetic judgment speech against the pride/arrogance of the nation under threat of the shame of exile. These themes of pride,[6] arrogance, glory-brought-low, humbled, shamed, reflect elements in 13.1-14 (13.15—אל תגבהו, 13.17—גוה, 13.18—עטרת תפארתכם, השפילו שבו/13.20—צאן תפארתך, 13.26—קלונך/13.9—שחת גאון, 13.11—תפארת/13.17—לא תשמעו/13.10—לתפארת, לתהלה, לשם/13.11—נתן כבר/13.16—לא שמעו; 13.11—מאן לשמוע and possibly a word-play 13.14—נפץ/13.24—פוץ).[7] Thus our overview would suggest that generally the units within 11–13 have been collected in a purposeful manner. The question remains whether this collective rationale is merely superficial and mechanical, or instead reflects a more significant editorial activity. This question must be considered in relation to the analysis of 11.18–12.6 and its place within the collection.

11.18–12.6: Compositional Function

Among the most recent studies of Jeremiah, that of Thiel appears to be the first to attempt an explanation of the redactional placement of the confessional complexes from the standpoint of their immediate literary setting.[8] He has detected a pattern of *Gerichtsbotschaft— Verfolgung—Klage* designed to effect stylized scenes of the prophet, suffering in the context of his preaching. More specifically, he views this patterning for 11.18–12.6 as *Anlass* (11.1-6), *Gerichtswort* (11.7-17), *Verfolgung* (11.18-23), and *Klage* (12.1-5).[9] Thiel's basic proposal has been accepted by Eichler[10] and Ahuis along with an attempt to lend more precision to it by developing the scheme to include all of the material in 11–20. Ahuis thus discerns a five-fold sectioning of 11–20 with each section consisting of seven parts. For the present complex the schema is *Gerichtsverkündigung Jeremias* (11.1-11), *Eintreffen des Gerichts* (11.11), *Klage des Volkes* (11.11-12), *Verbot der Fürbitten an Jeremia* (11.14), *Fortsetzung der Gerichtsverkündigung* (11.15-17), *Verfolgung Jeremias* (11.18f.), *Antwort Jeremias (Gerichtswort an die Verfolger*—11.21-23; *Klage zu Jahwe*—12.1-4).[11] While Thiel remains silent about the overall theological intention or result of these stylized scenes, Ahuis sees in it the Dtr. editorial concern to present Jeremiah as Yahweh's suffering servant.[12]

However, it is questionable whether Thiel's and Ahuis's attractive proposals really do provide an accurate description of the individual units. As Hubmann rightly points out, Thiel's subdivision of 11.1-17 into 11.1-6 as the rationale of the following judgment speech seems to be incorrect.[13] For vv. 7-8 also continue the function of the preceding; only vv. 11-13 formally constitute an announcement of judgment.[14] To this observation should also be added the difficulty of labelling the confession 11.18-23[15] differently from 12.1-5 as principally a report about persecution. No doubt it has to do with the prophet's persecution, but this is presented within the prophet's lament. And as we argued previously, 12.1-4 is not a complaint in the

first instance about the prophet's persecution but rather a response
to Yahweh's apparent failure to enact the preceding promise of
deliverance. Analogous problems adhere to Ahuis's development.
Besides the attempt to view 11.18-23 as Thiel does, it is not clear that
his view of v. 11 and vv. 11-12 respectively as *Eintreffen des Gerichts*
and *Klage des Volkes* can be sustained.[16] Formally, the verses
constitute the proclamation of judgment within the judgment oracle,
vv. 9-13, with the surrounding verses constituting the accusation and
grounds for that judgment. Their whole orientation is prospective,
announcing a *future* judgment during which the nation will petition
(זעק) Yahweh and their idols for succour. But this seems an
inadequate reason to view them separately from the preceding
judgment speech as depicting the realization of that judgment and
the nation's response to it. Ahuis's categories appear to be present
only implicitly, at best.[17] It may still be possible to speak of a stylized
scene of the prophet's mission involving Thiel's elements of
Gerichtsbotschaft—Verfolgung—Klage but only in a very general way
which still needs to be more carefully analysed in a manner
appropriate to the nature of the units involved.

Hubmann has sought to carry out such an analysis. Though
rejecting Thiel's model, he continues to find a programmatic
theological interest giving shape to the present arrangement of the
text.[18] Beginning first with the context preceding the confessions,
Hubmann discerns the logic of the prose sermon (11.1-14) developed
by two movements: vv. 1-8 proclaim the terms of the covenant,
providing a retrospective summary of Yahweh's faithfulness both to
the promises (vv. 4-5a) and to the enactment of the curses (vv. 7-8);
these constitute the basis upon which the following judgment speech
is pronounced to the present community (vv. 9-12, 13, 14). Thus the
effect created is an emphatic assurance that just as Yahweh proved
faithful to all the terms of the covenant and so judged earlier apostate
generations, so the present community of Judah will not escape
judgment.[19] Two intriguing features of the prose sermon are the
personal references to the prophet in 11.5b, 14. With the modelling of
11.3-5 upon the curse-ratification ceremony in Deuteronomy 27,[20] a
response by the whole nation would have been expected rather than
by the prophet alone. For Hubmann, this suggests that the prophet is
being viewed from a special theological perspective.[21] The prohibition
against intercession strengthens this impression further by evoking
comparison with 15.1—even the intercessory activity of a truly

faithful, spiritual leadership cannot avail to avert the judgment.[22] Jeremiah is set over against the nation as the only one affirming the terms of the covenant (11.5b). This contrast between nation and prophet, with the former apostate in its totality[23] and the latter the one faithful covenant member, matches the contrast between Judah and Yahweh with the latter innocent of any wrongdoing in his past relations to the nation. God and prophet are here drawn together in opposition (11.14) to the rejected and apostate community.[24] The remaining vv. 15-17 include a poetic fragment which constitutes a judgment speech related to cultic abuses.[25] This thematic link to 11.12, 13 and the accusations of idolatry plus explicit verbal echoes suggest that their function in the composition is to develop further and to illustrate that element of the nation's apostasy seen in idolatry as a *Beispiel des Versagens*.[26]

This leads Hubmann to postulate the editorial rationale for 11.18–12.6 in relation to 11.1-17. He observes that the nation's crime of idolatry receives further concrete illustration (vv. 15-17) on the one hand, while on the other the refusal to heed/obey the terms of the covenant (לא שמע בקול) did not receive such elaboration. This development, temporarily absent, is to be found in 11.18–12.6 which has its purpose in the concrete illustration of the nation's opposition to Yahweh (מאן לשמוע) through refusal to heed his prophetic messenger (11.21—לא תנבא בשם יהוה).[27] The redactional status of 11.21 enhances the explicit nature of the connection. 11.1-17 presents Yahweh's prophet in execution of his commission. The wording of the citation in 11.21 constitutes the outright rejection of the Yahweh prophet.[28] The contrast and opposition introduced initially by 11.5b and 11.14 are here brought to a climax as the persecution/opposition reaches from the prophet's clansmen even to members of his own family (12.6).[29] On this latter point, the links with the following context are established; for just as the prophet experiences alienation, treachery, and hostility from his own family[30] (בית אביך), so Yahweh experiences the enmity of the nation (12.7-13—נתן עלי בקולה, היה נחלתי כאריה, עזב ביתי).[31] As in 11.1-17, Yahweh and his prophet are set over against the nation. Jeremiah's fate at the hands of the nation participates in Yahweh's and provides an illustration of it.[32]

We find Hubmann's proposal attractive and convincing. Further features in the text can be mentioned which would seem to offer additional corroboration of his view. First, if our earlier exegesis of

12.6 in relation to 12.1-2 was correct, then the picture of the prophetic mission as a mirror of the conflict between Yahweh and Israel with the prophet participating in Yahweh's experience of treachery (12.1—בגד/12.6) and faithlessness (12.2 קרוב בפיהם ורחוק/ 12.6—רבר טוב אל) is already an internal constituent of 12.1-6. Thus this confession is admirably suited to the larger compositional purpose proposed by Hubmann. Then the picture of Yahweh, the object of a plot/conspiracy (11.9—קשר, 11.15—מזמתה), parallels the prophet's situation (11.18, 19—חשב מחשבות, מעלליהם). The picture of the prophet as the one loyal covenant member (11.5b, 14) set against the nation is stressed more emphatically in 11.19 (כבש אלוף) and 12.3 (לבי אתך). The common depiction of the prophet and nation with agricultural images permits a contrasting interplay in line with the illustrative role postulated for the confessional complex: the nation— a luxurious olive tree (11.16), planted by Yahweh (11.17; 12.2), flourishing and productive (11.16 יפה פרי תאר, 12.2—עשה פרי)—plot against the prophet—the innocent righteous (11.19 נשחיתה עץ בלחמו); and in contrast to his true piety (12.3a), their piety is hypocritical (12.2b),[33] masking their fundamental 'practical atheism' (12.4bβ).

Turning to the following passage (12.7-13), as noted the parallelism of the broken relationship experienced by both prophet and Yahweh is underlined through the numerous relational terms (12.7—ביתי; 12.7, 8, 9—נחלתי; 12.7—ירדות/cf. 11.15—ידידי; 12.10—כרמי, חלקתי) and the indications of hostility (12.8—כאריה, נתן עלי בקול/cf. 11.21— מבקשים נפשך; 12.6—קראו אחריך).[34] In addition, just as the prophet laments his circumstances, so the *Qina* metre[35] in the judgment speech (vv. 7-13) marks out Yahweh's lament over his own people's rejection of him. Finally, the repeated use of agricultural imagery to depict the land-nation may also serve to underline the contrast between the apostate nation and faithful prophet. The promise of a fertile land to the fathers (11.5) now falls under the curse and ruin as a result of the nation's wickedness (12.4—תאבל הארץ /מרעת ישבי בה. . . cf. 12.11—אבלה עלי שממה). Prophet and Yahweh both lament the spiritual blindness which has brought on this state of affairs (12.4— כי אין איש שם על לב/cf. 12.11—אמרו לא יראה). Thus, the prophet steps forward once again as the sole member of the community concerned for the dire consequences of the breach of the covenant bond (12.4— עד מתי). The evidence so far would suggest that as a literary complex 11.1-12.13 constitutes a significant editorial composition in which the confessions play an important theological role as Hubmann has argued.

The question still remains concerning the material in 11–13 left
for discussion, 12.14-17 and 13.1-27, that was raised earlier in the
overview of units. Is the more significant editorial activity discerned
so far continued in relation to these units? If such theologically
motivated composition can be discerned, there is the need to decide
whether a close relationship to the confessions is still present or
whether their significance is to be seen more generally within 11–13.
The immediate association of 12.14-17 with the preceding oracle
12.7-13 seems fairly clear as a further reflection and comment
motivated by the fate of Yahweh's inheritance (נחלה) at the hands of
their wicked neighbours (12.10—רעים רבים). Whether significance
beyond this immediate connection can be discerned is difficult to
decide. To my knowledge, no significant verbal, thematic, or
redactional links with the confessions are present. The only
possibility for an association may be present in the key terms of the
prose unit, בנה, אבד, נתש. The importance of this vocabulary in the
call-narrative for depicting the nature of the prophetic mission to the
nations (1.10 cf. 18.7, 9) may account in part for the association with
11.1-12.6 which reflects such a concern for depicting the nature of
the prophetic mission. It might be legitimate, then, to view the unit
as providing a more complete answer to the prophet's complaint in
12.2, 4[36] (cf. in 12.2 and 11.17 נטע the semantic opposite of נתש). The
re-establishment of the just order in the land suffering under the
curse lies beyond the judgment of exile in the hope of a future
restoration. Such a connection does not seem too obvious compared
to the immediate association of the passage with vv. 7-13.

On the other hand, a more general significance within the whole
collection seems more probable. While formally addressed to the
neighbouring nations, the assumption of exile common to all, even
Judah (v. 14) before any idea of hope or mercy becomes legitimate,
fits satisfactorily with the whole tenor of 11.1-12.13 to announce and
to vindicate the judgment of exile as an unavoidable doom. In this
line, the conditions of securing the situation of restoration, למד דרכי עמי
(v. 16), would seem to provide an appropriate parallel to the terms of
the covenant proclaimed in 11.1-8 (cf. שמע בקול to 12.12—אם לא ישמעו)
and serve to underline once again the only circumstances in which
the national life could expect a hope of maintenance in the land.
Nevertheless, this note of hope represents a new departure in the
thought of the composition.[37]

The situation for the units in 13.1-27 is similar. The rationale of this collection around the motifs of pride-glory/ruined-shamed was noted above. But discerning significant relationships with the confessions is difficult, especially for 13.12-14 and 13.15-27.[38] However, a stronger possibility than that suggested for 12.14-17 appears present for 13.1-11—the symbolic action of the linen waistcloth. Important key terms stating the significance of the symbolic action (13.7, 9—שחת; 13.9—נאון; 13.7, 10—צלח) provide verbal links with key terms characterizing the intentions, or actions, of the prophet's assailants in the confessions (11.19—שחת; 12.1—צלח; 12.6—נאון[39]) which could provide the focal point for the placement of 13.1-27 here. The concern may be to portray the judgment upon the nation as a reversal of fortunes and intentions of the assailants of the prophet in the manner of the punishment fitted to the crime.[40] The stylized scene of the prophetic mission as a mirror of the relationship between Yahweh and Israel receives further illustration in the nature of the symbolic action. God and prophet are again paralleled. Both prophet and Yahweh are victims of Judah's obdurate rebellion and hostility. The rejection of the prophetic mission is concrete proof of the same. So Yahweh's decision to judge the nation is given visible demonstration in prohibition of prophetic intercession (11.14) and the prophet's ruined waistcloth (13.9).

Beyond this possibility of a role in the further development of the stylized picture of Jeremiah's ministry, each of the three units in the chapter exhibits strong associations with what appears to be the central concern of the complex—i.e. to provide a theodicy of the judgment upon Judah as the legitimate and unavoidable punishment for the nation's breach of the covenant relationship.[41] Explicit links with the central accusations in 11.1-17 are present (13.10— ולא שמעו—13.11; הלך אחרי אלהים אחרים ,הלך בשררות לבם ,מאן לשמוע דברי and possibly 13.17—אם לא תשמעוה, 13.25-27—idolatry) as well as the motif of unavoidable judgment (13.14—לא אחמול ולא אחום ולא ארחם/ cf. 11.11, 14; 13.23). That the prose links are more than a matter of similarity based upon characteristic Dtr. motifs appears to be suggested by the zero variants in G, respectively at 11.7-8bα[42] and 13.10aα (החלכים בשררות לבם), which appear to represent explicit cross-linkages of the sections. If the additional suggestions of Thiel[43] relative to 13.10a, 11, and of W. McKane[44] relative to 13.14, as editorial expansions to the original units are valid, then the suggestion of explicit cross-linking would be further enhanced. Finally, the issue of providing an explanation and justification for the exile becomes an explicit feature in 13.22 (מדוע קראוני אלה).[45] The 'plus' of these portions of the complex are located in the development of the nation's stubborn rebellion (שררות לב) as pride/arrogance and the concrete specification of the judgment as political exile against the more general term of רעה. The description of 11-13 as a programmatic, theologically structured, editorial composition appears fully warranted.

Summary
11-13, as an editorial composition, is oriented to the issue of theodicy raised by the destruction of Judah. The theodicy offered is the justification of that judgment as an unavoidable divine punishment in response to Judah's persistent, unshakeable faithlessness and opposition to their covenant relationship with Yahweh. As a means of demonstrating this argument, a stylized scene of the prophetic mission is effected, particularly focused upon the confessional passages (11.18-12.6) but not exclusively so (11.5b, 14; 13.1-11). In this stylized scene the prophetic mission functions as a mirror of the relationship between Israel and Yahweh. God and prophet are paralleled. The confessions provide a concrete illustration of the nation's apostasy, witnessing to the national refusal to heed the divine word; thus the confessions are an integral part of the development of a theodicy.

2. Jeremiah 15.10-21; 17.14-18

Introduction

In keeping with the observations put forward in the preceding section, the presence of new editorial superscriptions at 14.1 and again at 18.1 would mark off 14–17 as the compositional block into which the two confession complexes of 15.10-21 and 17.14-18 have been incorporated. Once again there is the need to accumulate verbal-thematic echoes, logical and redactional developments across the whole, in order to place this proposal upon a more secure footing.

In addition, our results from the previous discussion on 11.18–12.6 can now lend a more precise focus to the analysis of the present complex. That is to say, does the focus upon the issue of theodicy, including the incorporation of a stylized scene of the prophetic mission to further that end, continue to exercise a controlling role in the organization and development of the units contained in 14–17? And if so, has this been carried out basically in the same manner or have new elements and perspectives been introduced?

14-17: Overview of Units

In contrast to the preceding complex, the present one under discussion contains two confessional complexes. Because of this, it seems preferable to carry out the analysis in two halves related to each confession block (14–15; 16–17) for the sake of efficiency in discussion. But prior to this approach, we can examine first the individual units throughout 14–17 with particular interest in their order of occurrence and signs of catchword and thematic echoes which indicate purposefulness in the formation of the collection.

14.1–15.9

Discussion of the material preceding the first block of confessions (15.10-21) can be simplified somewhat, since a number of recent studies of the material have appeared which convincingly recognize the compositional artistry employed.[1] Crucial notice should be taken of the structure of the drought liturgies which consist of two cycles of national lament and divine response (14.2-10; 14.17–15.4) connected by prose oracles effected in a similar dialogical manner (14.11-16). The remaining poetic judgment oracle (15.5-9) should be considered an integral part of the drought section[2] related to the issues of whether pity/mercy is available for Israel (15.5-6). Explicit connections with the preceding seem indicated by the conjunction כי (15.5)[3] and numerous verbal echoes (שחת—15.6 ;ירושלים—15.4 /ירשלים—15.5; שחת—15.3; חרב—15.9/15.3).[4]

16.1–17.27

Passing over the confession block (15.10-21) for the moment, it is followed by an extended prose section which appears to represent a compositional unit.[5] First there is the passage closely related to other narratives of prophetic symbolic actions (16.1-9). In this case the three prohibitions related to marriage, mourning rites, and feasting serve as signs of the total and irrevocable destruction of the nation. Next, a further oracle is explicitly connected to the preceding one as a justification of the judgment which has been announced (על מה). In v. 10 כל הדברים האלה seems to refer to the preceding symbolic report, and important verbal echoes can also be detected (16.11, 12, 13—לא אתן לכם חנינה/16.7; אביו, אבותם—16.13/אבותיכם—16.3, 7; כום תנחומים, לא יפרסו . . . לנחמו). The series of judgment oracles is continued in vv. 16-18, but an oracle of hope comes between it and the previous unit. Again explicit effort to integrate the oracle of hope[6] into the present context seems indicated by v. 18 ראשונה, omitted by G, which effects a pattern of assured future hope but first unavoidable judgment.[7] Verbal echoes with the preceding for both vv. 14-15 and vv. 16-18 are present (ארמתם אשר נתתי לאבותם—16.15/ נחלתי, הארץ הזאת—16.18/ארצי—16.11, 12, 13—אבות, עונם—18 ,16.17; חטאתנו, עוננו—16.10 /חטאתם—16.18; שקוצים, תועבות/16.11, 13—אלהים / אחרים). Appended to this prose block is a small poetic fragment (16.19-21) which looks forward to Yahweh's acknowledgment and reverence in repudiation of their former gods by the idolatrous nations. It is possible that the themes of idolatry and prospect of invasion (צידים, דוגים) have attracted[8] this unit to its present location.[9] As such, it seems to effect a contrast between faithless Israel and the reverent foreign nations.

The remaining material of 17 reflects a very heterogeneous character. The first unit is a poetic judgment speech (17.1-4) followed by units exhibiting proverbial and liturgical characteristics (vv. 5-8; vv. 9-10; v. 11; vv. 12-13). Then the second confessional passage in 14-17 occurs (vv. 14-18) followed by the prose sermon

enjoining observance of the Sabbath (vv. 19-27). Discerning indications for their associative rationale is very problematic.[10] In light
of these problems, we will postpone the attempt to discern
connective lines until a more careful analysis has been carried
through below.

15.10-21; 17.14-18: Compositional Function

15.10-21

In the attempt to extend the compositional pattern of *Gerichtsbotschaft—Verfolgung—Klage* discerned in relation to the confessions in
11.18ff., 18.18ff., and 20.7ff., to the present passage, Thiel encountered
difficulties in the lack of an explicit report of *Verfolgung* in 14-15;
and, while the prose material in 14.1-15.4 certainly constitutes
Gerichtsbotschaft, its association with the double cycle of national
liturgies has apparently obscured the aforementioned pattern if in
fact it is a controlling feature in the redactional placement of the
confessions.[11] The attempts by Eichler and Ahuis to make precise,
and strengthen, Thiel's view also seem to be problematic.[12] In order
to have judgment speech heading the series, they both take 13.1-21 as
the first unit of the complex, which requires them to ignore the
superscription in 14.1. In addition, our previous discussion of 13 in
relation to 11-12 suggests that it is more properly connected with
that complex. And problems similar to that observed in the
discussion of 11.18-12.6 are present here since their pattern requires
the labelling of individual units in a manner which obscures their
actual character.[13] Once again one of the prophet's laments is
labelled as *Verfolgung Jeremias*, while the second lament is labelled as
such, *Klage Jeremias*. The *Klage des Volkes* is present, but the
structure of a double cycle is obscured.[14] And again the *Eintreffen des
Gerichts* is implicitly present only if the boundaries of the complex
are ignored and 13.22 can be legitimately included within its scope.[15]
Before a stylized scene of the prophetic mission can be successfully
described, a more accurate discussion of the pattern of literary units
in the complex is required.

The discussion of 15.10-21 and its relationship to the tightly
structured drought liturgy (14.1-15.9) can be aided by first attempting
to discern the overall compositional intention of the latter and its
manner of execution. In each of the laments (14.2-6, 17-18) the
nation is depicted suffering under calamity, drought, and war. The

nation's complaints (14.7-9, 19-22) are directed to securing Yahweh's saving mercy. Alongside acknowledgment of national sin (14.7, 20) come reproachful questions as to Yahweh's faithfulness (14.8, 9, 19) and entreaties couched in covenantal and temple-cultic theology (14.8—ישראל מקוה, צרה בעת מושיעו 14.9—יהוה בקרבנו ואתה, ;אל תפר בריתך, כסא כבודך—14.21; למען שמך—14.7, 21; ושמר עלינו נקרא 14.22—אלהינו ונקוה לך).[16] This juxtaposition of confession with reproach may indicate that in the perspective of the nation's lament the true party at fault is Yahweh. At least, the appeals based upon covenant and temple suggest that the nature of their sins is not so serious as to require legitimately the perpetuation of this chastisement.[17] The responding divine oracles (14.10; 15.1-4) bring each cycle of national complaint to its climax and focal point. Yahweh rejects their petition. The judgment is to be inescapable and total. It is the nation's apostasy which has brought this calamity upon them, not any breach of fidelity on Yahweh's part. The remaining material which connects the two liturgies and rounds them off (14.11-16; 15.5-9) only serves to underline the import of the divine rejection of mercy as a possibility for Israel. Jerusalem is beyond mercy (15.5-9) for even Yahweh's compassion must be withheld because of her rebellion. The mediatorial role of the prophet is prohibited as a further sign that the nation is beyond help (14.11-12). And those prophets who are proclaiming the contrary have not been sent by Yahweh (14.13-16). Their message is a falsehood leading themselves and the nation into total destruction. As with 11-13, it appears legitimate to see the issue of theodicy as the controlling concern in the structure of 14.1-15.9.[18] At a number of points the theodicy motif becomes explicit. The first is in the notice in 15.4b[19] about Manasseh (בגלל; cf. 2 Kgs 24.3; 23.26) and then in the disputational questions (potential or actual) of the prophet (14.13)[20] and the nation (15.2)[21] in response to the preceding announcement of judgment without mercy.

In light of the primary interest of this discussion the manner in which this concern for theodicy has been executed is particularly significant. The dialogical pattern of the passage depicts a dispute between Yahweh and the nation into which the person of the prophet has been drawn.[22] A particular interest of the composition is in Jeremiah's role as intercessor or mediator between the people and Yahweh, for the divine prohibitions of intercession (14.11; 15.1) interpret the preceding complaint of the nation as the intercessory utterance of the prophet.[23] And in the development of the double

cycle the prophet is shown in the attempt to move in solidarity with
the nation in its dispute (cf. 14.13 and 15.2) by the attempt to avert
the judgment and contest the refusal of mercy. The divine response
to the prophet's attempts demands an alternative posture of the
prophet in his execution of his office. The theodicy motif has been
worked out through a dramatic focus upon the nature of Jeremiah's
prophetic mission.[24] The redactional introduction of the theme of
false prophecy only serves to highlight further this interest in the
nature of the prophetic mission. Jeremiah's dispute is portrayed as
spurred on by the alternative model of the prophetic office supplied
by his prophetic opponents. The false prophets appear as the
negative foil against which Yahweh's will in relation to Jeremiah's
mission is set forth.[25] Once again it seems legitimate to see a stylized
scene of the prophetic mission being incorporated into the theodicy
intention.

At this point it becomes possible to discern the place of the
confessional block within this stylized scene. That the confessional
block does play a part in the continued development of the stylized
scene becomes a distinct possibility since it too consists of a double
cycle of complaint and divine response. Our earlier exegesis of the
passage sought to show that the focus of each of these confessions
was upon a crisis in the prophetic mission. Numerous allusions to the
prophet's call ranging from biting ironic misinterpretations of the
prophet to Yahweh's reassertion of the original terms of Jeremiah's
commission were noted (cf. 15.12, 20 to 1.18). The struggle of the
prophet with the nature of his mission depicted within the confessions
matches that discerned in 14.1–15.9. Additional connection with the
preceding appears to be evoked by the common imagery of affliction
employed in the laments (15.18—מאנה הרפא, מכתי אנושה, כאבי נצח/
14.17, 19—מכה נחלה מאד, מרפא, עת מרפא) and by the common
motivation of the accusations against Yahweh's fidelity against the backdrop of covenantal expectations (15.16—נמצאו דברך,[26] כי נקרא שמך עלי;
for 14.1–15.9 see the vocabulary listed above and cf. esp. 14.9, 21).[27]
And finally in the divine rebuke of 15.19, the instruction,
ישבו המה אליך ואתה לא תשוב אליהם, invites comparison with the
preceding injunctions prohibiting Jeremiah's intercessory activity on
behalf of the nation (14.11; 15.1). In his prophetic mission Jeremiah
is to be permitted one role in relation to the nation—that of
opposition (לחומת נחשת בצורה).

In the discussion of the stylized scene in 11–13 a parallelism between prophet and Yahweh was observed. The prophetic mission was made a mirror of Yahweh's relationship to Israel. On this view we are largely in agreement with Hubmann's understanding of the compositional intention. In his discussion of the compositional function for 15.10-21, he has sought to extend the same conclusions, as redactional expansions 15.13-14 and vv. 20-21 effect a parallelism between prophet and God. The prophet is designated as Yahweh's messenger, set in opposition to the nation. The nation's doom is sealed by their opposition to Yahweh's prophet.[28] Jeremiah is made the *Prüfstein* for the nation's relationship to Yahweh. His suffering at the hands of the nation is a sign of their apostasy. At the same time his life is an expression of Yahweh's abandonment of Israel to judgment.[29]

However, this perception seems to represent only partially the nature of the stylized scene being developed in 14–15. It reflects that portion of the picture put forward in the responses and actions of Yahweh (15.11-14, 19-21; 14.10-11; 15.1-4, 5-6) but fails to consider the dialogical pattern running through 14–15 in which the prophet is portrayed in dispute with Yahweh over the nature of his prophetic mission. The issue of the prophet's persecution as a sign of national apostasy which was so much at the centre of the stylized scene in 11–13 appears to have a more subordinate role in 14–15. The elements of the previous portrayal are there but with a different focus. At the centre of the present stylized scene lies the attempt by Jeremiah to execute an alternative understanding of his prophetic office—one more in keeping with the covenantal-temple cult expectations of the nation which expects the beneficial mediatorial activity of the prophet in line with the activities of his prophetic opponents. The theodicy concern is aided once again by the stylized scene of Jeremiah's prophetic mission. The prophet's attempt to escape the way laid out for his mission and to substitute another failed. The failure of this alternative understanding of the prophetic office to achieve its ends by securing the nation from judgment did not, however, mean that there was a fundamental failure in the prophetic office per se; instead this alternative understanding is shown to be false—not rooted in the will of Yahweh—and a major contributor to the nation's destruction. In contrast, the manner of Jeremiah's mission is vindicated as legitimate and the only exercise of the prophetic office commensurate with the serious and intractable character of the nation's apostasy. Attention directed toward a crisis in the understanding of prophetic mission depicted by a stylized scene of Jeremiah's prophetic ministry has been incorporated into the larger concern of legitimizing Yahweh's withdrawal of mercy from the nation.

Before considering the second confessional block in 14–17 (17.14-18), we must first consider the material in 16 for signs that it is meaningfully related to the preceding confession and the whole of the editorial complex of 14–15. An affirmative answer can be given for both issues for the bulk of the material in 16. The frequent practice of viewing the connection between the symbolic actions in 16.1-9 and 15.10-21 as an attempt to illustrate and to explain further the motif of the prophet's isolation and alienation from the rest of the nation seems correct (cf. esp. 16.8-9 and 15.16-17).[30] The images of birth and parenting (ילד, אם) span across 15.5-9, 10[31] and 16.1ff. The prophet's manner of life is forcefully portrayed as a divine symbol of the judgment upon Israel. In this way, a further assertion of Yahweh's intention for Jeremiah's prophetic office is made; and the prophet's complaint and struggle against such a destiny (15.10) receive additional refutation.[32] This last point also suggests that 16.1-9 have been integrated into their position with a view to the whole of the preceding stylized scene. Substantial connections with the themes of bereavement by sword and famine and pestilence—no mourning, no burial, no mercy—are present.[33] The dialogical pattern is at least marginally continued by the shift to 2nd pers. pl. direct address in 16.9a[34] and anticipated questioning response of the people in 16.10. And it is just at this point (16.10-13) that the theodicy issue emerges in an explicit fashion.[35] The remaining judgment speech may legitimately find connections beyond its location in 16.1ff. In relation to the latter it lends greater concretion to the nature of the calamity announced in vv. 10-13[36] as well as further developing the notice of the nation's sin as idolatry (16.10, 11). These associations are primary for the unit, but the imagery of hunters/fishers sent to destroy the nation invites comparison with 15.3 with the analogous picture of judgment superintended by the four destructive terrors.[37] However, the intrusive oracle of hope (16.14-15; cf. its double 23.7-8) and the poetic fragment (16.19-21) which appears related to it[38] seem to relate only to the immediate context. No connections with 14–15 seem observable, and the note of hope seems on the surface to proceed in a manner extraneous to the stylized scene developed to that point under the over-arching concern of theodicy.

17.14-18

In the overview of the material in 17, the heterogeneous character of the material was noted. As a result, the attempt to discern a coherent redactional rationale is rendered highly problematic. Recent commentators, with few exceptions, treat the passage as a hotchpotch of isolated units and proverbial sayings.[39] Thiel was compelled by the nature of the material to give up the attempt to discern his stylized scene of the Jeremianic preaching.[40] And even Ahuis's attempt to extend Thiel's approach appears to be at its weakest with regard to the inappropriate labelling of textual units and the virtual absence of crucial aspects of his scheme. Some, at best, can be discerned as present only in a very marginal manner.[41] Alternatively, Holladay's attempt to isolate a limited portion of the material in 17 and to see it as part of the confessional material (17.5-10) alongside 17.14-18 constituting the prophet's repentance demanded in 15.19 is also unsatisfactory.[42] In our previous review of Holladay's structural analysis, we raised serious questions about the validity of his so-called initial stratum of confessional and quasi-confessional material.[43] And while he has usefully drawn attention to the partially dialogical character of the material (17.9-10, 14-18), its dialogical character is not sufficient indication that it constitutes a confession. For, as we attempted to show for 17.12-13, the dialogical pattern appears related here to one between Yahweh and Judah,[44] not to mention the drought liturgies in 14-15 and citations of the *vox populi* elsewhere in the book. It is also unlikely that 17.5-8 as curse and blessing formulations[45] are to be taken as the prophet's personal affirmations in prayer to Yahweh of a new-found attitude of faith. The messenger formula (v. 5) suggests that the editorial focus of the verses is distinctly different—i.e. they are presented as prophetic proclamation. Finally, with this view one is still faced with the difficulty of leaving unexplained those units within the chapter classified as secondary additions. Why would the editors interject them into the 'confessional' context and thereby obscure the original pattern? An analysis which more carefully explains the nature of the dialogical portions and their interaction with the wisdom and judgment oracle units seems required.

In this regard, some of the observations of A.H.J. Gunneweg and T.H. Polk offer promise in supplying a way through these difficulties.[46] Both attempt to see in the juxtaposition of the various units the development of a contrast between the prophet and nation[47] in terms

of wisdom motifs related to righteous/wicked, wise/foolish, blessing/
curse. The prophet's confession is integrated into a structure in
which he is depicted as one of the righteous/wise who relies upon
Yahweh while the nation in its opposition to him and his word are
shown to be among those who reject wisdom by forsaking Yahweh
and thus deserve judgment. If this view is correct, once again it
would be proper to speak of a theodicy intention which has
manifested itself in the editorial arrangement of the units in which
the prophet is given exemplary status.

A number of factors would seem to lend support to the basic
insight of these two scholars. Within the confession itself great stress
is laid upon the prophet's innocence and reliance upon Yahweh
(17.14—תהלתי אתה; 17.14—מחסי אתה; v. 16) and upon the opposition
and contrast between him and the people, his opponents (17.15, 18).
This contrast is complemented by the preceding judgment oracles
directed against Judah (17.1-4, 12-13)[48] which emphasize the
implacability of the nation's sin, its idolatry (17.2) and false
confidence in the temple (17.12-13a).[49] Framed within these
judgment oracles is the material with wisdom affinities, especially
the blessing and curse formularies with their focus upon the
contrasting destinies of the wicked and righteous (17.5-8). These run
parallel to the contrast between prophet and nation and invite
attention to a possible critical interpretive function for vv. 5-11 in
relation to the surrounding material. This connection between the
two types of material seems particularly enhanced by the repetition
of key terms across the units.[50] The blessing and curse formularies
centre a man's destiny upon his trust in Yahweh with the curse
awaiting anyone who turns away from Yahweh (יסור לבו). The divine
affirmation of the following unit (17.9-10) repudiates any objection to
the validity of the preceding based upon the depraved deceitfulness
of the human heart (לב). Yahweh's perception and evaluation of the
individual for the requital of justice is unerring. And it is just this
divine accusation and condemnation of Judah's wayward heart
which is the focus of the judgment oracles (17.1—לבם; 17.13b—יסורי).
The proverb about the deceptive 'blessing' of unjustly acquired
wealth (17.11) seems to function analogously to vv. 9-10 by countering an alternative objection to vv. 5-8. That is to say, the prosperity
of a wicked man is no contradiction of the divine retributive activity
since such 'blessing' is ephemeral and ultimately will be shown to be
a way of folly.[51] Significant association with the judgment oracles

also seems present with the loss of wealth echoing the motif of despoliation in 17.1-4[52] and the verbal echo with עזב (cf. 17.12-13) suggesting a punishment-fitted-to-the-crime schema.[53]

Thus it seems legitimate to see 17.5-11 as supplying the central interpretive and organizing principles of the material in 17. The judgment speech directed against Judah is interpreted in terms of the ideas of divine retribution—the meting out of curse and blessing— with the nation viewed abstractly[54] as deserving the fate of the wicked due to the folly of her apostasy. As such it is still possible to discern a theodicy[55] intention in the arrangement of the individual units. In addition, the contrast developed between prophet and nation is interpreted in an abstract manner with the prophet's identification as the one deserving of blessing through his fidelity. As such the prophet is vindicated over against his opponents. The contextual association between vv. 5-11 and vv. 14-18 would appear to resolve the sense of threat voiced by the prophet in his complaint in an anticipatory manner[56] through its strong affirmation of a positive destiny for the prophet. This contrast and vindication of the prophet in face of his opponents raises the question of whether a stylized scene of the prophetic mission has once again been employed in the promotion of the theodicy concern. The striking contrast between the nature of the material employed here and that encountered previously in 11-13 and 14-15 could make one dubious at first glance. However, though much reduced compared to 14-15, some dialogical material can be detected in 17. Embedded in at least two places are citations of the nation rejecting the prophetic message of judgment (17.12-13a;[57] 17.15), and because of the contextual interconnectedness of the units it would seem legitimate to speak of a stylized scene in which prophet and nation are depicted in dispute over the message of judgment. The prophet announces the un- avoidable destruction of Judah due to her intransigent apostasy (17.1-4) and seeks to legitimize the announcement through appeal to the alternatives of blessing and curse with the implication that Judah has forfeited any claim to blessing (17.5-8). Potential objections are then pre-empted by the following two units (17.9-10;[58] 17.11) which lead to the second judgment oracle (17.12-13). The citation carries the response of the nation to the foregoing. In it is reflected the failure to acknowledge the preceding accusations. Instead, the prophet's message is countered by appeal to the false national hopes in Zion as Yahweh's throne—the guarantee of divine presence and

shelter from the shameful fate of the wicked who forsake their God.[59]
The dispute is continued by the divine pronouncement (יסורי).
Within the confession the situation of delayed fulfilment allows the
nation to challenge the legitimacy of Jeremiah's prophetic mission,
and the prophet's petition exercises itself in regard to this dispute
about who will be shamed (בוש)—they or he.[60]

This recognition of the concern to effect a stylized dispute related
to the prophetic mission may also provide the means to explain the
rationale for locating 17.19-27 at the end of the section. The
difficulty of providing a satisfactory explanation is not to be
minimized. Polk and Gunneweg exclude this passage from consideration, as do most commentators, since they can detect no
apparent lines of connection to the preceding.[61] However, of
particular interest is the form of the Sabbath sermon after the initial
exhortation to observe the Sabbath injunction. It is elaborated in the
form of a positive and negative alternative with the keeping of the
Sabbath the only positive (17.24-27) means for ensuring the
continued life of the nation.[62] It is here in the proclamation of the
alternatives of life and death for the nation that the stimulus and
rationale for the association of the unit with the preceding may lie.
For, once again, the wisdom motifs in vv. 5-11 may provide the major
editorial attraction for the prose sermon, epecially since the prophet
is depicted there proclaiming the alternatives of blessing and curse
(כה אמר יהוה—17.5). The effect upon the stylized scene would be the
presentation of the prophet as the righteous sage counselling and
instructing the nation in the way of wisdom and life over against
their present course of folly. The dialogical elements discussed
above, where the nation rejects the prophetic analysis and counsel,
would serve to show its implacable commitment to the negative
alternatives. In this regard, the occurrence of the term לקחת מוסר
(17.23) with its overwhelming rootage in wisdom literature[63] may
also be significant in providing a basis and stimulus for the editorial
exploitation of a potential association between the prose sermon and
the preceding wisdom motifs.[64]

Finally, a brief comment should be made relative to the connections
of stylized scene with the preceding materials in 14–16. Numerous
points of contact seem present which suggest that 17 should not be
viewed in an isolated manner. The most extensive verbal and
thematic connections are with the immediately preceding material in
16 (17.1, 3—חטאת/cf. 16.10, 18; 17.4—נחלה/cf. 16.18; 17.2—idolatry /

cf. 16.10-13, 16-18, 19-21; 17.10—כדרכיו / cf. 16.17; 17.18—משנה שברון/
cf. 16.18—שלם משנה; 17.12-13—עזב/cf. 16.11; 17.1, 5, 9-10—לב / cf.
16.12—שרורות לבו הרע; 17.19-27—Sabbath law / cf. 16.11—לא שמר תורה[65]).
Still, some connections with the material in 14-15 can be discerned
(17.8—בשנת בצרת / cf. 14.1—הבצרות; and also the common images of
devastated fertility between 17.5-8 and the drought liturgy; 17.12-
13—כסא כבוד, כסא כבוד/מקוה ישראל, מקוה ישראל—cf. 14.8, 21; and
possibly the doublets 17.3-4 / cf. 15.13-14; 17.11—unjust wealth / cf.
15.10—unjust profiteering[66]). The points of contact with the second
half of 16 link on to, and underpin, a section which we have already
noted exhibits an explicit theodicy concern.[67] Similarly the connections
with 14-15 also aid the overall concern to vindicate the judgment by
interpreting the drought and national devastation depicted in the
liturgies in terms of the reward or curse accruing to the wicked.

Summary

Thus, it is possible to view 14-17 as a complex, integrated with few
exceptions (16.14-15, 19-21) as is 11-13 by a theodicy intention
which has incorporated within it stylized scenes of the prophetic
mission. In this case, two distinct stylized scenes centred upon each
of the confessions is present. The first (14-16) depicts the prophet in
dispute with Yahweh over the nature of his prophetic mission. The
triumph of Yahweh's intention for the prophet spells doom for any
expectations of mercy for Judah. In the second scene (17) a dispute is
once again present, but this time between prophet and nation over
the latter's destiny. The nation's folly is illustrated by her rejection of
the prophetic instruction and counsel in the way of life and blessing.
Consequently, her doom is secured as the legitimate recompense for
her reprobate way of life. Thus the stylized scenes vindicate the
prophetic mission and message, thereby promoting the theodicy
concern. Each scene is executed with a different, though related,
perspective from that discussed in 11-13. Of particular interest is the
more abstract character of the scene in 17 where employment of
wisdom mofits lends a heightened exemplary status to the person of
prophet.

3. Jeremiah 18.18-23; 20.7-18

Introduction

In keeping with our previous practice, we take the superscriptions in 18.1 and 21.1 as marking out the next section[1] which functions as the immediate context for the two confessional blocks, 18.18-23 and 20.7-18.[2] Additional corroboration of this approach seems indicated by the distinct shift of thematic focus in 21-24 to that of the nation's corrupt leadership and the cessation of any additional confessional materials. It remains to discern additional internal signs of an integrated complex in 18-20. In this regard the satisfactory analysis of Thiel, followed in part by Hubmann, will enable our discussion of this section to be much briefer since we are in substantial agreement with their analyses, especially their elucidation of the stylized scenes of prophetic mission.

18-20: Overview of Units

The delineation of units for this section is fairly straightforward. In 18, apart from the confession itself (18.18-23), there are two other units. The initial prose unit (18.1-12) relates the prophetic symbolic action (cf. 13.1ff; 16.1ff.) of the prophet's visit to the potter. This is followed by a poetic oracle accouncing national destruction and exile as punishment for Israel's apostasy and idolatry (18.13-17). In partial anticipation of the discussion to follow, we notice that all three units appear to be linked together by two major factors: verbal echoes and a dialogical pattern. For the verbal links see: 18.13—שעררת / cf. 18.12-שררות לבם; 18.13—גוים / cf. 18.7-9—גוי; 18.15—כשל / cf. 18.23—; מחשבותנו, חשב מחשבה, חשב—18.11-12 / cf. 18.8, 11—חשב מחשבות; 18.18—כשל. 18.20—רעה, מובה / cf. 18.8, 10—הרעה, המובה. For the dialogical framework: the symbolic action builds to its conclusion in v. 11 of the divine pronouncement of judgment and call to repentance. This is followed immediately by the negative response of the addressees (v. 12—ויאמרו). The following poetic oracle (vv. 13-17) again represents divine speech and in addition the initial conjunction[3] (v. 13—לכן) would suggest that it is meant to constitute the divine response to v. 12. A change of speaker is once again introduced by the citation of v. 18 (ויאמרו) and is to be identified with those of v. 12.[4] And finally in response to the plot to bring the prophetic mission into disrepute

(v. 18) follows the prophet's complaint and petition (vv. 19-23).[5]

In a manner similar to 18, the remaining units of 19-20 are bound together by an overall framework in addition to the verbal echoes. The bulk of the material consists of prose (19.1-20.6) with the only poetic portion that of the confessional block (20.7-18). For the prose units it is possible to discern an over-arching framework which ties them together. This time it is primarily a narrative one instead of dialogical. The first prose unit (19.1-13) consists again of a prophetic symbolic action concerning the smashing of a clay jar (19.1-2, 10-11a) interwoven[6] with sermonic judgment oracles (19.3-9, 11b-13). The next unit (19.14-15) provides the temporal and topical shift from the preceding episode, along with a prose judgment oracle that creates the transition[7] to the following unit and episode (20.1-6). The latter depicts the prophet in conflict with Pashur and provides an accompanying vindicatory judgment speech.[8] For the verbal links across this prose material see: התפת—מהתפת/cf. 19.6, 11b-13; 19.15—העיר הזאת/cf. 19.8, 11a, 12; 19.15 — הנני מביא רעה על/אל/cf. 19.3—הנני מביא רעה על; 20.1—את הדברים האלה/cf. 19.15; 20.1, 6— נבא/cf. 19.14—נבא; 20.5—העיר הזאת/cf. as cited above at 19.15; 20.4—בית יהוה—20.1; והפלתים בחרב לפני איביהם—20.7/cf. ונפלו בחרב איביהם cf. 19.14—בית יהוה. While the confessional block does seem to break the narrative framework, it also seems to introduce the prophet's response to the preceding conflict episode (note the verbal/thematic links: 20.10—מגור מסביב/cf. 20.3, 4—למגור, מגור מסביב; 20.7-8 persecution theme/cf. 20.2—episode of stocks).

Finally, the substantial links between 18 and 19-20 should also be observed providing further indication that an overall complex has been constructed. The most significant links relate to the potter/pottery motifs:[9] 19.1—בקק; 19.7—בקבק יוצר/cf. 18.1-6—יוצר; 19.11— כלי/cf. 18.4—כלי היוצר; 19.11—יצר רעה על/cf. 18.11—שבר הבקבק; 18.4—ושב ויעשהו כלי אחר/cf. אשר לא יוכל להרפה עוד— But other potential links seem present as well: 19.7—עצה יהודה וירושלים/cf. 18.21—גיא ההרגה; 19.6—עצתם, 18.23—עצה, 18.18—מחשבותנו—18.12; לשמה—18.16—שרק, ישם כל עובר עליה, לשרקה, לשמה; 19.8—הרג; 18.17—ערף ולא פנים אראם/cf. הקשו ערפם—19.15; ישם כל עובר עליה, שריקה; ואמרו—18.12, לבלתי שמע בקולי—18.10/cf. לבלתי שמוע את דברי—19.15; כשל—20/cf. 18.15, 20—כשל; 20.11—אל נקשיבה אל כל דבריו—18.18, נואש.

18.18-23 and 20.7-18: Compositional Function

The attempt by Thiel to see the confessions incorporated into

stylized scenes of the prophetic mission seems particularly appropriate
for the two blocks under immediate discussion. The general pattern
of *Gerichtsbotschaft—Verfolgung—Klage* finds its reflection in Thiel's
detailed analysis of material: *Anlass* (18.1-4; 19.1f.)—*Gerichtswort*
(18.5-17; 19.3-15)—*Verfolgung* (18.18; 20.1-6)—*Klage* (18.19-23;
20.7-12, 14-18).[10] However, this analysis requires certain additional
observations and qualifications if it is not to misrepresent two major
concomitant features of the patterning in 18–20. For efficiency of
discussion we will treat 18 and 19–20 separately.

18.1-23
As it stands, Thiel's pattern analysis for this chapter could obscure
the dialogical framework noted above which lends the stylized scene
its peculiar dynamic.[11] The scene presents a dispute between Yahweh
and Israel into which the prophet has been drawn. Within the scene
Yahweh and prophet are paralleled over against the nation.[12] The
nation's refusal of the summons to repent (v. 12) parallels their
rejection of the prophetic mission (v. 18).[13] The development of the
theodicy motif appears to be the controlling purpose of the stylized
scene. This becomes most explicit with the judgment oracle of
vv. 13-17. The latter's announcement of unremitting destruction
(v. 17b)[14] is presented as the direct consequence (v. 13—לכן) of the
preceding refusal of repentance (v. 12).[15] In this regard, the declaration
of divine sovereignty (v. 6)[16] and the explanation of Yahweh's
handling of a nation for רעה or טובה (vv. 7-10) also seem directed to
legitimizing the following announcement of judgment. In other
words, it defends the basis on which Yahweh could conceivably
entertain רעה for his own people.[17] As such, it provides the basis upon
which the ensuing dialogue is generated. The nation's refusal of
repentance (v. 12) logically progresses to the stated intention of
throwing the prophetic mission itself into disrepute as they contest
(נכהו בלשון) the prophetic proclamation (דבריו) of unremitting doom
(vv. 13-17).[18] The incorporation of the prophet's complaint into this
progression is fully appropriate according to our understanding of
v. 20aα (הישלם תחת טובה רעה; cf. רעה/טובה in 18.7-11) as a further
citation of his national opponents, contesting the possibility of any
purpose other than טובה for Israel on Yahweh's part.[19] The effect of
this stylized scene then would be to underscore once again the
validity of Israel's destruction at Yahweh's hands as the deserved,
inescapable punishment for her incorrigible impenitence.[20]

19.1–20.18

The close similarity is to be recognized between this section and the previous one in 18 and to a lesser extent that detected in 11–13 in presenting a picture of the preaching activity of the prophet falling upon deaf ears and issuing, as a consequence, in severe attacks upon and persecution of Jeremiah.[21] Nevertheless, the peculiar feature of the narrative framework binding all of the units together in 19.1–20.18 must be observed alongside Thiel's general pattern.[22] Particularly in need of modification is the *Verfolgung* section of Thiel's pattern (20.1-6); for in contrast to an open-ended report of the prophet's persecution (cf. 18.18) this one also includes a vindicatory oracle effecting a resolution to the report. The narrative begins with the symbolic action at the valley of Ben Hinnom (19.1-13) with the prophetic proclamation formulated[23] by a heaping up of general to specific accusations (centred on the nation's idolatry) and announcements of doom.[24] The shift of scene of the narrative to the temple court begins transitionally in vv. 14-15, again accompanied by a very brief prophetic oracle. The announcement of judgment itself is formulated in a general and summary fashion, and it is possible that the phrase כל הרעה אשר דברתי (v. 15a) refers to the catalogue of pronouncements in the preceding scene (1-13).[25] In this case the accusation is encapsulated in the unwillingness to heed the prophetic proclamation (v. 15b): כי הקשו את ערפם לבלתי שמע את דברי. The following narrative development (20.1-6) reporting the official opposition to Jeremiah's mission provides a concrete illustration of the nation's refusal to heed Yahweh (20.1—הדברים האלה). The accompanying oracle (vv. 3-6) vindicates the prophet in this conflict and illustrates the representative character of Pashur's action since it spells the doom for the whole nation. The concept of false prophecy is expanded to include even the attempt to silence Yahweh's messenger (אשר נבאת להם בשקר). With this latter note, the narrative of this stylized scene in the prophetic mission shows that it is particularly oriented to illustrate the nation in dispute over the prophetic word.[26] The theodicy concern appears once again to be served by this. The nation's doom was unavoidable because of her idolatry and unwillingness to heed Yahweh's warnings (19.15), concretely demonstrated by her opposition to the prophetic mission of Jeremiah.[27]

Strictly speaking, the narrative aspect of the stylized scene comes to a conclusion at 20.6 The recent work of G. Wanke has ably illustrated the parallels of this narrative sequence with some of the narratives elsewhere in the book. The pattern of narrated conflict situation in the prophetic mission resolved by a vindicating oracle in Jeremiah's favour is paralleled particularly by the narratives in 26–29, 36 (cf. esp. 28.15b, 16b; 29.31, 32b).[28] Wanke sees the focus of this narrative pattern upon the prophetic proclamation and its confirmation and vindication as true (*die Wahrheit der Verkündigung des Propheten Jeremia*).[29] By form and content, this block of narratives is to be distinguished from those in 37–43 which focus instead upon the prophet's experience of suffering in the concern to depict what it meant for Jeremiah to be a prophet (*die Wirklichkeit der prophetischen Existenz Jeremias*).[30] However, he did not consider in his discussion of 19.1–20.6 the association of the following confessional block with it. The presence of the incorporation of the latter into the narrative block seems to require some modification of Wanke's views for this passage and aids in the recognition of the compositional function provided by the confession. The verbal echoes (esp. מגור מסביב 20.3, 10) noted above between the confessional block and the preceding narrative provides indication that a catchword principle of association is at least in operation in the juxtaposition of the units. That a more explicit editorial concern is present seems indicated by the zero variant in G for 20.3, מסביב. The expansion in MT suggests a concerted attempt to strengthen the link betwen the two passages. With the incorporation of the confession into the narrative pattern, not only is a parallelism of pattern effected with 18 but also just that element of interest in the prophetic experience itself, alongside the prophetic proclamation, is introduced, which Wanke found to be characteristic of the narratives in 37–43 and not 26–29, 36.[31] As a result, the confessional block provides a stereoscopic effect with the preceding events. Not only is a scene of conflict described but the prophet's internal response and reflection upon it is constructed. Nevertheless, the content of the complaint is fully compatible with the import of the preceding dispute in its strident affirmation of the triumph of the divine word over all opposition and the expected vindication of the prophet. It would seem that the stylized scene within 19.1–20.18 now incorporates both of the thematic strands observed by Wanke (*Wahrheit* and *Wirklichkeit*).

Finally, as in 14–17 so in 18–20, two stylized scenes have been incorporated. However, in the latter the two scenes seem to be constructed in a much tighter relationship to one another. The

nature and extent of the verbal connections[32] noted above are a
strong indication of this, especially in the common potter/pottery
motifs. However, it also seems likely that this is more than just
simple catchword association. A broadly conceived narrative
progression appears discernible integrating the whole of 18–20
together. In the first portion of the complex (18) the dispute ends in
an unresolved manner with the petition of the prophet for vindication
and deliverance remaining unanswered. It is possible that the
following section (19.1-13) represents the editorially created answer[33]
with its ensuing narrative development (19.14–20.18) as the means of
bringing the dispute to its climax and conclusion. The resumption of
the potter/pottery imagery would aid such a connection and the
nature of the disaster announced echoes the content of the petition
within the confession. As such, the nature of the imprecations would
be clarified as not merely outbursts demanding personal revenge but
pleas for the fulfilment of the prophetic message upon a deserving
nation. And alternatively, the judgment speech would be clarified as
the necessary vindication and deliverance of Yahweh's loyal prophet.[34]
In this regard, corroboration of the proposal seems provided by the
alternate reading of the incipit, 19.1, by G as τοτε ειπε κυριος προς
με (אז אמר יהוה אלי) instead of MT, כה אמר יהוה. The reading in G
indicates a logical and possibly temporal relation to the preceding
and this links 18 into the following narrative sequence.[35] Whether or
not this represents a better reading is not clear, but at least it suggests
an interpretive move clarifying the contextual connections.[36]

Summary

Jeremiah 18–20 represents a complex characterized by a theodicy
intention. This has been achieved primarily through the composition
of stylized scenes of the prophetic mission (18; 19.1-20.18) articulated
through dialogue and narrative. The central focus of each scene is
upon the nation or one of its official representatives in dispute with
Jeremiah over the prophetic word. Jeremiah's message is rejected
outright and results in the attempt to silence his prophetic activity.
The confessions have been incorporated into the scenes in a way
which integrates the two stylized presentations together setting out
the prophet's plea for vindication and the assurance of the same
hand-in-hand. The overall effect is to provide an emphatic defence of
Jeremiah's prophetic mission, supplying a resounding rebuke to the

attempt to oppose Yahweh's word mediated through him, and providing concrete demonstration of the nation's incorrigible rebellion which rendered its destruction unavoidable before Yahweh.

Chapter 4

SYNTHESIS: 11-20 AS AN INTEGRATED LITERARY WHOLE

Introduction

In the exegesis of individual confessions numerous difficulties arose related to meaning and intention which pressed us to consider their contextual utilization. The initial stages of this exploration led us to examine their present literary sequence with the result that a double-cycled series appeared to be present. However, intervening materials and the ambiguous character of 20.14-18 presented problems to the validity of our analysis. So it was proposed that a legitimate contextual reading of the confessions would have to be carried out along a double axis—that of their literary sequence and immediate literary context. The assessment of this proposal and its impact on the interpretation and significance of the confessions must be the task of the present discussion.

The Validity of the Double-Axis Schema

The results of the two lines of exploring the contextual utilization of the confessions suggest the compatibility and co-ordination of the sequential pattern with that of the stylized scenes. In regard to the sequential pattern two progressive cycles (11.18-15.21; 18.18-20.18) were detected which are connected to one another by a transitional passage (17.14-18) and by concluding units possessing a synoptic character spanning the whole of the two cycles (20.7-13; 20.14-18). At the centre of the first cycle was the presentation of a dispute between the prophet and Yahweh over the nature of the prophetic mission. The second cycle shifted this focus to depict a dispute

between prophet and nation over the fate of his prophetic message
(i.e. as this held out the prospect of the nation's negative fate) which
was challenged and rejected by the nation. The transitional passage
(17.14-18) not only brought the preceding cycle to a close by
indicating the prophet's relinquishment of his dispute over his
mission, but it also initiated the ensuing cycle by raising the problem
of his message compromised and questioned before the eyes of the
nation. The final synoptic unit (esp. 20.7-13) once again linked the
two cycles together by mirroring the key issues in the course of both
progressions. It was the very nature of the prophet's mission and
message which became the basis for resolving the crisis points in
both cycles and brought them to a conclusion.

If the place of each confession within the stylized scene is now
compared to this preceding sequential pattern, a basic compatibility
and coordination of the two patterns can be observed. In the first
progressive cycle, the initial confessions (11.18-23; 12.1-6) begin a
dispute over the prophetic mission which has the delay in a promise
of vindication as its catalyst (12.1-4; cf. 11.21-23). In this part of the
cycle the prophet is challenged to consider the nature of his mission
as a mirror of the conflict between Yahweh and Israel (12.5-6). It is
precisely the latter feature which is reproduced at the level of the
stylized scene effected in 11-13. In order to promote the development
of a theodicy argument, the nation's negative response to the
prophetic mission is portrayed. Their attempt to oppose and to
destroy Jeremiah is a sign and consequence of their faithlessness to
the covenant relationship with Yahweh. The alienation and hostility
which Yahweh experiences from his people (12.7-13) display themselves against Yahweh's prophet. Conversely, Yahweh's intention to
judge Judah without mercy is displayed in the manner of the
prophetic mission by the prohibited intercession (11.14) and the
symbolic action of the linen waistcloth (13.1-12).

The remaining units of the first progressive cycle (15.10-12; 15.15-
21) intensify the dispute between prophet and Yahweh. The crisis
occasioned by the nature of the prophetic mission now occupies the
centre of attention and comes to its climax. The prophet, suffering
from the alienation and hostility of his community (15.10, 17) and a
sense of betrayal by Yahweh (15.18) occasioned by the nature of his
prophetic task, attempts to abandon the mission. Yahweh contests
the prophet's complaint, rebuking his bitter 'misinterpretations' of
the same and prohibiting the prophet from pursuing any course other

than that previously outlined for him if he is to continue as Yahweh's spokesman (15.11-14; 15.19-21). Ironically, it is only in the continued opposition of prophet over against Israel in his prophetic task that any hope of deliverance is offered. Again this dispute is paralleled at the level of the stylized scene in 14–16. For there, in support of the theodicy argument, the prophet is depicted in the attempt to exercise an alternative understanding of the prophetic mission in solidarity with the nation's attempt to avert Yahweh's wrath and secure mercy (14.1–15.4). The divine response (14.10-12, 14-16; 15.1-4) at every point rejects this attempt, prohibiting the prophet from any role other than one which signals the unavoidable destruction of Judah (16.1-9; 15.19b). As in the progressional sequence so in the stylized scene the prophet is depicted in dispute with the preceding definition of his mission outlined in 11–13.

Similarly, the transitional function detected for 17.14-18 at the sequential level seems to be matched at the level of the stylized scene. With reference to Cycle One, the confession presents the prophet once again appealing for the fulfilment of the message of judgment rather than attempting to avert it (17.14, 18b). No attempt is made to escape the mission (17.16), and the threat of discomfiture in the terms of his original commission is fended off (17.17-18a). Correspondingly, the stylized scene in 17 portrays the prophet once again in conflict with the nation. In the attempt to defend his proclamation of judgment (17.1-4) he counsels the nation in the way of life and death (17,5-11, 19-27) only to meet a total rebuff (17.12-13a). In this dispute over the fate of the nation, the prophet and Judah are contrasted with each other as the righteous versus the wicked with the prospect of the reward appropriate to each. Judah clings to the folly of its hopes in the Zion/temple theology and rejects the possibility of shame. The prophet, however, no longer attempts to exercise his office in solidarity with national desires.

This latter consideration also raises the point which exhibits the transitional character of 17.14-18 with regard to Cycle Two as well as its co-ordination with the stylized scenes in 18-20. The focus of Cycle Two upon the fate of the prophetic message is developed particularly in the series of citations beginning in 17 in which the nation's opposition and hostility to it are depicted in an increasing attempt to compromise its validity and to silence its bearer as a false prophet (17.15; 18.18, 20aα; 20.10). The three stylized scenes in 17, 18–20 are co-ordinate with this progression, depicting the identical dispute in response to the prophetic proclamation. The dispute portrayed in 17 is illuminated by the citation in 17.15 indicating the delay in fulfilment as a further basis for the nation's challenge of the message of doom. The stated intention to disregard and to contest the Jeremianic mission (18.18), grounded as it is in the outright rejection of judgment as a conceivable prospect (18.20aα), has been integrated into and co-ordinated with the stylized dialogue in which the nation rejects the call to repentance (18.12) which was grounded in the very explanation of Yahweh's way of טובה and רעה which the nation rejects (18.20aα). Then the plot to induce (פתה) the prophet to make censorable utterances in order to silence him (20.10) parallels the narrative scene in 19–20 which illustrates the official punitive action of Pashur in response to the preceding utterances of Jeremiah. The climactic and synoptic character of 20.7-13, which sets forth the triumph of the prophetic word against all opposition not only in dictating the manner of the prophetic mission but also in overcoming the nation's opposition to it, correlates with the climax of the narrative scene which sets forth an oracle vindicating the prophet and sealing the doom of his opponents at the same time (20.3-6). Further, the detected narrative framework integrating the two scenes of 18 and 19–20 into one complex matches the extent of the second progressive cycle of individual confessional units.

Finally, this pattern of two co-ordinated axes renders possible an explanation for the ambiguity of meaning encountered in the exegesis of 20.14-18. On the level of internal exegesis, a firm decision could not be reached for understanding the passage as either a self-curse in response to personal suffering or as a more objectified response to the unavoidable nature of Israel's doom and the prophetic mission as a harbinger of it. As a consequence, difficulties in the investigation of the literary sequence of the confessions were encountered. Given the synoptic and climactic character of 20.7-13 which seemed to resolve the issues of the double cycle in a triumphant manner, how was a second synoptic unit to be explained which appeared to conclude the series with an abrupt negative shift that seems to conflict with the tenor of the preceding? The immediate juxtaposition of 20.14-18 to 20.7-13 advises against excluding it from consideration in regard to the confessional series. But in light of our proposed double-axis pattern, the ambiguity of the unit may be seen in a more positive light—i.e. as a factor promoting its dual employment within the progressive cycles and within the stylized scene. In this regard, the more objective view seems most appropriate at the level of the confessional series as the immediate response and conclusion to the preceding declaration about the prophetic word. On the other hand, the more subjective reading of the unit seems to relate best as a function within the stylized scene 18–19 providing a further stereoscopic perspective of the prophet's response to the Pashur incident.

Thus the model of the two-axis schema permits the perception and interpretation of 11–20 as an integrated literary whole. By it, the validation problems presented by the intervening materials and the ambiguous character of 20.14-18 for the attempt to discern significance in the serial arrangement of the confessions receive an adequate solution. The only materials which seem extraneous to the compositional rationale are the oracles of hope in 11–13 (12.14-17) and 14–17 (16.14-15, 19-21). However, their presence does not seem fatal for our proposal since on first glance they appear to have been added on the basis of a separate and more restricted editorial rationale akin to that observable in other locations such as the prose 'commentary' in 3.[1] Our argument that 11–20 represent an integrated literary complex appears to receive further confirmation from the recent structural observations of Ahuis.[2] He has attempted to detect a concentric patterning of selected doublets (*Doppelüberlieferungen*) and allusions (*Anspielungen*) spanning the whole of 11–20 with 17.5-11 occupying the centre of the structure and providing the central thesis of it.[3] However, though attractive and compatible with our own proposals, his suggestion is not entirely convincing since the selection of texts passes over others equally appropriate but whose inclusion seems to obscure the concentric pattern.[4] Nevertheless, setting his concentric pattern aside, the numerous verbal links, allusions, and especially the doublets, do seem to sustain a cross-referencing function which enhances the appearance of 11–20 as a well-integrated literary composition.

The Double-Axis Pattern and the Theodicy Theme

Metaphorically speaking, the overall effect of the double-axis pattern could be styled as a prophetic drama.[5] For as a play, which apart from minor scenic comments relies primarily upon dialogue in order to create a sense of narrative development, so the literary complex 11–20 narrates or portrays the course of Jeremiah's prophetic mission as a dialogue in which prophet, Yahweh, and nation are the participants. The remaining task before us is to assess briefly the meaning and purpose of this portrayal. Our analysis of the stylized scenes in 11–13, 14–17, and 18–20 already permits an initial observation on this score, since in each case the theodicy theme suggested itself as the central, controlling principle in the composition.[6] And in retrospect a similar state of affairs appears to hold for the literary sequence. The co-ordination of the double progressive cycles with the stylized scenes makes this possible. The whole tenor of the sequence, with its picture of a crisis in the nature of the prophetic mission and conflict over the prophetic message resolved in the triumph of the divine word and intention for the prophet and against the nation, offers confirmation for the latter possibility. In both aspects of the double axis a justification for the destruction of Israel is offered which points to the incorrigible faithlessness and alienation of the nation in its relationship to Yahweh. The hopelessness of this situation is crystallized by the nation's response of obdurate rejection and opposition to Jeremiah's mission. The desperate nature of the national sinfulness, thus exposed, required a merciless, unavoidable judgment mirrored and presaged in the manner of the prophetic mission itself—i.e. as Yahweh's representative the prophet is permitted only the posture of combatant toward the nation as a sign of Yahweh's resolute intention to judge.

If this view of the theodicy function for the double-axis pattern is correct, then much that is characteristic in the normal approach to reading the confessions needs modification. While the increased appreciation for the stereotyped and traditional character of the language employed in the confessions has properly required a major adjustment from the older psychologically oriented exegesis to one that is more theologically formulated, the primary interest in the paradigmatic significance of the confessions has remained constant. On this reading, the confessions witnessed to the incorporation of the person or humanity of the prophet into his message. As such, they provide a model seen variously as one of personal spirituality or prayer,[7] or of the prophet as pastor exhibiting both the solidarity and empathy with his nation and the faithfulness to Yahweh's will that were required by his mission,[8] or especially in recent literature, as a model of obedient suffering;[9] and in the latter sense the confessions are comparable to the so-called Baruch narratives seen as a *Leidensgeschichte*.[10]

However, the incorporation of the confessions into the double-axis pattern would suggest that the previous approach to reading the confessions has pinpointed the primary significance of these texts in a manner which disregards the contextual framework in which they were placed, thus distorting the nature of the compositional interest in them. Though we have not followed Ahuis in his formal and redactional analysis of the confessions and their place within the stylized scenes, it is to his credit that he seeks to explore their contextual relationships and editorial employment in order to validate his view that Jeremiah is portrayed as a suffering servant in support of parenetic purposes.[11] Yet if our perception of their contextual utilization is correct, it is not their paradigmatic significance which is uppermost. In other words, it is not the personal experience of the prophet in the context of his mission per se and its value for the depiction of Jeremiah as an exemplary spiritual figure which lie at the heart of the editorial interest. Instead, the portrayal of the prophetic mission represents an element in the promotion of the theodicy theme and is subordinate to it.

The inadequacy of an exclusively paradigmatic reading of the confessions, even though theologically formulated and purged of psychologizing tendencies, is that it continues to treat the confessions as just that—a type of spiritual biography[12] with a theological and hortatory focus—when their contextual utilization has assigned them a more apologetic role rather than the purely biographical. Our criticism offered and the shift of focus suggested are parallel to the criticisms of interpretations of the so-called Baruch narrative as primarily biographical in import and more specifically viewed as a 'passion narrative' (*Leidensgeschichte*) of the prophet.[13] Just as it is the manner in which those narratives have been executed—that is, their inclusion of certain details and omission of others—which argues that more than a biographical interest is involved, so the confessions argue for an analogous adjustment in order to achieve a more appropriate reading of them. Repeatedly in the attempt to expound the individual confessional units the crucial role of their present contextual setting was indicated for the resolution of ambiguities and the fixing of meaning so that the necessity of investigating these contextual relationships was pressed upon us. As a result, a very deliberate and complex editorial activity was elucidated revealing the double axis as the primary contextual framework for the confessions with the theodicy theme as its central focus. Attempts to read the confessions apart from this context fail to interpret these texts in a manner which adequately considers the regulatory role of their contextual utilization.

But the question still remains whether this contextual framework of the double-axis pattern, and thus the editorial activity, has excluded the discernment of multiple levels of meaning within the confessions. In this regard the study of the confessions by R.P. Carroll would argue that the nature of these texts requires a 'multiplex hermeneutic' that allows for a number of levels of meaning in each particular confession.[14] The complexity of the editorial portrayal of the prophet has combined too many diverse elements from the tradition to allow a limitation of meaning to one perspective.[15] Carroll has in mind particularly the combination and interpenetration of individual and collective images which, for him, require an interpretation of the confessions in a dual aspect. So the referent of each confession is not only the prophet as victim and object of persecution but also the exilic community voicing its reaction to the circumstances of the exile.[16] While he is correct to note the applicability of the lament imagery in the confessions to both individual and corporate referents, their actual contextual employment, according to our analysis, would appear to rule out such a double sense as he has attempted to develop. It may be legitimate to see a potential association between prophet and nation based on the use of common imagery in the depiction of both, but the stylized scenes and double cycle progression have exploited the potential parallelization only to emphasize the contrast and non-representativeness between prophet and nation. This holds true particularly for the section 14–17 where the strongest parallelization in the type of imagery used as well as in the 'action' of the stylized scene occurs only to serve the emphatic point of dissociation and non-representativeness for the prophet and Israel. The type of polyvalence suggested by Carroll seems excluded by the double-axis pattern. His approach falters by failing to consider seriously enough the nature of the compositional or editorial employment of the confessions.[17] If an argument for polyvalence in the confessions and in the complex 11–20 is going to succeed, then it must do so with proper regard to the regulatory and excluding role offered in the presence of the double-axis pattern, focused upon the theodicy theme. And even so, the discovery of additional levels of meaning will have to result from the accumulative presence of features within the integrated literary complex, 11–20,

that impel one to speak of sub-themes subordinated to the primacy of
the theodicy theme and unexhausted by it.

Given the preceding discussion of the central focus of the double-
axis pattern and the qualifications imposed on the problem of
multiple levels of meaning, the presence of three legitimate sub-
themes seems discernible: prophetic conflict, prophetic iconoclasm,
and prophetic paradigm. All three themes are not only intertwined
closely with the central theodicy theme but also with each other. The
first concerns the problem of true and false prophecy.[18] The theme
emerges explicitly in five places (11.21—לא תנבא בשם יהוה; 14.13-
16—הנה הנביאים; 18.18—דבר מנביא; 20.6—נבאת להם בשקר; 20.10—
אולי יפתה) but presses for observation implicitly through the major
attention devoted to depicting the nature of Jeremiah's prophetic
mission. The double-axis pattern combines these elements into a
conceptualization of the prophetic office which presents Jeremiah as
a model of the true prophet of Yahweh.[19] Chief stress is laid upon the
reality of Jeremiah's divine commission (שלח; cf. 14.13-16) and the
absolute necessity of his fidelity to the terms and strictures of it. The
emphasis of the stylized scenes roots this fidelity in Jeremiah's
exclusive role of representing Yahweh's part in the struggle against
the nation. As such, he is the promoter and guardian of the covenant
relationship (11.1-17). Even the failure of Jeremiah to effect a
successful prophetic intercession, which otherwise could constitute a
legitimate expectation (cf. 27.18)[20] and thus avert the judgment, is
rooted in the prophet's loyalty to a divine interdict and not the
demonstration that Jeremiah himself was false to the prophetic task.
A note of realism is introduced into the model through recognition of
the susceptibility to subversion and perversion of the prophetic
mission. The prophet risks forfeiture of his commission as a true
spokesman through his struggle to escape the divine call (20.9; 15.15-
18) or to exercise an alternative understanding of the mission (14-17)
within the context of the coercive activity of his audience aided by
the delayed fulfilment of his proclamation and his membership in the
very community to which he has been sent.[21] However, this threat to
true prophecy is resolved by an understanding of the divine word as
an invincible power over against any threats presented by the
prophetic person or his community. With this understanding of
Jeremiah as a true prophet, it then becomes possible to expound the
concept of false prophecy as fundamentally any kind of attempt to
oppose or to subvert Jeremiah's ministry (20.6) as an implied claim

to possession and support of an alternative word. This ties the theme of prophetic conflict directly back into the theodicy theme.[22]

The second sub-theme, prophetic iconoclasm, refers to the dispute with, and refutation of, popular theology and expectations. It relates to the preceding theme since it indicates an additional element in the execution of Jeremiah's mission which involved him in conflict. The popular theology and expectations provided additional support for the attempt to discredit and to subvert the prophetic mission, and they even play a part in the representation of the prophet's own struggle with the mission. In addition, this theme is intricately connected with the theodicy theme since the successful vindication of the nation's judgment depends in part on the refutation of a misdirected confidence and exploitation of important traditions within Israelite faith. It is most visible in the citations of the *vox populi*[23] and the communal laments. The bulk of the citations report responses of shock, questioning, incredulousness, threat and rejection of Jeremiah's announcements of doom (15.2—אנא נצא; 13.22; 16.10— 11.21—; הישלם תחת טובה רעה —18.20aα ;לא יראה—12.4b ;על מה/מדוע לא תנבא; 18.12, 18; 20.10). The basis for this overall response appears to be correlated with the nation's firm conviction of Yahweh's fidelity to the choice of a special people and the Zion-temple cult as the guarantee of the divine presence, reflected especially in the communal laments and hymnic affirmations (14.7-9, 19-22; 17.12-13a). This conviction was corroborated in the proclamation of Jeremiah's prophetic opponents (14.13—שלום אמת) and by the delayed fulfilment of his own pronouncements (17.15). This problem posed by popular expectations is reflected more implicitly in the prophet's own struggle to escape and/or to alter his mission, especially in the first progressive cycle (11.18-15.21) and the stylized scene of 14–15. Much of the focus in the crisis at this point is the challenge represented by the nature of Jeremiah's prophetic mission, as this conflicted with the prophet's own expectations of divine faithfulness and justice (12.1-4; 15.10; 15.15-18) and of his own attempts to secure the nation's deliverance in intercession (14.1-15.4).[24] The failure of the prophet's attempts plus demonstration of the desperate character of Israel's sinfulness, cloaked by a superficial piety, constitute the emphatic refutation of these misplaced hopes and expectations.

The third theme, prophetic paradigm, returns us to a level of meaning which we scrutinized earlier. On the one hand it was necessary to argue that this theme was not to be seen as the central one in the editorial employment of the confessions; but on the other, numerous factors argue against its total exclusion from consideration and for its presence as a sub-theme within the complex.[25] Thus it becomes impossible to account for so much interest in portraying the prophet's personal reactions, struggles, and experiences within his mission. A concerted attempt has been made to construct a portrait of the prophet by use of the typical categories associated with the righteous, innocent supplicant of Yahweh and then to set him over against the nation as the epitome of the typical category unrighteous/ wicked. This is most explicit in the abstractly formulated stylized scene in 17 with its employment of the two ways of blessing/curse, righteousness/wickedness, wisdom/folly. In brief, the prophet is set forward as an exemplary pious-righteous man, as an exemplary Israelite and follower of Yahweh, and finally as a model of obedient suffering.[26] This theme has a particular parenetic focus, providing encouragement, comfort, and assurance of vindication in face of the suffering, hardship, and opposition entailed in the service of Yahweh. In the face of such undeserved suffering, continued loyalty is enjoined, accepting the struggle as a divine test or trial (20.12a) in the prospect of divine succour (20.13). However, this theme remains intricately related to the others. In terms of prophetic conflict, Jeremiah is vindicated as a model of righteousness in contrast to the nation's corrupt leadership (11.21-23; 14.13-16; 20.1-6) which promotes the nation in its wicked apostasy.[27] This vindication of the prophet also adds support to the manner in which his message included an iconoclastic element in relation to popular religion. And finally, Yahweh's destruction of his people is shown to have been an unavoidable necessity by the exposure of the nation's desperate wickedness through their unjustified persecution of the exemplary Jeremiah.

Conclusion

The primary goal of our discussion has been to consider the validity of discerning in 11-20 an integrated literary complex, structured around a double-axis pattern, and focused toward the development of the theodicy theme. With the establishment of the latter point, a consideration of its implications for the way in which the confessions are normally read and the question of detecting multiple levels of meaning was required. Further corroboration regarding the possibility and probability for the presence of such a compositional intention in 11–20 is provided by the existence of parallel compositional intention elsewhere in the prophetic book. This is reflected principally in the so-called Baruch narratives with their interest in documenting the fate of the prophetic message and mission, thus vindicating and justifying Israel's national demise—i.e. as due to obdurate apostasy manifested in her refusal to heed Yahweh's messenger (26–29; 36; 37–45).[28] Steck's[29] establishment of the Dtr. origin for the motif of Yahweh's prophets rejected by the nation as a type of theodicy for the exile, his *Prophetenaussage*—a motif present in Jeremianic prose sermons[30]—attracts attention to the complex 11–20 and its similar function, suggesting as a strong possibility that responsibility for the composition is to be attributed to the Dtr. editorial activity.

SUMMARY AND CONCLUDING POSTSCRIPT

The survey of Confession research highlighted the difficult problem of how a valid reading of these texts was to be achieved. Particularly problematic was the crisis reflected in post-Reventlow studies as to the proper interpretive context within which the confessions could be assessed. An attempt to resolve these problems has been the goal of this study. As a result, our primary point has been to argue that the Dtr. editors have incorporated the confessions into a significant interpretive framework. The double-axis pattern plays a dominant role in shaping the interpretation and aim of the passages. The confessions serve a distinctly apologetic purpose of constructing a theodicy of Yahweh's judgment upon Judah. A valid reading of the confessions must give primacy of place to this editorial framework. Conversely, the more the passages are isolated from their present literary setting, the more opaque and indeterminant become attempts to maintain a reading of them in relationship to the prophetic mission, especially the Jeremianic mission. The attendant problems of ambiguity relative to individual or corporate referents, prophetic or non-prophetic referents, and multiple levels of meaning, become impossible to resolve conclusively. The information necessary for such questions does not constitute the inherent characteristics of the individual units.

The last observation can be brought into relationship with the Dtr. character of the complex 11–20, with its double-axis pattern, to consider once again the question of authenticity from this wider perspective. As a result of our detailed exegesis a modification of total editorial transfer theories of origin was required. Given their stylistic compatibility and ease of 'fit', a greater allowance for basis in and/or incorporation of authentic material for the confessions seems a necessary minimum. The transfer theories address the problem, inherent in the traditional affirmation of authenticity, of adequately explaining the motivation for the prophet and/or his immediate supporters to have incorporated such prayers into the remaining 'public' aspects of the Jeremianic tradition. The problems affecting the elucidation of a preliterary setting in the prophetic mission continue to underline the existence of this problem. The question remains whether such transfer approaches, especially in their modified form, really do solve this problem.

Considered from the standpoint of the Dtr. editorial framework, it is not so clear that such transfer theories necessarily offer an overwhelmingly satisfactory solution. It remains unclear why the Dtr. would have executed so elaborate a development of their theodicy argument. We have in mind particularly the intensive attention to the 'inner' reactions of the prophet to his mission and its concomitant realities. In the remaining narrative cycles (esp. 26–29; 37–43) the narration of the prophet's experience in support of the theodicy argument is executed with extreme 'psychological' reserve in relation to descriptions of Jeremiah's reaction to the opposition and suffering entailed in his mission (apart possibly from 32.16-25). Similarly, in the prose sermons it was sufficient to appeal to the basic reality of the rejcted prophetic message (7.25; 25.4) without elaboration to buttress the theodicy argument (*Prophetenaussage*). Coupling the previous considerations with the implications of our diction analysis, and the accumulation of allusive elements to the Jeremianic mission, it may be preferable to continue the traditional ascription of substantial authenticity to the confessions. For on either approach a special development has to be assumed. The confessions either reflect a special development on the part of the prophet or upon the part of the Dtr. editors which is not entirely expected on the basis of their general features. The absence of similar indications of intense struggle with the prophetic mission in remaining portions of the Jeremianic poetic tradition may not represent an absolute barrier to the affirmation of authenticity. Without the vision reports of Amos's intercessory attempts to avert the divine wrath (Amos 7), that 'struggle' of the prophet with his message could hardly have been deduced from his remaining oracles. And some slight indications of prophetic struggle on the part of Jeremiah with his message and mission do appear to surface in 5.1-6 and 6.10-12 (esp. v. 11).

A firm conclusion concerning the authenticity problem is hard to reach. On balance, it may be more straightforward to affirm their basic authenticity. This would give full force to their stylistic compatibility and ease of 'fit' and at the same time provide an explanation for the special development in the elaboration of the Dtr. theodicy argument—i.e. it is a product of exploiting authentic material which was readily serviceable for incorporation into a double-axis pattern and the buttressing of apologetic interests. Still, one is left with only an assumption that the prophet must have perceived wider significance in these prayers in order to account for their preservation within the tradition. Given the employment of call narratives and vision reports plus prophetic-liturgy patterns in the service of prophetic speech, such an assumption is not entirely lacking in reasonable warrants for it.

Nevertheless, the authenticity question makes little difference in the attempt to establish a valid reading of these difficult passages. For this, we are dependent upon the Dtr. context-building which has effected a dramatic portrayal of the prophetic mission in the development of its theodicy argument.

NOTES

Notes to Introduction

1. We employ the usual label in accordance with the convention that has grown up around the discussion of these texts in awareness of its inappropriateness. A more technical classification of the passages will be discussed below in the detailed exegesis of the units.

2. This selection of passages represents the widest consensus of the texts to be included in the classification of Jeremiah's confessions. However, from time to time additional passages have also been included: von Rad, 'Konfessionen', p. 227 (8.18-23); Hyatt, p. 782 (10.23-24; 17.9-10); Bright, *Jeremiah*, p. LXVI (4.19-21; 5.3-5; 8.18-23); Berridge, p. 114 n. 1 (9.1-8); Holladay, *Architecture*, p. 152 (17.5-8, 9-10); Thompson, p. 88 (4.19-21; 5.3-5; 8.18-23). For a discussion of some of these additional passages not as confessions proper but as partial forerunners to them, see Ittmann, pp. 22-25; Ahuis, pp. 183-84.

3. No attempt at exhaustiveness or detailed exposition will be made. Detailed interaction with various positions will be provided in the course of the developing discussion throughout the monograph. See further the very fine detailed reviews of research in Wimmer, 'Experience' (1973); Ittmann (1981); Ahuis (1982). For excellent reviews of research on individual texts, see the studies by Hubmann, *Untersuchungen* (1978); *idem*, 'Jer. 18' (1981); *idem*, 'Anders' (1981).

4. For these, see the following, who viewed the confessions in total or in part as later interpolations: Bernhard Stade, 'Miscellen' (1886), p. 153; *idem*, *Geschichte* (1887), pp. 646 n. 481, 679 n. 1; N. Schmidt, 'Jeremiah' (1901), p. 2369; *idem*, 'Jeremiah (Book)' (1901), pp. 2388-89; G. Hölscher (1914), pp. 396-99; H.G. May (1942), p. 145.

5. Pre-Reventlow, see: standard commentaries; H. Ewald, *Die Propheten des Alten Bundes*, II (1840, 1868²), p. 65 (Eng. edn, p. 61); W. Baumgartner, *Die Klagegedichte des Jeremia* (1917); J. Skinner, *Prophecy & Religion: Studies in the Life of Jeremiah* (1922), pp. 201-30; G.A. Smith, *Jeremiah* (1923), pp. 317-35; H. Wheeler Robinson, *The Cross of Jeremiah* (1925), pp. 48-70; H.H. Rowley, 'The Text and Interpretation of Jer. 11.18–12.6'

(1926), pp. 217-27; G. von Rad, 'Die Konfessionen Jeremias' (1936), pp. 265-76; V. Herntrich, *Jeremia, der Prophet und sein Volk* (1938), p. 38; S.H. Blank, 'The Confessions of Jeremiah and the Meaning of Prayer' (1948); R.F. Kenney, 'Jeremiah's Distinctive Contribution to Hebrew Psalmody' (1952); J. Steinmann, *Le Prophète Jérémie. Sa vie, son œuvre et son temps* (1952), pp. 151-59; J. Leclercq, *'Les "Confessions" de Jérémie'* (1954), pp. 111-45; J.J. Stamm, 'Die Bekenntnisse des Jeremia' (1955), pp. 354-57, 370-75; H.J. Stoebe, 'Seelsorge und Mitleiden bei Jeremia' (1955), pp. 116-34; G.M. Behler, *Les Confessions de Jérémie* (1959); P. Bonnard, *Le Psautier selon Jérémie* (1960); J.L. Mihelic, 'Dialogue with God' (1960), pp. 43-50; H.J. Stoebe, 'Jeremia Prophet und Seelsorger' (1964), pp. 385-409.

   6.   *Die Klagegedichte des Jeremia.*
   7.   For further details of this discussion, see Baumgartner, pp. 1-5. This approach to the confessions has occasionally been continued post-Baumgartner: R.F. Kenney, 'Jeremiah's Distinctive Contribution to Hebrew Psalmody' (1952); P. Bonnard, *Le Psautier selon Jérémie* (1960); J. Coppens, 'Les Psaumes 6 et 41 dépendent-ils du Livre de Jérémie?' (1961), pp. 217-26; C. Hauret, 'Jérémie, xvii,14: Sana me, Domine et sanabor' (1962), pp. 174-84.
   8.   See esp. Stoebe, 'Seelsorge' (1955), pp. 119-20, 126, who de-emphasizes a psychological approach to the 'personalistic' utterances in the book based upon comparisons with similar motifs in other prophetic books and the Psalms. Subsequently, Stoebe, 'Jeremia' (1964), pp. 388-90, 392-93, repeated these observations and joined them to Reventlow's strictures against a psychological interpretation (p. 388 n. 16). To this may also be compared the study of Wolff (1937), who observes the indebtedness of citation and dialogical motifs with their personalistic appearance to speech forms of the law court and cult (pp. 41, 87-90). The pastoral and rhetorical function of such devices leads Wolff to observe the inadequacy of 'sentimental' interpretations of them (p. 83).
   9.   See n. 5 above. For a discussion of their positions with the exception of Mihelic, see Berridge, pp. 13-17. The latter also includes the work of Herntrich in this group though he is still heavily psychological in his interpretive approach.
   10.   For example, contrast the statements by Ewald, pp. 68-74 (Eng. edn, pp. 65-73), and Wellhausen, pp. 140-41, who speak of Jeremiah ushering in a dissolution of classical prophecy and view the confessions divorced from Jeremiah's prophetic office, to those of von Rad, 'Konfessionen', pp. 232, 234, where he stresses the intrinsic connection of the confessions to the prophetic office as well as seeing in Jeremiah the end of an old series and the beginning of a new series in prophecy.
   11.   *Liturgie und prophetisches Ich bei Jeremia.*
   12.   Prior to Reventlow, Weiser, *Jeremia*, pp. xxv, 169, 173, and Stamm, pp. 370, 374, postulated an actual cultic setting for Jeremiah's performance

of his confessions but continued to see them as his own petitions.

13. Reventlow, pp. 209-10, 259.

14. For detailed critiques of Reventlow's thesis, see esp. Bright, 'Jeremiah's Complaints', and Berridge.

15. S.E. Balentine, 'Jeremiah, Prophet of Prayer' (1981), pp. 331-44; J.V. Bredenkamp, 'The Concept of Communion with God in the Old Testament with special reference to the individual Laments in the Psalms and the Confessions of Jeremiah' (1970); J. Bright, *Jeremiah* (1965); *idem*, 'Jeremiah's Complaints: Liturgy or Expressions of Personal Distress?' (1970), pp. 189-213; *idem*, 'A Prophet's Lament and its Answer: Jeremiah 15.10-21' (1974), pp. 59-74; W.V. Chambers, 'The Confessions of Jeremiah: A Study in Prophetic Ambivalence' (1972); M. Fishbane, 'Jeremiah 20.7-12 / Loneliness and Anguish' (1979); *idem*, '"A Wretched Thing of Shame, A Mere Belly": An Interpretation of Jeremiah 20.7-12' (1982), pp. 169-83; G. Fohrer, *Die Propheten des Alten Testaments, II: Die Propheten des 7. Jahrhunderts* (1974), pp. 111-20; W.L. Holladay, *Jeremiah: Spokesman Out of Time* (1974), pp. 88-106; R. Jacobson, 'Prophecy and Paradox' (1976), pp. 49-61; J. Schreiner, 'Unter der Last des Auftrags. Aus der Verkündigung des Propheten Jeremias: Jer. 11,18-12,6 III. Teil', (1966), pp. 180-92; *idem*, 'Die Klage des Propheten Jeremias. Meditation zu Jer. 15,10-21' (1966), pp. 220-24; J.A. Thompson, *The Book of Jeremiah* (1980), pp. 88-92; C. Westermann, *Jeremia* (1967), pp. 38-44; W. Zimmerli, 'Jeremia, der leidtragende Verkündiger' (1975), pp. 97-111.

16. J.M. Berridge, *Prophet, People, and the Word of Yahweh* (1970); S.H. Blank, 'The Prophet as Paradigm' (1974), pp. 113-30; U. Eichler, 'Der Klagende Jeremia. Eine Untersuchung zu den Klagen Jeremias und ihrer Bedeutung zum Verstehen seines Leidens' (1978); N. Ittmann, *Die Konfessionen Jeremias: Ihre Bedeutung für die Verkündigung des Propheten* (1981); D.H. Wimmer, 'Prophetic Experience in the Confessions of Jeremiah' (1973); *idem*, 'The Sociology of Knowledge and the Confessions of Jeremiah' (1978), pp. 393-406.

17. These approaches which see the confessions as total editorial compositions are to be paralleled with the earlier attempts to deny their authenticity, note above in n. 4. Particularly striking is the manner in which the criteria of conventional psalm-expressions and their ambiguity as to individual or corporate referent employed in the current approaches were already anticipated in the analysis of Hölscher, pp. 396-99.

18. R.P. Carroll, *From Chaos to Covenant: Uses of Prophecy in the Book of Jeremiah* (1981), pp. 107-35; E. Gerstenberger, 'Jeremiah's Complaints: Observations on Jer. 15.10-21' (1963), pp. 393-408; A.H.J. Gunneweg, 'Konfessionen oder Interpretation im Jeremiabuch' (1970), pp. 395-416; J. Vermeylen, 'Essai de Redaktionsgeschichte des "confessions de Jérémie"' (1981), pp. 239-70; P. Welten, 'Leiden und Leidenserfahrung im Buch Jeremia' (1977), pp. 123-50.

19. This is not to exclude the possibility that the tradition may have also exercised some influence in the fact and manner of its transmission.

20. F. Ahuis, *Der klagende Gerichtsprophet: Studien zur Klage in der Überlieferung von den alttestamentlichen Gerichtspropheten* (1982); F.D. Hubmann, 'Anders als er wollte: Jer 20,7-13' (1981), pp. 179-87; *idem*, 'Jer 18,18-23 im Zusammenhang der Konfessionen' (1981), pp. 271-96; *idem*, *Untersuchungen zu den Konfessionen: Jer. 11.18–12.6 und Jer. 15.10-21* (1978); D.J.A. Clines and D.M. Gunn, 'Form, Occasion and Redaction in Jeremiah 20' (1976), pp. 390-409.

21. Geoffrey Hartman, 'Jeremiah 20.7-12: A Literary Response' (1982), pp. 184-95; T.H. Polk, 'The Prophetic Persona and the Constitution of the Self: A Study of First Person Language in the Book of Jeremiah' (1982). Particularly illustrated in the latter study is the indebtedness of this approach to the theoretical contributions of rhetorical criticism, canon criticism, and the wider literary and hermeneutical discussions of the New Criticism and Structuralism. Cf. with Polk's study the analogous approach of W. Brueggemann, 'The Book of Jeremiah: Portrait of the Prophet' (1983), pp. 130-45, who discusses the depiction of the prophet as an 'imaginative literary' construct (p. 132) and also P. Miller Jr, 'Trouble and Woe: Interpreting the Biblical Laments' (1983), pp. 32-45, who stresses the importance of the narrative setting or context for interpreting the confessions more concretely in relation to Jeremiah.

22. See for example, Ewald, pp. 68-74 (Eng. edn, pp. 65-73); Wellhausen, pp. 140-41; Baumgartner; Skinner, pp. 201-30.

23. See for example, von Rad, 'Konfessionen', pp. 224-35.

24. See esp. the approaches of Skinner; Smith, *Jeremiah*; Robinson; and most recently, Ittmann.

25. Especially Ittmann, pp. 1-4, 18-20; Eichler, pp. 6, 15, 152, 200.

26. See n. 18 above.

27. Especially the studies of Ahuis; Clines and Gunn, 'Form'.

28. Polk, p. 13.

29. By 'intention' Polk, p. 21, understands: 'In sum, "the text intends" is a shorthand way of saying that one reading is to be preferred to another on the basis of what is perceived as the text's comprehensive structure, thematic concerns, points of view, tone, diction, and whatever other internal literary features are deemed as relevant and recognized as impelling text and reader to "the point"'.

30. We have adopted this term from Geoffrey Leech, *A Linguistic Guide to English Poetry*, pp. 56-57, who uses it of artistic deviations from the normal conventions of the particular medium involved.

31. For wider discussion of the importance of such an analysis of a given biblical text plus the concepts of typicality and particularity, see Rolf Knierim, 'Old Testament Form Criticism Reconsidered', pp. 435-68 (esp. p. 461); J. Muilenburg, 'Form Criticism and Beyond', pp. 1-18; R.F.

Melugin, 'The Typical Versus the Unique among the Hebrew Prophets', pp. 331-41.

32. For example, contrast the divergent analyses of Ittmann, Ahuis, and Hubmann to be discussed in detail in each relevant section of the initial exegetical portions of this study:

	Original Kernel	Editorial Expansion
Ittmann	11.18-20, 22-23a	11.21, 23b
	12.1-3, 4bβ-6	12.4abα
	15.10-11, 15-20	15.12-14, 21
	17.14-18	17.12-13
	18.18-22	18.23
	20.7-11, 13	20.12
Ahuis	12.1-4bβ, 5	11.18-23; 12.4a-bα, 6
	15.10, 17, 18, 19b, 20a	15.11-16, 19a, 20b-21
	17.14-18	17.12-13
	18.19-20, 22b-23	18.18, 20aβ, 21-22a
	20.7-9	20.10-13
	20.14-15, 16b, 17-18	20.16a
Hubmann	11.18-20, 22-23	11.21, 23b (אל אנשי ענתות)
	12.1-5	12.6
	15.10-12	15.13-14
	15.15-19	15.20-21
	17.14-18	—
	18.19-23	18.18
	20.7-11	20.12-13
	20.14-18	—

33. In the initial stages of our research and prior to the appearance of T. Polk's dissertation, we had already begun to consider the potential significance and necessity of a contextually oriented reading of the confessions. Differently from Polk, we have not sought to focus the investigation in a rigidly synchronic fashion; and, as well, the scope of our study takes in the entire block of the confessions, whereas Polk's more hermeneutical theory focus considers only two of the passages (17.12-18; 20.7-18) as an intensive illustration of his theoretical discussion (p. 2).

Notes to Chapter 1.1

1. In the interest of economy text-critical discussion has been kept to a minimum. However textual issues have been evaluated in light of the studies of Janzen, *Studies*; and Tov, *Septuagint*; *idem*, 'Aspects', pp. 145-67; *idem*, 'notes', pp. 73-93. Particularly critical are the implications of the zero variants in G which suggest a blending of text-editorial and text-transmissional stages. MT may well represent a second expanded edition of the *Vorlage* of G. To the extent that such issues arise for the confessions, such

theoretical possibilities will need to be tested. See, further, Bogaert, pp. 168-73.

2. ויהוה—G omits copula—α' Targ V follow MT. The expansion could reflect an editorial attempt to connect the confession with the preceding context. So Hubmann, *Untersuchungen*, p. 51; Ittmann, p. 89 n. 294; Thiel, p. 158, or more likely, the omission is a question of stylistic variation in response to the overall interpretation of v. 18a as vocative and imperative. The latter accords with normal expectations of lament structure but the narrative mode in MT reflects the harder reading.

3. נשחיתה עץ בלחמו—The versional evidence is very divergent. By literal retroversion G Targ V read נשליכה or נשיתה (ἐμβαλωμεν; נרמי; *mittamus*) for the initial verb. σ' follows MT. The remainder of the consonantal text of MT is followed by all but σ' (ξυλων ἀρτον αὐτου) which suggests עץ לחמו with עץ as an instrumental accusative. The main difficulty appears to rest with the expression עץ בלחמו.

The traditional translation of 'tree with its fruit' runs counter to the normal usage of לחם which never refers to the fruit of trees (cf. Ps. 104.14). Usually solutions have been reached through emendation to עץ/בלחו 'vigorous tree' (see standard commentators); by appeal either to Arabic *lahm*/'fleshiness of things, pulp of a tree' (Guillaume, p. 343; Reventlow, pp. 251-52); or to an explanation of the *mem* as enclitic with suffix (Dahood, 'Ugaritic', p. 66; Bright, *Jeremiah*, p. 84). An entirely different result has been achieved by viewing the variant witnesses as the effect of improper division of consonants, proposing as the original, עצב לחמו/'let us make trouble his food' (Burkitt, p. 373; Houberg, pp. 676-77).

Evaluation of the proposals is difficult. The resultant images can be paralleled elsewhere. Cf. Pss. 1; 52.10; 92.13 to Pss. 42.4; 127.2; Job 3.24. None of them disturbs the metre of the verse. Based upon the strength of external evidence, a solution which resorts to the least emendation seems best. Of the various proposals the suggestion of an enclitic *mem* seems the best way to accomplish this.

4. ויהוה צבאות—G omits צבאות. οι γ' Targ V follow MT. MT has the tendency to expand divine epithets. Omission in G is preferred. See Janzen, *Studies*, pp. 75-76.

5. נפשך G την ψυχην μου. O L' σ' θ' Targ V follow MT. MT preserves the compositional pattern of lament and answer to lament that is part of the context.

6. לכן כה אמר יהוה צבאות—G omits. O οι γ' Targ V follow MT. MT has the tendency to add headings to prophecies or to fill out implicit details. The messenger formula has been added due to its frequent occurrence before הנני פקד. G is preferred. See Tov, 'Aspects', pp. 152, 159; Janzen, *Studies*, p. 85. Commentators generally follow MT. The הנני clause does occur elsewhere without the messenger formula (Jer. 5.14; 12.14; 23.2; 29.21).

7. Muilenburg, pp. 1-18; Knierim, pp. 435-68; Greenwood, pp. 418-26; Melugin, pp. 331-41.

8. Blank, 'Confessions', pp. 332-37; Wimmer, 'Experience', pp. 86, 104.

9. Ittmann, pp. 62-79. Though we shall be evaluating Ittmann's analysis of each unit, it will be helpful to summarize his analysis and register our general response to it at the outset. Ittmann reclassifies the confessions into three groups (Nos. 1—18, 11, 12; Nos. 2—17; Nos. 3—15, 20). Against Baumgartner, he emphasizes that no uniform structural pattern, such as cultic lament, is common to the three groups. Instead there is a progressive breakdown in form as one proceeds through the groups. Group No. 1 is the most stable, exhibiting the closest affinities to cultic lament, and is characterized by *prophetische Situationsbeschreibung mit Anrede an Jahwe* (11.18a, 19; 18.18; 12.1b-2); *Appellation an Jahwe mit Gerichtswunsch und Begründung* (11.20; 18.20-22; 12.3, 4bβ); and a *Reaktion Jahwes* (11.22-23a; 12.5f.). Groups No. 2 and 3 lack this pattern as a result of the changing problem in view. While the first group is concerned primarily with the prophet's enemies and the desire for God's intervention (p. 68), the second group is transitional, shifting to the problem of the prophetic mission and understanding of God. These themes become central in the third block.

There are many helpful observations in his analysis. Still, it is not clear that his reclassification actually represents an improvement; and in some cases, it leads to a misrepresentation of the texts. For example, his structural categories for Group No. 1 seem only to represent the pattern of a complaint psalm in other terms. But granted the new classification, the passages in it do not form a unity. Jeremiah 18 lacks a divine oracle. The narrative description of prophetic situation in 11 and 18 is countered by direct address in 12. For Group No. 3 he must recognize a certain similarity of pattern to Group No. 1 (p. 70) which is difficult if stable forms are supposed to break down. If a distinction between the two groups is still to be maintained, as he argues, on the basis of emphasis in content, then the bitter and ironic accusation of God in 12 (see below) could warrant its inclusion with 15 and 20. Even Ittmann recognizes a shift of focus within 12 *vis à vis* 11 and 18 (p. 78). In our view, Ittmann has not given sufficient weight to the explicit contacts with lament psalms. It is precisely in the passages where he sees the lack of a stable, common pattern (15; 20) that the best parallels to the overall lament pattern can be found (see below). There are admittedly differences between the confessions and Psalm laments, particularly at the level of content and emphasis. Thus, Ittmann may be correct to argue that complaint Psalms do not provide the only source to which appeal can be made in the analysis of the confessions (p. 79) but it is not clear that he has disproved the central role of laments in this regard, nor that his reaction to Baumgartner's approach is necessary or successful.

10. For an excellent review of rearrangement proposals, see Hubmann, *Untersuchungen*, pp. 24-42.

11. So Baumgartner, p. 32.

12. *Ibid.*, pp. 30, 32.

13. Texts such as 1.11, 13; 24.1; 32.8; and 38.21 could help; but the poetry-prose distinctions in the Jeremiah tradition should probably be observed. Thus caution is needed before simple cross-linking is employed between these strata, particularly in this case, where parallels in the poetry are completely wanting.

14. Reventlow, pp. 253-54. As supporting evidence, he observed formal parallels to psalm style in v. 18: adversative *waw*; the undetermined suffix on מעלליהם comparable to oblique references to enemies in Psalms; use of אז introducing the new situation as a result of divine intervention (Pss. 19.14; 51.21; 56.10; 96.12; 126.2); its tone comparable to the certainty of hearing motif; the transition from v. 18 to 19 comparable to the retrospective review of the distress in a thanksgiving. See also Weiser, p. 99, who observes a blend of lament and thanksgiving style.

15. For the primary elements of the thanksgiving genre, see Gunkel-Begrich, p. 269.

16. For example, note the correspondence of the portrayal of distress and cry to God within thanksgiving to complaint and petition in lament, or *vice versa* the correspondence of vow and assurance of hearing in lament to celebration of the divine aid and fulfilment of the vow in thanksgiving. In a number of laments the vow and certainty of hearing take on more of a past-oriented perspective comparable to thanksgiving rather than the future-oriented perspective, anticipating help (Pss. 6.9; 28.6; 54.9; 56.14; 61.6; and esp. 3.5; 32.7-9, 23; 22.23ff.). In the case of Ps. 22, it could be described as a mixed form or even answered lament.

17. The difficulty of genre analysis experienced by the commentators especially for Ps. 120 illustrates its borderline character. Kraus, pp. 830-31; Weiser, *Psalmen*, p. 511 (Eng. edn, p. 742); Dahood, *Psalms III*, pp. 195-96.

18. Particularly in light of the narrative mode of v. 18 and the retrospective orientation of v. 19. Also, in light of Ps. 120, there is no need to view the passage as a fragment (against Reventlow, p. 254).

19. Blank, 'Confessions', p. 332; Wimmer, 'Experience', pp. 120-21; Hubmann, *Untersuchungen*, pp. 162-63. Blank views the trial pattern as 'narrative and plea' and 'expression of confidence'. Wimmer analyses the pattern as 'v. 18 introduces the matter; v. 19 sets forth the details of the case and begins defense; v. 20 requests sentence and rests his case; v. 21 Judge gives verdict and charge; v. 22 sentence; v. 23 closing statement'.

20. Blank, 'Confessions', p. 33; Hubmann, *Untersuchungen*, p. 162. In Deut. false witnesses are inflicted with the penalty which they intended for the falsely accused; and in Jer. 11.22, 23 the sentence on the men of Anathoth corresponds to their plans for murder, v. 19b. Wimmer, 'Experience', p. 126, sees the correspondence as v. 19—'destroy the tree' / v. 22—'die by famine', v. 19—'cut off from the land' / v. 22—'die by sword'; v. 19—'name remembered no more' / v. 23—'no remnant'. Cf. Hubmann, *Untersuchungen*, pp. 80-81, 162.

21. Particularly surprising is the absence of motifs and idioms associated with the 'pre-trial encounter', 'speeches before the court', the 'court's decision', and 'summary'. Alteration of plaint and counterplaint among litigants is absent. The pronouncement of the judgment lacks the shift from third person speech of accusation before the court to a verdict constructed in direct address to the guilty party (see Ramsey, p. 53, listed below). Seminal analyses of trial language and process go back to Köhler (pp. 149-75) and Boecker. For survey and refinement of their details see Gemser, pp. 120-37; H. Huffmon, 'Covenant', pp. 285-95; Limburg, pp. 291-304; North, pp. 31-67; Blenkinsopp, pp. 267-78; Ramsey, pp. 45-58; Clark, pp. 125-27; Nielsen.

22. Gemser, pp. 127-28.

23. Blank, 'Confessions', pp. 336-37, recognized this possibility and still continued to view the confessions as prayer. Wimmer, 'Experience', pp. 120-21, perhaps went too far when he attempted to deny any contacts with cultic psalm genre in the passage. Finally, Ittmann's analysis of the confession (see above, n. 9) is helpful in its recognition of the anomalous character of v. 18 but in the final analysis offers no real improvement over the mixed lament and thanksgiving genre view.

24. For the discussion of this form and its employment of the cultically rooted genre of lament and salvation oracle, see Begrich, pp. 81-92; Gunkel–Begrich, pp. 408-11; Westermann, *Lob*, pp. 44-48 (Eng. edn, pp. 59-64); Schoors, pp. 1-31. Though lists of prophetic liturgies vary, the following are generally accepted: Hos. 6.1-6; 14.2-9; Hab. 1-2; Isa. 33; 51.9-16; Mic. 7; Joel 1-2.27. If Hos. 6 is legitimate, then it provides the only extra-Jeremianic example where the petition is rejected.

25. So noted by Mowinckel, p. 77. The principal difference from the oracle in the confession is that their oracles reject the petition or only conditionally accept it.

26. Additional indirect evidence exists attesting to collocation of individual lament and divine salvation oracle and the possibility of its occurrence as a legitimate variant to the other liturgies cited above (n. 24). The salvation oracles of Dt.-Isa. have been shown to presuppose the lament of the individual (Schoors, pp. 42, 45-46). And extra-biblical parallels attest explicitly to the divine oracle as an answer to individual prayer as well as its rootage in the cult. See esp. the Zakir Inscription A.11-14 (text and translation in Gibson, pp. 8-9). For the phenomenon in Mesopotamia, see Wilson, pp. 115-19.

27. To our knowledge the most recent attempt to produce a structural analysis of 11.18-20 was by Hubmann, *Untersuchungen*, pp. 77-79. Most of his detailed observations are very helpful, but we have not followed him in the discernment of a chiastic pattern (ABC/A'B'C') as the over-arching framework. His c/c' members are only superficially parallel, having different grammatical function (יכ‎-clauses). The B member (v. 19a) has no parallel since A'B' (v. 20ab) are paralleled to A (v. 18). Finally, the A' member is

taken as a statement, but it could equally be viewed as vocative (see below).

28. Our analysis is in agreement with Hubmann, *Untersuchungen*, p. 82.

29. For this and the following observations, see Hubmann, *Untersuchungen*, pp. 79-81. See also Wimmer, 'Experience', p. 126, cited in n. 20 above.

30. Hubmann, *Untersuchungen*, p. 82, also saw as an over-arching pattern the alternation of the divine name alone with its expansion to include the epithet צבאות (v. 18—יהוה; v. 20—יהוה צבאות; v. 21—יהוה; v. 22—יהוה צבאות). The zero variants in G at vv. 20, 22 complicate the validity of the observation. Given the nature of the textual developments, the zero variants could reflect explicit editorial activity in MT to tie the sections together. However, more mechanical explanations seem preferable to the aesthetic in this case (see above, notes 4-6).

31. Eichler, pp. 68-69; pp. 86-87. Eichler does not view vv. 18-20 as prose. She relies mainly on alleged structural parallels and the doublet in 20.10-12. See below on 20.7-13 for criticism.

32. The doublet phenomenon in the book of Jeremiah represents a complex problem which we will discuss more fully at the confessional units in 15. See below.

33. Vermeylen, pp. 242-65. In total he finds four major stages in 11.18–12.6. The first and oldest layer is the Jeremianic kernel 12.4abα, 5. The second stage is 11.21-22, offered as a Dtr. commentary to 11.1-17. Third is the post-exilic addition of 11.18-19 which fixed vv. 21-22 in reference to Jeremiah as confession proper. Fourth, the confessional appearance was intensified further by a second post-exilic layer represented by 11.18b—אז הראיתני; 20, 23—כי אביא רעה שנת פקדה; and 12.1-3, 4bβ, 6. The redaction upon which the enhanced picture of the material as confession rests took place within the inner Jewish conflicts of post-exilic Judaism (i.e. between the 'pious' and the 'wicked').

34. See Vermeylen, pp. 252-53, 256-57. The formal, verbal, and thematic relationship between vv. 18-19 and v. 20 seems to provide little internal basis for discerning editorial seams. The external evidence of the doublet is Vermeylen's strongest point, but it can be explained as a repeated formulaic expression. The shift from 3rd pers. sg. to 2nd pers. sg. in v. 18 has its parallel in the formally analogous Ps. 120 and seems to reflect stylistic technique. Note it parallels the direct address in v. 20. אז seems to reflect semantic parallelism with the preceding result clause indicated by ואדעה and constitutes an elaboration of it.

35. See the diction analysis below. The closest parallels to some of the rare expressions in v. 19 are to be found in Isa. 52–53, but direction of influence cannot be decided solely on this basis. His main appeals are to post-exilic Psalm parallels (Vermeylen, pp. 253-54). But the majority of his examples are of unclear date (Pss. 27.13; 34.17; 38.14; 42.4; 52.7, 10; 109.13; 142.6; see Kraus, BK.AT, in place); and one, 83.4-5, seems to be pre-exilic (see 83.9—Asshur; cf. Kraus, BK.AT, in place). In the light of this, plus the many

widespread contacts of diction and theme between vv. 18-20 and the psalter, Vermeylen's remaining evidence loses its force (Hos. 5.12; Mic. 7.5; Job 3.24; 28.13; Isa. 38.11; Ezek. 26.20; 32.23ff; Prov. 10.7). Vermeylen himself recognized the difficulty of locating the vocabulary of vv. 18-19 in any one period (p. 254). Similar difficulties afflict his vocabulary analysis of v. 20 (p. 257).

36. Just this feature has been taken as evidence against a connection between the units. See Baumgartner, p. 33; Reventlow, p. 256. If the citation motif (v. 21) is taken as interpretive and not verbatim quotation explaining the ultimate intent and character of the opponents' plot, then the dissonance between the citations would be reduced somewhat. See Chambers, pp. 44-45; Overholt, p. 273; Crenshaw, *Conflict*, pp. 23-38; Wolff, p. 68. Other attempts to reduce the tension by appeal to a supposed progression in the historical events must go outside the passage for an explanation and misconstrue its compositional intention. See Volz, p. 138; Weiser, p. 100 n. 1; Berridge, p. 166.

37. So esp. Thiel, p. 159. He is followed by Eichler, pp. 69-70; Ahuis, p. 87; Vermeylen, pp. 248-51; Nicholson, *Jeremiah*, p. 114. For those who recognize the tension in situation between the units, see Duhm, p. 113; Gunneweg, pp. 400-401; Carroll, p. 108 (see n. 31 above). Thiel, p. 160, granted the possibility of an original poetic oracle lying behind the present one, since explicitly clear Dtr. characteristics were lacking.

38. Hubmann, *Untersuchungen*, pp. 60-74. He reconstructs the poetic kernel thus:

לכן כה אמר יהוה צבאות
הנני פקד עליהם
הבחורים ימתו בחרב
בניהם ובנותיהם ימתו ברעב
ושארית לא תהיה להם
כי אביא רעה
שנת פקדתם

39. *Ibid.*, pp. 65, 69.

40. *Ibid.*, pp. 72, 69-70. For the problem of 12.6, see below on 12.1-6.

41. *Ibid.*, p. 65 n. 18.

42. Ittmann, pp. 37-38, has also attempted to excise v. 21 and v. 23b. His argument is based on the demonstration of stylistic divergence from the normal prose expressions and style in Jeremiah. In the light of our analysis below, Ittmann has only succeeded in illustrating further the presence of some affinities to Jeremianic poetry without eliminating the primary relationships to Jeremianic prose, which underlines our contention of a composition employing poetic precursors and affecting oracular style. In v. 21 his primary evidence is בקש (את) נפש in shortened form (cf. 4.30) without the associated אויב/ביד (cf. 19.7, 9; 21.7; 22.25; 34.20, 21; 38.16; 44.30; 46.26; 49.37). For v. 23b, הביא על רעה contravenes the more common

prose construction with ptc. + הנני (to 11.23b cf. 23.12b, 17).

43. Diction and style analysis: פקד is generally used in prose and poetry but the participle is used only in prose and only with הנני (6x—11.22; 23.2; 29.32; 44.29; 46.25; 50.18):

	Poetry	Prose
General constr. הנני + ptc	14	37
בניהם	3 (3.24; 17.2; 18.21)	7
בנותיהם	1 (3.24)	4
(The latter always coordinated with בניהם.)		
בחרב	1 (5.17)	23
ברעב	0	17
(Double assoc. of preceding frequent in prose, with the triad דבר-רעב-חרב exclusively prose.)		
מות	2 (20.17; 22.10)	0
שארית	3	17
בחור	10	1

44. For others who reconstruct poetry with various emendations, see Volz, p. 135; Cornill, p. 152; Baumgartner p. 29; Holladay, *Architecture*, p. 139. The contacts with Jeremianic poetry (see notes 42, 43) lend probability to Thiel's suggestion of an original Jeremianic oracle or material as precursor to the present text: 3.24; 4.6; 5.12, 17; 6.11, 19; 9.20; 12.12; 14.18; 17.2; 18.21; 20.17; 22.10.

45. For the problems in poetry/rhythmic prose distinctions, see Kugel, pp. 59-95. For poetic precursors and reconstructed poetry in Jeremiah, see Holladay, 'Recovery', pp. 401-35; and *idem*, 'Prototype', 31-67. For affected prophetic speech, cf. the analogous situation in Chr. —von Rad, 'Predigt', p. 122 (Eng. edn, p. 278): 'When the writer wishes to present such sermons as prophetic pronouncements, he will occasionally employ a style akin to poetic parallelism, although we are always conscious that prose is the essential medium of this form-category' (translation from Eng. edn).

46. Nielsen, pp. 2-4; Fohrer, *Einleitung*, p. 364 (Eng. edn, p. 333).

47. We leave aside the cultic theories of Reventlow and Weiser. The criticisms of Berridge and Bright directed to Reventlow's approach seem valid. Weiser, like Reventlow, has failed to distinguish adequately between the primary and secondary uses of a genre. With regard to the present confession, esp. vv. 18-20, its complete lack of reference to national concerns provides serious difficulty to Reventlow. Reventlow, p. 256, conceded that this passage was of no help for his theory.

48. Berridge, pp. 155-58.

49. Clines and Gunn, 'Form', pp. 401-402; Wimmer, 'Experience', p. 135.

50. So Berridge, p. 30; Clines and Gunn, 'Form', p. 402. On the call narrative, see Habel, pp. 297-323.

51. Wimmer, 'Experience', p. 84.

52. Eichler, pp. 142, 147-48, 213, was content to understand the confessions

within this general framework, while Ahuis has taken it further; see below.

53. This point represents Ahuis's contribution to the theory.

54. Ahuis, pp. 38-42, discusses these examples.

55. *Ibid.*, pp. 58-59, 211.

56. *Ibid.*, pp. 60-74. The following confessions are assigned to the first pattern, *Botenvorgang*, as the *Rückmeldung*: 12.1-4 (p. 84); 11.18-20 (p. 87); 15.10ff. (p. 94); 20.7ff. (p. 109). The rest of the *Botenvorgang* elements are drawn from the surrounding symbolic actions, respectively (13.1, 2, 4-7; 16.5, 7; 18.2-4/19.1-2a, 10.11a). To the second pattern, *Warten auf das Gericht*, are related 17.14ff. (p. 118) and 18.18ff. (p. 36).

57. Recognized by Ahuis, p. 42. He explains this as due to the narrative form in which it is now reported. But if the present form has obscured the original, how will we infer what may or may not have been the case? The problem is not the occasional omission, or alteration, as with other elements of the form, but almost total exclusion.

58. Ahuis, pp. 45-56.

59. Note also that David as the commissioner-sender is not accused.

60. Also Moses' commission is pastoral in focus and not as messenger. So recognized by Ahuis, p. 55.

61. Of all the examples, only 1 Kgs 19.10, 14, and Isa. 6.11 exhibit language apparently related to lament language.

62. We have in view the approaches of Gerstenberger, 'Complaints'; Gunneweg; Carroll; Vermeylen; Welten.

63. The strongest considerations offered by the traditional approach as an explanation of these difficulties are to assume that Jeremiah or at least his disciples had seen paradigmatic significance in these personal prayers and, based upon the antiquity of cultic genre, to see no theoretical objection in the prophet expressing personal concerns through prayers utilizing traditional forms. See Stoebe, 'Seelsorge', pp. 126, 131; *idem*, 'Jeremia', p. 393.

64. For example, the key verbs which help integrate the prayer occur frequently as word pairs or in co-ordination elsewhere in Jeremianic poetry but never so in the Psalms: ידע + ראה—2.19; 5.1; 12.3; ידע//ראה 2.23; 11.18; 12.3;—בחן//ראה + ידע 20.12; ראה//בחן—17.9; בחן//ידע—6.27; ידע + בחן; ראה//גלה—11.20; 20.12.

65. Though Gunneweg, pp. 413-15, denies the authenticity of the confessions, he does see warrant for this editorial development within authentic tradition.

66. See the standard commentaries for Psalm parallels, esp. Baumgartner, pp. 28-33; Reventlow, pp. 252-57; Carroll, p. 109.

67. For this motif in Psalms see 3.3; 13.5; 22.9; 35.21, 25; 64.7; 71.11; esp. 83.5. The last text is the closest parallel.

68. We take v. 20a as a vocative (cf. Ps. 59.6; 69.7; 89.5, 8, 15; 84.2, 4, 9, 13) which seems to fit the following petition best. But it could also be a

descriptive statement (cf. Ps. 125.2). The phrase is ambiguous.

69. See notes 42-44 above for diction and style analysis of vv. 21-23. See further Hubmann, *Untersuchungen*, pp. 65-67; Ittmann, pp. 37-38. Besides the very general and common nouns, the following expressions/words never occur in the psalter:

הנה פקד על
מות ביד
מות בחרב
מות ברעב
שנת פקרה (only Jer. in O.T.)
נבא בשם יהוה
הביא רעה על
לכן כה אמר יהוה

But for the remaining:

	Psalms
בקש את נפש	7 (35.4; 38.13; 40.15;54.5; 63.10; 70.3; 86.14)
פקד (alone, non-ptc.)	9
בחור	3
חרב (alone)	17
רעב (alone)	2
שארית (office)	1

70. But depictions of treacherous plots (Pss. 5.9-10; 10.7-9; 55.13-14, 20-21; 64.37), unawareness (Ps. 35.8, 15), and Yahweh's knowledge of human schemes (Ps. 94.11) are present. Since *hi.* ראה occurs in Jeremiah only at 24.1 and 32.8, it may be legitimate to see editorial exploitation of the ambiguity by the present location of the confession in the context as an allusion to revelatory experience. In Psalms ראה/ידע in the *hi.* are associated more with hymnic motifs related to manifestations of divine saving actions (25.14; 60.5; 75.15; 78.11; 85.8; 91.16; 98.2; 106.8). מעללים—41x O.T., 5x Pss., 16x Jer.; 11x prose, 5x poetry.

71. Cf. Pss. 9.6; 21.11; 34.17; 41.6; 52.7; 109.13, 15; Job 18.17.

72. *Ni.* and *hi.* of כרת are used in Psalms to describe the fate and judgment of the wicked. See 34.17; 37.9, 22, 28, 34, 38; 108.8; 109.13, 15. שחת is frequently associated with divine judgment (Pss. 78.38, 45; 106.23; Lam. 2.5, 6) and prominently so in Jeremiah (2.30; 4.7; 5.10; 12.10; 13.7, 9, 14; 15.3, 6; 22.7). The association of many of these images with corporate and national concerns has encouraged some to see explicit paralleling of prophet and nation (so Reventlow, p. 256; Carroll, p. 109). The issue of how such overtones may or may not have been exploited by the editors will be the subject of our analysis later on, when the contextual utilization of the confessions will be considered.

73. The attempt to find a concrete reference behind עץ בלחמו to the prophet's activity or progeny seems an unnecessary pressing of the imagery. Appeal to vv. 22-23 below is precarious since the parallelism of the crime-

punishment scheme is not entirely harmonious. In any case, v. 21 relates the opposition to an attempt to prohibit the prophetic mission by a threat on the prophet's life. Cf. 20.1-6, where judgment upon progeny (punishment) bears no relation to the crime (arrest and pillory). See Hubmann, *Untersuchungen*, pp. 160-61.

74. כבש אלוף occurs only here in OT. The closest parallels are Jer. 12.3; 51.40; Isa. 53.7; Ps. 44.23; Prov. 7.22. Only the Proverbs text makes the point of the imagery on the element of deception. For עץ בלחמו see text. It too is unique. For the righteous as a fruitful tree, see Ps. 1; 52.10; 92.13-15; Jer. 17.8.

75. For the remaining diction of v. 19:

	O.T.	Pss.	Total	Poetry	Prose	f.n.o.
הוביל לטבוח	2 (cf. Isa. 53.7)		1 (11.19)			0
יבל	18	6	2	2	0	0
טבח	11	1 (inf.)	3 (inf.)	2	0	1
חשב מחשבות	see on 18.18					
שחת	140	9	19	8	6	5
כרת	285	14	26	3	18	5
זכר	222	52	15	9	5	1

76. The closest parallel to v. 20 is 20.12; see further there. Diction analysis:

	O.T.	Pss.	Total	Poetry	Prose	f.n.o.
שפט צדק	2	1 (9.5)	1	1		
בחן כליות ולב	2	0	2	2 (11.20; 17.10)		
כליות ולב	4	1 (7.10)	3	3 (11.20; 17.10; 20.12)		
ראה נקמה	3 (Lam. 3.60)	0	2	2 (11.20; 20.12)		
גלה ריב	2	0	2	2 (11.20; 20.12)		

However, the theme of Yahweh as judge and avenger is common in Psalms (18.48; 35.23; 43.1; 58.11; 74.22; 99.8; 119.54).

77. As, for example, Ittmann does in his formal analysis; see above n. 9.

78. For divine oracles in the psalter, see above on Form.

79. See Hubmann, *Untersuchungen*, pp. 168-69, for the ironic usage of לא נבא בשם יהוה as an outright prohibition of authentic Yahweh prophecy just as one might prohibit anyone who spoke in the name of 'another god' (cf. Deut. 13.2-6).

80. See Wimmer, 'Experience', p. 134, who notes this quality of the

confession. For him this necessarily implied the concrete historical realities
of the hypothetical setting as a public declamation.

   81. Cf. Jer. 22.12; 48.44. So also Reventlow, p. 256; Berridge, p. 168.

Notes to Chapter 1.2

   1. תראני—G omits. οι γ' Targ V follow MT. Though MT could be viewed
as an editorial expansion to link back to the preceding confession, it is more
likely that the omission has occurred by homoioteleuton (ידעתני . . . תראני).
Textual evaluation is complicated by the various proposals for rearrangements between 11.18-23 and 12.1-6, but most follow MT.

   2. התקם כצאן לטבחה—G omits. O L' Q C θ' 4QJer.ᵃ Targ V follow MT. If
G has intentionally struck the clause, it is hard to see why. The link with
11.19a could indicate that MT represents an editorial expansion connecting
the two confessions. However, if it were a redactional addition, we should
most naturally have expected כבש instead of צאן. Intentional deletion or
expansion seems equally problematical. Perhaps the omission resulted from
homoiarchton (התקם . . . הקרשם). Most follow MT.

   3. יראה את אחריתנו—G + o θεος/οδους ημων. α' σ' Targ V follow MT.
MT is preferred. G is interpreting for clarity (cf. 4QJerᵃ, which apparently
reflects יהוה; Janzen, p. 176). For οδους, it is unlikely that a *Vorlage* of ארח is
indicated since G normally translates דרך and ארח is not used in Jeremiah.
The general tendency is to follow G if the verse or at least v. 4bβ is retained.
See standard commentators. For recent advocates of MT, see Reventlow,
p. 242; Hubmann, *Untersuchungen*, p. 55.

   4. So Baumgartner, p. 53, grouped 12.1-6 with 'Hiobdichtungen'.

   5. Psalms 37 and 49 have set the problem within the framework of wise
counsel and encourage the faithful to 'fret not'. Ps. 73 perceives the threat to
divine justice and the problem for faith occasioned by the prosperous wicked
but holds back from formally levelling explicit accusations at God (cf. vv. 2,
15).

   6. 'Near-lament' derives from the category of Baumgartner, p. 52:
'Gedichte, die den Klageliedern nahestehen'. Parallels with disputational
motifs in Job have also been noted by Eichler, pp. 84-88. This problem of
genre analysis is parallel to similar difficulties encountered in the complex
interweaving of lament, wisdom, hymn, legal speech forms in Job. See
Crenshaw, *Wisdom*, pp. 121-23; Westermann, *Aufbau*, pp. 27-39 (Eng. edn,
pp. 1-13).

   7. Blank, 'Confessions', pp. 331-54; Reventlow, pp. 243, 246-47; Schreiner,
'Last', p. 190; Wimmer, 'Experience', p. 157; *idem*, 'Sociology', pp. 400-
403.

   8. Still a consistent analysis of the trial process as reflected in the
confession has not been reached: contrast Wimmer, 'Experience', p. 157, and

Blank, 'Confessions', p. 332: v. 1—'presentation of brief', v. 2—'evidence', v. 3a—'precedents', v. 3b—'demand', v. 4—'argument', vv. 5-6—'verdict and challenge' (Wimmer); v. 1a—'veiled accusation', v. 1b—'rhetorical question', vv. 2-3a—'prayer narrative', v. 3b—'direct appeal' (Blank).

9. Reventlow, pp. 246-47.

10. Boecker, pp. 66-67, 72: Normally accusations of the plaintiff in the pre-trial stituation are addressed to the accused in the 2nd pers. but shift to 3rd pers., about the accused, before the court.

11. See Boecker, pp. 98 n. 3, 131-32, on Jer. 12.1 and its deviation from normal legal practice. For his discussion of the idioms, see: pp. 66-67, on מדוע as a shortened accusation formula; pp. 98, 124, esp. 131-32, on ריב אל and צדיק אתה. The translations of the verse by Blank, 'Confessions', p. 333, and Wimmer, 'Experience', pp. 147-48, obscure the ironic usage of the idioms.

12. In some cases the trial analysis seems to misrepresent the passage. For example, Wimmer's analysis of v. 2 as evidence and v. 4 as argument suggests distinct functions for what seem to be parallel elements in the prayer. See below, Particular Form.

13. See also Baumgartner, p. 59, and Berridge, p. 161 n. 252, who viewed the lawsuit classification as inadequate. In this regard, whereas Wimmer wants to distinguish the passage from lament, Blank, Reventlow, and Schreiner are content to speak of the transfer of legal imagery and trial process into a lament. Our disagreement is not that the lament has utilized legal imagery, for this it has. We disagree, however, that this has shaped its overall pattern. Finally, there is no need to follow Ittmann's classification either, since it primarily reflects lament typicalities in other terms. See on 11.18-23, n. 9.

14. We are basically in agreement with Hubmann, *Untersuchungen*, pp. 82-88.

15. So Hubmann, *Untersuchungen*, p. 82 n. 11.

16. The practice of viewing v. 4abα or the whole verse as a gloss among commentators (see standard commentaries) has been modified by some recent redactional studies which view it now as an editorial expansion. The primary rationale has remained the same in any case: i.e. logical incoherence within the context. Redactional approaches have expressed this variously, seeing the mixing of lament accusation and descriptions of divine judgment as inappropriate (Eichler, pp. 68-70) or viewing the judgment in v. 4abα as a past event while the remainder of the context represents it as outstanding (Ahuis, pp. 81-84). Both Eichler and Ahuis see the Dtr. active here. The latter scholar lays great stress upon the prose character of the half-verse, which he nowhere demonstrates. The ease of scansion for the whole verse and its terse chiastic structure (in part) make this suggestion unlikely. There is nothing distinctive of Dtr. or Jeremianic prose in it. Vermeylen, pp. 244-48, 259-64, has gone in an entirely different direction by viewing 12.4abα, 5

as an original Jeremianic oracle to which a post-exilic editor has added 12.1-3, 4bβ, 6. As with his approach to 11.18-23, his view here is seriously vitiated by inappropriate methodology. He assumes a uni-directional influence in late literary contacts, appeals to Psalm parallels of unclear date, and inappropriately discounts contacts with Jeremianic poetry. See diction analysis below. Finally, his analysis does not account for the high degree of logical coherence and structural integrity in the passage that our formal analysis indicates.

17. For a detailed review of these older approaches, see Hubmann, *Untersuchungen*, pp. 32-46 (summary chart p. 42). Besides the redactional solutions discussed below, additional studies after Hubmann continue the older alternatives. See Bredenkamp, p. 263 (rearrangement); Wimmer 'Experience', p. 150 (unity without rearrangement); Chambers, p. 50; Ittmann, pp. 63-64 (radical separation).

18. Thiel, pp. 157-58, 161-62.

19. Hubmann, *Untersuchungen*, p. 72.

20. *Ibid.*, p. 64 n. 16.

21. *Ibid.*, p. 63.

22. *Ibid.*, p. 71.

23. This point is underlined by seeing the use of בגד in v. 6 as different from its usage elsewhere in Jeremiah. *Ibid.*, pp. 64 n. 16, 90.

24. *Ibid.*, pp. 71, 90. Hubmann argues against rearrangement in spite of this because the triple גם presupposes a concrete antecedent upon which it depends (p. 63). So also Ittmann, p. 64.

25. *Ibid.*, p. 74. Similar dissonances between vv. 5 and 6 are noted by Vermeylen, p. 263; Eichler, p. 69.

26. *Ibid.*, p. 71. Similar arguments are used by others who see connections between 12.6 and preceding verses adjuged as secondary: Eichler, p. 68 (11.18-20); Ahuis, p. 85 (11.18-23); Vermeylen, p. 263 (12.1-3, 4bβ).

27. A variety of redactional studies have reached similar conclusions to that of Thiel and Hubmann, though minor differences in argumentation are present: Nicholson, *Jeremiah*, pp. 114, 117; Gunneweg, p. 401; Reventlow, p. 255; Carroll, p. 110 n. 9; Eichler, pp. 68-70; Ahuis, pp. 81-85; Vermeylen, pp. 263-64.

28. Classified as such by Thiel, p. 158; Hubmann, *Untersuchungen*, p. 63; Ahuis, p. 85. Cf. Ittmann, p. 64, who classified 12.6 as prose but continued to maintain its originality.

29. Hubmann, *Untersuchungen*, p. 64 n. 16. Thiel, p. 158, provided no vocabulary analysis. Ahuis, p. 85, also noted the lack of Dtr. features.

30. Distribution as follows:

	Prose	Poetry
אח	11	3
בית	84	10 (excluding the formula 'House of PN')
אב	42	13

	Prose	Poetry
המה	24	16
קרא	42	15
אחר	34	10
טובות	24	10
דבר	8	24
אמן	2	1
מלא	1	5
בגד	2	6

Distribution in the foreign nation oracles has been excluded.

31. Distribution reflecting precise morphological parallels and/or word combinations:

	Only here in *Jeremiah*	Other
אחיך	x	
בית אביך	x	
קרא אחר		Cf. 1 Sam. 20.37, 38; 24.9 as the only parallels in OT (Still these texts are semantically distant, lacking the sinister overtones of 12.6)
קרא מלא	x but cf. Jer. 4.5	
אמן ב		Only here in OT
דבר טובות אל		Cf. Jer. 52.32 (דבר טובות את)

32. See esp. Jer. 14.18; 23.11; 12.2. For כי גם or גם המה beginning a poetic line, see Jer. 6.11; 14.5; 46.21.

33. So assumed by Thiel, p. 158; Hubmann, *Untersuchungen*, p. 63.

34. For this pattern, plus examples in Ugaritic and Hebrew verse, see Loewenstamm, pp. 176-96; Avishur, pp. 1-10. A certain fluidity in terms is to be noted ('climactic parallelism', 'repetitive parallelism', 'expanded colon').

35. Vermeylen, p. 263, attempts to remove the force of this parallel by finding signs of post-exilic additions in Jer. 9.1-8 (i.e vv. 2a, 3-5, 7-8). But the close intertwining of the two themes of falsehood between men and falsehood toward Yahweh provides a strong case for the structural integrity of the passage instead of viewing them as unrelated intrusions (so Vermeylen). Note that v. 5 weds the two themes together. The validity of his argument for the redactional character of 9.8 because of the doublet with Jer. 5.9, 29 is possible, but it does not demonstrate post-exilic character or inauthenticity. His supposed literary contacts with late Psalms are unclear as well in regard to firm post-exilic dating (Pss. 12.1-5; 28.3; 41.10; 57.5; 64.4; 120). Vermeylen's objection to vv. 7-8 renewing the accusation section after the announcement of judgment (v. 6) seems misplaced given the freedom in the order of elements in prophetic judgment oracles and their susceptibility to modification and expansion (so Westermann, *Grundformen*, pp. 23, 27-30 (Eng. edn, pp. 173, 176-81). The doubling of parts in an oracle is attested

elsewhere and esp. in Jeremiah (so Westermann, *Grundformen*, pp. 29-30 (Eng. edn, pp. 180-81). Cf. Jer. 5.7-11; 2.4-11 (12, 13); Mic. 3.1-4; Hos. 4.4-10; 5.8-14) and in this specific passage seems to follow as a natural development in response to the rhetorical questions of v. 6b.

36. For others who take v. 6 as poetry, see Duhm, p. 114 (explicitly); Baumgartner, p. 52; Bright, *Jeremiah*, p. 83; Thompson, p. 348 (implicitly).

37. It could be argued that this is too selective an analysis since it does not include all the word links (אתה—vv. 1, 2; ארץ—vv. 4, 5) which if included would disrupt the chiasm. Still, in the complex structure of the poem, more than one structural device could be at work. That is, the אתה and ארץ links could limit their role to the smaller sub-units while the chiasm functions over the whole poem.

38. A possibility considered by Berridge, p. 126 n. 76.

39. This seriously weakens Hubmann's point about the different points of comparison involved in v. 5 and v. 6.

40. Cf. similarly Reventlow, p. 248; Baumgartner, p. 58. Contrast Eichler, p. 69, who sees incongruity between the rebuke and promise.

41. Editorial-transfer views encounter difficulty in v. 6 in light of our preceding analysis of diction, style, and theme. See above nn. 30-32 and Jer. 9.1-8 (theme). Similar problems for vv. 1-5 will emerge below (see statistics in Interpretation) which could permit the discernment of some signs of authenticity.

42. See Setting on 11.18-23.

43. So Bright, 'Jeremiah's Complaints', p. 208. For Reventlow's exegesis, see pp. 242-51.

44. McKane, 'Jeremiah 12.1-5', p. 46; and Baumgartner, p. 59 n. 3, argued that the affinity with Job rendered the corporate interpretation of 12.1-6 unlikely since the former was concerned more with the individual.

45. Ahuis's original kernel appears to fare no better (12.1-4bβ, 5). He classifies it as *Rückmeldung* within the *Botenvorgang* pattern (p. 84). He also notes the motif of delayed fulfilment but does not comment upon its implication for his proposal of two patterns of *gerichtsprophetische Klage*. His interpretation of the רשעים as a sub-group within the nation is also unlikely—see below on Interpretation.

46. This lack of explicit inherent prophetic references seems to be the Achilles heel of any attempt to speculate about settings within a prophetic mission. For example, besides a public apologetic role or a special prophetic lament, an additional hortatory function could be postulated. Assuming a close circle of disciples or supporters, the failure of the prophetic mission to effect national repentance, the unchecked progress of sections of society inimical to national religious health, and delay of the threatened judgment could have greatly agonized such a group. This passage could function as an exhortation to perseverance and courage in view of Yahweh's presence to defend them in such hostile and troubled conditions.

47. On v. 6 see above n. 41; to v. 4 cf. 14.2ff.; to the theme of hypocritical piety in v. 2b cf. 3.1-5; 5.2; 6.20; to דבר משפט את in v. 1 cf. 1.16; 4.12.

48. Instead of a reference to Yahweh's general righteousness (cf. Ps.11.7; 119.37; 129.4; 145.17), צדיק אתה should be given the nuance of 'innocent'/ 'acquitted' (cf. 2 Kgs 10.9; Deut. 25.1; Exod. 23.7; Prov. 24.24). The precise expression דבר משפט את, unique to Jeremiah, should be translated juridically as 'pass sentence upon' (Jer. 1.16; 4.12; 39.5; 52.9). See the following analogous expressions for corroboration of the juridical nuance: דבר משפט sentence, verdict (Deut. 17.9); משפטי צדק/ just verdict (2 Chron. 19.6); דבר משפט/ make a just plea (Isa. 32.7). See further, Holladay, 'Lawsuit', pp. 280-81. A double meaning should probably be seen for ריב אל in 12.1, as Boecker, p. 98, observed; for appeal is made both to Yahweh and against him. For the nuance 'bring charges before', see Judg. 21.22 and the analogous Mic. 6.1 (את ריב—the context requires an understanding of את as 'in the presence of', Gen. 20.16; Isa. 30.8; cf. BDB, p. 86; Mays, p. 131). For 'contend with' (normally ריב את/ב), see Job 33.13; Jer. 2.29. The interchange of אל/את suggests that the alternate nuances depend more on context than anything else. Word frequencies:

צדיק	as an epithet of God in Pss. 5x
צדיק	3x Jer.; only poetic
ריב אל	4x OT, Ox Pss., 2x Jer.; only poetic

49. Hubmann, *Untersuchungen*, pp. 134-35. A survey of the wicked and their fate across Psalms, Proverbs, and Job produces a helpful comparative pattern to the employment of this motif in 12.1-6: In the psalter the wicked (רשעים) are consistently viewed in a negative light. God is never arrayed on their side. He may be accused of delaying (Ps. 10); but never is he depicted directly superintending their success, as in Jer. 12.1-6. Some Psalms exhibit faltering confidence in a divine just order (Pss. 37; 49; 73); but they never level harsh accusations, and resolve themselves in confidence. When the prosperity of the wicked is considered, it is viewed as temporary and ephemeral in character (Pss. 37.2, 10, 35; 73.18-20). Agricultural imagery is employed not only for this purpose but also to depict the blessings of the righteous. The latter fits with Jer. 12.1-6. The same picture holds for Proverbs and the speeches of Job's friends (Prov. 10.3, 6, 7, 11, 16, 20, 24, 30, 32; 11.31; 21.19-20; Job 8.13-22; 15.20-35; 18.5-21; 20.5-29; 22.18; 34.18, 26). However, in the speeches of Job blame is laid upon God as the immediate cause of the wicked's success and innocent suffering (9.22, 24; 10.3; 21.7-33; 16.11).

50. The various proposals range from the men of Anathoth to the whole nation or prophetic opponents. See standard commentaries, esp. Hubmann, *Untersuchungen*, p. 133. The description of the רשעים in Psalms remains largely generic, with a more explicit identification offered four times: Pss. 9-

10 (enemy nation); 55.4 (trusted friend); 50; 106.18 (national sub-groups). The situation for בגדים is equivalent (Pss. 25.3; 59.6; 73.15; 78.57; 119.158; cf. Prov. 2.22; 21.18).

51.

	Only here in O.T.	Other	Jeremiah			
			Total	Poetry	Prose	f.n.o.
רשעים		52× Pss.	5	5		
			Referents: wicked rich (5.26);			
			false prophets & nation (23.19);			
			nations of earth (25.31; 30.23)			
בגד (verb)		5× Pss.	8	6	2	0
בגוד (adj.)	x		2	0	2 (3.7, 10)	0
דרך רשעים		2× Pss. (1.6; 146.9)	1	1		
		2× Prov. (4.19;				
		12.26; cf. 15.9—רשע)				
בגדי בגד	x					
צלח		3× Pss. (cf. esp. 1.3)	8	5	3	0
שלה		1× Pss.	1	1		
מרוע		72× O.T.; 0x Pss.	16	10	3	3

Finally, the conjunction כי is ambiguous representing a temporal, conditional (see standard commentaries), frequentive (Berridge, p. 161 n. 253) or concessive (BDB, p. 473 2c) clause. On any of these views the opening statement is lent a note of frustration.

52. Hubmann, *Untersuchungen*, p. 135.

53. This precise formulation of the hypocrisy motif is unparalleled. For the general idea, see Pss. 50.16, 17; 78.36; Isa. 29.13; Ezek. 33.31. Only Ps. 50 has a sub-group of the nation in view. To the divine planting motif, cf. Isa. 5.2; Amos 9.15; 2 Sam. 7.10 (Israel as vine or vineyard).

	O.T.	Pss.	Jeremiah			
			Total	Poetry	Prose	f.n.o.
נטע		2 (in this motif—				
		44.3; 80.16)				
שרש	8	2	1	(cf. Ps. 80.10; Isa. 27.6; 40.24)		
עשו פרי	8	1 (107.37)	2	2 (12.2; 17.8) (cf. 2 Kgs 19.30//		
				Isa 37.31; Hos. 9.16—relating to		
				national well-being or loss)		

54. For the adversative-*waw* construction with this motif, see the discussions at Jer. 15.15; 17.16; 18.23; cf. Pss. 31.8; 40.10; 69.6, 20; 139.2, 4. In light of the parallelism ראה/בחן, emphasis seems to be placed upon the poet's innocence. In Psalms, see בחן—7.10; 11.4, 5; 17.3, etc.; ראה—14.2; 53.2; 119.159; 139.24.

55. This difficulty occasioned frequent rearrangement attempts. See standard commentaries.

56. Each employs the motif differently. Ps. 73 testifies to questioning of

the value of righteousness (vv. 13, 14) but then affirms that the poet's integrity has not collapsed (vv. 15-17). Ps. 37 employs the motif in the form of an exhortation to innocence (vv. 1, 5, 27).

57. So Duhm, p. 115.

58. So Hubmann, *Untersuchungen*, p. 136. Such allusions occur in other confessions (see below on 15.12, 20; 17.18). The only other occurrence of *hi.* קדש in Jeremiah is at 1.5. Still the allusion does not seem particularly underlined in the present context.

59. So Hubmann, but the link to 11.19 has arisen through the secondary association of the two confessions. No necessary allusion to the wicked kinsmen seems involved in v. 3b. The latter associations reflect a growth in meaning affected by the redaction. For the diction analysis of the general vocabulary in v. 3a, see on 11.18, 20. For v. 3b:

	O.T.	Pss.	*Jeremiah*			
			Total	Poetry	Prose	f.n.o.
נתק	26	2	7	6	1	0

Used only here in O.T. in relation to slaughter of sheep

	O.T.	Pss.	Total	Poetry	Prose	f.n.o.
קדש (verb)	171	0	7	2	3	2

Idea of simple designation the focus here (against Hubmann, *Untersuchungen*, p. 137 n. 15)

יום הרגה   Only here in O.T. (cf. Isa. 30. 25; Zech. 11.4, 7)

For the remaining vocabulary, see 11.19.

60. Hubmann, *Untersuchungen*, p. 136, employs the allusions to the call narrative to see a crisis in prophetic office as the central theme, thus requiring complementary opponents (i.e. prophets). This is unnecessary. The terms of Jeremiah's call array him against the whole nation.

61. Inner Jeremianic usage corroborates this, see 6.12; 10.18; 4.7; 8.16; 9.10 (poetry); 1.14; 13.13; 25.9, 29 (prose).

62. For this view, see Hubmann, *Untersuchungen*, p. 143.

63. So similarly, Berridge, p. 165.

64. For further details, see Hubmann, *Untersuchungen*, pp. 138-43.

65. *Ibid.*, p. 141.

66. *Ibid.*, p. 142.

67. The subject of יראה is ambiguous, but the structural parallelism between vv. 1-2 and v. 4 favours Yahweh as subject. Observe that v. 2b is characterizing the posture of the wicked toward Yahweh. Also in the inclusio between vv. 3 and 4 with ראה, the subject of the former is God. So standard commentaries; but Wimmer, 'Experience', p. 151, identifies Jeremiah as the subject. For אחרית as 'end'/'doom', see Deut. 32.20, 29; Ps. 73.17; Num. 23.10; Jer. 17.11.

68. Apart from the plaintiff question and the citation motif, the diction and imagery find their major parallels in prophetic texts (Jeremiah and

others) and not in the psalter. See examples above. Such parallels add to the accumulation of inner-Jeremianic allusions and poetic affinities for the whole prayer. The effect is to enhance the warrants for seeking a setting within Jeremiah's mission. Though a precise determination appears excluded, the citation's rejection of the divine warnings suggests a situation of popular opposition to the prophetic announcement of judgment as the background of the text. Diction analysis:

	O.T.	Pss.	Jeremiah			
			Total	Poetry	Prose	f.n.o.
אבל	39	0	5	5	0	0
יבש	61	6	4	2 (cf. 23.10)	0	2
עשב השדה	8	0	1			
ספה	21	1	1			
בהמות ועוף	only here					
עוף	71	4	9	4 (cf.4.25; 5.25; 9.9; 7.33/15.3/16.4/ 19.7/34.20)	5	
בהמה	190	10	18	3	13	2
ראה אחרית	only here					
אחרית	61	5	10	6	1	3 (meaning un-differentiated)

69. So Baumgartner, pp. 56-57; Rudolph, p. 86; Weiser, *Jeremia*, p. 105; McKane, 'Jeremiah 12, 1-5', p. 45.

70. See standard commentaries, esp. Hubmann, *Untersuchungen*, pp. 145-49, for a detailed review. The basis of this position is the appeal to inner-Jeremianic allusions for both סוסים and גאון הירדן which are used in military contexts of attacking nations, esp. the foe from the north (cf. 4.13; 6.23; 8.16; 46.4, 9; 49.19/50.44; 50.37, 42). The remaining key nouns of the verse provide no possibility of veiled allusions:

	Only here in O.T.	O.T.	Pss.	Jeremiah			
				Total	Poetry	Prose	f.n.o.
רגלי (pl.)	x						
ארץ שלום	x(cf. Jer.25.37—נאוה שלום)						
סוסים		83	1	12	5	3	4
גאון הירדן		4	0	3	1	0	2
	(cf. Zech. 11.3)						

71. So Hubmann, *Untersuchungen*, pp. 151-55. The basis of his view points first to the parallel chiastic structures in v. 5a and v. 5b to v. 1b and v. 4a respectively. The significance of the correspondence between v. 5a/ v. 1b is found in the veiled allusion of the verb רוץ to the prophetic office (cf. Jer. 23.21; 51.31). So also Thompson, p. 355. Additional support for this is found in the identification of the רשעים as prophetic opponents. They constitute the present lesser threat. The future and greater threat is left

unspecified; its function is for shock. Similarly the significance of the correspondence, v. 5b/v. 4a, is found in the verbal link of ארץ שלום. ארץ and גאון הירדן are taken as symbols of a situation of security, and one of insecurity and threat. Verse 5b criticizes the criterion for confidence in the divine rule as the ארץ שלום by challenging the prophet to discover a faith capable of sustaining itself in the גאון הירדן.

	O.T.	Pss.	Jeremiah			
			Total	Poetry	Prose	f.n.o
רוץ		6	5	2	0	3
לאה	19	1	5	5	0	0 (cf. 6.11; 15.6; 20.9)
כי...אין (cstr.)		0	1			
תתחרה	2 only here in Jer. (cf. 22.15)					
בטח		44	15	6	6	3

72. That is, רגלים and ארץ שלום linked to רשעים (v. 1) and ארץ (v. 4) respectively. Notice ארץ שלום must be handled inconsistently to the pattern of veiled allusions and be taken at face value.

73. So similarly Berridge, p. 165.

74. For a review of research, see Hubmann, *Untersuchungen*, pp. 97-101. Either מלא is taken as a straight adverb or as an abbreviation for קול מלא. However there are no parallel examples, unless Jer. 4.5—קראו מלאו applies. מלא and קול never occur together. The versions all diverge in their translation: G επισυνηχθησαν; α'σ'—ενεπλησθησαν; Targ—מלן בישן; V—*plene voce*. Cf. BDB, p. 571; *HALAT* p. 533.

75. So Thomas, pp. 47-52, who saw the expression here and in Jer. 4.5 as military idioms repointed as the noun מְלָא, or inf. abs., producing a meaning of 'mass', 'multitude', 'mustering'. Besides comparative semitic evidence, he could also appeal, convincingly, to such texts as Jer. 51.11, Job 16.10, Gen. 48.19, and Isa. 31.4 in support of such a nuance. G (see above n. 74) appears to be reflecting a similar understanding. Cf. Driver, pp. 177-78, for a similar approach, though he took it as an actual cry with the meaning 'all together', through comparison with an Arabic idiom.

76. So Driver, pp. 177-78.

77. Note in these examples the presence of לאמר/אמר is optional. The phrase in these contexts does not carry a negative connotation. It is neutral. Cf. Hubmann, *Untersuchungen*, p. 97.

78. Cf. Hubmann, *Untersuchungen* pp. 96-97, for a similar line of reasoning. We do not follow his redactional reconstruction nor appeal to the pattern of citations with a descending frequency of words.

79. So Thomas's and Driver's development of the interpretation.

80. An alternative proposal of Hubmann, *Untersuchungen*, p. 105, views מלא as an abbreviated death threat (מלא ימיו למבחה)—Jer. 25.34; cf. Jer. 6.11; Lam. 4.18; 2 Sam. 7.12). In the last analysis, this attractive proposal fails to explain the need for a warning of treachery since קרא אחר suggests direct address.

81. To אל טובות דבר cf. 2 Sam. 7.28; 1 Kgs 12.7; Jer. 52.32/2 Kgs 25.28.
The Samuel text is explicitly concerned with a covenant or pact. For the
cognate expressions in Akkadian and Aramaic treaty idiom, see *Ṭābūta itti
dabābu* and מבתא (Sefire). See for further details and texts: Moran, pp. 173-
76; Fox, pp. 41-42.

82. Fox, p. 42.

83. In light of the potential quality of ידברו in the concessive clause (כי), it
seems best to take בגד/קרא as perfects of certainty referring to the imminent
future (cf. GKC, §106n). A further objection of Hubmann, *Untersuchungen*,
p. 64, to the integrity of the connection between v. 5 and v. 6 drops away
since the supposed future (v. 5)—past (v. 6) tense shift need not be in
view.

84. Lines of association for a subtle interplay at this level are set up along
the axis of false speech/profession. External protestations of piety/friendship
(דבר טובות אל, מלא/קרוב אתה בפיהם) are shown to be utterances of deceit
בגד/רחוק מכליותיהם. The treaty-covenant idiom becomes suggestive coupled
with the use of בגד, for the latter is a metaphor of Israel's betrayal of Yahweh
(Jer. 3.20).

85. See above, nn. 30-32, for diction analysis of v. 6.

Notes to Chapter 1.3

1. ואיש מדון—omit איש 2° with G σ′ pc. MSS. O α′ θ′ Targ V follow MT.
Most follow the shorter reading. See standard commentators. As exceptions,
note Baumgartner, p. 60; Hubmann, *Untersuchungen*, p. 205.

2. כלה מקללוני—Follow the *Qere* כלה מקללני as the harder reading. The
images are of the whole land as a collection of individuals by synecdoche.
The *Kethib* arose probably under influence of the idea of plurality and
misdivision of consonants, כלהם קללוני. Most follow the *Kethib*. See
standard commentators. As an exception, note Hubmann, *Untersuchungen*,
p. 205.

3. אמר יהוה—G γενοιτο δεσποτα (אמן יהוה). α′ σ′ Targ V follow MT.
The text of v. 11 is very disturbed. MT marks the verse as divine speech. G
continues the prophetic complaint. Both alternatives are possible. אמן is
usually a concluding confirmatory response, but in Jer. 28.6 (G—αληθως)
and 1 Kgs 1.36 it introduces oaths. אמר יהוה normally concludes an oracle,
though medial and introductory occurrences exist (descending frequency—
Jer. 46.25; esp. Pss. 50.16; 68.23; Isa. 36.10). Given the influence of the
prophetic liturgy pattern on three other confessional units (11.18-23; 12.1-6;
15.15-21), MT אמר is tentatively preferred. G probably derives from
confusion of ר and ן, facilitated by the oath character of the immediate
sentence. Most follow G. See standard commentators. As recent advocates of
MT, note Reventlow, p. 211; Hubmann, *Untersuchungen*, p. 206. Talmon's

attempt (pp. 124-29) to exclude MT does not sufficiently come to terms with the overall pattern of the text in light of other confessional parallels. We hope to show that MT makes the best sense in its present literary setting (see below, Interpretation). The appeal to אמן יהוה in Jer. 11.5 (Talmon, p. 127) misconstrues the latter passage for there it is a concluding confirmatory formulation.

4. אם לא שרותך לטוב—G—καταθυνοντων αυτων. α' ει μη το υπολειμμα σου ην μοι εις αγαθον. σ' ει μη υπελειφθης εις αγαθον. Targ— אם לא סופך יהי לטב. V—*Si non reliquiae tuae in bonum*. Besides the problem of אמן/אמר, the centre of the disturbances in v. 11 appears to lie in the obscure שרותך. We tentatively suggest preservation of MT *Kethib*. The various witnesses attest to the present consonantal text. α' σ' Targ V imply some form of שארית/שאר with their assumption of an elided quiescent א in MT. G probably reflects changes contingent upon its understanding of the verse as prophetic speech reading ישר/אשר through haplography of the *Alephs* (אם לא). See Hubmann, *Untersuchungen*, pp. 180-99, for a review of scholarship. For explanation of שרותך, see below, Interpretation.

5. As a doublet with 17.3-4, vv. 13-14 are generally treated as intrusive to 15.10ff. and to be excluded (so Baumgartner; Duhm; Volz; Cornill; Weiser; *Jeremia*; Rudolph; Bright, *Jeremiah*; Ittmann) or at least to be seen as a deliberate redactional insertion (so Gerstenberger; Gunneweg; Hubmann, *Untersuchungen*; Reventlow. For defence of their integrity, see Smith, 'Quotations', pp. 229-31; Thompson, pp. 393-94). Detailed discussion of this problem will be postponed to the section on Redaction. Of more immediate interest is the consideration of the widespread doublet phenomenon (*Doppelüberlieferungen*) in Jeremiah (for discussions, see Driver, *ILOT*, p. 227; Bright, *Jeremiah*, pp. LXXV-LXXV1; Hubmann, *Untersuchungen*, pp. 218-22; Marx, pp. 106-20). The textual criticism of doublets must exercise great caution before simple excision or emendation to smooth differences between them is employed. The variant readings may relate to the intentional alteration and adaptation of the doublets to their respective settings (so Hubmann, *Untersuchungen*, pp. 208-209. For a summary of his position, see below, n. 28). Thus on this specific text, the reading with עבר should be preserved as a possible adjustment to the context as address to the prophet. Witnesses to עבר probably arose by assimilation to 17.4. For עבר ב meaning 'pass over into', cf. Judg. 9.26 (So also Gerstenberger, 'Complaints', p. 395 n.10. Most read העברתיך/תי. See standard commentators. Besides Gerstenberger, Hubmann, *Untersuchungen*, p. 209, follows MT). Though the G zero variant of 17.1-4 is probably due to haplography (16.21—יהוה/17.5—יהוה) (so Janzen, *Studies*, pp. 117, 133) it could be an indication that it has been drawn from 15.13-14 rather than the reverse.

6. לא במחיר—G ἀνταλλαγμα(>לא). α' σ' Targ V follow MT. G apparently translates to harmonize the overall logic interpreting בכל חטאות as δια πασας suggesting the despoliation as 'payment for'. See below for the

interpretation of בכל. Most omit the negative. See standard commentators. As exceptions, note Volz, p. 183; Thompson, p. 393; Hubmann, *Untersuchungen*, p. 209.

7. So Wanke, 'אוי', p. 15. For the use of the הוי/אוי formulae in the prophets and determination of their setting, see: Gerstenberger, 'Woe-Oracles', pp. 249-63; Clifford, pp. 458-64; Williams, pp. 75-91; Clements, pp. 17-29; Janzen, *Mourning*; *THAT* I, pp. 474-77.

8. The address to the 'mother who bore' can be taken as an oblique address and implied petition to Yahweh. So Blank, 'Confessions', pp. 331, 347; Reventlow, p. 216. Still the difference from what is normally encountered stands. So Baumgartner, p. 61, who classified it as near lament related to *Hiobdichtungen*. On the latter relationship the formal distinction between self-curse (cf. Jer. 20.14-18; Job 3.3-10) and the woe-cry must be maintained. Job never uses the latter. There seems to be no suggestion in v. 10 that calamitous results of evil deeds are anticipated so that it approaches the anticipatory function of curse as a cry of anguish. See further Wanke, 'אוי', p. 217; Gerstenberger, 'Woe-Oracles', p. 250; Clifford, p. 459. For self-curse, see on Jer. 20.14-18.

9. See Gen. 24.38; Num. 14.28; Josh. 14.9; Ps. 137.6; and GKC §149. Blank, 'Confessions', p. 348 n. 24, saw it as a basis for the suitability of G אמן versus MT אמר.

10. The reference is to the form of speech. No claim is intended regarding Jeremiah's relationship to the 'wise' or wisdom tradition in general. The use of rhetorical questions containing appeals to natural phenomena occurs elsewhere in Jeremianic poetry (18.14; 13.23; 2.11, 32; 8.4; perhaps 3.1-5). Note too the proverbial character of the challenge in 12.5. So Baumgartner, p. 62 (*Gleichnis in Frageform*). See further Brueggemann, 'Rhetorical Questions', pp. 358-74; Hobbs, 'Reflections', pp. 62-72; *idem*, 'Jer. 3.1-5', pp. 23-29; Crenshaw, *Wisdom*, p. 233.

11. Cf. Gerstenberger, 'Complaints', p. 395, who views the whole of vv. 13-14 as a judgment speech remodelled into a salvation oracle to the nation.

12. For labels and analysis of form, see Schoors, p. 42.

13. For example, note Jer. 8.18-23 (9.1) with alternation of speakers: prophet (vv. 18-19aα), exiles (v. 19aβ), Yahweh (v. 19b), exiles (v. 20), prophet (vv. 21-23). See, further, Holladay, *Architecture*, pp. 67, 74-75, on the phenomenon in the 'foe from the north' oracles. In our text, the alternation of addressees could be seen analogously as the figure of speech, apostrophe. Cf. Pss. 6.9; 114.1-5; 2 Sam. 1.19-21.

14. Previous commentators have offered various understandings of such an alternation (noted in Hubmann, *Untersuchungen*, pp. 180-87): S. Schmidt (1685) following Kimchi, saw vv. 11b-14 addressed to the nation; E.F.C. Rosenmüller (1826) saw v. 11 addressed to Jeremiah, vv. 12-14 addressed to the nation; C.F. Schnurrer (1793) saw vv. 11b, 13, 14b addressed to the

nation; W. Neumann (1856) saw vv. 13-14 addressed to Jeremiah as representative of the nation. Hubmann has modified the latter viewing עליכם (v. 14b) as including both prophet and nation separated. See on Interpretation below.

15. Argued by Blank, 'Confessions'; Wimmer, 'Experience'; and Reventlow. See Form on 11.18-23 for summary of their positions. Ittmann's formal analysis (pp. 70-74) of the unit is marred by the excision of 15.12-14 (pp. 44-49) based upon the doublet phenomenon and the joining of 15.10-11, 15-21 together as one unit.

16. So Hubmann, *Untersuchungen*, pp. 252-53. Our structural schema is in general agreement with his. We have preferred labels indicating formal/logical functions without anticipating decisions of a redactional nature. The alternative structural analysis by Smith, 'Quotations', pp. 229-30, which treats 15.10-21 as one unit and understands vv. 11-12 and vv. 13-14 as two previous contradictory divine sayings cited by the prophet as the basis of his complaint is attractive. However, הפגע ב probably is not to be given a positive nuance. Thus it cannot be taken as a promise that the prophet will be favourably received (see Interpretation below). Verse 14a makes best sense as direct address to the prophet. Adjustment of 17.3-4 would not have been necessary had the intention been to cite a previous judgment speech against Yahweh. The double cycles of prophetic liturgy patterns in 11.18-12.6 and in the immediate context (14.1-15.4) create an expectation of a similar pattern here. Further 15.15-21 seems to constitute a formally integrated unit on its own. See below on 15.15-21.

17. This feature led Gerstenberger, 'Complaints', p. 402, to see vv. 10-12 as the oldest element of the unit.

18. The possible exception, ארץ in vv. 10 and 14, does not seem likely since the word is used in entirely different senses.

19. Interpreting v. 12, alternatively, as a reference to the foe from the north would remove its transitional nature, associating it with vv. 13-14 to render the shift from rebuke to promise more abrupt. See below on Interpretation for an evaluation.

20. So most redactional studies: Gerstenberger, 'Complaints', p. 402; Gunneweg, pp. 404-405; Hubmann, *Untersuchungen*, pp. 255-57; Carroll, p. 112; Vermeylen, p. 266. The latter is instructive, for though he finds two post-exilic editorial stages, the first consists of vv. 10-11 as a unit. His post-exilic dating again rests upon the inappropriate data observed on 11.18-12.6 and does not give sufficient weight to inner-Jeremianic contacts. The standard commentators retained these verses as a unit in some fashion.

21. Eichler, pp. 92-96; Ahuis, pp. 90-91, 98-100.

22. Eichler, pp. 95-96, 70, does not reach a firm decision about v. 11 in regard to the MT vs. G reading. The force of her argument is to show that either way the text is unintelligible. For the MT reading, she draws attention to 1 Kgs 19.18 as its model. However, there is no resemblance between the

verses. No oath clauses are present in 1 Kings. The only possible connection is the occurrence of שאר if the *Kethib-Qere* reading in 15.11 is derived from this root. We think not. See below on Interpretation. Also, even on the interpretation of G, the second profession of innocence is not an entirely unsatisfactory development of the first, illustrating that the basis of the conflict with the community lies in their perversity and not for want of the supplicant's attempt to side with them.

23. The basis for Ahuis's classification (p. 91) appears to lie in his contention that the poetic kernel (vv. 10, 17, 18) of the complaint is executed in a *Qina*-metre. However, to support this he must then engage in conjectural emendations to produce the required metrical pattern (p. 91 n. 3). It seems preferable to accept a mixed metre for the passage. The only over-balanced line is produced by את האיב in v. 11, but this is probably not a sufficient reason to reclassify the whole as prose.

24. See diction analysis below.

25. A reason given by many for engaging in emendation, if not for judging the verse secondary: so Duhm; Volz; Cornill; Weiser, *Jeremia*; Rudolph; Bright, *Jeremiah*; Vermeylen, p. 266; Carroll, p. 112; Ittmann, p. 49; Ahuis, p. 99.

26. Only ברזל and מצפון seem correspondent while the other examples offered by Rudolph, p. 104, and Ahuis, p. 99, seem too superficial to represent material links. If 15.12 is derived from 17.1, it represents a complete rewriting of it rather than a corruption.

27. See above note 20 for advocates of their redactional status. As defenders of originality, see Reventlow, p. 213; Thompson, p. 393; Chambers, p. 62; Wimmer, 'Experience', p. 196. Reventlow and Chambers do so on the basis of the formulaic character of the expressions.

28. It is beyond the scope of our study to enter into a detailed analysis of the Jeremianic doublets, but a summary of Hubmann's observations (*Untersuchungen*, pp. 217-44) will be helpful. The doublets occur in poetry and prose, between poetic and prose material, within Jeremiah, and between Jeremiah and other biblical texts (p. 218). The relationship between any particular doublet and its parallels can consist of basic identity, slight differences, or major alterations. The doublets within prose material or between poetry and prose provide the majority of cases where major alterations occur. For the most part, poetic doublets are confined to identical or near identical repetitions (p. 224). An interesting feature that occurs across all types of doublets, accounting for almost half of them, is the change of addressee either by alteration of name or labels, or simply arising from the new context (p. 224). When it comes to suggestions about the cause and origin of various doublets, Hubmann argues that careful distinctions must be made. The short formulation of some texts can be viewed as 'standing phrases' capable of multiple utilization (p. 224). Unaltered doublets are best regarded as due to multiple anchoring in various tradition complexes

(p. 243). However, signs of intentional re-use through conscious alteration of addressees are best understood as redactional productions arising from the concern to actualize the doublet for needs of a later time (p. 243). Noticing that doublets between Jeremiah texts and other biblical texts, on the whole, exhibited major alterations, Hubmann argued that these may be traced back to the prophet himself. This was based upon the relatively greater freedom in the use of traditional material as opposed to the reserve exhibited toward the inner-Jeremianic doublets (pp. 237, 243). Since the majority of these examples occur in the foreign nation oracles, this point remains unconfirmed since the authenticity of many of these texts is in dispute (cf. p. 238). Whether he can be followed in every point for the rest or not, Hubmann's analysis shows that the doublets cannot be treated on the same level. There is a need for careful analysis of each example before a decision in regard to originality or the opposite can be made.

29. Note the absence or alteration of the following in 17.3aα—חררי בשדה; 17.3bα—במתיך; 17.4aα—entirely; 17.4bα—קרחתם changed to קרחה; 17.4bβ—עד עולם changed to עליכם.

30. For example, vv. 1-2 contain the concrete accusation of idolatry which balances with במתיך in v. 3. The corporate addressee is clear between vv. 3-4 and vv. 1-2.

31. For the text, see Hubmann, 'Textgraphik', pp. 30-36.

32. So Hubmann, *Untersuchungen*, p. 257.

33. See Reventlow and Chambers, n. 27 above.

34. See n. 28 above.

35. Its length may disqualify it from classification as 'stock formula'. So Hubmann, *Untersuchungen*, p. 224. He sees it as due to multiple anchoring in separate complexes.

36. See above n. 28 for the possibility of the prophet using earlier tradition in a free manner.

37. See diction analysis in Interpretation.

38. In passing, we note that the consistent corporate interpretation of Reventlow, p. 212, is not required by vv. 10-12; v. 13 is ambiguous; v. 14b is explicitly corporate but could be explained in relation to an alternating pattern of addressees (see below); and v. 14a (MT) definitely excludes a corporate interpretation. For the latter, Reventlow inappropriately adjusts the verse to read according to 17.4. Similarly, Gerstenberger, 'Complaints', p. 396, defends his view of 15.13-14 as a salvation oracle addressed to the nation by partial adjustment to 17.3-4.

39. For review, see on 11.18-23.

40. Proposals for a total transfer in a post-exilic setting (Carroll, Vermeylen) seem highly improbable in light of the contacts with Jeremianic poetry already noted. Other transfer approaches may need to be modified, at least, to allow for a significant relationship to and/or incorporation of authentic materials. For example, Gunneweg's so-called biographical

elements interwoven with psalm motifs may need to be related more closely
to authentic material (p. 405). Still the presence of stylistically and verbally
compatible elements affecting each of the verses would not be explained.

41. So also Hubmann, *Untersuchungen*, p. 260; Ittmann, p. 271.

42. Advocates of total editorial transfer views took the figurative and
stereotyped imagery as signs of inauthenticity (so Gunneweg; Gerstenberger,
'Complaints'). However, the poetic method by which such figurative
transfers obscure the concrete nature of the difficulty indicated in such
imagery is not only common to the Psalter but also in Jeremianic poetry. Cf.
the language of physical affliction in Psalms used to represent problems
ranging from physical disease to persecution and spiritual ailment (30.3;
31.11; 32.3,4) to similar usage in Jer. 15.15-18. See the latter unit for analysis
of image use elsewhere in Jeremiah to depict national apostasy and
destruction.

43. Cf. as well the similar language in 20.14-18 and its apparent echoes of
the call narrative: 20.18—מרחם מרחם יצאתי/1.5—תצא מרחם. So also Thompson,
p. 392; Hubmann, *Untersuchungen*, p. 259 n. 2; Ittmann, p. 72. The latter's
additional appeal to vv. 11, 12 and 1 Kings 19 as part of the prophetic
background of Jer. 15.10 seems unlikely since any possible relationship
between the passages is too general to be helpful. Further contacts to the call
narrative may be present in על כל הארץ (note 15.10 לכל
הארץ כל/cf. 1.18 —כל הארץ) instead of על כל). Jeremianic poetry also uses the term to refer to the nation
(4.20, 27; 8.16; 12.11; 23.15).

44. The practice of taking איש ריב as 'legal adversary' (cf. Job 31.35) is
unlikely in light of the connection with מדון suggesting a more general
nuance of 'strife'/'contention'. The latter, used mainly in Proverbs, (9x; OT
13x—Pss. 1x—Jer. 1x) never has a legal connotation (cf. 6.14; 15.8; 16.28;
26.20; etc.). Against Bright, *Jeremiah*, p. 109; Thompson, p. 392; Wimmer,
'Sociology', p. 404; Ittmann, p. 71 n. 233.

45. For example, in the call narrative note: 1.10—הפקיד על; 1.18—
עיר מבצר, etc.; 1.19—נלחמו אל. In this regard cf. איש ריב in Judg. 12.2,
referring to a state of war, and איש מדון (*Qere*) in 2 Sam. 21.20, analogous to
איש מלחמה. The latter is textually uncertain and such parallels as Prov.
21.9, 19; 25.24; 26.21; 27.15 indicate that a military connotation is not
required.

46. Diction analysis: The distance from normal complaint psalms should
be stressed:

	O.T.	Pss.	Jer.
woe-cry	25 (common in Prophets)	1 (120.5)	8 (4.13, 31; 6.4; 10.19; 13.27; 15.10; 45.3; 48.46)
איש ריב	3 (Job 31.35; Isa. 41.11)	0	1
איש מדון	2 (2 Sam. 21.20-*Qere*)	0	1
נשה	13	1 (109.11)	2 (only 15.10)
קלל (*pi.*)	43	3	1

For אם, ילד see 20.14-18.

47. The ambiguity of איש ריב (objective or subjective genitive) also affects the allusion to the call narrative for the latter requires a subjective genitive while the parallel with כלה מקללני suggests the objective genitive. For advocates of the subj. gen., see Bright, *Jeremiah*, p. 106; Thompson, p. 392; Hubmann, *Untersuchungen*, p. 260.

48. For a detailed survey of research, see Hubmann, *Untersuchungen*, pp. 179-99.

49. Extensive discussion of the problems can be found in Reventlow, pp. 211-12; Cornill, pp. 193-94. As advocates of שרר/'strengthen', see Ewald; von Orelli; Lamparter; Nicholson, *Jeremiah*.

50. A certain amount of ambiguity *vis à vis* divine or prophetic spech afflicts this proposal. As divine speech, see Baumgartner, p. 60; Gerstenberger, 'Complaints', p. 402 n. 37, though the latter's translation implies שרה. As prophetic, see Duhm, p. 134; Bredenkamp, p. 268.

51. So Volz, p. 171; Weiser, *Jeremiah*, p. 130; Rudolph, p. 104; Condamin, p. 131; Blank, 'Confessions', p. 348 n. 24; Bright, *Jeremiah*, p. 106; Eichler, pp. 95-96; Ahuis, p. 90; Ittmann, p. 48 n. 144.

52. So first Hitzig, p. 122, but revived recently by Holladay, *Spokesman*, p. 96; Thompson, p. 393; Hubmann, *Untersuchungen* p. 262. Before them, cf. Nägelsbach, p. 119. Isolated solutions can be found in Cornill, p. 194 ('zu ihren Verwünschungen'); Reventlow, p. 216 n. 81 ('ich habe dir geholfen'); Carroll, p. 112 ('entreat'). The last two provide no justification for their translations.

53. So הפגיע ב with ל/'for what' in Jer. 36.25 (cf. Isa. 53.12; 59.16). For the *qal* in Jeremiah with ב of the person interceded plus ל/'for what', see 7.16; 27.18. As the most recent advocate of this view, see Ittmann, pp. 46-48. And before him Duhm; Cornill; Volz; Weiser, *Jeremia*; Rudolph; Bright, *Jeremiah*. More traditionally a causative nuance was assumed ('cause the enemy to make entreaty') without, however, the support of any parallels. So BDB, p. 803, and analogously Baumgartner, p. 60; Gerstenberger, 'Complaints', p. 402.

54. Ittmann, p. 48 n. 145, wants to emend the text to לאיב which would produce the required construction. But G (πρός) and V (*adversum*) do not necessarily support this since they could be interpreting את as the preposition meaning either 'with'/'for help' (BDB, p. 85 la) or 'with'/'against' (BDB, p. 86 lab).

55. Ittmanns attempt, p. 46 n. 131, to exclude this verse from consideration seems too hasty in light of the precise grammatical correspondence.

56. So Reventlow, p. 212; Holladay, *Spokesman*, p. 95; Hubmann, *Untersuchungen*, p. 262; Thompson, p. 391. Given the complex blend of challenge, rebuke, and warning in 12.5-6, there seems to be no theoretical presumption for an exclusively promisory answer here as Ittmann, p. 46, argues. Similarly, attempts to see a change of address in v. 11b because of its negative tone are not necessary. So for example, Reventlow, pp. 213-14

(addressed to Israel). For others, see Hubmann, *Untersuchungen*, p. 180.

57. So Holladay and Hubmann above n. 56. The phrase לטוב does not appear to be decisive in reaching a solution, since, whatever the meaning of שרותך (positive or negative), it only asserts that this is directed to a good purpose, against Ittmann, p. 46.

58. This postulaled geminate root is problematical in light of the derivation from שור, a hollow root, in BDB, p. 1004, offered for the ptc. שוררי. However, *KBL*, p. 958, offers a derivation from שרר. The *Kethib* in 15.11 implies a geminate verb (note the anapyctic vowel 'ו'). And since BDB views the ptc. as a *po.* the elision of preformative *Mem* (cf. GKC § 52s), a root שרר could still be implied since the ptc. forms of hollow and geminate roots would be identical. Though such a root is not widely attested, there does appear to be an appropriate cognate in AKK. *šāru* III ('hostile', 'enemy'). See *AHw*, p. 1193. It is attested frequently in Amarna AKK., adjectively and substantively (see VAB 2; 5. 1518). The more widely attested form of the word is sarru (*AHw*, p. 1030), which is also attested in Amarna AKK. (VAB 2; 1500). these considerations provide some basis for postulating a root שרר ('be hostile'/'be an enemy').

59. However, GKC § 67 1 n. 1 observes the existence of both *pi.* and *po.* forms for the same root with a more causative nuance for the former. This may account for the *Kethib* in 15.11 which resembles a *qal* stem. Alternatively, an abstract nominal formation could be postulated to avoid the difficulty (cf. GKC § 86k), translating שרותך as 'your situation of enmity'. The postulation of inf. cstr. (so Hitzig, p. 122) would encounter difficulty in explaining an inf. שרות from שרר.

60. More precise identification of האיב is difficult. The overwhelming usage in Jeremiah refers to the foe from the north (6.25; 12.7; 15.9; 17.4; 18.17; 19.7, 9; 20.4, 5; 21.7; 30.14; 31.16; 34.20, 21; 44.30) which could permit a similar interpretation in 15.11. So Reventlow, p. 214; Carroll, p. 114. However, the tight logical and thematic relationship of vv. 10-11 seems to exclude such a view. Instead a link between האיב and כל הארץ seems more likely. In this regard, the generic character of the label fits the usage in the other confessions, though איב is used only here. The reference to 'northern iron and bronze' in v. 12 also need not be seen as a reference to Babylon, thus providing no support for איב as national foe (see below on v. 12). Advocates for איב as the prophet's opponents range on both sides of the question of the speaker of v. 11: Hubmann, Thompson (Yahweh); Duhm; Cornill; Volz; Weiser, *Jeremia*; Rudolph; Bright, *Jeremiah*; Ittmann (Prophet).

61. Diction analysis: Distance from the psalter should be stressed. The oath pattern and messenger formula each occur twice in Pss. שרר occurs only here, unless it is legitimately related to שוררי (Pss. 5x).

	O.T.	Pss.	Jeremiah			
			Total	Poetry	Prose	f.n.o.
הפגיע ב...את	2 (Isa. 53.6; Jer. 15.11)		1			
פגע	46	0	4	1	3	
איב	279	74	19	8	10	1
עת רעה	8	1 (37.19)	4	3 (2.27, 28: 15.11)	1 (11.12)	
עת צרה	7	1 (37. 39)	3	3 (14.8; 15.11; 30.7)		

Co-ordinate phrases—only here

	O.T.	Pss.	Total	Poetry	Prose	f.n.o.
רעה		31	83	24	52	7
צרה		22	8	5	1	2

The latter terms are ambiguous in Psalms. They refer to general situations of distress. But in Jeremiah the reference is usually to Yahweh's judgment upon Judah (possible exceptions: 14.8; 16.19; 17.17, 18).

62. Three potential referents are indicated according to usage. ברזל מצפון is unique in the OT. מצפון could reflect a reference to Babylon, the foe from the north, since מצפון refers elsewhere in Jeremiah exclusively to this (1.13, 14; 4.6; 6.1, 22; 10.22; 13.20; etc.). However, ברזל ונחשת is never so used and could imply a reference to the prophet (1.18; 15.20) or national spiritual depravity (6.28). See Hubmann, *Untersuchungen*, p. 181 n. 8, for a review of positions taken. The understanding northern foe/Babylon has been by far the most popular.

63. In addition, the reading in Jer. 6.28 which suggests the possibility is textually problematic. See further Bright, *Jeremiah*, p. 49; Thompson, p. 266. The only basis upon which such a view would work in 15.12 would be if v. 12 is prophetic speech. But the only reason for requiring the latter would be if no other possibilites exist which would permit the continuance of the divine speech from v. 11. The remaining possibilities do just that.

64. For the probable spread of high quality iron from Asia Minor south into Syria-Palestine, see 'Iron' in *IDB*, p. 725.

65. So Hubmann, *Untersuchungen*, p. 265. For the use of iron/bronze as a symbol of strength, hardness, and permanence, see Lev. 26.19; Deut. 33.25; Isa. 48.4; Jer. 6.28; 11.4; 17.1; 28.13, 14; Mic. 4.13; Ps. 2.9; Job 40.18.

66. Diction analysis:

	O.T.	Pss.	Jeremiah			
			Total	Poetry	Prose	f.n.o
רעע	14	1 (2.9)	3	3 (2.16; 11.16; 15.12)		
ברזל	76	5	8	4	4	
נחשת	133	1	14	3 (9 × Jer. 52)	2	
מצפון	34	1 (107.3)	3	2 (4.6; 6.1)	1 (1.14)	
צפון	153	3	20	7	4	9
ברזל ונחשת	14	0	2	2 (6.28; 15.12)		

We view the relationship of the repeated ברזל as synonymous rather than as subject-object, based upon the stylistic characteristic of doubled expressions in the unit. So Hubmann, *Untersuchungen*, p. 253. An intransitive sense for רעע is attested (BDB, p. 949; Jer. 11.16; Prov. 25.19). No explicit parallel to the rhetorical question exists in the OT.

67. The only reading which could permit a consistent corporate addressee is העבדתיך, but emendation would constitute an inappropriate conflation of the doublets.

68. For collective singulars, see GKS §123. In Jeremianic poetry the nation is frequently represented as an individual (2.28; 3.12-13; 5.15-17; 4.1, 2; 30.8, 11).

69. So Hubmann, *Untersuchungen*, p. 269.

70. *Idem*, p. 271, and, independently of him, Wimmer, 'Experience', p. 200.

71. *Idem*, pp. 268-69. He is countering older approaches which either ignored the *waw* or omitted it (cf. 17.3) and subordinated the second phrase to the first: 'because of all your sins in all your borders'.

72. For this understanding of ו . . . ו see GKC §154a n. 1 and cf. Ps. 76.7— נרדם ורכב וסום. Hubmann, *Untersuchungen*, p. 203, translates: 'Deine Habe und deine Schätze gebe ich zur Beute, ohne Bezahlung, sowohl für deine Sünden, als auch für dein Land'.

73. *Idem*, pp. 269 and 272: 'Die Weissagung kündigt dem Propheten den ersatzlosen Verlust seiner privaten Güter an. Mit ihnen war er zwar vor Menschen einwandfrei umgegangen, wie er sich in v. 10c rechtfertigt, vor Jahwe hat aber dann der Verlust rechtfertigende Wirkung, doch nicht nur für Jeremia allein, sondern auch für sein Land'.

74. גבול could refer to property unjustly acquired, but there are more explicit ways of expressing this. Verse 10c is against it. Hubmann's appeals to various narratives are precarious. For example, Jeremiah 32 indicates that the prophet was propertied, and that such experiences, as related there, could have symbolic significance. But it does not show why possession of property would be culpable nor does it match the present passage which announces actual judgment rather than providing a symbolic chastisement of the prophet in anticipation of imminent judgment (against Hubmann, *Untersuchungen*, p. 269 n. 40). Similarly, Jer. 39.12 and 40.4-6 show the exile of the prophet's enemies with the prophet remaining in the land. However, in 43.1-6, the prophet goes into Egyptian exile shortly after Gedaliah's assassination which would conflict with the interpretation proposed by Hubmann. And that the addition of vv. 13-14 is a reflection of these very events is unlikely for the same reason (*ibid.*, p. 270).

75. For explicative *waw*, see BDB, p. 252 1b, and Williams, §434. For pleonastic *waw*, see Williams, §435, and esp. Wernberg-Møller, 'Pleonastic', pp. 321-26. It is documented in biblical and Qumran Hebrew, and Ugaritic (2 Sam. 7.10f.; 1QIsa.ª 9.19; 24.20; Ug. 51. v. 107). The examples noted

involve the usage with prepositional phrases. In Jer. 15.13 the two phrases
would represent a usage with non-synonymous components. For further
Ugaritic examples, see Gordon, §13.103.

76. Our approach is paralleled by the older commentator (cited in
Hubmann, *Untersuchungen*, p. 183) C.F. Schnurrer (1793). We differ from
him in that he also saw v. 11b as addressed to the prophet's enemies.

77. The disjunctive placements of the objects in v. 13a could represent a
slight notification that an addressee-shift had occurred.

78. Hubmann's remaining objections to our position are inconclusive. The
most they can show is that v. 13 need not have a corporate addressee. גבול
could mean either the border of a country or territory/possession, but the
latter does not say whether or not an individual's or nation's property is in
view (against Hubmann, *Untersuchungen*, p. 270). Given the doublet
phenomenon, simple appeal to 17.3 to decide the issue is ruled out since a
new addressee could be intended in 15.13; so *ibid.*, p. 268. However, the
omission of many explicit national references from 17.1-4 to 15.13-14 need
not indicate an exclusive individualizing trend. Contrast 17.4b—עד עולם to
15.14b עליכם. It may be more correct to say that alteration of judgment
speech to function as a promise of salvation is the governing factor for the
readjustments (against *ibid.*, p. 269 n. 42).

79. Cf. כי אש קדח באפי ותיקד. So also Hubmann, *Untersuchungen*, p. 271.

80. For אש, see Jer. 4.4; 5.14; 11.16; cf. Ps. 18.9; 50.3; 78.21, 23; 97.3. For
אף, see Jer. 2.35; 4.8; 12.73; 18.23; 23.20; 30.24; cf. Pss. 7.7; 78.21; Hos. 8.5;
Zech. 10.3; Job 19.11.

81. Diction analysis: Apart from general vocabulary usage, distance from
Psalm idioms should be stressed:

V.13	O.T.	Pss.	Unique	Jeremiah Total	Poetry	Prose	f.n.o.
חילך ואוצרותיך	(co-ord.)		x				
ובכל חטאותיך ובכל גבוליך	(co-ord.)		x				
חילך (wealth)		10		1	1		
לא במחיר	1 (Isa. 45.13)	0		1	1	(cf. Isa. 51.1—בלא; מחיר; Ps. 44.13—ולא רבית במחיריהם)	
לבו אתן	2 (cf. Ezek. 23.46; 25.7)	0		3	3 (15.13; 17.3; 30.16)		
V. 14a							
עבר ב/'pass over into'	1	0		1	1 (cf. Judg. 9. 26)		
בארץ לא ידע	3	0		3	3 (15.14; 17.4; 14.18)		
חיל	244	17		31	2	22	7
אוצר	79	2		12	3	3	6

	O.T.	Pss.	Unique	Total	Poetry	Prose	f.n.o.
בז	24	0		5	4	0	1
מחיר	15	1	(44.13)	1	1		
חטאת ('sin')	95	13		13	7	5	1
גבול	240	5		4	4		
עבר	547	29		28	14	9	5
קרח	5	0		2	2 (15.14; 17.4)		
יקר	8	0		2	2 (15.14; 17.4)		
אש	379	28		39	8	23	8
אף (anger/wrath)	—	32		24	13	8	3

For איב, ארץ see vv. 10-11. For ידע, see 15.15.

82. Hubmann, *Untersuchungen*, p. 271, saw a tension between איביך/האיב since the former referred to a national enemy, and the latter the prophet's opponents. But see n. 60 above where האיב most probably links to כל הארץ. No conflict is present. Hubmann apparently found this meaning for האיב by seeing the reference to a future opponent (p. 266). However, the parallel oaths suggest that הפגעתי refers to a past occurrence rather than constituting a prophetic perfect.

Notes to Chapter 1.4

1. On the whole, the text is in good condition. By and large the versions support MT with the principal exceptions provided by G. For the latter, numerous alternative readings arising from incorrect division of letters or free interpretive translation are to be noted. These probably do not reflect a *Vorlage* different from MT.

2. אתה ידעת—G omits. οι γ′ Targ V follow MT. MT is to be preserved as a probable editorial expansion designed to link up with the preceding unit. The phrase is commensurate stylistically with other confessions (12.3; 17.16; 18.23) but normally specifies the object either following or preceding (Pss. 31.8; 69.6; 20; 139.2, 4; 40.10). Here it occurs absolutely.

3. לארך—G εἰς μακροθυμιαν (אֶרֶךְ). Targ ארכה. V *patientia*. Retain MT as a divine epithet (Exod. 34.6; Pss. 86.15; 103.8). The use of adjectives in poetry for substantives and as objects of a preposition is legitimate (GKC §132 n. 3). Though handled variously, MT is retained by most in some fashion. See standard commentators.

4. דברך/דבריך—read *Qere* with mlt. MSS and versions. However, the *Kethib* is grammatically possible (GKS §145.0). Only Reventlow, p. 212, and Berridge, p. 118, read the *Kethib* on the basis of their special understandings of דבר—the former as divine commandments, the latter as prophetic literary works.

5. ופריתיך; והצלתיך; נאם יהוה—G omits. οι γ′ Targ V follow MT. Retain

MT. Omission in G probably due to haplography (ולהצילך ... והצלתיך) and homoioteleuton (ופריתיך). So Janzen, *Studies*, p. 117. Standard commentators generally follow MT. The issue is complicated by redactional problems. See below.

6. See previously our discussion of Form and Redaction for 15.10-14 and views surveyed there. For an excellent and detailed review of approaches to the structure of 15.10-14, 15-21, see Hubmann, *Untersuchungen*, pp. 179-99.

7. So Baumgartner, p. 38.

8. See our earlier summary of their positions in Form on 11.18-23.

9. Berridge, p. 114.

10. Noted already by Baumgartner, pp. 36, 39, who described v. 17 as a profession of innocence remodelled into complaint.

11. See Reventlow, pp. 222-25, who attempted such a classification for v. 17a by interpreting the roots עלז/שחק as references to godless scoffers. For a convincing critique of his approach, see Bright, 'Jeremiah's Complaints', p. 202; Berridge, pp. 123-29.

12. See below on Interpretation.

13. On the despairing tone of Ps. 88, see Kraus, p. 608; Weiser, *Psalmen*, p. 399 (Eng. edn, p. 586); Dahood, *Psalms II*, p. 302. See Westermann, *Lob*, pp. 55-56 (Eng. edn, pp. 74-75) where he observes that none of the Psalm laments consists exclusively of lament and petition.

14. Categories according to Schoors, p. 42.

15. The problem of the syntactical relationship to v. 19 complicates the analysis of formal typicalities. See below on Redaction.

16. For a general discussion of the form, see Raitt, pp. 34-35. He identifies as the primary elements: admonition, promise, accusation, and threat. While most of his examples contain both promise and threat, some omit the threat: Isa. 55.6-7; Joel 2.12-13; Amos 5.14-15; Zech. 1.2-6; Mal. 3.7. For examples where the promise is omitted, he cites only Jeremiah texts. A major difficulty in his analysis is the failure to distinguish adequately the prose and poetic traditions in Jeremiah. In light of Thiel's subsequent isolation of the alternative preaching form in the prose sermons, the relationship of the latter with the summons to repentance requires clarification. See Thiel, pp. 290-95.

17. However, interesting parallels in the Mari prophetic correspondence can be noted. ARM X.8 contains a conditional promise and summons to *Zimri-lim* (however, translation of the *šumma*-clause is disputed). A.1121 contains both a positive and a negative summons (cf. Thiel's alternative-preaching, above n. 16). Still, none of these also includes elements comparable to the oracle of salvation motifs to be found in the Akkadian prophetic oracles to Esarhaddon and Ashurbanipal (see *ANET*, pp. 449-51; 604-606). For translation and bibliography on the Mari texts, see Huffmon, 'Prophecy', pp. 199-224. For a general survey of Mesopotamian prophecy with biblio-

graphic survey, see Wilson pp. 89-124.

18. Schoors, p. 47.

19. However the delineation of the passage is contested. See Raitt, pp. 37-38, who divides it into smaller units. See Weiser, *Jeremia*, p. 32; Hyatt, pp. 829-30; Thompson, pp. 205-206, for unity and liturgical affinities.

20. So Berridge, p. 209, who explains the absence of the assurance formula as evidence of prophetic freedom in the employment of traditional forms. For other uses of the salvation oracle patterns in the Jeremiah tradition, see 1.17-19, 30.10-11, and 42.7-17, where it has been incorporaated into an alternative preaching sermon.

21. For particularly helpful analyses, see Hubmann, *Untersuchungen*, pp. 247-48; Jüngling, pp. 17-20.

22. So, similarly, Hubmann, *Untersuchungen*, p. 248, who observes the stylistic feature of doubled expressions related to actions and conditions.

23. Cf. the similar approaches of Volz, p. 171, amd more recently Jüngling, pp. 17-20. They, however, treat 15.10-14, 15-21 as a single unit.

24. See notes on text, above.

25. Eichler, pp. 92-100; Ahuis, pp. 90-101.

26. Eichler, p. 98, emphasizes the loose logical connection; Ahuis, p. 91, the prose character of the verses.

27. Eichler, pp. 92, 100; Ahuis, pp. 100-101. On our view that v. 15 contains an ironic play on a divine epithet (see below) the verse would enhance the attack upon Yahweh rather than reduce it.

28. So admitted by Eichler, and Ahuis, in regard to other confessional passages and even their reconstructed kernel of 15.10, 17, 18.

29. Verse 15b: דע שאתי עליך חרפה already provides the point of integration for the two themes.

30. His assumption of a rigid *Qina*-metre in the original kernel is weakened by the necessity of conjectural emendation in order to support it: vv. 10a, 18a (Ahuis, p. 91 n. 3).

31. Ahuis, p. 100, views the allusion of v. 16 to Jer. 1.9 and 16.9, plus the phrase נקרא שמך עלי, as evidence of its Dtr. character. He cites no evidence for v. 15. Cf. Gerstenberger, 'Complaints', p. 401. The validity of his arguments depends in part on one's understanding of דבר. For evaluation, see the diction analysis, note 49 and Interpretation below.

32. Eichler, pp. 190-91; Ahuis, p. 101; Vermeylen, p. 266; Hubmann, *Untersuchungen*, p. 289-99; Ittmann, p. 49. Prior to redaction critical models aspects of the verses were treated as glosses: Baumgartner, p. 34 (vv. 19b, 20aβb); Blank, Confessions', p. 347, n. 22 (v. 21).

33. Gerstenberger, 'Complaints', pp. 397-98.

34. Comparison is made to the prose sermon pattern of alternative preaching (Thiel, pp. 290-95): Eichler, pp. 187-88; Gerstenberger, 'Complaints', p. 398. As a Dtr. expansion, it is seen as a further attempt to reduce the blasphemous statements in the lament (Eichler, pp. 190-91; Ahuis, p. 101).

35. This appears to be stylistically paralleled elsewhere within Jeremianic poetry: 3.12, 22; 8.4, 5; 31.18, 21-22 (cf. [prose] 3.7, 14). None of the other diction is distinctively Dtr. or characteristic of Jeremianic prose. See below.

36. Eichler, pp. 190-91; Ittmann, p. 49; Ahuis, p. 101, who also stresses the prose character of the verse without demonstration.

37. See diction analysis below.

38. Hubmann, *Untersuchungen*, pp. 179-307.

39. *Ibid.*, pp. 233-34. The parallel with the call narrative has constituted the major basis for the exclusion of all or part of v. 20 by other scholars.

40. *Ibid.*, pp. 290-91.

41. *Ibid.*, pp. 278-81. This point will be evaluated below on Interpretation. Thus a certain tentativeness in the present discussion must be observed.

42. *Ibid.*, pp. 254-56. This point is inconclusive since 15.20-21 as original components of the oracle could have served as the model for the subsequent addition of 15.13-14. Cf. 12.5-6 and 11.21-23.

43. Particularly instructive are the inclusion in 1.18 of היום and the expanded series of opponents to mention not only the nation in general, but also its official leaders. The former is appropriate to the issue of the call event; the latter accords with the overview character of Jeremiah's mission provided by Jeremiah.

44. See Schoors, pp. 45-46, for a list of common expressions and formulas.

45. For a critique of Reventlow's attempt, pp. 24-77, to see a common ordination liturgy as the basis of a prophetic call with the salvation oracle at its centre, see Berridge, pp. 26-30. None of the other call narratives contains a salvation oracle or its elements as in Jeremiah 1, especially those closest in pattern (Exod. 3.10-12; Judg. 6.11-17; 1 Sam. 10.1-7). It is questionable whether a single pattern exists controlling every call narrative. See further, Zimmerli, *Ezechiel*, pp. 24-31 (Eng. edn, pp. 16-21); Yost, p. 45.

46. So Bright, *Jeremiah*, p. 6; Thiel, pp. 78-79; Ahuis, pp. 177-81; Carroll, p. 51. But see Yost, p. 80, and Jüngling, pp. 11-17, whose analyses of the intricate structure and relationships between 1.4-10 and 1.17-19 could be used to support an argument for unity. Thus, for example, Hubmann, *Untersuchungen*, p. 292, argues that 15.20-21 is only intelligible if they were originally connected with the call narrative. But the point of these verses in 15.19-21, to set forth the manner of the prophet's task and divine enablement seems clear enough without the necessity of an allusion back to Jeremiah 1. Their character as reassertion of the original terms of the prophet's call is due more to the present shape of the book than to some intrinsic connection in the statements.

47. For the *waw* consecutive perfect introducing result, see GKC §112pq. ישבו could be taken as a jussive or hypothetical imperfect. תשוב is an imperfect of prohibition.

48.   The idioms in v. 19 referring to an official function, כפי/עמד לפני, are complemented in v. 20 by the idiom of designation and appointment, נתן ל/ב (Jer. 6.27; Isa. 49.6; Ezek. 3.17; 12.6; Ps. 89.28).

49.   Those redactional models which argue for the transfer of a pre-existing lament, or the total *ad hoc* composition of the confession, by the editors of the book run into difficulty in light of the diction analysis. It exhibits continuity and discontinuity with Psalm laments. There is nothing distinctive of Dtr. or Jeremianic prose. On the other hand, the numerous points of stylistic and thematic contact with Jeremianic poetry could provide evidence of authenticity or, at least, that authentic materials lie behind the present confession. The details as follows:

	Unique O.T.	Pss.	*Jeremiah*				*Other*
			Total	*Poetry*	*Prose*	*f.n.o.*	
V.15							
אתה ידעת		7	4	4			
ידע		89	72	43	25	4	
זכר		51	16	10	5	1	
פקד		9	48	9	28	11	
נקם		3	7	4	0	3	
רדפי		7	3	3			
אֶרֶךְ אפים	11	3	1	1			
לקח		13	63	5	54	4	
נשא חרפה	6	2	2	2 (15.15; 31.19)			
חרפה		20	12	4	6	2	
V.16							
נמצא דבר			0	1 (only parallels 2 Kgs 22.13; 23.2; 2 Chr. 34.30)			
אכל דבר	x						
מצא		18	26	13	19	4	
אכל		30	40	19	13	8	
ששון		5	6	2	4	0	
שמחה		13	7	2	4	1	
ששון ושמחה	12	1	5	1	4	0	
שמחת לבב	3	0	1	1			
נקרא שם על	19	0	8	2 (14.9; 15.16)	6	0	
V.17							
ישב		50	82	16	52	14	
סוד משחקים	x						
שחק	35	5	3	3			
סוד	21	6	4	4			
עלז	16	7	4	2	0	2	
מלאו זעם	x						
זעם	22	4	3	1	0		1 (lx-10.10)
ישב בדד	4	0	1	1 (cf. Lam. 1.1: 3.28)			
V.18							
למה		17	11	6	5	0	
כאב	6	1	1	1			

	Unique	O.T.	Pss.	Jeremiah				
				Total	*Poetry*	*Prose*	*f.n.o.*	*Other*
נצח		45	18	3	2	0	1	
מכה		44	1	10	7	1	2	
אנושה		8	0	5	5			
מכה אנושה		2	0	1	1 (cf. Mic. 1.9)			
כאב נצח	x							
מאנה הרפא	x							
רפא			7	12	7	2	3	
מאן			2	12	7	4	1	
היו תהיה		6	0	1	1			
אכזב		2	0	1	1 (cf. Mic. 1.4)			
מים לא נאמן	x							
מים מים	x							

V.19

	Unique	O.T.	Pss.	Total	Poetry	Prose	f.n.o.	Other
לכן כה אמר יהוה			0					
עמד לפני ('attend upon')		25	0	4	1	3	0	
				(cf. 7.10; 15.1; 18.20)				
היה כפה	x	(cf. Exod. 4.16 - לפה)						
הוצא יקר מזולל	x							
יקר		36	4	1	1			
זולל		6	0	1	1			
שוב		1059	17	109	41	60	8	206—Dt.Hist. 16—Dt.Isa.
שוב אל (to person)			2	10	5	4	1	21—Dt.Hist. 2—Dt. Isa.

V.20

	Unique	O.T.	Pss.	Total	Poetry	Prose	f.n.o.	Other
עם הזה			0	31	6	25	0	
חומת נחשת בצורה	x			2	1	1 (1.19- חומת נחשת)		
נחשת			1	15	3	12	0	
						(mostly Jer. 52)		
חומה			2	12	1	7	4	
בצורה			0	2	1	1	0	
נלחם אל	x			2	1	1 (1.19)		
יכל			10	17	10	7	0	
אתך אני			0	5	3	1	1	2—Dt. Isa.
ישע			52	17	13	3	1	
נצל			45	10	3	7	0	
פרה			13	2	2			
להושיע		21	4	4	3	1	0	
להציל		23	3	4	1	3	0	

V.21

	Unique	O.T.	Pss.	Total	Poetry	Prose	f.n.o.	Other
נצל מיד		26	2	3	2	1	0	
פרה מכף	x	(cf. מיד 3× O.T.)						
עריץ		20	3	2	2			
רעים		34	1	3	3			
מיד רעים	x	(cf. מכף - Hab. 2.9)						
מכף עריצים	x	(cf. מיד - Job 6.23)						

50. See our previous critique of the major theories in Setting on 11.18-23.

51. See below on Interpretation.

52. The allusion to the call narrative is more a factor of setting within the present book rather than of intrinsic unambiguous allusions.

53. The value of עמד לפני in the sense of 'attend upon', 'serve' is ambiguous since it can refer not only to a prophet (1 Kgs 17.1, 18, 15; 2 Kgs 3.14; 5.16) but also to cultic (Num. 16.9; Deut. 18.7; Judg. 20.28; 2 Chron. 29.11; Ezek. 14.15, 11) and secular, political officials (Gen. 41.46; Deut 1.38; 1 Kgs 12.8; 2 Chron. 10.6, 8; Dan. 1.5, 19). Though היה כפה occurs only here, the analogous expression in Exod. 4.16 suggests an official spokesman and therefore 15.19, a divine spokesman (cf. Num. 22.38; Deut. 18.18).

54. See n. 49 above for statistics. Especially note the vocabulary of pain and healing in v. 18, and cf. Jer. 3.22; 6.14; 8.11, 22; 10.19; 14.17, 19; 17.16; 19.8; 30.12, 14, 15, 17; 31.15; 33.6.

55. For summary of their positions, see above in Setting on 11.18-23. Eichler views the two crisis points in prophetic mission as the potential of outright rejection in response to the message and the potential of opposition and persecution in response to delayed fulfilment of the message (Eichler, p. 200).

56. Hos. 6.1-6; 14.2-9; Isaiah 33; Micah 7; Joel 1-2.27; Habakkuk 1-2; Jer. 3.22-4.2(4); 14.1-15.4.

57. See above, n. 49.

58. For discussion of standard parallels with psalms, see Baumgartner, p. 35; Reventlow, p. 219; Weiser, *Jeremia*, p. 132; Gerstenberger, 'Complaints', p. 400; Carroll, p. 116.

59. So similarly, Berridge, p. 118; Reventlow, p. 219. The preposition (ל) should probably be taken in the sense of 'on account of' (BDB, p. 514 5f). An alternative understanding would be 'according to' (BDB, p. 516 ib), which would remove the poetic irony and supply a positive nuance, but this does not seem as contextually appropriate.

60. For discussion of standard Psalm parallels, see Baumgartner, p. 37; Reventlow, p. 225; Gerstenberger, 'Complaints', p. 400. For the collective use of the imagery, see Berridge, pp. 129-30; Carroll, pp. 118-19.

61. So, similarly, Eichler, p. 100; Hubmann, *Untersuchungen*, p. 284; Ahuis, p. 93; Ittmann, p. 166.

62. It may be legitimate in this regard to compare אכזב to the usage of the related noun, כזב, in Amos. 2.4, where it refers to foreign deities/idols.

63. See standard commentators.

64. For attempts to see דבר, as in the Psalm references of a divine commandment or promise, see Reventlow, p. 220, and those who follow him such as Gunneweg, p. 405, Carroll, pp. 116-17. For critique, see Bright, 'Jeremiah's Complaints', pp. 200-201. The chief difficulty for an approach such as Reventlow's is in the usage of מצא דבר, which nowhere occurs in the

Psalms to support his contention.

65. Cf. Baumgartner, p. 35, and Hyatt, p. 942, who follow the alternative reading of G for this very reason.

66. Contrast the active expressions in Amos and Lam. The normal expression for reception of the prophetic word in Jeremiah is היה דבר יהוה אלי/ירמיהו (2.1; 13.3, 8; 16.1; etc.), and description of responsiveness to the prophetic word is primarily indicated by the verbs חפץ, ירא, קשב, שמע (6.10; 23.18, 22). Nevertheless, such texts as 1.9, 5.14 (נתן בפה) and 6.10 (חפץ) might render 15.16 intelligible as a further development of such imagery. On the other hand, 6.19 (תורתי//דברי); 8.8-9 (תורת יהוה//דבר יהוה) and 23.9 (דברי קדשו) might provide references of the sort suggested in our argument for 15.16—i.e. not prophetic word but the traditional law of Yahweh.

67. So Holladay, 'Jeremiah and Moses', p. 23. See the analogous positions of Stoebe, 'Seelsorge', pp. 120-23; *idem*, 'Jeremia', p. 404; Berridge, p. 119; and Hubmann, *Untersuchungen*, p. 276, who see a reference to prophetic traditions/words in general. Holladay's additional attempt (pp. 23-24) to connect the remaining vocabulary of the verse to the prophet's call is not necessary. The vocabulary usage would favour interpreting the idioms as general expressions of loyalty to covenantal piety. נקרא שם על, a term of ownership transferred to express relationship to Yahweh (2 Sam. 6.2; 12.28; 1 Kgs 8.43; 2 Chron. 7.14; Isa. 4.1; 63.19; Jer. 7.10, 11, 14, 30; 14.9) asserts the poet's status as a member of the people of God (cf. Jer. 14.9). In light of the liturgical affinities of the confession ששון and שמחה should probably be understood in relation to general cultic thanksgiving (Pss. 16.11; 21.7; 63.12; 119.111; cf. Deut. 12.7, 12, 18; 14.26; 16.11, 14, 15).

68. There seems to be no theoretical reason for excluding knowledge of such historical events from the prophet on any view of the date of his prophetic call. Cf. Deut. 8.3 as the kind of background to the sentiment suggested for Jer. 15.16.

69. See below.

70. Its chief difficulty lies in the lack of clear data elsewhere in the book indicating the prophet's relationship to the Josianic reform and a supposed Ur-Deuteronomy. A further question which arises, if this interpretation is taken, is whether or not such an allusion constitutes evidence of Dtr. redactional activity. The preceding observation complicates a decision. The usage of נקרא שם על coupled with the allusion could provide strong testimony to Dtr. activity. The phrase occurs primarily in Dtr. or texts dependent upon Dtr. (see Deut. 28.10; 1 Kgs 8.43; 1 Chron. 13.6; 2 Chron. 6.33; 7.14; Isa. 63.19; Jer. 7.10, 11, 14, 30; 14.9 25.29; 32.34; 34.15; Dan. 9.18, 19; Amos 9.12). Still, v. 16a as an expression of loyalty to the covenant and its status is uncharacteristic of Dtr. (cf. the list in Weinfeld, pp. 332-39). And the occurrence of the idiom in v. 16b at Isa. 14.1 applied to an individual (non-theologically), plus its theological usage in the ark narrative (2 Sam.

6.2), suggest that the term need not be considered Dtr. in origin or that its transfer into a theological sphere was a Dtr. product. If Jer. 14.9 is considered authentic, the occurrence of the idiom in a pre-exilic, non-Dtr. text would find additional attestation. See further Bright, 'Jeremiah's Complaints', p. 201. There seems to be no necessity for viewing v. 16 as Dtr. in part or *in toto*.

71. For יד see Pss. 32.4; 38.3; 39.11. For מלאו זעם see Isa. 30.27 (*qal* not *pi.*). Cf. Isa. 51.20—המלאים חמת יהוה. For זעם in general, see Pss. 69.25; 78.49; 102.11; Isa. 10.5; 13.5.

72. For יד see Isa. 8.11; Ezek. 1.3; 3.14, 22; 8.1; 33.22; 37.1; 40.1; 1 Kgs 18.46; 2 Kgs 3.15. For זעם cf. Jer. 6.11—מלא חמה (*qal*, not *pi.*).

73. For further details of the debate between the alternative nuances, see Reventlow, pp. 222-25, who interprets the expressions in an exclusively non-prophetic manner, and against him see Bright, 'Jeremiah's Complaints', p. 201; Berridge, pp. 123-29.

74. A similar blend of stereotyped and more concrete references to the opponents was noted for 12.1-6. See above.

75. Hubmann, *Untersuchungen*, pp. 278-81.

76. *Ibid.*, pp. 248, 278.

77. *Ibid.*, p. 278. He follows Bright, 'Jeremiah's Complaints', pp. 202-204, and Berridge, pp. 123-28, in rejecting Reventlow's attempt, pp. 222-25, to interpret the terms as a reference to 'godless scoffers'.

78. *Ibid.*, pp. 279-80. He derives the negative connotation not from the verbal roots but the nature of the false prophet's message (p. 280 n. 92).

79. I find no association of this root with prophets in the OT. Similarly for עלז, none of the other occurrences in Jeremiah or OT pertains to prophets.

80. So Hubmann, *Untersuchungen*, p. 280 n. 92.

81. While Hubmann sees the whole verse as a profession of innocence, Reventlow, pp. 224, classified only v. 17a as such. Baumgartner, pp. 36, 39 noted the similarity of v. 17a to a profession of innocence but classified it as one remodelled into complaint.

82. This understanding of the סוד משחקים also appears reflected by the redactional association of this passage with 16.1-9. On Hubmann's view a more general correspondence between the two textual blocks must be envisaged. See Hubmann, *Untersuchungen*, pp. 304-305.

83. A smooth transition between v. 16 and v. 17 is still in force: profession of covenantal piety (v. 16)—frustrated expectations of commensurate blessings (v. 17). A satisfactory antithesis between v. 17a and v. 17b is still present since it is the prophetic mission which has proved a barrier to the realization of the previous expectations.

84. Also the basis for the supposed tension between v. 16 and v. 20 over the identity of the prophet's opponents drops away.

85. More precise explanation of v. 19bc is difficult on any view of the

whole passage. הוצא יקר מזולל is normally taken as a rebuke of the prophet's preceding accusation and so a rebuke directed to the character of his speech. So standard commentators. See esp. Hubmann, *Untersuchungen*, pp. 285-86, for a review of interpretations. This seems to fit the context the best but the uniqueness of the expression prohibits appeal to corroborative examples. Comparison to 17.16—מוצא שפתי is attractive (so Ittmann, p. 181) and would fix the intent of the rebuke toward ensuring the prophet's proclamation as one unadulterated by base (זולל) motives. On our view, the זולל might be specified more particularly as the prophetic 'misinterpretations' of his mission. Ittmann, p. 181, views זולל as falsification of the prophetic word through community influence.

In v. 19c, שוב אל is likewise difficult. Hubmann, *Untersuchungen*, pp. 289-90, interprets it in light of המה as false prophets and thus a call to the latter to join with the tenor of Jeremiah's mission and not vice versa. Our critique above rules out such a view. With המה equivalent to עם הזה, the issue becomes one of a positive nuance for שוב אל (so Holladay, *Šubh*, p. 131) or a negative one (so Eichler, p. 189). Is it a reference to his enemies 'turning against' or 'turning to' (for support) the prophet? What is prohibited to the prophet, a 'turning to' or a 'turning against'? Does the parallelism require synonymity between the first and second שוב אל? The context in v. 20 (נלחמו אליך abd v. 15b) could argue for a negative nuance for the first but the prohibition (v. 19cβ) seems to require a positive nuance in order to fit the following (v. 20 נתתיך). Such separate nuances might parallel the word plays on שוב best (Carroll, p. 120). However, שוב אל in reference to persons in Jeremiah normally has a positive sense (3.1, 7, 10; 4.1; 24.9; 40.5; 46.16). Still a negative force is attested elsewhere (Judg. 20.48). The contrast המה . . . ואתה permits either nuance for the first שוב אל but v. 20aα seems to exclude any but the positive for the second. On balance, a negative nuance for the first seems to be contextually more appropriate.

Notes to Chapter 1.5

1. יסורי—The *Kethib* is morphologically possible (see GKC §85d) and though unattested elsewhere in the OT, 4QJer.,[a] supports it (Janzen, p. 178). The *Qere* is attested widely but the *Kethib* should be followed as the more unusual form. The normal emendation of MT to וסוריך is predicated on the 'illogic' of the apparent shift to divine speech (so most commentators). Such an emendation is not supported by the textual witnesses, which at least reflect the consonantal text of the *Qere*. And the illogic of this shift depends greatly upon one's view of the nature and function of vv. 12-13 in their relationship to vv. 14-18. We hope to show below that MT represents not only a difficult reading but also an intelligible one. Among recent commentators, only Reventlow follows MT. The alternative of Duhm, p. 147, and Cornill,

p. 215, of reading וסוּרִי as pl. cstr. before a prepositional phrase is possible (see GKC §130a) and though supported by G σ′ V, requires the improper separation of באָרֶץ from יכתבו and the misconstruing of that idiom. See below, Interpretation.

2. לא אצתי מרעה—However they understood it, all the witnesses reflect the present consonantal text. The core problem is determination of an appropriate meaning for מרעה in relation to אוץ. Major emendation to a clearer text seems unwarranted and would not explain why the versions had so much difficulty. A solution simply upon textual considerations is not desirable. See below on Interpretation. Of recent commentators, I find only three who maintain MT: Weiser, *Jeremia*, p. 148; Berridge, p. 140; and P. Wernberg-Møller, 'Observations', p. 64. Most would follow α′ σ′ (απο κακιας) and emend at least to מרֵעָה and preferably לרעה or יום רעה. See standard commentaries.

3. Baumgartner, p. 43. See our review of formal classifications on 11.18-23. The lawsuit approach is at its weakest here for there is a virtual absence of legal imagery employed; and even if one were to grant a legal background as the ultimate origin of the lament pattern, that influence of the origin has been reduced to the minimum in vv. 14-18. The relevance of such a background for explaining this particular passage appears inconsequential. Also, Ittmann's analysis of this passage (p. 77), though acceptable, in reality does not represent an analysis significantly different from that of Baumgartner.

4. Baumgartner, p. 41. In addition to his example of Ps. 80.2 (national lament) and Assryo-Babylonian practice, appeal can also be made to Pss. 44; 85; 125 (national laments); and Pss. 9/10 (individual lament) if the latter constitute properly one psalm. For the 'heaping up' of predications, cf. the similar stylistic character in the Zion-hymns, Pss. 48.2-3 and 76.2-3 (so Weiser, *Jeremia*; Reventlow). For others who take this approach, see: Berridge; Wimmer, 'Experience'; Kenney; (apparently) Carroll; Polk, p. 210.

5. See standard commentators.

6. For example, some defend authenticity and still exclude from the confessional unit: Nicholson, *Jeremiah*; Thompson. Others leave the authenticity question open and exclude on formal grounds: Gunneweg; Hubmann, 'Jeremiah 18'. On the other hand, Ahuis views them as a Dtr. expansion but still a constituent part of the unit.

7. Reventlow, pp. 232-33. For 'we-I' shift in national lament, see Ps. 44.

8. *Idem*, p. 235. See the criticisms in Berridge, pp. 137-51, and Bright, 'Jeremiah's Complaints', pp. 205-207.

9. On this view, the judgment speech would be complementary to Jeremiah 7. For affirmations about the destruction of the wicked in hymns and festival psalms, see Pss. 11.4-5; 145.20; 146.9; 36.13; 68.2-3; 132.18; and

esp. 97.7; 104.35; 135.18. If יבושׁו, Jer. 17.13a, were a jussive (cf. G), the tone of implicit confidence on the part of the community would be enhanced. For accusation in the 3rd pers., see Jer. 2.8, 11, 13, 32; 4.22; 5.2-5. For announcement of judgment in the 3rd pers., see Jer. 4.27, 28; 5.6; 6.15.

10.   The matter of the extent of the confessional unit has also been raised in relation to vv. 9-10. Duhm, p. 148, and following him, Cornill, p. 216; Skinner, pp. 205, 213, relocated the unit before vv. 14ff. Bredenkamp, p. 283, accepted this as second best to placing them as the sequel to vv. 14-18. Finally, Holladay, *Architecture*, p. 99, argues that vv. 5-8, 9-10, and 14-18 constitute three distinct confessions arranged in a progressive series. For criticisms of Duhm and Cornill, see Baumgartner, p. 44, who rejected their view. In our view, the fundamental problems of these approaches are either the failure to explain how the present incorrect arrangement came about or the improper assumption that any dialogical material is meant to represent solely dialogue between Jeremiah and Yahweh in the book (contrast Jer. 8.19; 9.16-21; 10.19-22; and even 17.12-13 if our exegesis is correct). For further criticism of Holladay's view, see below, the Literary Sequence of the confessional material.

11.   Features also noted by Ittmann, p. 77.

12.   For the idea of the 'three subjects of Lament' and 'negative petition', see Westermann, *Lob* pp. 47 and 56-57 (Eng. edn, pp. 169, 181). So also the work of Eichler, pp. 81, 83; Ahuis, p. 115. As further features of style, note the lament section is articulated as a citation of the enemy; repetitive verbal sequences (vv. 14, 18) and assonance (משׁנה שׁברון שׁברם; מחסי/מחתה).

13.   So noted by Baumgartner, p. 43; Weiser, *Jeremia*, p. 149; Reventlow, p. 239. For further criticism of Duhm and Cornill employing theological and psychological explanations, see Skinner, pp. 223-24; Rudolph, p. 119; Chambers, pp. 75-76.

14.   Vermeylen, pp. 266-67.

15.   Ahuis, p. 118.

16.   In keeping with our normal practice, the issues of original-secondary and authentic-inauthentic have been kept separate. On the latter issue, some evidence from consideration of setting and vocabulary usage must await further discussion in the appropriate sections. Initially, we may observe though that the stylistic features already noted are completely compatible with Jeremianic style elsewhere. See further, Holladay, 'Style', pp. 45-47. Such evidence is short of demonstration, but at least no obstacles are raised for the possibility of authenticity.

17.   See review, Setting, 11.18-23.

18.   See Berridge, p. 138; Bright, 'Jeremiah's Complaints', pp. 206-207; and below on Interpretation.

19.   So Gunneweg, pp. 406-407; Welten, p. 141.

20.   Our observations at this point serve to point out the problems for deciding this question of setting as one takes the characteristics of this

confession on its own. Once we have completed our exegesis of all the units, we will want to consider the question of authenticity and setting from that overall perspective. It may be that decisive criteria cannot be generated on the basis of the confessions alone, but rather evaluation in the light of wider literary relationships is required—i.e. other layers/'sources' in the book (so the arguments of Welten, pp. 144-45). See Polk, p. 204 n. 15, for critique of Welten's so-called distinct 'theologies'.

21. Reventlow, pp. 236-38. We also note that the success of approaches like Gunneweg's and Welten's depend in part as well on the viability of much of Reventlow's exegetical approach.

22. See Jer. 28.9; cf. Deut. 18.22; 13.3; Ps. 105.19; Isa. 5.19; Ezek. 24.14; 33.33. For further texts and criticism, see Berridge, p. 138, and Bright, 'Jeremiah's Complaints', p. 207 n. 45. Also see our previous criticism of Reventlow's analogous argument for דבר in Jer. 15.16. The Psalm text coming closest to our present passage which also fits Reventlow's needs is Ps. 119.41; but אמרה is used, not דבר. Further, we find the phrase דבר יהוה only 2x in the Psalms (Ps. 33.4, 6), and these refer only to the divine creative power. In contrast, the phrase occurs 52x generally in Jeremiah and 7x (8x if 17.15 is allowed) in poetic texts where it refers to the prophetic proclamation (see esp. 2.4, 31; 6.10; 8.9; 9.19; 20.8; 31.10).

23. Reventlow, pp. 237-38.

24. Translated literally: 'But I have not hurried away from being a shepherd after you'. Weiser's translation, *Jeremia*, p. 143, appears to represent the sense well: 'Ich habe mich doch nicht entzogen dem Amt des Hirten in deinem Dienst'. The singularity of the clause complicates its explanation. רעה אחר occurs only here in the OT. The verb אוץ occurs only once in Jeremiah and never in Psalms. For the rendering of the ptc. plus מן, see GKC §119x. The figurative use of רעה for Yahweh or the king is dominant, but some indication of extension in unrelated directions is indicated by Prov. 10.21, 'guide/lead'—i.e. 'instruct'. If אחריך could be viewed as related in some way to הלך אחר a deity, then more justification for Weiser's translation would emerge.

25. Note the depiction of the prophet as iron-bronze wall or pillar, appointed for war with and under siege by the nation (1.17-19; 15.11, 12, 20). The prophet is given authority (הפקיד על, 1.10) over the nations and is to pass sentence/judgment (1.16) on Israel. It is interesting that some see royal motifs in Jeremiah's call. If this were a valid observation, the use of רעה in 17.16 would fit with it. See Ahuis, p. 136 n. 1; Reventlow, pp. 36-41; Yost, pp. 130-31.

26. Berridge, p. 140. However, his exegesis of 2.8 is not absolutely compelling. Contrast Rudolph, p. 16; Thompson, p. 168.

27. This is the only occurrence of the phrase יום אנוש. Its closest parallel would be Isa. 17.11 which is still not what we have here. Five of the eight occurrences of the adjective are in Jeremiah (15.18; 17.9, 16; 30.12, 15)—all

poetic texts. Mic. 1.9 fits the usage in Jeremiah. Job 33.6 indicates the appropriate association of the term within complaint. Further interplay in the mutual description of the prophet and nation was also discussed for 15.18. Finally, the adjective is never used in the Psalms, which raises a difficulty for Reventlow's interpretation.

28. Berridge, pp. 144-45, offers another interpretation of v. 16aβ by comparison to Amos 5.18 הוי המתאוים יום יהוה. The prophet would be separating himself from this improper expectation of the day of Yahweh. Presumably this would distinguish him from the prophets of false peace. However, in light of the usage of אנוש in Jeremiah, this is unlikely.

29. That this phrase can have the connotation of approval is illustrated by Judg. 18.6 and Ezek. 14.3, 4, 7. This is the only use of the construction in Jeremiah. For פנים alone in reference to divine favour or wrath in the Psalms, see 19.15; 4.7; 11.7; 18.7; 41.13; 21.10. We have followed *BHS* in the scansion of the cola though MT *athnach* at אתה ידעת would also be permissible in light of the usage of this phrase (see on 15.15). The scansion followed is more appropriate to the general length of bi-cola in the lament.

30. For the ambiguity of יום רעה, see the discussion for 15.11 and Berridge, pp. 141-43.

31. For further examples of the verb היה plus divine epithet used positively in Psalms, see: Pss. 9.10; 33.22; 119.76; 173. Also cf. the similar ironic reversal of epithets noted at 15.18. מחתה is used as a 'divine epithet' only here in OT.

32. For ישע/רפא (1.14), see: Jer. 2.27, 28; 3.22; 6.14; 8.11, 22; 14.8, 9, 19; 30.10, 11, 17; 31.7. The roots are common in Psalms. For אנוש (v. 16), see n. 27. For חתת (vv. 17, 18), see: 1.17; 8.9; 14.4; 23.4; 30.10. For יום רעה (vv. 17, 18), see in n. 30. For שבר/שברון (v. 18), see: 4.6; 6.1; 14.17 (noun-שבר); 8.21; 14.17. For בוש (v. 18), see: 2.36; 6.15; 8.12; 9.18; 12.13; 20.11; 22.22; 31.19. The appeal for the shaming of one's enemies is common in Psalms. The use of מחסה as a divine epithet is very common in Psalms (61.4; 71.7; 91.2, 9; 142.6). For יום רעה see: Jer. 2.3; 4.6; 5.12; 6.19; 17.18; 23.12, 17. The expression בוא/הביא על in reference to יום רעה/רעה never occurs in Psalms relative to general distress or divine judgment (cf. 35.8; 37.13; 44.18). For the irregular impf. in v. 18, see GKC §72y; 74 1. General diction:

	Unique	Pss.	*Jeremiah*			
			Total	Poetry	Prose	f.n.o.
רפא			13	8	2	3
ישע			17	11	5	1
חתת		0	21	7	2	12
שברון	x					
שבר (verb)		(cf. Pss. 10.15; 37.15, 17; 60.14)	26	9	8	9
בוש			17	17		
מחסה		12	1	1		
ירם רעה/רעה			20	7	10	3

33. One could also argue that his opponents are prophetic ones (cf. אמרים המה Jer. 14.15; 27.9). However, the broad usage of the 3rd pers. pl. pronoun in Jeremiah permits our view, for it is more generally used either of Jeremiah's opponents or in accusation of the nation. This coupled with the vocabulary cluster already discussed is more suggestive of a national identity in Jeremiah 17. Jer. usage: (המה) 17x poetry—24x prose; (הם) 3x poetry—13x prose.

34. Berridge's criticism (p. 144) of older views of the passage (see Baumgartner; Rudolph) which saw Jeremiah defending himself against accusation of being an anti-patriot or doom-monger is well placed. In this case, appeal to external historical background (accurate or not) introduces considerations which disturb the internal integration of the lament.

Notes to Chapter 1.6

1. אל—Its omission by G is probably to be traced to its *Vorlage*. However, MT should be retained with 4QJer[a], Targ, O L V as an editorial expansion in light of the overall redactional intention in Chapter 18. So Hubmann, 'Jer. 18', p. 292 n. 102. The interpretation of נכהו בלשון does not appear to be the critical factor in its absence or presence (contrast G and Targ). Commentators are divided.

2. יריבי—G Targ imply ריבי. MT is morphologically possible (GKC §85d) and attested elsewhere in OT (Isa. 49.25; Ps. 35.1). MT is the better reading. The variant arose on the basis of the paralellism with v. 19a and normal lament practice. Commentators are generally divided. In actuality, v. 19b introduces a citation of the opponents (v. 20aα) and is not simply parallel. So Hubmann, 'Jer. 18', p. 284. See below, Interpretation. 4QJer.[a] has a lacuna here, but it might permit a reading equivalent to MT (see Janzen, *Studies*, p. 179).

3. כי כרו שוחה/שיחה—The textual history is particularly complicated for vv. 22aβ, 22b. The *Kethib-Qere* in v. 22b merely represents permissible variants for 'pit' (שיחה—Pss. 57.7; 119.85; שוחה —Jer. 2.6; Prov. 22.14; 23.27). The translation of G (λογον, ρηματα) appears to have arisen by a confusion of שיחה (pit) with the homonym שיחה (speech, complaint). The translation and expanded reading of G in v. 20aβ appears to have resulted from conflation with v. 22b. This seems the most straightforward explanation. α′ σ′ Targ V support MT. 4QJer.[a] reads *Kethib*. O Q 86 ÷ κατα ψυχης. But there is such a discrepancy in the translation of G for the doublets that a conflation of separate traditions has been suggested relative to the shifted location of the bi-cola (see esp. Janzen, *Studies*, pp. 27-28). Many commentators have excised v. 20aβ entirely. But cf. the similar phenomenon in other doublets of Jeremiah where translation variants are offered for identical phrases (see Hubmann, *Untersuchungen*, pp. 336, 339, 341, and cf.

G 20.12; 11.20). For supporters of MT, see: Weiser, *Jeremiah*; Bright, *Jeremiah*; Thompson; Carroll; Eichler; Hubmann, 'Jer. 18'. See below, Redaction.

4. Cf. the analyses of Baumgartner, p. 48; Eichler, p. 77; Ittmann, pp. 67-68; Hubmann, 'Jer. 18', p. 296; Ahuis, p. 34.

5. See as cited in the previous note. For general review of approaches, see Form on 11.18-23.

6. Discerning the prose or poetic character of some verses is difficult, as we have seen in relation to other confessions. Verse 18 certainly has a rhythmic flow and the motif of a citation of the enemy; the seditious plot (with חשב) and some of the vocabulary (לכו; קשב; חשב) have analogues in Psalms (Baumgartner, p. 46; Gunneweg, p. 408). But the most formidable obstacle is the difficulty of casting the verse into parallel lines in a convincing way. As it stands, it produces three bi-cola of 3+2, 4+4, and 3+2 metre. The parallel לכו exhortations would be easiest to take in a poetic fashion, but the middle line כי לא ... מנביא is awkward. It would seem easier to view it as prose (so Thiel) and view its rhythmic character as a function of its nature as direct speech. For problems of poetry-prose distinctions, see Kugel, pp. 76-84. The vocabulary usage is basically inconclusive, though its generalized character and the breakdown for Jeremiah and Psalms indicate a certain weight in favour of the prose side:

	Unique O.T.	Pss.	Total	Poetry	Prose	f.n.o
				Jeremiah		
יאמרו			21	5	16	0
לכו		41 (הלך)	3	2	1	0
חשב מחשבות		0	3	1	2	0
verb alone		18	4	0	4	0
noun alone		6	4	2	2	0
אבד		26	15	6	9	0
תורה מכהן	x					
עצה מחכם	x					
דבר מנביא	x					
נכהו בלשון	x					
קשב		8	7	7		

7. This very feature in Ps. 39 is unusual, and the formal classification of the Psalm is difficult. Contrast Kraus, p. 300, and Weiser, *Psalmen*, p. 221 (Eng. edn, p. 328). The former views it as individual lament; the latter views the Psalm as unclassifiable.

8. Baumgartner, p. 48, was aware of this difficulty but attempted to explain the irregularity as a sign of the prophetic character of the confession. Of the prophetic texts cited as parallels, only Isa. 40.6 comes close to the nature of Jer. 18.18.

9. Baumgartner, p. 47; Gunneweg, p. 408.

10. Metrical scansion: v. 19—3+3; v. 20—3+3, 3+3+3; v. 21—4+3+4, 4+4;

v. 22—3+4, 3+3; v. 23—3+3, 3+3, 3+3. We also note that imprecations in Psalms can function as an extended literary block (see esp. Pss. 35; 69; 109) but metrically remain fairly homogeneous with the prevailing metre of the whole psalm. The change in the poetic lines has been noted by both Baumgartner, p. 45, who resorted to textual emendation in order to produce uniformity, and apparently also by Ahuis, p. 33, who reclassifies vv. 21-22a as prose. However, he provides no justification for the latter; and the parallelism which is there would argue against his approach. See further on Redaction.

11. Though the vocabulary of v. 18 is stylistically compatible and logically connected with the preceding prose, it is interesting to notice the lack of any distinctive Dtr. contacts in it, so that one could hardly argue on this basis for its redactional status (see Thiel, p. 218, for discussion of these difficulties). It is not clear, however, that the way is cleared by this for Ittmann, pp. 51-52, to argue for the originality of v. 18. His chief appeal is that קוֹל יְרִיבִי (v. 19) demands a citation in the near context which v. 18 supplies. However, if the approach of Hubmann, 'Jer. 18', pp. 284ff., to v. 20aα as a citation is correct (see below), then v. 18 is no longer as essential to the internal requirements of the lament. Ittmann's approach must also discount the wider contextual role of v. 18 and its external formal character over against the following lament.

12. Ittmann, pp. 39-40.

13. *Ibid.*, pp. 51-52.

14. *Ibid.*, p. 39. Note that he also views v. 20aβ as an editorial doublet drawn from v. 22bα.

15. Baumgartner, p. 47.

16. His appeals to vocabulary usage could also work against his position. Instead of illustrating editorial character, points of contact between v. 23 and other confessions could serve as illustrations of style consistent with confessional material. For example, v. 23aα as a motif of confidence in Yahweh's knowledge of the prophet's situation (cf. 12.3; 15.15; 17.16); the murder plot, v. 23aβ (cf. 11.19, 21); for use of כשל as fate of the opponents (cf. 20.11) generally as description of nation's judgment, cf. 6.15, 21; 8.12; 18.15; 31.9. Also the occurrences of expressions unique to Jeremianic poetry are difficult to evaluate since one has to allow for the possibility that an author can employ expressions only once or infrequently alongside other more predominant modes of expression (cf. v. 23 כפר עון; מחה חטאת only here in Jeremiah). Note the latter expressions are infrequent in the OT generally, כפר עון only 6x and מחה חטאת only 3x besides our passage. Similar evaluative problems exist for expressions unique to this confession (cf. עת אפר only here).

17. The traditional understanding of נכחו בלשון as 'slander' would strengthen this observation (cf. Pss. 35; 109). However, Hubmann, 'Jer. 18', p. 291, has argued that it has nothing to do with false legal witness but should be taken, in light of his view of v. 20aα, as simply 'dispute'. But even

here a successful refutation of Jeremiah's message would constitute at least his 'destruction' as prophet. Comparison to the situation of Jeremiah 26 may also be appropriate, especially if we are right about the relationship of v. 18 to Jeremianic prose materials.

18. Ahuis, pp. 33-35.

19. For expressions unique to this passage in the OT: מכי חרב; הרגי מות. For those unique to Jeremianic poetry: גרור; זעקה; שכול; הגר על ידי חרב; שיחה; פח טמן; פתאם. It is also worth observing that while individual vocabulary of the imprecations is generally attested in the Psalms, its formulation into closely parallel curses is attested only for v. 21aγ תחינה נשיהם (cf. Ps. 109.8). For distribution statistics in Jeremiah, see previously on 11.21-23 and 17.18, where relevant. For the remaining:

| | | | Jeremiah | |
	Total	Poetry	Prose	f.n.o.
נשים	24	4	18	2
אנשי	47	2	36	9
מות	11	4	5	2
מלחמה	24	5	7	12
לכר	21	4	7	10

20. Without it one would lack a parallel colon for v. 20aα or produce a four-cola stanza which would run counter to the mix of bi- and tri-cola in the lament.

21. Eichler, p. 71.

22. *Ibid.*, p. 73.

23. See our previous observations on evaluating Jeremianic doublets at 15.10-14.

24. So the working definition proposed by Hubmann, *Untersuchungen*, p. 217.

25. If we were correct to argue for the redactional status of 11.21-23, then the parallel with 18.21-22a is not an automatic demonstration of the latter's secondary status as Eichler and, to a certain extent, Ahuis suppose. Cf. Thiel, p. 159, for whom our text provides part of the background for 11.21-23.

26. Correctly noted by Ahuis, p. 35, as never being so used in Psalms.

27. See further, Kuhl, p. 1.

28. See review on 11.18-23.

29. Wimmer, 'Experience', pp. 279-80. His argument is coupled with the contention noted previously for him that a legal/ריב process is to be discerned for the genre pattern of the confessions. On p. 268, he offers the following schematic: v. 18 'functions as request for a hearing'; v. 20 'opening question', vv. 21-22a 'suit for damages', v. 22b 'specific accusation'; v. 23a 'demand for sentence', v. 23b,c 'false end to case', v. 23d 'time of execution'.

30. Ahuis, p. 36.

31. See *ThWAT*, I, pp. 448-51 (Eng. edn, pp. 416ff.) for details of the setting of curse in the ancient Near East and the Old Testament. Particularly illustrative in the OT for curse as oral threat are Lev. 5.1 and Judg. 17.2. For discussion, see Brichto, pp. 42-45.

32. See n. 19 above and cf. esp. 11.21-23.

33. It might also compensate for the weakness imported into other developments of the 'apologetic' role which emphasize the importance of an answering oracle.

34. Ahuis, pp. 119-20, observes parallels to the negative petition in Jeremianic judgment speech. Cf. esp. 2.22; 14.10.

35. An intercessory function for prophets is certainly attested. See further, Rhodes, pp. 107-28. But the activity is also predicated of Abraham (Gen. 18.22); Moses and Samuel (Jer. 15.1; Ps. 106.23); David (2 Sam. 24.17); even theoretically anyone from leaders to individuals of the nation (Ezek. 22.30). Note the ambiguities of other potential prophetic characteristics; though עת אף occurs only here, the phrase could be read similarly to the ambiguous expressions עת רעה and עת צרה which need not refer specifically to the judgment announced by the prophet. As for the parallels between the curses and Jeremiah's imagery of judgment, the broad correspondences between prophetic announcements and ancient Near Eastern treaty curses and *Kudurru* inscriptions suggest caution is needed in face of such widespread contexts before one concludes that the imprecations are distinctively prophetic. See, further, Fensham, pp. 155-75. Finally the explicit parallels to the curses are infrequent though the vocabulary employed in them is widely attested in Psalms except for some of the expressions in vv. 21-22a (see also n. 19): גדור—1x; זעקה—never; בחור—3x; שכול—3x; נגר—3x; רעב—2x; לכד—3x; פתאם—2x.

36. It should be noted, though, that the stylistic compatibility and ease of reading the passage in terms of a prophet and Jeremiah in particular also raise problems for approaches like Gunneweg's, Welten's, and Vermeylen's. Granted there is ambiguity in the expressions, yet it is to be wondered whether the appeal to this feature alone is sufficient to explain why there is such a 'nice fit' if the lament originally had no connection at all with Jeremiah. One may contrast similar 'transfers' with regard to 1 Sam. 2.1-10 and Jon. 2.3-10, which display a more generalized type of relationship with the narrative than this Jeremianic confession does with other materials in the book.

37. See the standard commentaries. Hubmann, 'Jer. 18', pp. 276-80, provides a helpful review of the traditional interpretation.

38. See esp. Hubmann, 'Jer. 18', pp. 276-78, for a review of scholarship on this problem.

39. *Ibid.*, pp. 280-84.

40. *Ibid.*, pp. 290-93.

41. Hubmann (*ibid.*, p. 283), also observes that elsewhere in the book of

Jeremiah where there are comparable texts, it is not a question of literal dependents but the whole nation is drawn into judgment through the misrule of their representative leaders (cf. Jer. 20.4, 6; 14.15-16; and similarly 29.32).

42. Hubmann's contention here appears to be basically borne out by the various expressions for intercession. התפלל בעד—7.16; עמד לפני—15.1; 11.14; 14.11. However, the occurrence of the aforementioned expression in 42.2, 20 with reference to a remnant of the nation could be viewed as providing a possible exception to Hubmann's claim; and one would have to be open to a similar possibility for 18.20—i.e. a sub-section of the nation. Though one may argue that intercession is to be distinguished from enquiring an oracle (so Hubmann, 'Jer. 18', p. 283 n. 78), this may only represent a technical distinction, with overlap between the two activities fully possible. In 37.3, 7 the one activity is represented both by התפלל בעד and דרש בעד. Perhaps the factor which permits such overlap is that expectations of relief from distress are involved for both (cf. *ThWAT*, III, p. 324 [Eng. edn, p. 303]). In this light one may also compare דרש בעד (21.2) and שאל דבר (37.17; 38.14).

43. Further problems noted for the older view are: the undemonstrated assumption that נכהו בלשון means slander (cf. Targ); the necessity of resorting to various external psychological and theological considerations in order to explain an apparent shift of attitude in the prophet toward his enemies; and failure to account for the renewed petition in v. 23. However, these last two considerations only become significant if one views the general theological offence of imprecation as a legitimate exegetical tool.

44. If Hubmann is correct, then Jer. 18.20 would represent the only poetic example of טוב used this way. The usage of טובה in this sense is predominantly prose: 12x Jer.: 10x prose; 2x poetry.

45. Hubmann, 'Jer. 18', p. 286. At first glance, the many parallels to the phrase would suggest that a specialized nuance is ruled out (Pss. 35.12; 38.21; 109.5; Prov. 17.13; Gen. 44.4; 1 Sam. 24.21; 2 Sam. 16.12). However, the word order is unusual, for the normal רעה תחת טובה is not followed, which may indicate a more particular usage. In addition, the masculine passive verb appears to rule out either following phrase as the subject (contrast GKC §145 o for initial predicate) and might best be construed as an impersonal passive with implicit personal agent (GKC §121a, b). This would complement well the idea of an oblique reference to Yahweh.

46. *Ibid.*, p. 286 n. 88. If this is correct, the situation would find an appropriate analogue in Jeremiah 26.

47. *Ibid.*, p. 287. Cf. Jer. 27.18. Understood this way, the statement might better be seen as a mixture of innocence declaration and a subtle complaint against the necessities of the prophetic mission.

48. *Ibid.*

49. *Ibid.*, p. 289.

50. So observed by Ittmann, p. 51, who sought to employ it as an argument for retaining the citation of v. 18.

51. Hubmann, 'Jer. 18', p. 282, also noted this strong possibility and observed, p. 280, that such an approach was characteristic for much of the older exegesis of the passage.

52. Hubmann's observation (p. 290) that the theological character of the citation requires someone competent in such matters and not just anyone is invalid in light of similar 'theological' statements placed on the lips of the nation (Jer. 2.35; 3.4, 5; 5.12, 13).

53. Hubmann, (*ibid.*, pp. 285-86) recognizes the unavoidable nuance of intercession for the third colon of v. 22b but seeks more specialized nuances for the first two cola which will aid his understanding esp. of טובה and רעה. He first observes correctly that דבר טובה על is never used elsewhere of making intercession. The closest analogue is 1 Sam. 19.4: דבר טוב ב. Then observing that עמד לפני has reference to the prophetic office/mission *per se* (cf. 15.19), he argues that טובה must be related to this as a proclamation of 'ein von Jahwe her kommendes Heil' (p. 286). It is not clear, though, how Hubmann understands the basic sense of the first two cola. His understanding of the phrases implies that the prophet is claiming to be a prophet of טובה, which seems to make nonsense of the crisis portrayed by the lament, to say nothing of material elsewhere in Jeremiah. However, Hubmann clearly does not mean this, for he wants to compare v. 22b with 17.16, 'I did not desire the evil day' (p. 286). Further difficulty lies in his approach to עמד לפני, which can also stand on its own for intercession (Jer. 15.1), and the parallel with להשיב would appear to confirm this. So far, Hubmann's attempt seems problematical.

54. See n. 42 above.

55. דבר טוב על elsewhere has a very distinct connotation of 'promise good to', esp. of divine promises of blessing within covenantal contexts (Jer. 32.42; 39.9; Num. 10.29; 1 Sam. 25.30; 2 Sam. 7.28) or, slightly differently, of a positive prophetic oracle (1 Kgs 22.13). If we accept some such nuance here, continue to view עמד לפני on its own as intrinsically related to intercessory activity, view as acceptable an overlap between intercession and the request for an oracle (see n. 42 above), then we might paraphrase the profession of innocence thus: 'remember I interceded with you, that I might proclaim hope/blessing to them, thus turning your wrath from them'. This approach would appear to provide a more intelligible rationale for mention of prophetic intercession in the face of the supposed citation of v. 20aα.

56. For further Psalm parallels, see Baumgartner, pp. 44-48, and the texts cited there.

Notes to Chapter 1.7

1. The textual condition of this passage is good. Apart from the odd

minor variant and G, the versions witness to the present consonantal text. More intriguing are the numerous alternative readings of content against MT in G. In our view, most of these are to be explained as mistaken readings of consonants or vowels, or represent a significantly different interpretation of the passage on the part of G, which nevertheless does not indicate a different *Vorlage*. Except for vv. 9-10, commentators generally follow MT. A composite approach drawn from MT and G is taken for the former.

2. G reads entirely differently: οτι πικρω λογω μου γελασομαι, αθεσιαν και ταλαιπωριαν ἐπικαλεσομαι. A different *Vorlage* seems most likely unless מרי has been read as מרי and זעק as צחק. MT represents a more complex meaning and is preferable. So the majority of commentators.

3. בלבי—G omits. If MT is an explanatory gloss, it is difficult to see the motivation since the meaning was already clear. Perhaps G has arisen through homoiarcton with ב and כ (כאש . . . . ב). Of recent commentators, only Duhm and Cornill follow G.

4. צבאות—Omit with G. MT has the tendency to expand divine epithets (cf. Janzen, pp. 79-80). Most commentators follow MT.

5. צדיק—pc. Mss G α′ Targ V read צֶרֶק probably under influence of the doublet 11.20. MT is the more difficult reading (cf. σ′ο δικαιος). The ambiguity of צדיק as purely adjectival or as personal object makes evaluation of the versions uncertain. On the whole, commentators appear to preserve MT.

6. Of recent commentators, only Cornill, Rudolph and Wimmer ('Experience') treat vv. 7-18 as a unit once allowances for redactional additions are made. Most have divided the passage into two blocks, vv. 7-13 and 14-18; but a few have attempted a triple subdivision (vv. 7-9; 10-13; 14-18): so, Baumgartner, Volz, von Rad ('Konfessionen'), Berridge, Hyatt, Carroll.

7. In our view, it has been the cultic lamentation genre which has provided the dominant literary force in shaping the text. Alternative classification attempts are unconvincing. Legal imagery is so reduced that it does not play a dominant role. Even Wimmer, 'Experience', observes that the juridical has been subordinated in 20.7-18 (p. 313), so that the literary structure of the lawsuit is lacking (p. 312). Ittmann's approach is countered by the ease with which Clines and Gunn were able to analyse the passage in terms of formal lament (see below). And finally, Ahuis's attempt, pp. 27ff., to see the messenger process (event) as the dominant patterning force also must be questioned (see below). The basic question and problem for these alternatives is whether the various elements of imagery do constitute the more prominent genre influence over against that of cultic lament. See further on 11.18-23.

8. The chief difficulty of the former was the improper use of shifts in tone as a criterion of subdivision. See, for further criticisms, Clines and Gunn, 'Form', pp. 394-97. Verses 14-18 are to be classified as a distinct genre from

cultic lament—i.e. self-curse. Cf. Clines and Gunn, 'Form', p. 393; and
Westermann, *Aufbau*, p. 58 n. 1 (Eng. edn, p. 37 n. 12).

9. Clines and Gunn, 'Form', p. 392.

10. Cf. Ps 22.23-25 and see Clines and Gunn, 'Form', p. 393; Westermann,
Lob, p. 44 (Eng. edn, pp. 58-59); Gunkel–Begrich, pp. 257-58.

11. So Berridge, p. 155; Clines and Gunn, 'Form', p. 396; Hubmann,
'Anders', p. 183; Fishbane, 'Wretched Things', p. 178.

12. This theme is not only underlined by the verbal repetitions but also the
latter are further emphasized by tonal-assonantal clusters around k-l, q-l, g-l
sounds running right through the passage to v. 12. So Fishbane, 'Wretched
Thing', p. 178 n. 16.

13. Clines and Gunn, 'Form', pp. 396-97.

14. *Idem*, 'Violence, Outrage', p. 26.

15. Hubmann, 'Anders', p. 183.

16. *Ibid*.

17. For those viewing one or both verses as secondary, or at least unsure of
their status, see: Baumgartner (only v. 12); Duhm; Volz; Cornill; Rudolph
(only v. 12); Bright, *Jeremiah* (v. 12 unsure); Hyatt (v. 12 secondary, v. 13
unsure); Blank, 'Confessions'; Holladay, *Spokesman* (only v. 13 unsure);
Fohrer, *Propheten*; Thiel; Fishbane, 'Wretched Thing' (only v. 13 unsure);
Ittmann (only v. 12); Hubmann, 'Anders'.

18. So Cornill (v. 11); Thiel (v. 10 unsure); and recently Eichler, Ahuis,
Vermeylen.

19. Weiser, *Jeremia*, p. 172; and Bredenkamp, p. 304, attempted to remove
this difficulty by rearrangement of v. 12 before v. 11. Clines and Gunn,
'Form', p. 392 n. 10, argue that variability in the order of elements must be
allowed.

20. Unless one counted כי הציל.

21. Those who have stressed these features have usually found no
compelling reason for questioning the originality of vv. 12-13. So Weiser,
Jeremiah; Bredenkamp; Wimmer, 'Experience'; Clines and Gunn, 'Form';
Thompson.

22. See standard commentaries.

23. Eichler, p. 68.

24. See above, 11.18-23; 12.1-6.

25. We are not arguing against the existence of certain parallels between
the passages. But these extend beyond vv. 10-13 into vv. 7-9 and thus do not
help for separating out an original kernel. Cf. Ittmann, p. 75, who also
discerns formal parallels between the passages.

26. The use of citation in portrayal of enemies is too frequent an element
of lament to be a very decisive criterion. Also the presence of catchwords in
the preceding context (11.19 to 11.16; 20.10 to 20.3) says nothing about the
redactional origin of each juxtaposed unit (against Eichler, p. 68).

27. Eichler, p. 69.

28. *Ibid.*

29. Ahuis, p. 111.

30. See standard commentaries. Exceptions to be noted are: Volz (both vv. 10-11); Cornill (only v. 11); Fishbane, 'Wretched Thing' (v. 11). But they also make no attempt at demonstration. Presumably it is the metrical irregularity of the verses which has stimulated such a judgment.

31. See Baumgartner, Duhm, Cornill.

32. It is very questionable that a rigid *Qina*-metre can be required for the confession as Ahuis apparently implies (p. 27 n. 4). Even for vv. 7-9 one has to resort to a number of emendations and rearrangements to produce it. It would seem better to accept that a canon of rigid metre has not been employed in the composition of this lament.

33. Ahuis, p. 111.

34. Like Eichler, Ahuis sees the Dtr. character of the verse in the use of citations, אולי introducing direct speech and the doublet of v. 10aα with Ps. 31.14a. Such criteria are not very convincing: citations are too common a feature in cultic lament to be labelled as distinctive Dtr. features; though אולי occurs mostly in Jer. prose (4x) and is used 8x in the Deuteronomistic history, its frequent occurrence elsewhere in the OT (45x) and in non-Dtr. material (e.g. Genesis 12x) argues against a Dtr. identification. Similarly the doublet phenomenon in Jer. cannot be restricted to the prose editors since one also most allow for the multiple use of formulaic expressions by the prophet or other editors besides Dtr. As for Ps. 31.14, if one dates it later than Jer. 20.10, the issue drops away entirely; but if it is earlier, there is no intrinsic reason why the prophet could not have borrowed and reformulated the idiom. In addition, מגור מסביב appears to be a distinctive of Jer. poetry (6.25; 20.10; 45.6; 49.29;). The one Jer. prose occurrence (20.3) appears to be a redactional expansion for the editorial linking of 20.1-6 to vv. 7-13 (G omits מסביב; cf. Janzen, *Studies*, p. 73). Finally, the remaining vocabulary and idiom do not exhibit any striking Dtr. provenance:

	Unique	O.T.	Pss.	Total	Jeremiah Poetry	Prose	f.n.o.
דבת רבים (cstr. chain)		2	1 (31.14)	1	1		
נגד (*hi.*)			20	28	7	15	6
אנוש שלומי (cstr. chain)	x	(cf. Ps. 41.10; Jer. 38.22; Ob. 7 - (אנשי/איש שלומו					
צלע		4	2	1	1		
לקח נקמה/נקם		2 (cf. Isa. 47.3)		1	1		

For remaining vocabulary, see v. 7 below.

35. Ahuis, pp. 111-12.

36. Of course, this is what Ahuis attempts to argue in his analyses of the respective texts with the exception of 17.18.

37. גבור עריץ—double expression only here in OT. The adjective is never used elsewhere of Yahweh. Ahuis (p. 111 n. 9) cites Isa. 49.24f. incorrectly for neither is the reference predicated of Yahweh nor do the words occur in series. For Yahweh as גבור, see Jer. 14.9; 20.11; 32.18; Ps. 24.8; Deut. 10.17; Zeph. 3.17; Job 16.14; Isa. 42.13; 9.21; Neh. 9.32. For עריץ in Ps. (3x), see 37.35; 54.5; 86.14; and in Jer. (2x), 15.21; 20.11. כשל—12x Ps., 6x Jer. (3x poetry, 2x prose, 1x f.n.o.), 8x Deut.—Kings and predominantly in wisdom genre. For בוש, יכל, כשל, רדפי, see on previous occurrences.

38. Cf. Holladay, 'Prototype', pp. 351-67; and McKane, 'Relations', pp. 220-37. Also note that 20.40 is slightly different using כלמות not כלמת. Frequencies: כלמה (alone)—7x Pss.; 3x Jer. (3.25; 20.11; 51.51). שכח (all stems)—32x Pss.; 13x Jer. (6x poetry, 4x prose, 2x f.n.o.).

39. See Clines and Gunn, 'Form', p. 392 n. 10, and cf. esp. Ps. 54.5-7; 59.7-14.

40. Clines and Gunn, 'Form', p. 398.

41. Notice that in both locations, thematic and verbal connections are sustained with the context.

42. For details, see our earlier treatment on 11.20.

43. See below on Interpretation. 11.20 has שפט צדק for בחן צדיק and ראה כליות ולב for בחן כליות ולב.

44. Cf. similar observations by Baumgartner, p. 66; and Weiser, *Jeremiah*, p. 169.

45. Hubmann, 'Anders', p. 184. Cf. Gunkel–Begrich, pp. 268ff., who comment on the centrality of this feature in psalms of thanksgiving.

46. Hubmann, 'Anders', p. 184.

47. *Ibid.*, pp. 185-86.

48. *Ibid.*, p. 187.

49. I.e. the evidence of the doublet takes on more weight.

50. Hubmann, 'Anders', p. 182.

51. *Ibid.*, p. 182. See further below on Interpretation.

52. For discussion and examples, see Gunkel–Begrich, p. 215.

53. The perfect verbs in vv. 7-9 could be viewed as present perfects. So Gunkel–Begrich, p. 215, on complaint in form of 'Erzählung'.

54. So observed by Hubmann, 'Anders', p. 184.

55. Cf. 11.18-20. Weiser, *Jeremiah*, p. 169, speaks of this confession as a combination of lament and thanksgiving psalm.

56. See Clines and Gunn, 'Form', pp. 397-98.

57. Hubmann's view of v. 13 is also not required. It is not as obviously dependent upon v. 12 as claimed and could equally follow on v. 11 however the whole genre is classified. The stylistic compatibility with other confessions and Jeremianic poetry cautions against its exclusion (cf. 15.21; 23.14; 21.12). Thus Ittmann, p. 53, only treats v. 12 as secondary.

58. See Clines and Gunn, 'Form', p. 401, for an excellent critique of Gunneweg's attempt to dissolve the 'prophetic' features of the passage.

59. Clines and Gunn, 'Form', p. 402. For review of 'apologetic' approaches, see 11.18-23.

60. Ahuis, pp. 28-31.

61. Ahuis discounts too much the contacts with psalm lament in these verses. Cf. Clines and Gunn, 'Form', p. 395, for details of these contacts.

62. The strength of the Clines and Gunn approach can be seen in its ability to explain just these features.

63. For review of this approach, see on 11.18-23.

64. The proposal of a total editorial transfer also suffers from drawbacks: the stylistic compatibility of the passage with Jeremianic poetry and failure to demonstrate total ambiguity of the content *vis à vis* a prophet (see below on Interpretation). Vocabulary statistics for vv. 10-12 have already been given. For the remaining:

	O.T.	Pss.	Total	Jeremiah Poetry	Prose	f.n.o.
V.7						
פתח		1	3	3		
חזק		5	14	9	2	5
יכל		10	19	6	7	2
שחוק		1	4	1	0	3
כל היום		26	2	2		
לעג		4	1	1		
כל + pt.			9	9		
V.8						
דבר		55	117	27	80	10
זעק		5	8	2	3	3
קרא		56	63	17	42	4
חמס ושר (co-ord.)	5	0	2	2 (cf.Ezek.45.9; Amos 3.10; Hab. 1.3)		
חרפה		20	12	4	6	2
קלם	3	2	1	1		
V.9						
זכר		51	16	10	5	1
לב		28	54	25	23	6
אש		28	39			
בער		7	7	3	4	0
עצר		1	4	1	3	0
עצם		15	3	2	1	0
לאה		1	5	5		
כול		2	4	4		
V.13						
שיר		25	1	1		

	O.T.	Pss.	Total	Jeremiah Poetry	Prose	f.n.o.
הלל	74		11	3	4	4
נפש אביון (cstr. chain)	3	1 (72.13)	2	2 (cf. 2.34)		
אביון (alone)	22		4	4		

For נצל and מיד מרעים, see on 15.20.

65. Excellent lists of these parallels can be found in Baumgartner, pp. 48ff., 63ff.; and Clines and Gunn, 'Form', pp. 394-96.

66. See on 11.18-23 for review.

67. For usage, see discussion on 17.15.

68. No occurrence of this idiom in the psalter is attested (10x in OT), and usage elsewhere has the prophetic proclamation in view (4x Jer.—20.9; 26.20; 29.23; 44.16): see esp. Exod. 5.23; Deut. 18.19, 20, 22; Zech. 13.3. Gunneweg's emendation (p. 411) of דבר to קרא has neither textual support nor corroboration for זכר with a proposed meaning of 'im Kult anrufen'.

69. For excellent detailed discussions of these problems, see Baumgartner; Bright, 'Jeremiah's Complaint', pp. 212-13; Clines and Gunn, 'Form', p. 401.

70. See standard commentaries and esp. Berridge, pp. 151-54.

71. For sexual associations, see Exod. 22.15 (פתה); Deut. 22.25; 2 Sam. 13.14 (חזק); Jer. 13.22 (verb חמס).

72. Cf. 1 Kgs 22.21, 22; Ezek. 14.9. Non-sexual connotations are predominant for the other terms (e.g. 1 Kgs 16.22 [חזק—military]; Jer. 6.7; Ezek. 45.9; Amos 3.10; Hab. 1.3 [חמר ושד—violations of general social justice]). Any idea that we have to do with technical sexual vocabulary appears to be ruled out.

73. Clines and Gunn, 'Jeremiah xx 7-8', pp. 21-22. It would seem though that the nuance of 'deceive' cannot be entirely ruled out (cf. Ps. 78.36).

74. Note the range of connotations, positive and negative: Hos. 2.16— 'coax', 'allure'; Judg. 14.15; 16.5—'cajole'; Ezek. 14.9—'induce', 'compel'; Ps. 78.36—'beguile'.

75. So Clines and Gunn, 'Jeremiah xx 7-8', p. 21.

76. Note esp. the association of קרא and זעק with the cries of distress of the innocent (Pss. 22.6; 107.13, 19; 142.1, 6; 14.14; 17.6; 31.18; 88.10).

77. See esp. Job 19.7; Hab. 1.2 for parallel usages of this idiom as a dramatic cry for help and of protest. The legal implications of the Job context should not be missed. See further *THAT*, pp. 584-85.

78. As Clines and Gunn, 'Jeremiah xx 7-8', pp. 25-26, argue. See there for detailed critique of alternatives. This approach requires a view of the כי conjunction as not strictly subordinate to the immediately preceding colon (cf. BDB, p. 473 §3c).

79. Ahuis, pp. 30-32, views vv. 7-8 as reflecting the 'commissioning— execution' elements and v. 9, the 'report'. The validity of such general comparisons also depends partly upon the validity of seeing the messenger

function as *the* central determinant of the prophetic office.

80. See the standard commentaries. מגור מסביב could be viewed as appositional to דבת or as the mocking employment of Jeremiah's expression by the enemies in order to signify their intention for him—i.e. reversal of judgment proclamation back upon the prophet.

81. Hubmann, 'Anders', p. 181.

82. *Ibid.*, pp. 180-81.

83. *Ibid.*, p. 186.

84. *Ibid.*, pp. 181, 186, is also reluctant to do this.

85. These stages need not represent a consistent organic progression.

86. *GKC* §110f. does not take Hubmann's view but sees a telic nuance in the construction. For adverbial usage of the imp., see *GKC* §120d, but no examples of נגד, so used, are provided. At least Jer. 35.11 suggests the possibility of Hubmann's approach.

87. Jer. 4.5; 5.20; 31.10; 46.14; 48.20.

88. Lev. 5.1; Josh. 2.14, 20; Judg. 17.5; Prov. 29.24.

89. Similarly observed by Clines and Gunn, 'Form', p. 397 n. 31.

90. Verse 10aα—narrative report of plot; 10aβ dramatic portrayal in direct speech; 10aγ—narrative report; 10b—dramatic portrayal.

91. MT תחרגנו הרג. For discussion of the text in Deut., see Weinfeld, pp. 94-96, who draws the comparison to Jer. 20.10. This textual difficulty in Deut. introduces a problematic feature for the comparison.

92. See Weinfeld, pp. 92ff., for parallels with Ancient Near Eastern treaties.

93. Cf. also Jer. 38.22, where a more formal political nuance of 'friends' as 'political advisers' seems indicated. However, the political connotation is not required (cf. Ps. 41.10).

94. So Clines and Gunn, 'Form', p. 399.

95. Helpfully discussed by Hubmann, 'Anders', pp. 185-86.

96. So Clines and Gunn, 'Form', p. 397, and *idem*, 'Jeremiah xx 7-8', p. 27.

97. The irony of this combination should not be missed. One is a term associated with divine salvific actions (גבור—Ps. 24.8; Isa. 42.13; Zeph. 3.17; Deut. 10.17) and the other with the acts of the wicked ruthless (עריץ—Pss. 37.35; 54.5; 86.14; Jer. 14.21). So Clines and Gunn, 'Form', p. 397.

98. So Hubmann, 'Anders', pp. 185-86.

99. *Ibid.*, pp. 185, 187, observes the résumé character of this confession. In a sense, it sums up and resolves many of the tensions of the preceding confessions.

100. *Ibid.*, p. 187, though for him this interpretation of the prophetic way is redactional.

Notes to Chapter 1.8

1. מרחם—G εν μητρα (ברחם) α′ σ′ Targ V follow MT. On the basis of the parallelism, the reading of G is most natural. Yet, if G is original, it is difficult to see how MT could have arisen, especially in view of its wide attestation. Perhaps G has rendered MT due to contextual constraints. MT could involve a mixed metaphor or the preposition may represent the 'perspective' of 'on the side of ' (positional) and be equivalent to 'in the womb'—'from the side of the womb' (cf. BDB, p. 578 1c and מחוץ/מבית). Most emend MT to ברחם. See standard commentaries.

2. Baumgartner, p. 67.

3. For the most significant formal analysis and comparison of this curse to other examples of the genre, esp. Job 3, see: Schottroff, pp. 48 n. 3, 56, 74-77, 84-85; Horst, pp. 40-42; Westermann, *Aufbau*, p. 58 n. 1 (Eng. edn, p. 37 n. 12); Clines and Gunn, 'Form', p. 393; Ittmann, pp. 25-26.

4. So Schottroff, pp. 74-75.

5. See further Schottroff, p. 56, but who sees no element of *Fluchbegründung* present. However, the similarity of function of the relative clause to that of the formula developed with a ptc. should be noted. For the latter, Schottroff does recognize an element of *Fluchbegründung*.

6. On the problem presented by האיש and its usual emendation, see below.

7. This fits the function generally of the curse-development element. For further examples, see Schottroff, pp. 156-57, and for analysis of their function, see p. 130.

8. *Ibid.*, pp. 77-75.

9. Baumgartner, p. 67. His remaining vocabulary contacts can stand: עמל—Pss. 10.14; 25.18; 55.11; 90.11. יגון—Pss. 13.3; 31.11; 116.3. Verse 18b—Pss. 31.11; 102.4.

10. Total occurrence 17x Pss. of which 13x are in sense noted (e.g. 10.1; 22.2; 42.10; 43.2; 74.11; 79.10; 80.13). Frequencies for Jer.: 11x (6x poetry, 5x prose).

11. Westermann, *Aufbau*, p. 59 n. 1 (Eng. edn, p. 61 n. 14); Schottroff, pp. 76-77. Note that the references in Maccabees and Esdras relate to the destruction of the temple and nation.

12. Bright, 'Jeremiah's Complaints', pp. 213-14.

13. Note the complementary metrical pattern: 2 + 3 + 3 + 2.

14. Again, note the metrical pattern: 2 + 4 + 4 + 2. However, the 1st and 4th cola are not as strictly parallel as in v. 14; coupling this with the synthetic logical development may render the alternate scansion in BHS preferable. My scansion is favoured by the parallelism with the structure of the other curse formulary.

15. See Duhm, p. 167. In addition to the problem of digression from the true subject of the curse, Duhm also finds difficulty in the comparison of a

man to cities and the possibility that a third party could be viewed as having the right of destroying a child.

16. See standard commentaries. For recent discussions, see esp. Schottroff, p. 48 n. 3; Horst, p. 40; Ittmann, p. 25.

17. See *GKC* §144d and cf. Blank, 'Confessions', pp. 351-52 n. 29.

18. Probably the standard practice of emendation just mentioned obviated the need for such an approach among earlier scholars.

19. Ahuis, p. 109 n. 5.

20. *Ibid.*, p. 110 n. 2.

21. A parallelism apparently felt by both G (+ ἐν θυμῳ) and Targ. (ברוגזיה).

22. Note that in some older scholars irregularity of metre was observed: Duhm, p. 166; Volz, p. 210; Cornill, p. 239.

23. As noted in earlier discussions of his approach in the preceding confessions.

24. The bi-colon balances nicely with a 4 + 4 metre.

25. Ahuis, p. 110 n. 2. He points to the usage of נחם in Jeremianic prose plus the parallel of הפך in Deut. 29.22. However, *ni.* and *pi.* of נחם ocur 48x in the OT out of which the Dtr. Hist. has only 12x—usage comparable to usage in Pss. 10x; Jer. 10x (4x poetry; 6x prose). For הפך—10x Pss.; 6x Jer. (5x poetry; 1x prose). The remaining vocabulary also appears too generalized to be of use for detecting Dtr. character. For further distribution statistics throughout the OT, see *THAT* II, pp. 60-61.

26. For examples, see: Isa. 1.9, 10; 3.9; 13.19; Jer. 23.14; 49.18; 50.40; Ezek. 16.46, 48, 49, 53, 55, 56; Amos. 4.11; Zeph. 2.9.

27. Fensham, pp. 155-75.

28. So Hillers, *Treaty Curses*, pp. 74-76. Further analogies to ANE curses are also discussed in Schottroff, p. 154, though explicit use of the Sodom-Gomorrah motif represents a distinctive OT development.

29. Duhm's additional objections (see above n. 15) seem less decisive. Is the comparison of a day to cities any less odd than that of a man? The so-called irrational expectation that a third party would have had the right to slay a new-born may reflect an approach to this poem which unfairly requires rationality of what is essentially a reversal of normal expectation.

30. So Ahuis, p. 110; Eichler, p. 154.

31. Job 3 functions in a similar fashion.

32. On this question of the logic proper to this type of utterance compare the similar difficulty in Job 3.3, where ילד precedes הרה/the day of birth—the night of conception. See the commentaries by Horst, Rowley, Pope, and Gordis for a discussion of problems arising out of such poetic logic.

33. *ThWAT* I, pp. 448-51 (Eng. edn, pp. 416-18), and Schottroff, p. 199-230.

34. As discussed in the exegesis of 20.7-13, Wimmer, 'Experience', had to recognize the lack of a trial process pattern for all of vv. 7-18 (p. 312). Also

Blank, 'Confessions', p. 351 n. 29, had to classify this passage separately from the other 'law court'-influenced passages. Ittmann, pp. 25-26, disengaged this unit from inclusion among the confessions.

35. Clines and Gunn, 'Form', pp. 405-407, distinguish the pre-literary setting of this passage from that of vv. 7-13, where they did see an apologetic concern. Berridge, p. 168 n. 287, does not discuss this passage in detail though he sees some type of proclamatory function for it.

36. It is interesting that Ahuis, pp. 111, 114, does not view this unit as integrally bound up in a *Botenvorgang* as *Rückmeldung* but rather sees it as the literary climax to the original collection and series of the confessions, as a statement which results from his unsuccessful bid to escape the messenger commission. Eichler, on the other hand, sees the unit as a rejection of wisdom values, related to normal expectations of a meaningful, just order in the face of his prophetic situation of suffering. The poem is designed to force Yahweh to address the issue of theodicy raised by the tensions within the prophetic mission (pp. 172, 182, 192-93).

37. So observed by Ittmann, p. 26; Baumgartner, p. 67; and Schottroff, pp. 77-78, who explains the opaque character of the language as a result of Jeremiah's having employed 'eine "agendarisch" vorgeprägte Selbstver-fluchung'.

38. Clines and Gunn, 'Form', pp. 405-407.

39. See further, Hillers, 'Reaction', pp. 86-90.

40. Clines and Gunn, 'Form', pp. 406-407. For critique of their anti-psychological reading of the curse, see Polk, p. 247.

41. *Ibid.*, p. 406, for further details.

42. *Ibid.*, p. 407, followed by Hubmann, 'Anders', pp. 187-88, and slightly modified by Ittmann, pp. 23, 25-26, 294-95, who sees a strong personal element.

43. So Lundbom, p. 28; Holladay, *Architecture*, p. 18; Eichler, p. 172.

44. Hubmann, 'Anders', p. 187. On the relationship and/or distinction of woe-cry to curse, see Janzen, *Mourning*, p. 39; Schottroff, pp. 116-17. The latter completely divorces the two from one another.

45. In keeping with the problems raised by total editorial composition approaches, we list word frequencies for the passage which (at least) suggest a basic compatibility with Jeremianic poetry elsewhere:

	Unique O.T.	Pss.	Jeremiah Total	Poetry	Prose	f.n.o.
V.14						
ארור	40	1 (119.21)	6	3 (cf. esp. 17.5)	1 (11.3)	2 (48.10)
ילד		9	23	14	6	3

For the birth theme employed as reaction to bad news, see Jer. 6.24; 22.23; 30.6; 49.24; 50.43.

	Unique	O.T.	Pss.	Jeremiah Total	Poetry	Prose	f.n.o.
ברוך		71	17	2	2 (cf. 17.7)		

Curse formula

    with יום   x   plus negated blessing formula.

V.15

| ארור האיש | | 6 (Deut. 27.15 Josh. 6.26; 1 Sam 14. 24, 28) | 0 | 2 | 1 (20.15) | 1 (11.3) | 0 |
| בשר | | 24 | 3 | 1 | 1 | | |

Never used elsewhere in relation to annunciation of birth.

| בן זכר | x | | | | | | |
| שמח | | 154 | 52 (not with birth theme) | 6 | 4 | 1 | 1 |

    inf. cstr.   x

V.16a (see above n. 25)

V.16b

זעקה בבקר	x						
זעקה		18	0	6	2	0	4
בקר		214	16	2	2 (20.16; 21.12)		
תרועה		35	5 (related to noise of cultic cele-bration)	3	2	0	1 (cf. esp. 4.9; 49.2- תרועה (מלחמה
בעת צהרים	x						
צהרים		23	3	3	3 (6.4; 15.8)		

V.17

רחם		26	3	4	4		
קבר		67	3	4	2	2	0
הרת עולם	x						
הרה		54	1 (7.15)	2	2 (31.8)		

V.18

למה			17	1	6	5	0
יצא מרחם			0	cf. Jer. 1.5; 20.18; Job 3.11; 10.18; 24.20; 31.15; 38.8; Num. 12.12.			
עמל ויגון (co-ord.)							
עמל		55	13	1	1		
יגון		14	4	4	3	1	0

For usage with national calamity, see Jer. 8.18; 31.13; 45.3.

| כלה (qal) | | 64 | 14 | 5 | 3 | 2 | |
| בשת | | 30 | 7 | 6 | 2 | 4 | |

                (predominantly of the nation's shame)

כלה בבשת   x

For further psalm parallels, see above n. 9.

46. See previous note and n. 9.

47. The grammatical subject in v. 17 can be construed either impersonally (*GKC* §144d) or with reference to אִישׁ (v. 15). If our suggestion about the role of the imagery is correct, then the latter seems contextually better.

48. Clines and Gunn, 'Form', p. 408, do, in fact, allow for some preservation of this thrust in relation to Jer. 21-24 as a presage to the latter's announcement of impending doom. So also Hubmann, 'Anders', pp. 187-88, in a similar way.

49. Clines and Gunn, 'Form', pp. 407-408.

50. *Ibid.*, p. 408.

51. Prijs, pp. 106-107. Usage of the Sodom-Gomorrah theme in Jer. 23.14; 4.6, plus military imagery in 20.16b and the potential national associations of the diction (see above n. 45) lend plausibility to Prijs's approach.

52. Prijs, p. 105, attempts to read the statements of the self-curse without any optative nuance. But he fails to reckon seriously enough with the formal typicalities already observed plus the parallel with אַל יְהִי (v. 14). For further criticisms, see Schottroff, p. 48 n. 3; Rudolph, p. 132 n. 1.

53. Prijs, p. 107.

54. Hubmann, 'Anders', pp. 187-88.

55. See also Ittmann, p. 26, who also discusses the problems of pinning down the details of the passage relative to Jeremiah.

Notes to Chapter 2

1. Skinner, p. 208.

2. *Ibid.*, p. 210.

3. *Ibid.*, p. 214.

4. *Ibid.*, p. 209.

5. However, not all those who have taken a psychological-biographical approach to the texts have followed Skinner at this particular point. For example, Bright, *Jeremiah*, pp. LXVI-LXVII, insists on their treatment as isolated units.

6. For example, Chambers, p. 205, has interpreted the fluctuations of hope and despair, faith and doubt against the model of prophetic ambivalence instead of the crisis-resolution model. While he does not reconstruct a confessional series, presumably his assumption about the nature of the psychological process reflected by them would produce an entirely different reconstruction to Skinner's. Divergent logical rearrangements have been produced by Fohrer, *Propheten*, pp. 111-20, and Blank, *Jeremiah*, pp. 106-11, respectively as follows: 11.18ff.; 12.1ff.; 15.10.; 17.14ff.; 18.18ff.; 20.7ff.; 15.15ff.; and 17.14ff.; 18.18ff.; 11.18; 12.6; 11.19ff.; 20.7ff.; 15.10-11, 15-20; 12.1-5.

7. A specific chronology for the confessions is notoriously difficult.

Suggestions range from Skinner's view of Josiah's reign to that of Jehoiakim (Rudolph) or spanning the prophet's entire ministry (Bright, *Jeremiah*). Reventlow, p. 210, also raised serious questions about the ability to date the confessions and the assumption of a chronological order. Baumgartner, p. 87, was also pessimistic about the temporal setting.

8. See above on 11.18-23.
9. See above on 11.18-23.
10. See review in 11.18-23. Ahuis, p. 113.
11. *Ibid.*, p. 123.
12. *Ibid.*, p. 121.
13. *Ibid.*, p. 114. He has in mind 16.5, 15.17, and 12.5.
14. *Ibid.*, p. 121. He argues that 18.19 materially links to 17.18; dangers to the prophet represented as possibilities in 17/18 are lamented as realities in 20.7-9 and the appeal of 17.14 links back to 15.18 and the divine promise of deliverance in 15.20a (p. 117).
15. Von Rad, *Theologie*, II, p. 215 (Eng. edn, p. 203). In his earlier study of the confessions he did not discuss this question, see *idem*, 'Konfessionen', pp. 224-35; Wimmer, 'Experience', p. 357. While Wimmer sees the confessional order as a direct reflection of the prophet's experience, von Rad (p. 216 n. 19—Eng. edn, p. 204 n. 19) grants the possibility that such a close connection may not be sustained, however much he is of the opinion that they do.
16. *Ibid.*, pp. 214-15 (Eng. edn, p. 203). Cf. Ahuis's perception above that the original complex ended with a despairing cry.
17. *Ibid.*, p. 216 (Eng. edn, p. 204).
18. Cf. Ittman's similar understanding above.
19. Wimmer, 'Experience', p. 357.
20. *Ibid.*, p. 337. See also p. 329 for his view of the self-curse as a 'negative way of expressing absolute dependence'.
21. See below.
22. See the earlier exegetical discussion.
23. Holladay, *Architecture*, pp. 125-63.
24. In his earlier popular study, *Jeremiah: Spokesman Out of Time*, he viewed the confessions as Jeremiah's private prayers without attention to their present arrangement.
25. His theoretical exposition of his method can be found in Holladay, 'Recovery', pp. 401-35, and *idem*, *Architecture*, pp. 20-26.
26. By 'initial stratum' he means: 'the earliest material in a given section of the book of Jeremiah, material that was then incorporated into the growing collection of Jeremianic material' (*Architecture*, p. 127).
27. *Ibid.*, pp. 145-50; 160-63.
28. *Ibid.*, p. 133.
29. *Ibid.*, p. 128.
30. *Ibid.*, p. 130.

31. *Ibid.*, pp. 129-30. References to parents in 12.6; 15.10; 20.14-18; echoes between the Father complex and funeral section: קרב/רחק—12.2 and קבר/ קרח—16.4, 6; sound plays by permutation of consonants; between the Mother complex and wedding section: שמח—15.16; 16.19; ששון-15.16; 16.9; אכל, ישב—15.16, 17; 16.8.

32. *Ibid.*, pp. 131-32. In the Man complex ארור הגבר אשר (17.5) and ברוך הגבר אשר (17.7) are echoed in 20.15 ארור איש and 20.14 ברוך respectively. The sequence of time-related words in the Day complex יום (17.16, 17, 18), בעת (18.23), יום (20.7, 8) is echoed in the same order in 20.14, 16, 18 respectively. He also notes the word play between בְשָר (17.15) and בְשַר (20.15).

33. *Ibid.*, pp. 132-33. The Father/Mother complexes are echoed Mother/ Father (20.14, 15). The Man/Day complexes are echoed Day/Man (20.14, 15).

34. *Ibid.*, p. 131. A שנת (11.23)—יום (12.3)—עת (15.11) sequence is paralleled in the Man/Day complex by a שנת (17.8)—יום (17.16-18)—עת (18.23)—יום (20.7, 8) sequence and reflected again in 20.14-18.

35. In part, Holladay offers frequency counts of a proposed marker with the relative infrequency of the term enhancing the probability of a given suggestion (pp. 25-26).

36. For example, the term אבות is particularly frequent in Jeremianic prose, and burial motifs occur elsewhere in the doubleted Topeth sermons (8.30ff.; 19.1ff.).

37. Holladay, *Architecture*, pp. 131 n. 6, 141 n. 17, 154 n. 46, 155-56.

38. For example, see Thiel's view of the place of the confession within complexes designed to produce stylized scenes of Jeremiah's preaching (pp. 161-62).

39. Holladay, *Architecture*, pp. 20-26, is aware of some of these difficulties for his approach. But given the seriousness of these problems, he does not seem to have been rigorous enough in analysis or validation of his proposals.

40. The following discussion depends heavily upon our previous exegetical analyses at many points. The necessity for conciseness prevents us, however, from reproducing the details of that exegesis. We can only refer the reader back to the relevant points in that section for details and documentation.

41. This appears to have been the consensus until recently with reference to the arrangement of the entire book (Bright, *Jeremiah*, p. LVI). Holladay, *Architecture*, pp. 13-20, provides a helpful summary on this pessimism among exegetes of Jeremiah. Pessimism of opinion specifically in reference to the confessions can be found in Robinson, p. 50; or Blank, 'Prophet', pp. 125-26.

42. See below.

43. If Hubmann's view of redaction turned out to be correct, our basic point would receive only that much more corroboration.

44. See below.

45. See the previous review of Wimmer, 'Experience', above.

46. Note in particular the common depiction of the prophet and opponents as fertile plants and the legal imagery in relation to Yahweh used conventionally and unconventionally.

47.

11.19	.התקם כצאן לטבחה—12.3//כבש אלוף יובל לטבוח
11.19	.עשו פרי—12.2//עץ בלחמו
11.18	— 12.1//ריב, ראה, בחן כליות ולב, שפט צדק—11.20; ידע, ראה—
12.4—	בחן לב, ראה, ידע—12.3; מכליותיהם—12.2; ריב, צדיק,
	.ראה

48. So Lundbom, pp. 100-101. He also finds a chiastic arrangement of key terms between 11.18-20 and 12.1-3.

49. See Wimmer, 'Prophetic Experience', p. 143; and Gunneweg, p. 401, who also see the point of the connection in the issue of delay.

50. For the idea of the three subjects of lament, see Westermann, *Lob*, p. 47 (Eng. edn, p. 169). Expressed in more formal terms: 11.18-23 stress *Feindklage* and absorb *Ichklage* in signs of the divine support; 12.1-6 shift the stress to *Anklage Gottes*.

51.

12.1	—איש ריב—15.10//אריב
12.4	.איש מדון לכל הארץ—15.10//ארץ שלום—12.5; אבל ארץ—

Logical considerations might strengthen the associations, with 15.10 lamenting the loss of an existence in the ארץ שלום.

52. Cf. Wimmer, 'Experience', p. 222, who sees 15.10 as questioning the viability of his call.

53. Formally expressed: an oblique *Anklage Gottes* is developed by placing the stress upon *Ichklage*.

54. If Hubmann's view of 15.20-21 as an editorial expansion is correct, then this would provide an even more explicit character to the link.

55. See also Hubmann, *Untersuchungen*, p. 307.

56. More schematically conceived: The prophet opens his complaint focused upon his enemies and moves to the ironic interpretation of his mission; the divine answer responds first to this interpretation of mission and moves to its conclusion with response to the issue of the enemies.

57. Wimmer, 'Experience', p. 222, emphasizes the element of threat in the oracle.

58.

15.18	.רפא—17.14//מאנה הרפא—
15.18	.אל תהיה לי—17.17//היו תהיה לי—
15.19	.מוצא שפתי נכח פניך היה—17.16//תוציא יקר מזולל, כפי, לפני—
15.21	.ישע—17.14//ישע—

59. Similarly Wimmer, 'Experience', pp. 259-60.

60. See n. 58 above.

61. Also in the approaches of Ittmann and Ahuis attempts were made to discern a transitional role for this passage.

62. With the exception of 12.4, citations in the first cycle are directed principally against the prophetic person.

63. 18.20b could be viewed as an expansion upon the meaning of 17.16—ויום אנוש לא התאויתי.

64.

18.18	דבר יהוה—20.8//דבר מנביא—
18.23	יכשלו—20.11//מכשלים—.
18.19	ריבי—20.12//וריבי—.
18.18	נכהו בלשון//(possibly the terms of verbal abuse)— קלם, חרפה—20.8—לעג, שחוק—20.7.

65.

11.21	לא אדבר עוד בשמו—20.9//לא תנבא בשם יהוה—
11.20	doubletted with 20.12 (cf. 20.10—נקמתו ממנו).
12.1	דבר—20.12//דבר ריב, צדיק; 20.8, 9—ריבי, צדיק, צדיק—
12.3	ראה כליות ולב, בחן—20.12//בחן לב, ראה—
12.4	כלמת עולם—20.11//אחרית—
12.6	קרא—20.8//קרא—
15.10	ריבי—20.12//איש ריב—
15.10	כלה לעג לי—20.7//כלה מקללני—
15.15	חרפה—20.8//חרפה—
15.16	דבר יהוה לי—20.8//דברך לי—
15.20	יכל//20.7, 9, 10, 11—
15.20	ויהוה אותי—20.11//אתך אני—
15.21	עריץ—20.11//עריצים—
15.21	נצל מיד מרעים—20.13//נצל מיד רעים—
17.18	בוש—20.11//בוש—
17.15	דבר יהוה—20.8//דבר יהוה—

For links with 18.18-23, see n. 64.

66. But not as rigidly as Holladay's index-integrating passage idea suggested.

67. Note the strong verbal echoes:

15.10	ילד, אמי//20.14, 15, 17, 18—
15.15	בשת, יגון, עמל//20.18—חרפה—
15.16	שמח//20.15—
15.18	מכה, כאב//20.18—

68. Observe the verbal links in Cycle Two related to the nation's judgment: 17.18—בוש; 18.22—תשמע זעקה/20.16—שמע זעקה and possibly תרועת בעת צהרים with גדוד פתאם (military cry). However, the ambiguity in some of these terms would allow for either an objective or subjective nuance which renders ambiguous some of the verbal links as well —esp. בוש (17.18) and the terms of verbal abuse in 20.7-8.

69. The links begin midway in Cycle One, at 15.10ff. See n. 67 above. For

the principal links in 17.14ff. and 18.18ff., see n. 68 and possibly 17.16—
יום אנוש, 17.17, 18, יום רעה//20.14—היום.

70. For example, Skinner, p. 201; Eissfeldt, p. 402 (Eng. edn, p. 357);
Weiser, *Einleitung*, pp. 193-94 (Eng. edn, pp. 213-14); Fohrer, *Einleitung*,
p. 433 (Eng. edn, p. 395); Lindblom, p. 162.

71. For example, the zero variants in G at 12.3b and 15.21 or the
additional doublet passages of 11.20-20.12 and 1.18-15.20.

72. For comprehensive treatment of the Dtr. redaction of Jeremiah, see the
works of Thiel; and Nicholson, *Preaching*.

73. So our criticism, above, of Holladay, *Architecture*.

Notes to Chapter 3.1

1. We follow recent attempts which view the superscriptions in this
manner: Hubmann, *Untersuchungen*, p. 109; Thiel, pp. 106-107; and argued
at length, Neumann, p. 210. Older commentators have handled the
superscription in different ways, either discounting their structural value
(Duhm) or similar to these recent positive evaluations taking them as major
section markers (Keil, Rudolph, Payne).

2. The remaining occurrences comparable to the pattern in 11.1 seem to
have taken on a different type of function in relation to the needs of the
narrative cycles in which they occur (34.1; 34.8; 35.1; 40.1; 44.1).

3. A detailed exegesis of each of the units cannot be attempted in light of
the present scope of the study. Nor can a detailed analysis of redaction-
critical questions for each unit be attempted. Generally speaking, we will be
operating within the redactional framework as worked out in the studies of
Thiel, and Nicholson, *Preaching*. However, our primary interest in discerning
the compositional function and significance of the confessional complexes in
the nature of the case requires close attention to be given to the final shape
and placement given them through the editorial process. This will mean on
the one hand that the most important features of explicit editorial linking
will need to be noted; but, on the other, extensive interaction with competing
redactional theories will not greatly affect or promote discernment of the
compositional function adhering to the final shape of the text.

4. So Thiel, p. 166.

5. Unless the following should also be included: 12.16—שבע בבעל/
לא שמע, מאן לשמע—11, 13.10/לא שמע—12.17; הלך אחרי אלהים אחרים—13.10.

6. So Holladay, *Architecture*, pp. 148-49.

7. Note the versional translation of נפצתים in G—διασκορπιω and V—
dispergam with nuance of 'scatter', 'disperse'. McKane, 'Jeremiah 13.12-14',
p. 11, offers two possible explanations for the variants: (a) נפץ is understood
as a variant root of פוץ; or (b) the smashing is understood in terms of the
exile. The latter would fit the context as far as 13.15-27 is concerned. The

possibility of phonological association for פוץ/נפץ could also have promoted the interactions in the arrangement of units. However, פוץ in 13.24 is not translated in the same way which would have provided stronger indication of the suggestion.

8. Prior to Thiel's attempt, analogous proposals were made by Stone and Jacoby, though Thiel has worked this out independently (p. 161 n. 70). I have not had access to Jacoby's study; but that of Stone, while markedly similar to Thiel's and Ahuis's proposal (see below), suffered from the attempt to find in Jer. 11; 12; 14–20; 22.1-23; 26 seven chronologically successive temple sermons parallel to a preceding block of seven sermons in Jer. 7–10 (p. 92).

9. Thiel, pp. 161-62. He finds a similar pattern in Jer. 18, 19 and 20. For 14.1–15.21, he encounters greater difficulty in isolating the same pattern and in 17.14-18 views it as entirely absent (p. 161 n. 71). Subsequently, we will take up his approach for each of these sections.

10. Eichler, p. 64, basically has followed Ahuis with the proviso of an alternating pattern of divine action—human response. Consequently, we will concentrate upon Ahuis for the purposes of review.

11. Ahuis, p. 131. Subsequently, we will discuss his approach to the four remaining sections which he views as follows: 13.1–15.21; 16.1–17.18; 17.19–18.23; 19.1–20.12.

12. *Ibid.*, p. 182.

13. Hubmann, *Untersuchungen*, p. 166.

14. *Ibid.*, pp. 109-19, views 11.1-12 as a unit with vv. 13, 14 as redactional additions. However, it seems preferable to see the unit division coming after v. 13, with v. 14 the transition and initial framing verse for the unit vv. 14-17 related to the ineffectual cultic activity of Judah. Verse 13 could be taken as the concluding characterization for the judgment oracle vv. 9-13. For terminology and discussion of the structure of judgment oracles, see Koch, pp. 210-13. Evaluation of the redactional status of these verses would not affect this understanding. For evaluation of the doubletted character of the verses, see Thiel, pp. 153-54 (cf. v. 11b to Judg. 10.13b-14; v. 13 to Jer. 2.27-28; v. 14 to Jer. 7.16; 14.11).

15. Thiel, p. 158, attempted to view this passage as largely prose with only v. 20 poetry. See our previous criticisms in the exegesis.

16. In his chart (p. 131), Ahuis implies a slightly implicit status in the presence of his categories by placing 11.11, the *Eintreffen des Gerichts*, in parentheses.

17. Ahuis apparently requires these categories in order more successfully to incorporate the material in 14.1–15.4 into a consistent pattern across the five sections.

18. Hubmann, *Untersuchungen*, pp. 165-73.

19. *Ibid.*, pp. 113-15.

20. *Ibid.*, p. 112. Also argued at length by Thiel, pp. 142-44.

21. *Ibid.*, pp. 112-13.

22. *Ibid.*, p. 118.

23. Note the terms for the addressees of the sermon emphasize this: יהודה/
חצות/ערי. So *ibid.*, p. 119. or ישבי/איש—ירשלם

24. *Ibid.*, p. 118.

25. On the vexed textual problems of vv. 15-16, see standard commentators and Hubmann, *Untersuchungen*, pp. 125-29.

26. Hubmann, *Untersuchungen*, p. 131, provides a detailed list of the verbal echoes integrating 11.1-17 together. Thiel, pp. 154-56, also sees a similar function for the verses with v. 17 an editorial *Klammer* for all of 11.1-17.

27. *Ibid.*, pp. 167-68.

28. *Ibid.*, p. 168.

29. *Ibid.*, pp. 167, 172. While he views 12.6 as editorial, we argued in the exegesis that this was not the case. Either way his basic point would stand—though as an editorial addition it would be more explicit.

30. *Ibid.*, pp. 169-71, finds the background for the redactional pattern in the legal stipulations of Deut. 13.2-6. The threat of 11.21 is ironic, labelling true Yahweh prophecy in effect as a word in the name of 'another god'. The Anathothites are introduced as the proper court of execution—i.e. the family/clan of the 'false prophet'. This is possible; but, without explicit verbal links to the Deut. passage, the influence of the immediate context around the themes of covenant-house-family, etc. may account more significantly for the nature of the editorial shaping.

31. *Ibid.*, p. 172.

32. *Ibid.*, p. 173.

33. Also 11.15, if the normal understanding of the verse is followed instead of Hubmann's. See commentaries.

34. So Hubmann, *Untersuchungen*, p. 173.

35. Thompson, p. 357. The poem is viewed as a divine lament also by Weiser, Rudolph, Bright, Cornill, Volz.

36. In this light, the comment of the older commentator Keil, p. 169 (Eng. edn, p. 228), is interesting, though of course not uttered in consideration of redaction-critical issues: 'By this discovery of His world-plan the Lord makes so complete a reply to the prophet's murmuring concerning the prosperity of the ungodly (vers. 1-6) that from it may clearly be seen the justice of God's government on earth' (translation of Eng. edn).

37. Hubmann, *Untersuchungen*, p. 173, sees the intention of vv. 14-17 as an attempt to show that, while unavoidable, the judgment was not the last word. Rather, it is a means to a new beginning.

38. The only possibility for 13.12-14 is שחת (cf. 11.19) and for 13.15-27 is צאן—12.4, כבש—11.19/צאן, ערד—13.17, 20.

39. Though semantically different, 12.6 as a characterization of the familial hostility could have permitted the touch-point for the pride-glory motifs.

40. A similar pattern was noted for the redactional linking of 11.18-23 and 12.1-6 (cf. 11.19 and 12.3).

41. The idea of theodicy as the controlling issue of the complex, 11–13, is also supported by Thiel, pp. 156-57. Once again the older commentator, Keil, p. 16 (Eng. edn, pp. 21-22) is interesting in that he too views the rationale of the complex in an analogous manner. Alternative suggestions for the controlling idea of the complex are helpful in isolating subcategories within the theodicy motif but fail to provide a precise enough analysis of the organizing principle: Lamparter, p. 122, 'Verderbtheit des Volkes'; Neumann, p. 211 n. 1, 'Bund(esbruch)'.

42. This one, however, is possibly a result of haplography. See Janzen, *Studies*, pp. 39-40, 94, 119 for a vigorous defence of G. Thiel, pp. 149-50, prefers MT but allows that G may indicate editorial activity.

43. Thiel, pp. 170-73.

44. McKane, 'Jeremiah 13.12-14', pp. 116-17.

45. This passage would be similar to the Dtr. prose form isolated by Thiel, pp. 295-300, as *Gerichtsbegründung im Frage-Antwort-Stil*.

Notes to Chapter 3.2

1. Beuken–van Grol, pp. 297-342; Kessler, 'Drought', pp. 501-25; Castellino, p. 407; Holladay, *Architecture*, pp. 145-48; Reventlow, pp. 185-87; Gerstenberger, 'Complaints', pp. 403-408; Thiel, pp. 179-80. The major difference among these studies is whether the section constitutes an original unity (so Reventlow, Kessler, Holladay, Beuken–van Grol) or an editorial composition (so Gerstenberger, Thiel). However, those who argue for the original unity of the passages in our view, do not deal adequately with the nature of the poetry-prose shifts including the strong signs of Dtr. characteristics in the prose (so Thiel), and with the incipit of 14.17 which seems to break the unit in half. Attempts to view this incipit as referring to the preceding (so Kessler, Holladay, Beuken–van Grol) go against the consistent use of this formula elsewhere in the book to introduce what follows.

2. So convincingly Holladay, *Architecture*; Reventlow; Gerstenberger, 'Complaints'; Thiel; Beuken–van Grol.

3. Cf. Janzen, *Studies*, p. 25. G omits the conjunction, so that MT could represent an editorial expansion directed to underpinning the connection of 15.5-9 to the preceding.

4. Further echoes with 14.1-15.4 can be noted:

15.7	שערי הארץ//14.2—שעריה—
15.8	עיר ובהלות//14.19—בעתה—
15.9	14.2//אמל—
15.9	חרב//14.12, 13, 15, 16, 18; 15.2.—
15.9	בוש, ילד//14.4, 5.—

5. That this prose unit represents an editorially created unity rather than an original one seems most probable. See Thiel, pp. 195-201, for a detailed analysis of the composition.

6. This is generally taken as a later insertion into the context. See Thiel, p. 199, who also views this as a post-Dtr. editorial product. That this oracle is a doublet of Jer. 23.7-8 provides more explicit indication of the possible editorial character of the oracles.

7. So Thiel, p. 200.

8. The analogous motif in the hope oracle of 12.14ff., which similarly considers a turning of the pagan nations to the keeping of Torah should be noted.

9. Thiel, p. 200, attributes the unit to the same hand that added the oracle of hope (vv. 14-15).

10. This is illustrated well by Bright's comment (*Jeremiah*, p. 119) that it is as if the chapter represents the prophet's 'miscellaneous file'. Cf. standard commentaries and Thiel, pp. 202-203.

11. Thiel, pp. 194, and 161 n. 71.

12. Eichler, p. 65; Ahuis, p. 131.

13. Ahuis, p. 131, schematizes as follows; *Gerichtsverkündigung Jeremias* (13.1-21); *Eintreffen des Gerichts* (13.22); *Klage des Volkes* (14.2-6); *Verbot der Fürbitte an Jeremia* (14.11f.; 15.1-4); *Fortsetzung der Gerichtsverkündigung* (14.12b; 15.3f.); *Verfolgung Jeremias* (15.10); *Antwort Jeremias (Gerichtswort an die Verfolger*—15.12-14; *Klage zu Jahwe*—15.15-18, *mit Antwort Jahwes* —15.19-21).

14. Eichler, p. 65, gives greater recognition to the double cycle.

15. Alternatively, the national lament-dirge could be seen as implying the occurrence of the judgment. But even so, this spans the whole of 14.1-15.9 and cannot be isolated to one unit in the series.

16. See Reventlow, pp. 149-87, for a detailed exegesis of the covenantal and cultic background of these terms. This background has also been noted by Kessler, 'Drought', pp. 508, 509 n. 17, 512; Beuken-van Grol, p. 325.

17. So, similarly, Beuken-van Grol, pp. 327, 337.

18. For others who detect a theodicy concern, see Kessler, 'Drought', p. 520; Gerstenberger, 'Complaints', pp. 406-407; Thiel, p. 195; Beuken-van Grol, pp. 324-23, 341.

19. If the general view of v. 4 or at least v. 4b as an insertion is correct, then the compositional intention becomes even more explicit. See Thiel, p. 189 n. 27.

20. So *ibid.*, p. 184. For the disputational nature of the formal pattern, *Einwand*, see Eichler, pp. 105-11, 130; and Ahuis, pp. 187-204, who distinguish this from lament genre.

21. Thiel, p. 190, sees an analogy in vv. 1-2 to the *Gerichtsbegründung im Frage—Antwort—Stil*. See *idem*, pp. 295-300, for a detailed discussion of this form.

22. The dialogical nature of the text is widely recognized. So Holladay, *Architecture*, p. 148; Kessler, 'Drought', p. 518; Gerstenberger, 'Complaints', p. 405; Beuken–van Grol, p. 341. The latter speak, not inappropriately, of a 'prophetic drama'.

23. Thiel, p. 182.

24. So also, Gerstenberger, 'Complaints', p. 406; Beuken–van Grol, p. 341.

25. Thiel, p. 188, speaks of the issue of false prophecy as a special case of theodicy.

26. For this as an allusion to the rediscovered law book and not the reception of the prophetic word, see our earlier exegesis.

27. For additional verbal echoes:

15.11	בעת צרה—	// 14.8.
15.20, 21	ישע— // 14.8, 9—מושיע, ישע.	
15.20	לא יוכל—	// 14.9.
15.14	ארץ לא ידע—	// 14.18.
15.15	פקד, זכר—	// 14.21; 15.3.
15.10	ילד, אם— // 15.8, 9—אם, ילדת שבעה.	

28. Hubmann, *Untersuchungen*, pp. 297-98. See our earlier exegesis for our disagreements with his views of various points. Principally, we do not follow him in viewing 15.20-21 as a redactional addition.

29. *Ibid.*, pp. 306-307. Cf. similar statements in Gerstenberger, 'Complaints', pp. 398-99, 406.

30. See standard commentaries; Berridge, pp. 125-27; Thiel, p. 198; Hubmann, *Untersuchungen*, pp. 304-305, in a modified manner due to his exegesis of 15.17. See our earlier exegesis.

31. On the link between 15.5-9 and 15.10 Hubmann, *Untersuchungen*, p. 303, suggests that in this association the further element of the prophet's lament over the hapless fate of the nation has been added to his struggle against the mission. The observation is in line with older commentators of the passage.

32. *Ibid.*, p. 305.

33. Cf. 16.4 / 14.16, 18; 15.3, and 16.5-7 / 14.13, 16; 15.5, 6. Thiel, p. 201, has reconstructed an original kernel (16.1-3a, 4a, 5-8, 9*) to which the Dtr. editors have added vv. 3b, 4b, and in v. 9 לעיניכם ובימיכם. If this reconstruction is valid, then some of the links to the preceding material would fall within this category of explicit editorial activity. In addition, the zero variant in G, 16.5b-6a (נאם יהוה את החסד ואת הרחמים ומתו גדלים וקטנים בארץ הזאת לא יקברו) offers similar potential evidence of a similar type (cf. Janzen, *Studies*, p. 98).

34. Thiel, pp. 197-98 takes the phrase לעיניכם ובימיכם as a Dtr. expansion to link vv. 1-9 to 10-13.

35. Note as possible verbal echoes to 14–15:

16.10   רעה//14.16; 15.11.
16.13   שלח מעל—15.2//יחיו משלכים—14.16//הטל מעל.
16.13   ארץ לא ידע—15.14 ;14.18 // על הארץ אשר לא ידעתם.

36. So Thiel, p. 200.

37. A verbal echo tying the unit back to 14–15 is also possible: 16.17—
מדרכיהם לא שבו—15.17/כל דרכיהם.

38. So Thiel, p. 200. However, as noted in the overview 16.19-21 may effect a contrast between the nations and Israel with the latter shown to be intransigent in her idolatry. This would relate the verses more closely to the theodicy concern. Cf. von Orelli, pp. 276-78 (Eng. edn, pp. 141-42).

39. See standard commentaries.

40. Thiel, p. 161 n. 71.

41. Ahuis, p. 131, schematizes thus: *Gerichtsverkündingung Jeremias* (16.1-13), *Eintreffen des Gerichts* (16.13), *Klage des Volkes* (16.10; 17.12f.), *Verbot der Fürbitte an Jeremia* (17.16), *Fortsetzung der Gerichtsverkündigung* (17.15), *Verfolgung Jeremias* (17.15), *Antwort Jeremias* (*Gerichtswort an die Verfolger*—17.18, *Klage zu Jahwe*—17.14-18). Only for 16.1-13 and 17.14-18 do his labels seem appropriate. And while his section at 16.1 does not run against a major section marker as in his previous two series, his scheme fails to account for the strong connections of Jer. 16 with the preceding.

42. Holladay, *Spokesman*, pp. 99-100, and *idem*, *Architecture*, pp. 152-54. Thompson, p. 419, has followed Holladay in this. For Holladay, the remaining material is taken as secondary insertions.

43. See above, Chapter 2.

44. See our previous exegesis on 17.12-18.

45. For a detailed formal and tradition-historical analysis of the verses, see Schottroff, pp. 130-34, who also argues against their authenticity and ascribes them to Dtr.

46. Gunneweg, pp. 411-12; Polk, pp. 226-34.

47. The older commentators Ewald, pp. 171-74 (Eng. edn, pp. 163-68), and von Orelli, p. 278 (Eng. edn, p. 143), also detected such a contrast. Occasionally allusions to Jeremiah's experience and the experience of various kings are detected in more recent commentators: Cornill, p. 212; Rudolph, p. 115 (Zedekiah); Weiser, *Jeremia*, p. 146 (Jehoiakim); Lamparter, pp. 162-63; Keil, pp. 210-11 (Eng. edn, p. 285).

48. Note the verbal links in 17.12-13—בוש, עזב / contrasted to 17.16—
לא אץ.

49. Cf. similarly Gunneweg, p. 411.

50. So also Polk, p. 226.

51. Our remarks here on v. 11 as well as on vv. 9-10 suggest a fairly logical progression of thought for vv. 5-11. Such a progression has also been observed by older and more recent commentators: Kimchi (cited in Cornill, p. 214); Keil, pp. 209-10 (Eng. edn, p. 283); von Orelli, p. 278 (Eng. edn, pp. 142-43); Volz, p. 185; Weiser, *Jeremia*, p. 146; Rudolph, pp. 115-16;

Wimmer, 'Experience', pp. 245-58. The latter seeks to interpret the progression as the prophet's debate with the wisdom assumptions of the retribution scheme. Our arguments related to the nature of vv. 12-13 raise serious difficulties since it appears to introduce the nation as the explicit partner of the dispute over these wisdom motifs.

52.   So Polk, p. 226.

53.   Cf. Polk, p. 226. However, the connection may simply be a matter of mechanical catchword association. Similar verbal repetitions which may create significant associations or simply provide mechanical associative bases can be multiplied through the passage:

17.2   רענן— // 17.8.
17.8   פרי— // 17.10.
17.9   אנוש—//17.16—יום אנוש.
17.1   כתב—//17.13.

54.   Polk, p. 226, speaks of the particularizing and universalizing character of the context.

55.   Cf. Volz, p. 185, and Weiser, *Jeremia*, p. 146, who both detect the issue of theodicy lying behind vv. 9-10.

56.   Cf. similarly, Polk, p. 230.

57.   Polk, p. 228, sees this as part of Jeremiah's complaint, but see our earlier exegesis in support of their distinction from the confessional unit.

58.   It would be helpful to see the rhetorical question of v. 9 as a third citation of the *vox populi* reflecting a cynical denial of the retributive scheme outlined in vv. 5-8. This would make it parallel to the dialogical pattern in vv. 12-13. But this is difficult to prove. Normally, v. 9 is viewed as Jeremiah's (Polk; Holladay, *Architecture*; and standard commentaries); and this is attractive in light of the other 'heart' utterances in the prophetic oracles (4.4, 14, 18; 5.21, 23). Yet the uncertain character of the genre of the unit makes an affirmative decision difficult. To my knowledge, the only analogously structured utterances of a question plus divine pronouncement in response are to be found in Dt.-Isa. (41.4; 45.21). This would suggest that 17.9 is purely rhetorical and part of the divine speech itself.

59.   See our exegesis on 17.12-18.

60.   Rudolph, p. 117, suggests as well the editorial design to connect the prophet's petition for the fulfilment of his message as a response to the failure of the curse-blessing scheme to be realized upon the nation as they deserve.

61.   Polk, p. 225; Gunneweg, pp. 411-12; and the standard commentaries with the exception of Rudolph, p. 119, who suggests a connection to 16.11 לא שמר תורה.

62.   For a detailed discussion of this form of alternative preaching in Jeremiah and its Dtr. affinities, see Thiel, pp. 290-95.

63.   The noun occurs 30x in Prov. out of a total occurrence in the OT of 50x. Note esp. its occurrence 3x in Prov. with לקח (1.3; 8.10; 24.32). See

further *THAT*, pp. 739-41, for the wisdom context of מוסר in its relation to the formation of character and as well in a religious sense as holding out a way of life.

64. In this regard, the sharing of motifs between the wisdom literature and Dtr. literature as pointed out by Weinfeld (see part III, esp. pp. 303, 316-19, and Appendix A. VII. B.4; XII.12) would enhance the probability that the Dtr. editors would have perceived and exploited such potential associations. Polk, p. 229, already suggested that the blessing-curse formulary was to be understood in covenantal terms rather than merely secular wisdom. And, Schottroff, pp. 133-34, also points to Deut. 11.26-29; 30.19, and the alternative preaching forms in the Jeremianic prose sermon as the possible background for the unusual combination of the blessing and curse formulas (strictly speaking on vv. 5, 7) with developments (vv. 7 and 8) drawn from the wisdom sphere. But this raises wider issues about the ultimate connections between legal, treaty, covenant, and wisdom literature which cannot be entered into here. What is important is not the presence of intrinsic treaty/covenantal associations in the wisdom materials but rather the likelihood of the Dtr. editors effecting such associations through their compositional procedure.

65. So Rudolph, p. 119, and Weiser, *Jeremia*, p. 149. Contrast Thiel, p. 209, who grants this as a possibility but considers the distance to be too great for the proposal to be entirely satisfying. However, the extent of the links between the two chapters compensates for this problem.

66. Both these last two examples would aid in the demonstration of Judah's apostasy by linking her punishment with both her idolatry and her antagonism to the prophet, and in stressing the contrast between the prophet's innocence and the nation's guilt.

67. Rudolph, p. 113, notes at least for 17.1-4 the extensive contacts with 16.1-13, 16-18 related to 'cultic sins' and the 'exile as punishment'.

Notes to Chapter 3.3

1. So also Thiel, p. 211.

2. Contrast Ahuis, p. 131, who divides the material into two blocks: the first beginning with 17.19-27 and ending with 18.19-23; the second comprising 19.1-20.12. His seven-fold pattern is seriously hampered by a total absence of a *Klage des Volkes, Verbot der Fürbitte an Jeremia*; and a *Fortsetzung der Gerichtsverkündigung*. In addition, other aspects are produced only by disregarding the integrity and order of units in the appeal to their implicit character in line with his proposed schema: *Eintreffen des Gerichts* (18.17; 19.3, 6-9, 11b-13, 15); *Verbot der Fürbitte an Jeremia* (18.20b); *Antwort Jeremias—Gerichtswort an die Verfolger* (18.21, 22a, 23). If our proposal for the function of 17.19-27 within 14-17 is valid, then this too

raises problems for Ahuis's analysis.

3. The messenger formula and conjunction are frequently treated as an editorial addition (so Thiel, p. 217, and standard commentators). If this is correct, explicit compositional intention would be indicated in the patterning of units.

4. So Thiel, p. 217.

5. See our earlier exegesis on 18.18-23 for a discussion of the redactional status of v. 18 and its relation to the preceding context.

6. For detailed source and redactional analysis of this section, see Thiel, pp. 218-26; Wanke, *Baruchschrift*, pp. 8-19, who basically come to the same results.

7. So also Thiel, p. 226.

8. This narrative framework is generally recognized; see standard commentators.

9. So also Thiel, p. 212; cf. Holladay, *Architecture*, pp. 158-60, who also notes some of these verbal links but then downplays their significance in favour of his theory about 'adjunction by pre-existing association'. In this way, he treats 18.1-12, 13-17; 19.1–20.6 as secondary insertions into his supposed initial stratum of confessional passages. However, his proposals fail to recognize the dialogical and narrative patterns observed above and the presence of the stylized scenes which we shall seek to elucidate below.

10. Thiel, pp. 161, 212. For our disagreements with his analysis of the final confessional block, see the previous exegesis of 20.7-13, 14-18.

11. Thiel, p. 217, protects himself from this problem by noting these very features. Similar recognition of the dialogical pattern and the place of the confessions within it is given by Gunneweg, p. 408; Hubmann, 'Jer. 18', pp. 291-92.

12. Cf. the stylized scene in Jer. 11–13.

13. See the verbal links noted above.

14. The zero variant in G could provide indication of the editorial intention to underscore the unremitting unavoidable character of the disaster. G—δειξω αυτοις ημεραν απωλειας αυτων—omits MT—ערף ולא פנים.

15. So also Thiel, p. 217

16. The meaning of v. 6 is complicated by one's view of the redactional process. On the normal practice of treating 18.1-6 as the original kernel, two other possibilities arise for interpretation besides that cited in the text: it can be taken as an oracle of hope or of doom. See further Thiel, pp. 213-14, for details. He takes it as an oracle of doom through appeal to v. 4—כלי אחר as a sign that the nation/spoiled vessel is totally set aside. But the preceding שב ויעשהו seems to indicate the renovation of the spoiled vessel. In any case, the present connection to vv. 7-10 orients or re-orients the verse to a figurative statement of Yahweh's sovereignty over a nation which is then developed more abstractly in vv. 7-10. Cf. Brekelmans, p. 346; Hubmann, 'Jer. 18', pp. 291-92.

17. Cf. Brekelmans, p. 346; 'The symbolic action in vv. 2-6, 11a, thus seems to have been directed against such members of the people who were doubting that Yahweh would ever carry through what the prophet announced . . .'

18. Cf. Hubman, 'Jer. 18', p. 292, who speaks of v. 18 along with the confession setting forth Jeremiah's persecution as a consequence of and, at the same time, an example of Israel's unwillingness to repent.

19. For details, see our earlier exegesis of 18.18-23.

20. For a discussion of the redactional development and further literature, see Thiel, pp. 210-18. Any of the proposals for isolating an original kernel from the existing passage would only intensify the explicit character of the editorial design in the production of the dialogical framework. For Thiel, vv. 1-6 in the prose, and vv. 13-17, 19-23 in the poetry are the authentic portions, with the rest (vv. 7-12, 13aα, 18) a product of Dtr. The most problematic aspect in his analysis relates to the symbolic action, vv. 1-12. Recently, Brekelmans, pp. 343-50, has attempted to correct Thiel's analysis by detecting three stages of growth: the original symbolic action, vv. 2-6, 11a; an exilic redaction, vv. 11b-12; and a post-exilic one, vv. 7-10. In contrast to this approach remain those affirming the unity of the present passage: Rudolph, pp. 121-23, who assigns the passage to source C but reckons with the presence of a now unrecoverable kernel lying behind its present form; Weippert, pp. 48-67, who argues for authenticity as well as unity. The strong verbal and logical connections across the narrative coupled with the localization of Dtr. affinities to vv. 7-12 suggest that a clear decision of the matter is not to be reached.

21. So Thiel, p. 212; and following him, Clines and Gunn, 'Form', p. 404; Hubmann, 'Jer. 18', pp. 292-93; *idem*, 'Anders', p. 188; Polk, p. 243.

22. Thiel, p. 228, gives due notice to this feature of the text.

23. Convincing redactional analyses of 19.1-13 have been carried out by Thiel, pp. 228-29, and Wanke, *Baruchschrift*, p. 19, isolating 19.1-2a, 10-11a as the original kernel interwoven with the editorial sermonic judgment oracles, 19.2b-9, 11b-13. Particularly instructive are the zero variants in G. (19.5, 11) and the doublets with material from other prose sermons (esp. Jer. 7.31-33) as corroborative evidence that the material is secondary in its present context.

24. Cf. Thiel, p. 223.

25. Thiel, pp. 226-27, views vv. 14-15 as entirely the product of Dtr., which would heighten the deliberate character of the editorial design in the production of the narrative framework. Usually most of the verses are preserved as part of the original narrative (see Thiel, p. 219). Cf. for example Wanke, *Baruchschrift*, p. 13, who views מהתפת (v. 14a) as the only secondary part binding 19.14b-20b with the preceding.

26. Thiel, p. 229, views הדברים האלה (v. 1) and אשר נבאת להם בשקר (v. 6) as Dtr. editions which would again underscore the explicit intention of

the editorial process. Contrast Wanke, *Baruchschrift*, p. 15, who views only
20.4-6 as secondary.

27. So Thiel, p. 229.

28. For details, see Wanke, *Baruchschrift*, pp. 6-91, esp. pp. 19, 34, 58, 72.
He detects a common pattern throughout: Action—Jeremiah, counteraction
—opponent; confirmation of Jeremiah and threat toward opponent. For an
extensive review of Wanke's study, see Holladay, 'Fresh Look', pp. 394-
412.

29. Wanke, *Baruchschrift*, p. 156.

30. *Ibid.*, p. 155.

31. This raises implications for the composition history of these narrative
blocks as outlined by *ibid.*, pp. 151-53. He distinguished two separate cycles
of narratives 19.1-20.6, 26-29, 36 and 37-43 which were not to be traced to
the same editorial hand. In regard to the first cycle, he noted that the present
separation of 19.1-20.6 from its original location illustrated how tradition
collected into a common block could subsequently become isolated again
(p. 153). However, no explanation of why such a separation occurred was
provided. Our present attempt to detect stylized scenes into which the
confessions have been incorporated across Jer. 11-20 would provide some
rationale for such a process. At the same time, the affinity of this stylized
scene to the narrative cycles in 37-43 could be an indication that the
editorial hand responsible for the latter was also involved in the present
composition of the scene in 18-20.

32. Especially instructive in this regard is the verbal/thematic link noted
earlier between 19.15 and 18.17. The zero variant in G at 18.17, ערף ולא פנים,
could represent an editorial attempt to tie the complex together around the
central idea of refusal to heed Yahweh (19.15—הקשו את ערפם) and the
corresponding judgment suited to the crime (ערף ולא פנים אראם—18.17).
Cf. the previous note 14. All the versional evidence reads the full MT text
(Hexaplaric, 4QJer^a, V, Targ). The closest parallels to 18.17 are the converse
statements in 2.27 and 32.33 (ויפנו/פנו אלי ערף ולא פנים). The expression in
19.15 occurs only in Jeremianic prose: 7.26; 17.23.

33. This may provide some explanation for the abandonment of the
prophetic liturgy pattern observable in 11.18-12.6 and 15.10-21.

34. Cf. Hubmann, 'Jer. 18', p. 293, who observes that seen contextually
the imprecations are nothing more than the request for what Yahweh had
already announced.

35. Ahuis, pp. 102-107, has attempted to show an original connection
between 18.1-6a; 19.1-2a, 10-11a; and 20.7-9 based upon form-critical
reasons. The validity of this proposal would be somewhat helpful in relation
to the present discussion. However, his dependence upon the conjectured
Botenvorgang process, which we have found wanting previously, seriously
weakens his approach. In addition, it is to be wondered whether his other
schema of vision of judgment (18.1-6a)/announcement of judgment (19.1ff.)

and intervention of Yahweh (18.1-6a)/consequences of intervention (19.1ff.) really do compensate for the fact that we appear to have two *formally* distinctive narratives of symbolic action. Still the possible influence of such logical patterns upon the arrangement of 18.1ff and 19.1ff cannot be totally excluded.

36. The Greek evidence admits of no internal variants. V and Targ (except 1 MS) follow MT. G—τοτε is unrepresented by any other witnesses but προς με is supported by 10 MSS Syr. and 1 MS Targ. Thiel, pp. 220, 226-27, has suggested that the elimination of אלי in MT could reflect the editorial adaptation of the 1st pers. report to fit with the 3rd pers. narrative of 19.14–20.6. But τοτε is viewed as a consequence of the translator engaging in an interpretive assimilation of the two situations in 18 and 19–20. The weak textual attestation for τοτε would tend to support this. However, if G—MT variants do witness to editorial stages with the text becoming increasingly smoothed out into consistent narrative, then would not the presence of אי/ τοτε have been more expected in MT? Is it possible for G actually to reflect a mixed text, editorially speaking?

Notes to Chapter 4

1. In this regard, see McKane, 'Relations', p. 229, who argues for limited exegetical interests in certain prose pieces in relation to prior, mainly poetic, units. However, further analysis of the oracles of hope in the book might render their placement in 11–20 intelligible in a way compatible to our double-axis schema.

2. Ahuis, pp. 134-39. However, as our previous criticisms illustrate, we do not see his analysis of the stylized scenes necessarily connected to the present observations about the proposed concentric structure.

3. *Ibid.*, pp. 138-39. He constructs the following two concentric patterns: (doublets underlined)

11.1-17		-17.5-8-	20.14-18
11.18+19		-	20.13
<u>11.20</u>		-17.10-	<u>20.12</u>
11.21		-	20.1-6
<u>11.22-23</u>		-	<u>18.21-22a</u>
14.8		-	17.13
14.21		-	17.12
15.13-14		-	17.3-4

and:

Gerichtspredigt	11.1-17	-	19.1-13
Alternativ-Predigten	12.14-17	-	17.19-18.12
Schuldaufweis	13.22	-	16.10

4. As even stronger allusions which are not considered, note: 15.21/20.13; 15.5-9/16.1-9; 12.14-17/16.14-15, 19-21; 12.4/14.1. Also his second concentric

pattern is difficult to mesh with the other and it is not clear that treating the two *Alternativ-Predigten* in 17.19-27 and 18.1-12 as one block is legitimate. The failure of some texts to appear within the scheme is not explained; 12.1-6, 7-13; 15.15-21; 18.13-17; 19.14-15.

5. We extend the fitting description of 14.1–15.9 by Beuken–van Grol, p. 341, with this term to the whole complex.

6. So also Thiel, p. 229.

7. See the studies of Skinner and Blank, 'Confessions of Jeremiah and the Meaning of Prayer'.

8. See the studies of Stoebe, Stamm, Berridge.

9. See the studies of von Rad, 'Konfessionen' (and cf. his *Theologie*, II); Mihelic; Gunneweg; Blank, 'Prophet', Welten; Ittmann; Ahuis; Eichler.

10. Argued by Kremers.

11. Ahuis, pp. 142-69, basically argues that the intention of the stylized scene relates to the problem of the exiles over the question of the proximity of the restoration. The answer given is negative in relation to a speedy end to the exile. But they are given the model of Jeremiah as suffering servant with the implied exhortation that their only hope in the meantime is to affirm and emulate the prophet's pattern of obedience with its concomitant suffering.

12. This appears to hold no matter what one assumes about their origin and character—authentic/inauthentic; private outbursts/stereotyped complaint—for the paradigmatic reading still assumes a common intention either way. For example, contrast the approaches of Blank, 'Prophet'; and Gunneweg. The latter specifically rejects the biographical and psychological reading in contrast to the former; and yet both discern paradigmatic significance in them.

13. For criticisms of the 'passion narrative' approach, see Kessler, 'Jeremiah 26–45', p. 87; Ackroyd, p. 52; Nicholson, *Preaching*, pp. 104-105.

14. Carroll, pp. 123, 130.

15. *Ibid.*, p. 130.

16. *Ibid.*, pp. 109, 117-18, 120, 123.

17. *Ibid.*, p. 112. He stresses the critical importance of the redactional activity in fixing the meaning of the text and yet argues that the multiple employment of the tradition in different contexts renders the context useless in determining meaning. These observations seem at odds with one another. But it appears to allow Carroll to exegete a given passage (illegitimately) strictly in terms of the traditional background of images employed disregarding the use and import attached to such tradition by its incorporation into its present setting.

18. A full discussion of this complex issue in the OT is beyond the scope of our present study. See further Crenshaw, *Conflict*; and Carroll, pp. 158-97.

19. See Carroll, p. 192, for Jeremiah as the editor's standard of Jeremiah as a true prophet.

20. Cf. Carroll, p. 183, on Jer. 27.18—effectual intercession as a constituent of true prophecy.

21. See Crenshaw, *Conflict*, pp. 64ff., on the causes leading to the subversion of true prophecy; and Ittmann, p. 194, for the threat to prophecy posed by the community.

22. Crenshaw, 'Living Tradition', p. 127, sees the contribution of the prophetic conflict theme in the book of Jeremiah to the development of theodicy.

23. For further details on this motif in the prophets and Jeremiah, see Crenshaw, *Conflict*, pp. 23-38; and for additional discussion of popular religion and the prophetic dispute with it, see Brueggemann, 'Rhetorical Questions', p. 371; Overholt, pp. 262-73.

24. Also to be considered are stated intentions in conflict with his commission: 17.16aβ; 18.20b; 20.9.

25. Kessler, 'Jeremiah 26-45', p. 85, allows a similar subordinate role for this theme in these narratives.

26. See further the many valuable insights in the exposition of this theme in the studies of Gunneweg; Blank, 'The Prophet'; Ittmann, and Ahuis.

27. See Carroll, pp. 166-67, 180, on the prophet as a model of morality.

28. For details, see the studies of Wanke, *Baruchschrift*; Kessler, 'Jeremiah 26-45'; Ackroyd; Nicholson, *Preaching*; and Thiel.

29. Steck, pp. 60-80. Especially instructive is his observation that the attention given to the negative personal fate of the prophets is done not merely for the sake of the prophet but serves as an element in the demonstration of Israel's obdurate apostasy, thus contributing to theodicy (pp. 79-80).

30. See Nicholson, *Preaching*, pp. 55-56; and Jer. 7.25; 25.4.

BIBLIOGRAPHY

Ackroyd, Peter R., 'Historians and Prophets', *SEÅ* 33 (1968), pp. 18-54.

Ahuis, Ferdinand, *Der klagende Gerichtsprophet: Studien zur Klage in der Überlieferung von den alttestamentlichen Gerichtspropheten* (CThM, 12), Stuttgart: Calwer Verlag, 1982.

Avishur, Y., 'Addenda to the Expanded Colon in Ugaritic and Biblical Verse', *UF* 4 (1972), pp. 1-10.

Baker, David W., 'Further Examples of the Waw Explicativum', *VT* 30 (1980), pp. 129-36.

Balentine, Samuel E., 'Jeremiah, Prophet of Prayer', *RExp* 78 (1981), pp. 331-44.

Baumgartner, Walter, *Die Klagegedichte des Jeremia* (BZAW, 32), Giessen: Alfred Töpelmann, 1917.

Baumgartner, W., *et al.* (eds.), *Hebräisches und Aramäisches Lexicon zum Alten Testament*, 3 vols.; 3rd edn; Leiden: E.J. Brill, 1967, 1974, 1983.

Begrich, Joachim, 'Das priesterliche Heilsorakel', *ZAW* 52 (1934), pp. 81-92.

Behler, G.-M., *Les Confessions de Jérémie* (BVC), Tournai, 1959.

Berridge, John Maclennan, *Prophet, People, and the Word of Yahweh* (BST, 4), Zürich: EVZ-Verlag, 1970.

Beuken, W.A.M., and Grol, H.W.M. von, 'Jeremiah 14, 1-15, 9: A Situation of Distress and its Hermeneutics, Unity and Diversity of Form—Dramatic Development', *Le Livre de Jérémie*, ed. by P. M. Bogaert; Leuven: University Press, 1981.

Blank, S.H., 'The Confessions of Jeremiah and the Meaning of Prayer', *HUCA* 21 (1948), pp. 331-54.

—*Jeremiah, Man and Prophet*, Cincinnati: Hebrew Union College Press, 1961.

—'The Prophet as Paradigm', *Essays in Old Testament Ethics*, ed. by J.L. Crenshaw and J.T. Willis; New York: KTAV, 1974.

Blenkinsopp, Joseph, 'The Prophetic Reproach', *JBL* 90 (1971), pp. 267-78.

Boecker, Hans Jochen, *Redeformen des Rechtslebens im Alten Testament* (WMANT, 14), Neukirchen-Vluyn: Neukirchener Verlag, 1964.

Bogaert, P-M., 'De Baruch à Jérémie: Les deux rédactions conservées du livre de Jérémie', *Le Livre de Jérémie*, ed. by P.-M. Bogaert; Leuven: University Press, 1981.

Bonnard, Pierre E., *Le Psautier selon Jérémie*, Paris: Les Editions du Cerf, 1960.

Bredenkamp, Victor Julius, 'The Concept of Communion with God in the Old Testament with Special Reference to the Individual Laments in the Psalms and the Confessions of Jeremiah', Unpublished Ph.D. dissertation, Princeton University, 1970.

Brekelmans, C., 'Jeremiah 18, 1-12 and its Redaction', *Le Livre de Jérémie*, ed. by P.-M. Bogaert; Leuven: University Press, 1981.

Brichto, H.C., *The Problem of 'Curse' in the Hebrew Bible* (JBL.MS, 8), Philadelphia: Society of Biblical Literature, 1963.

Bright, John, *Jeremiah* (AncB, 21), New York: Doubleday, 1965.

—Jeremiah's Complaints: Liturgy or Expressions of Personal Distress?', *Proclamation and Presence*, ed. by J.I. Durham and J.R. Porter; London: SCM, 1970.

—'A Prophet's Lament and its Answer: Jeremiah 15.10-21', *Interp* 28 (1974), pp. 59-74.

Brown, Francis; Driver, S.R.; and Briggs, Charles A., *A Hebrew and English Lexicon of the Old Testament*, Oxford: Clarendon Press, 1906.

Brueggemann, Walter A., 'The Book of Jeremiah: Portrait of the Prophet', *Interp* 37 (1983), pp. 130-45.

—'Jeremiah's Use of Rhetorical Questions', *JBL* 92 (1973), pp. 358-74.

Burkitt, F.C., 'Justin Martyr and Jeremiah xi 19', *JTS* 33 (1932), pp. 371-73.

Carroll, Robert P. *From Chaos to Covenant: Uses of Prophecy in the Book of Jeremiah*, London: SCM, 1981.

Castellino, G.R., 'Observations on the Literary Structure of Some Passages in Jeremiah', *VT* 30 (1980), pp. 398-408.

Chambers, W.V. 'The Confessions of Jeremiah: A Study in Prophetic Ambivalence', Unpublished Ph.D. dissertation, Vanderbilt University, 1972.

Clark, Malcolm W., 'Law', *Old Testament Form Criticism*, ed. by John H. Hayes; San Antonio: Trinity University Press, 1974.

Clements, R.E., 'The Form and Character of Prophetic Woe Oracles', *Semitics* 8 (1982), pp. 17-29.

Clifford, R.J. 'The Use of Hôy in The Prophets', *CBQ* 28 (1966), pp. 458-64.

Clines, D.J.A. and D.M. Gunn. 'Form, Occasion and Redaction in Jeremiah 20', *ZAW* 88 (1976), pp. 390-409.

—'"You tried to persuade me" and "Violence! Outrage!" in Jeremiah xx 7-8', *VT* 28 (1978), pp. 20-27.

Condamin, Albert, *Le Livre de Jérémie* (EtB), 3rd edn; Paris: J. Gabalda, 1936.

Coppens, J., 'Les Psaumes 6 et 41 dépendent-ils du livre de Jérémie?', *HUCA* (1961), pp. 217-26.

Cornill, Carl Heinrich, *Das Buch Jeremia*, Leipzig: Chr. Herm. Tauchnitz, 1905.

Crenshaw, James L., 'A Living Tradition: The Book of Jeremiah in Current Research', *Interp* 37 (1983), pp. 117-29.

—*Old Testament Wisdom: An Introduction*, London: SCM, 1982.

—*Prophetic Conflict* (BZAW, 124), Berlin: Walter de Gruyter, 1971.

Dahood, Mitchell J., *Psalms I: 1-50* (AncB, 16), New York: Doubleday, 1966.

—*Psalms II: 51-100* (AncB, 17), New York: Doubleday, 1968.

—*Psalms III: 101-150* (AncB, 17A), New York: Doubleday, 1970.

—'Ugaritic Studies and the Bible', *Gr* 43 (1962), pp. 55-79.

Driver, G.R., 'Jeremiah XII 6', *JJS* 4 (1954), pp. 177-78.

Driver, S.R., *An Introduction to the Literature of the Old Testament*, 9th edn; Edinburgh: T. & T. Clark, 1929.

Duhm, Bernhard, *Das Buch Jeremia* (KHC), Tübingen: J.C.B. Mohr, 1901.

Eichler, Ulrike, 'Der klagende Jeremia. Eine Untersuchung zu den Klagen Jeremias und ihrer Bedeutung zum Verstehen seines Leidens', Unpublished Ph.D. dissertation, University of Heidelberg, 1978.

Eissfeldt, Otto. *Einleitung in das Alte Testament* (NTG), Tübingen: J.C.B. Mohr (Paul Siebeck), 1934. (*The Old Testament: An Introduction*, 3rd Germ. edn trans. by Peter R. Ackroyd; Oxford: Basil Blackwell, 1965.)

Ewald, Heinrich. *Die Propheten des Alten Bundes*, II: *Jeremja und Hezeqiel mit ihren Zeitgenossen*, 2nd edn; Göttingen: Vandenhoeck & Ruprecht, 1868. (*Commentary on the Prophets of the Old Testament*, III: *Nahûm SSephanya, Habaqqûq, 'Zakharja' XII.-XIV., Yéremjà*, trans. by J. Frederick Smith; London: Williams & Norgate, 1878.)

Fensham, Charles F., 'Common Trends in Curses of the Near Eastern Treaties and Kudduru-Inscriptions Compared with Maledictions of Amos and Isaiah', *ZAW* 75 (1963), pp. 155-75.

Fishbane, Michael, 'Jeremiah 20.7-12/Loneliness and Anguish', *Text and Texture: Close Readings of Selected Texts*, New York, Schocken: 1979.

—'"A Wretched Thing of Shame, A Mere Belly": An Interpretation of Jeremiah 20.7-12', *The Biblical Mosaic* (Semeia St.), ed. by Robert M. Polzin and Eugene Rothman; Philadelphia: Fortress, 1982.

Fohrer, Georg, *Die Propheten des Alten Testaments*, II: *Die Propheten des 7. Jahrhunderts*, Gütersloh: Gütersloher Verlagshaus, 1974.

Fohrer, Georg, and Sellin, Ernst, *Einleitung in das Alte Testament*, 10th edn; Heidelberg: Quelle & Meyer, 1965. (*Introduction to the Old Testament*, trans. by David Green. London: SPCK, 1970.)

Fox, Michael, 'Tōb—as Covenant Terminology', *BASOR* 209 (1973), pp. 41-42.

Gemser, B., 'The Rîb-Or Controversy-Pattern in Hebrew Mentality', *VT.S* 3 (1955), pp. 120-37.

Gerstenberger, Erhard, 'Jeremiah's Complaints: Observations on Jer.15 10-21', *JBL* 82 (1963), pp. 393-408.

—'The Woe-Oracles of the Prophets', *JBL* 81 (1962), pp. 249-63.

Gibson, John C.L., *Textbook of Syrian Semitic Inscriptions*, II: *Aramaic Inscriptions*, Oxford: Clarendon Press, 1975.

Gordon, C.H., *Ugaritic Textbook*, Rome: Pontifical Biblical Institute, 1965.

Greenwood, David, 'Rhetorical Criticism and Formgeschichte: Some Methodological Considerations', *JBL* 89 (1970), pp. 418-26.

Guillaume, A., *Prophecy and Divination* (Bampton Lectures), London: Hodder and Stoughton, 1938.

Gunkel, Hermann, and Begrich, Joachim, *Einleitung in die Psalmen* (HK), Göttingen: Vandenhoeck & Ruprecht, 1933.

Gunneweg, A.H.J. 'Konfession oder Interpretation im Jeremiabuch', *ZThK* 67 (1970), pp. 395-416.

Habel, N. 'The Form and Significance of the Call Narrative', *ZAW* 77 (1965), pp. 297-323.

Hartman, Geoffrey, 'Jeremiah 20.7-12: A Literary Response', *The Biblical Mosaic*, ed. by Robert M. Polzin and Eugene Rothman, Philadelphia: Fortress, 1982.

Hauret, C., 'Jérémie, XVII, 14: Sana me, Domine, et Sanabor', *RScRel* 36 (1962), pp. 174-84.

Herntrich, V. *Jeremia, der Prophet und sein Volk*, Gütersloh: Gütersloher Verlag, 1938.

Hillers, Delbert R., 'A Convention in Hebrew Literature the Reaction to Bad News', *ZAW* 77 (1965), pp. 86-90.

—*Treaty-Curses and the Old Testament Prophets*, Rome: Pontifical Biblical Institute, 1964.

Hitzig, F., *Der Prophet Jeremia* (KEH, 3), 2nd edn; Leipzig, 1846.

Hobbs, T.R., 'Jeremiah 3.1-5 and Deuteronomy 24.1-4', *ZAW* 86 (1974), pp. 23-29.

—'Some Proverbial Reflections in the Book of Jeremiah', *ZAW* 91 (1979), pp. 62-72.

Holladay, William L., *The Architecture of Jeremiah 1-20*, Lewisburg: Bucknell University Press, 1976.

—'A Fresh Look at "Source B" and "Source C" in Jeremiah', *VT* 25 (1975), pp. 394-412.

—'Jeremiah and Moses, Further Considerations', *JBL* 85 (1966), pp. 17-27.

—*Jeremiah: Spokesman Out of Time*, Philadelphia: United Church Press, 1974.

—'Jeremiah's Lawsuit with God', *Interp* 17 (1963), pp. 280-87.

—'Prototype and Copies: A New Approach to the Poetry-Prose Problem in the Book of Jeremiah', *JBL* 79 (1960), pp. 351-67.

—'The Recovery of Poetic Passages of Jeremiah', *JBL* 85 (1966), pp. 401-35.

—*The Root Šûbh in the Old Testament*, Leiden: E.J. Brill, 1958.

—'Style, Irony, and Authenticity in Jeremiah', *JBL* 81 (1962), pp. 44-54.

Hölscher, Gustav, *Die Profeten: Untersuchungen zur Religionsgeschichte Israels*, Leipzig: J.C. Heinrichs'sche Buchhandlung, 1914.

Horst, F. *Hiob* (BK.AT, 16.1), Neukirchen-Vluyn: Neukirchener Verlag, 1968.

Houberg, R., 'Note sur Jérémie XI 19', *VT* 25 (1975), pp. 676-77.

Hubmann, F.D., 'Anders als er wollte: Jer 20.7-13', *BiLe* 54 (1981), pp. 179-87.

—'Jer 18,18-23 im Zusammenhang der Konfessionen', *Le Livre de Jérémie*, ed. by P.-M. Bogaert; Leuven: Leuven University Press, 1981.

—'Textgraphik und Textkritik am Beispiel von Jer 17.1-2', *BibNot* 14 (1981), pp. 30-36.

—*Untersuchungen zu den Konfessionen Jer. 11, 18-12, 6 und Jer. 15, 10-21* (FB, 30), Echter Verlag, 1978.

Huffmon, Herbert B., 'The Covenant Lawsuit in the Prophets', *JBL* 78 (1959), pp. 285-95.

—'Prophecy in the Mari Letters', *The Biblical Archaeologist Reader*, III, ed. by Edward F. Campbell, Jr, and David Noel Freedman; New York: Doubleday, 1970.

Hyatt, J.P. and Hopper Stanley R., 'Jeremiah', *The Interpreter's Bible*, V, ed. by G.A. Buttrick; New York: Abingdon Press, 1956.

Ittmann, Norbert, *Die Konfessionen Jeremias: Ihre Bedeutung für die Verkündigung des Propheten*, Neukirchen-Vluyn: Neukirchener Verlag, 1981.

Jacobson, R., 'Prophecy and Paradox', *LingBib* 38 (1976), pp. 49-61.

Jacoby, G., 'Glossen zu den neuesten kritischen Aufstellungen über die Composition des Buches Jeremja (Capp. 1-20)', Unpublished Ph.D dissertation, Königsberg, 1903.

—'Zur Komposition des Buches Jeremja', *ThStKr* 79 (1906), pp. 1-30.

Janzen, J. Gerald, *Studies in the Text of Jeremiah* (HSM, 3), Cambridge, Mass.: Harvard University Press, 1973.

Janzen, W., *Mourning Cry and Woe Oracle* (BZAW, 125), Berlin: De Gruyter, 1972.

Jenni, Ernst and Westermann, Claus (eds.), *Theologisches Handwörterbuch zum Alten Testament*, 2 vols.; Munich: Chr. Kaiser Verlag, 1971, 1976.

Jüngling, H.W., 'Ich mache dich zu einer ehernen Mauer. Literarkritische Überlegungen zum Verhältnis von Jer 1.18-19 zu Jer 15.20-21', *BiB* 54 (1973), pp. 1-24.

Kautzsch, E. (ed.), *Gesenius' Hebrew Grammar*, 2nd edn; trans. by A.E. Cowley; Oxford: Clarendon Press, 1910.

Keil, Carl Friedrich, *Biblischer Commentar über den Propheten Jeremia und die Klagelieder* (BC, 3.2), Leipzig: Dörffling und Franke, 1872. (*The Prophecies of Jeremiah*, I, trans. by David Patrick; Edinburgh: T. & T. Clark, 1953.)

Kenney, R.F., 'Jeremiah's Distinctive Contribution to Hebrew Psalmody', Unpublished Th.D. dissertation, Southern Baptist Seminary, Louisville, 1952.

Kessler, Martin, 'From Drought to Exile: A Morphological Study of Jer 14.1-15.4', *Proceedings of the Society of Biblical Literature*, II, Los Angeles, 1972.

—'Jeremiah Chapters 26-45 Reconsidered', *JNES* 27 (1968), pp. 81-88.

Knierim, Rolf, 'Old Testament Form Criticism Reconsidered', *Interp* 27 (1973), pp. 435-68.

Köhler, Ludwig, *Der hebräische Mensch*, Tübingen: J.C.B. Mohr (Paul Siebeck), 1953. (*Hebrew Man*, trans. by P.R. Ackroyd; London: SCM, 1956.)

Köhler, Ludwig, and Baumgartner, W., *Lexicon in Veteris Testamenti Libros*, Leiden: E.J. Brill, 1953.

Kraus, Hans-Joachim, *Psalmen* (BK.AT, 15.1, 2), 2nd edn; 2 vols; Neukirchen-Vluyn: Neukirchener Verlag, 1961.

Kremers, Heinz, 'Leidensgemeinschaft mit Gott im Alten Testament: Eine Untersuchung der "biographischen" Berichte im Jeremiabuch', *ZThK* 13 (1953), pp. 122-40.

Kugel, James L., *The Idea of Biblical Poetry: Parallelism and its History*, New Haven: Yale University Press, 1981.

Kuhl, Curt, 'Die "Wiederaufnahme"—ein literarkritisches Prinzip?', *ZAW* 64 (1952), pp. 1-11.

Lamparter, Helmut, *Prophet wider Willen: Der Prophet Jeremia* (BAT), Stuttgart: Calwer, 1964.

Leclerq, J., 'Les "Confessions" de Jérémie', *Etudes sur les prophètes d'Israël* (LeDiv, 14), Paris, 1954.

Leech, Geoffrey N. *A Linguistic Guide to English Poetry*, London: Longman, 1969.

Limburg, James, 'The Root ריב and the Prophetic Lawsuit Speeches', *JBL* 88 (1969), pp. 291-304.

Lindblom, J., *Prophecy in Ancient Israel*, Oxford: Basil Blackwell, 1962.

Loewenstamm, S.E., 'The Expanded Colon in Ugaritic and Biblical Verse', *JSS* 14 (1969), pp. 176-96.

Lundbom, Jack R., *Jeremiah: A Study in Ancient Hebrew Rhetoric* (SBL.DS, 18), Missoula, Montana: Scholars Press, 1975.

McKane, William, 'The Interpretation of Jeremiah 12.1-5', *TGUOS* 20 (1963/64), pp. 38-48.

—'Jeremiah 13.12-14: A Problematic Proverb', *Israelite Wisdom*, ed. by John G. Gammie, Walter A. Brueggemann, W. Lee Humphreys, and James M. Ward; New York: Union Theological Seminary, 1978.

—'Relations Between Poetry and Prose in the Book of Jeremiah with Special Reference to Jeremiah III 6-11 and XII 14-17', *VT.S* 32 (1981), pp. 220-37.

Marx, A., 'A propos des doublets du livre de Jérémie. Réflexions sur la formation d'un livre prophétique', *Prophecy*, ed. by J.A. Emerton; Berlin: Walter de Gruyter, 1980.

May, H.G., 'Towards on Objective Approach to the Book of Jeremiah: The Biographer', *JBL* 61 (1942), pp. 139-55.

Mays, James Juther, *Micah: A Commentary* (OTL), London: SCM, 1976.

Melugin, Roy F., 'The Typical versus the Unique among the Hebrew Prophets', *SBL Proceedings*, II, Los Angeles, 1972.

Mihelic, Joseph L., 'Dialogue with God', *Interp* 14 (1960), pp. 43-50.

Miller, Jr, Patrick, 'Trouble and Woe: Interpreting the Biblical Laments', *Interp* 37 (1983), pp. 32-45.

Moran, W.L., 'A Note on the Treaty Terminology of the Sefire Stelas', *JNES* 22 (1963), pp. 173-76.

Mowinckel, Sigmund, *The Psalms in Israel's Worship*, 2 vols.; trans. by D.R. Ap-Thomas; Oxford: Basil Blackwell, 1962.

Muilenburg, James, 'Form Criticism and Beyond', *JBL* 88 (1969), pp. 1-18.

Nägelsbach, C.W.E., *Der Prophet Jeremia* (THBW, 15), Leipzig, 1868.

Neumann, Peter K.D., 'Das Wort, das Geschehen ist . . . zum Problem der Wortempfangsterminologie', *VT* 23 (1973), pp. 171-217.

Nicholson, Ernest W., *The Book of the Prophet Jeremiah: Chapters 1-25* (CNEB), Cambridge: CUP, 1973.

—*Preaching to the Exiles*, Oxford: Basil Blackwell, 1970.

Nielsen, Kirsten, *Yahweh as Prosecutor and Judge: An Investigation of the Prophetic*

288   *The Confessions of Jeremiah in Context*

Lawsuit (Rîb-Pattern) (JSOTS, 9), Sheffield: JSOT, 1978.

North, Robert, 'Angel-Prophet or Satan-Prophet?', *ZAW* 82 (1970), pp. 31-67.

Orelli, Konrad von, *Die Propheten Jesaja und Jeremia* (KK), Nördlingen: Beck'sche Buchhandlung, 1887. (*The Prophecies of Jeremiah*, trans. by J.S. Banks [CFThL, 39], Edinburgh: T. & T. Clark, 1889.)

Overholt, Thomas W., 'Jeremiah 2 and the Problem of Audience Reaction', *CBQ* 41 (1979), pp. 262-73.

Payne, J. Barton, 'The Arrangement of Jeremiah's Prophecies', *BEvThSoc* 7 (1964), pp. 120-30.

Polk, Timothy Houston, 'The Prophetic Persona and the Constitution of the Self: A Study of First Person Language in the Book of Jeremiah', Unpublished Ph.D. dissertation, Yale University, 1982 (now published as *The Prophetic Persona: Jeremiah and the Language of the Self* [JSOT, 32], Sheffield, JSOT, 1984).

Prijs, L., 'Jeremia XX 14ff: Versuch einer neuen Deutung', *VT* 14 (1964), pp. 104-108.

Pritchard, J.B. (ed.), *Ancient Near Eastern Texts Relating to the Old Testament*, Princeton: Princeton University Press, 1950.

—*The Ancient Near East: Supplementary Texts and Pictures Relating to the Old Testament*, Princeton: Princeton University Press, 1969.

Rad, Gerhard von, 'Die Konfessionen Jeremias', *Gesammelte Studien zum Alten Testament*, II, ed. by Rudolph Smend; Munich: Chr. Kaiser Verlag, 1973. (ET in *Theodicy in the Old Testament*, ed. by J.L. Crenshaw; Philadelphia: Fortress, 1983.)

—'Die levitische Predigt in den Büchern der Chronik', *Festschrift Otto Procksch*, ed. by Albrecht Alt, *et al.*; Leipzig: A. Deichert'sche Verlagsbuchhandlung, 1934. ('The Levitical Sermon in I and II Chronicles', *The Problem of the Hexateuch and other Essays*, trans. by E.W. Trueman Dicken; London: Oliver & Boyd, 1965.)

—*Theologie des Alten Testaments*, II: *Die Theologie der prophetischen Überlieferungen Israels*, 2nd edn; Munich: Chr. Kaiser Verlag, 1960. (*Old Testament Theology*, II, trans. by D.M.G. Stalker. London: Oliver & Boyd, 1965.)

Raitt, Thomas M., 'The Prophetic Summons to Repentance', *ZAW* 83 (1971), pp. 30-49.

Ramsey, George W., 'Speech-Forms in Hebrew Law and Prophetic Oracles', *JBL* 96 (1977), pp. 45-58.

Reventlow, Henning Graf, *Liturgie und prophetisches Ich bei Jeremia*, Gütersloh: Gütersloher Verlagshaus (Gerd Mohn), 1963.

Rhodes, Arnold B., 'Israel's Prophets as Intercessors', *Scripture in History and Theology*, ed. by A.L. Merrill and T.W. Overholt; Pittsburg, Penn.: Pickwick Press, 1977.

Robinson, H. Wheeler, *The Cross of Jeremiah*, London: SCM, 1925.

Rowley, H.H., 'The Text and Interpretation of Jer. 11.18–12.6', *AJSL* 42 (1926), pp. 217-27.

Rudolph, Wilhelm, *Jeremia* (HAT, 12), 3rd edn; Tübingen: J.C.B. Mohr, 1968.

—'Liber Jeremiae', *Biblia Hebraica Stuttgartensia*, ed. by K. Elliger and W. Rudolph. Stuttgart: Württembergische Bibelanstalt, 1970.

Scharbert, J., 'אָרַר', *ThWAT*, I, ed. by G. Johannes Botterweck and Helmer Ringgren; Stuttgart: W. Kohlhammer, 1973. (*TDOT*, I, rev. edn; trans. by John T. Willis; Grand Rapids, Mich.: Eerdmans, 1974.)

Schmidt, N. 'Jeremiah', *Encyclopaedia Biblica*, II.

—'Jeremiah (Book)', *Encyclopaedia Biblica*, II.

Schoors, Antoon, *I Am God Your Saviour* (VTS, 24), Leiden: E.J. Brill, 1973.
Schottroff, Willy, *Der altisraelitische Fluchspruch* (WMANT, 30), Neukirchen-Vluyn: Neukirchener Verlag, 1969.
Schreiner, J., 'Die Klage des Propheten Jeremias. Meditation zu Jer 15.10-21', *BiLe* 7 (1966), pp. 220-24.
—'Unter der Last des Auftrags. Aus der Verkündigung des Propheten Jeremias: Jer, 11.18-12,6, III. Teil', *BiLe* 7 (1966), pp. 180-92.
Skinner, John, *Prophecy & Religion: Studies in the Life of Jeremiah*, Cambridge: CUP, 1922.
Smith, George Adam, *Jeremiah*, London: Hodder & Stoughton, 1923.
Smith, G.V. 'The Use of Quotations in Jeremiah XV 11-14', *VT* 29 (1979), pp. 229-31.
Soden, Wolfram von (ed.), *Akkadisches Handwörterbuch*, 3 vols.; Wiesbaden: Otto Harrassowitz, 1965, 1972, 1981.
Sperber Alexander (ed.), *The Bible in Aramaic*, IV B: *The Targum and the Hebrew Bible*, Leiden: E.J. Brill, 1973.
Stade, Bernhard, *Geschichte des Volkes Israel*, I, Berlin: G. Grote'sche Verlagsbuchhandlung, 1887.
—'Miscellin', *ZAW* 6 (1886), p. 153.
Stamm, J.J., 'Die Bekenntnisse des Jeremia', *KBRS* III (1955), pp. 354-57, 370-75.
Steck, Odil Hannes, *Israel und das gewaltsame Geschick der Propheten* (WMANT, 23), Neukirchen-Vluyn: Neukirchener Verlag, 1967.
Steinmann, J., *Le Prophète Jérémie. Sa vie, son œuvre et son temps* (LeDiv, 9), Paris, 1952.
Stoebe, H.J., 'Jeremia Prophet und Seelsorger', *ThZ* 20 (1964), pp. 385-409.
—'Seelsorge und Mitleiden bei Jeremia. Ein exegetischer Versuch', *WuD* 4 (1955), pp. 116-34.
Stone, Pearle Felicia, 'The Temple Sermons of Jeremiah', *AJSL* 50 (1933/34), pp. 73-92.
Talmon, Shemaryahu, 'Amen as an Introductory Oath Formula', *Textus* 7 (1969), pp. 124-29.
Thiel, Winfried, *Die deuteronomistische Redaktion von Jeremia 1-25* (WMANT, 41), Neukirchen-Vluyn: Neukirchener Verlag, 1973.
Thomas, D.W., 'מלאי in Jeremiah IV,5: A Military Term', *JJS* 3 (1952), p. 47.
Thompson, J.A., *The Book of Jeremiah* (NICOT), Grand Rapids, Mich.: Eerdmans, 1980.
Tov, Emanuel, 'Exegetical Notes on the Hebrew Vorlage of the LXX of Jeremiah 27 (34)', *ZAW* 91 (1979), pp. 73-93.
—*The Septuagint Translation of Jeremiah and Baruch* (HSM, 8), Missoula, Mont.: Scholars Press, 1976.
—'Some Aspects of the Textual and Literary History of the Book of Jeremiah', *Le Livre de Jérémie*, ed. by P. M. Bogaert; Leuven: Leuven University Press, 1981.
Vermeylen, J., 'Essai de Redaktionsgeschichte des "Confessions de Jérémie"', *Le Livre de Jérémie*, ed. by P. M. Bogaert; Leuven: Leuven University Press, 1981.
Volz, Paul, *Der Prophet Jeremia* (KAT, 10), Leipzig: A. Deichertsche Verlagsbuchhandlung, 1922.
Wagner, S., 'ידרש', *ThWAT*, II, ed. by G. Johannes Botterweck and Helmer Ringgren; Stuttgart: W. Kohlhammer, 1977. (*TDOT*, rev. edn, III, trans. by John T. Willis, Geoffrey W. Bromiley, and David E. Green; Grand Rapids, Mich.: Eerdmans, 1978.)

Wanke, Gunther, 'אוי und הוי', *ZAW* 78 (1966), pp. 215-18.
—*Untersuchungen zur sogenannten Baruchschrift* (BZAW, 122), Berlin: de Gruyter, 1971.
Weber, Robert O.S.B. (ed.), *Biblia Sacra: Iuxta Vulgatam Versionem*, II: *Proverbia— Apocalypsis, Appendix*, Stuttgart: Württembergische Bibelanstalt, 1969.
Weinfeld, Moshe, *Deuteronomy and the Deuteronomic School*, Oxford: Clarendon, 1972.
Weippert, Helga, *Die Prosareden des Jeremiabuches* (BZAW, 132), Berlin: de Gruyter, 1973.
Weiser, Artur, *Das Buch Jeremia: Kapitel 1–25,14* (ATD, 20), 7th edn; Göttingen: Vandenhoeck & Ruprecht, 1976.
—*Einleitung in das Alte Testament*, 6th edn; Göttingen: Vandenhoeck & Ruprecht, 1966. (*Introduction to the Old Testament*, 4th Germ. edn trans. by Dorothea M. Barton; London: Darton, Longman & Todd, 1961.)
—*Die Psalmen* (ATD, 14/15), 2 vols.; 4th edn; Göttingen: Vandenhoeck & Ruprecht, 1955. (*The Psalms: A Commentary* (OTL), Germ. 5th edn trans. by Herbert Hartwell; London: SCM, 1962.)
Wellhausen, J., *Israelitische und jüdische Geschichte*, 9th edn; Berlin: de Gruyter, 1958.
Welten, Peter, 'Leiden und Leidenserfahrung im Buch Jeremia', *ZThK* 74 (1977), pp. 123-50.
Wernberg-Møller, P. 'Observations on the Hebrew Participle', *ZAW* 71 (1959), pp. 54-67.
—'"Pleonastic" Waw in Classical Hebrew', *JSS* 3 (1958), pp. 321-26.
Westermann, Claus, *Der Aufbau des Buches Hiob* (CThM, 6), 3rd edn; Stuttgart: Calwer, 1977. (*The Structure of the Book of Job*, 2nd Germ. edn trans. by Charles A. Muenchow; Philadelphia: Fortress, 1981.)
—*Grundformen prophetischer Rede* (BeT, 31), 2nd edn; Munich: Chr. Kaiser Verlag, 1964. (*Basic Forms of Prophetic Speech*, trans. by Hugh Clayton White; London: Lutterworth, 1967.)
—*Jeremia*, 2nd edn; Stuttgart, 1972.
—*Lob und Klage in den Psalmen*, 5th edn; Göttingen: Vandenhoeck & Ruprecht, 1977. (*Praise and Lament in the Psalms*, 1st Germ. edn trans. by Keith R. Crim and Richard N. Soulen; Edinburgh: T. & T. Clark, 1981.)
Williams, James G., 'The Alas-Oracles of the Eighth Century Prophets', *HUCA* 38 (1967), pp. 75-91.
Williams, R.J., *Hebrew Syntax: An Outline*, Toronto: University of Toronto Press, 1967.
Wilson, Robert R., *Prophecy and Society in Ancient Israel*, Philadelphia: Fortress, 1980.
Wimmer, D.H. 'Prophetic Experience in the Confessions of Jeremiah', Unpublished Ph.D. dissertation, Univ. of Notre Name, 1973.
—'The Sociology of Knowledge and the Confessions of Jeremiah', *SBL Proceedings*, Missoula, Mont.: Scholars Press, 1978.
Winnett, F.V. 'Iron', *Interpreter's Dictionary of the Bible*, II.
Wolff, H.W., 'Das Zitat im Prophetenspruch', *Gesammelte Studien zum Alten Testament* (TB, 22), Munich: Chr. Kaiser Verlag, 1964.
Yost, Burton George, 'A Form and Motif Analysis of Jeremiah 1.4-19', Unpublished Ph.D. dissertation, Vanderbilt University, 1975.
Ziegler, Joseph (ed.), *Jeremias, Baruch, Threni, Epistula Jeremiae*, Vol. XV of

Septuaginta: Vetus Testamentum Graecum, ed. by Auctoritate Academiae Scientiarum Gottingensis; 2nd edn; Göttingen: Vandenhoeck & Ruprecht, 1976.

Zimmerli, Walther, *Ezechiel*, I: *Ezechiel 1–24* (BK.AT, 13.1), Neukirchen-Vluyn: Neukirchener Verlag, 1969. (*Ezekiel I* [Hermeneia], trans. by Ronald E. Clements; Philadephia: Fortress, 1979.)

—'Jeremia, der leidtragende Verkündiger', *Communio* 4 (1975), pp. 97-111.

INDEX

INDEX OF BIBLICAL REFERENCES

INDEX OF AUTHORS

JOURNAL FOR THE STUDY OF THE OLD TESTAMENT
Supplement Series

* Out of print